Stephan Joubert

Paul as Benefactor

Reciprocity, Strategy and Theological Reflection in Paul's Collection

WIPF & STOCK · Eugene, Oregon

Wipf and Stock Publishers
199 W 8th Ave, Suite 3
Eugene, OR 97401

Paul as Benefactor
By Joubert, Stephan
Copyright©2000 Mohr Siebeck
ISBN 13: 978-1-5326-0267-2
Publication date 7/16/2016
Previously published by MoMohr Siebeck, 2000

To Andrie du Toit, Jan van der Watt
and Hans-Josef Klauck

Preface

After the completion of my doctoral studies in 1987, I had always wanted to analyse the Pauline Collection from a different angle. I wish to thank the Alexander von Humboldt Foundation for the scholarship in 1997, which enabled me to study in Germany. During my stay at the University of Würzburg, Hans-Josef Klauck encouraged me to re-examine the collection critically, incorporating an understanding of the social background(s) of the New Testament, with a close reading of relevant texts. His two short but significant commentaries on 1 and 2 Corinthians, as well as his influential *religionsgeschichtlichen* studies on the world of the New Testament served as examples, and paved the way for indepth research.

The influential works on the Pauline Collection by Georgi and Nickle, have for long been the standard authorities on the subject. Apart from a few less prominent voices attempting to participate in the debate, their insights went unchallenged. Without disregarding the contributions of Georgi and Nickle, it is hoped that this study will express the need for an on-going search for new answers to old questions regarding the Pauline Collection.

This project would not have been possible without the assistance and encouragement of Hans-Josef Klauck, with whom I had the opportunity of spending pleasant hours in discussion during 1997. My thanks also go to Frau Hannelore Ferner, secretary in the Department of New Testament Studies at the University of Würzburg, for all her assistance in practical, everyday matters while I was resident in Germany.

I would also like to thank the members of the "Oberseminar" (1997) at Würzburg, who painstakingly assisted me in the long process of reading numerous primary texts on patronage and "euergetism". A word of gratitude is also due to my colleague at the University of Pretoria, Prof. Jan van der Watt, for his words of advice throughout the course of this project. In the same breath, I would like to mention Proff. Bruce Malina, Jerome Neyrey and Thomas Söding for their friendship and formative theological advice. A last word of appreciation to our Dean at the Faculty of Theology of the University of Pretoria, Prof. Cas Vos, for his kind assistance, and Me. Elize Henning as well as Mr Petrus Maritz, who, in their own ways, contributed to the completion of the manuscript. Not least, I am indebted to the immanent Proff. Martin Hengel and Otfried Hofius for including this study in their WUNT series.

To Marietjie, Tarien and Elani, thank you!

Stephan Joubert
Department of New Testament Studies
Faculty of Theology
University of Pretoria
0002
South Africa
E-mail: stefan@ccnet.up.ac.za

Table of Contents

Preface VII
Abbreviations XIII

Chapter 1: Introduction The Current Communis Opinio on Paul's Collection 1
1.1. Uniting body and soul again 3
1.2. Hypotheses and aims of the investigation 6
1.3. Theory underlying a 'holistic' understanding of the collection 8
   1.3.1. Ideological factors and the collection 8
   1.3.2. The ideological and social frameworks for Paul's collection 11
1.4. The larger picture: using models 14

Chapter 2: Benefactor or Patron? Social Exchange in the Graeco-Roman World as the Interpretative Framework for the Collection 17
2.1. Introduction 17
2.2. Gift-exchange and social relations in primitive societies 18
   2.2.1. Marcel Mauss 19
   2.2.2. C.A. Gregory's model of gift-exchange in clan-based societies 20
2.3. The social embededness of exchange in the Graeco-Roman world 22
2.4. Patronage: a system of social control 23
   2.4.1. Patronage before the principate 24
   2.4.2. Patronage in the early empire 26
      2.4.2.1. The princeps as patron 26
      2.4.2.2. Brokerage: Pliny the Younger as an example of a 'middle order' patron 28
      2.4.2.3. Patronage and friendship 29
      2.4.2.4. Patronage of communities 31
      2.4.2.5. Patronage and collegia 32
      2.4.2.6. Plebs and patrons: patron-client relations from the 'bottom' and from the 'top' 34
   2.4.3. Patronage: a summary 36
2.5. Benefaction 37
   2.5.1. Aristotle on 'magnificence' and benefaction 38
   2.5.2. Seneca on interpersonal benefit-exchange 40
      2.5.2.1. The aim and structure of De Beneficiis 40
      2.5.2.2. The true nature of a benefit 42
      2.5.2.3. The role of the benefactor: benefits are gifts, not loans 43
      2.5.2.4. Benefit-exchanges are not agonistic competitions 43
      2.5.2.5. Choose worthy recipients 44
      2.5.2.6. Internalised reciprocity and social approval 45
      2.5.2.7. What benefits should be given? 46
      2.5.2.8. Should the benefactor ask for a return? 46

        2.5.2.9. Benefits and the recipient: choose the right benefactor.................................47
    2.5.3. Ingratitude and obligations 47
        2.5.3.1. Gratitude is sufficient reward, but one's debt must still be repaid...............48
        2.5.3.2. The agonistic contest of benefit-return..49
        2.5.3.3. What kind of benefits should be returned?.......................................49
    2.5.4. The social embededness of benefit-exchanges 50
    2.5.5. Collective benefaction (euergetism) 51
        2.5.5.1. Benefactors and beneficiaries in honorary inscriptions............................51
        2.5.5.2. The agonistic context of benefit-exchange..54
        2.5.5.3. Bread for the hungry 56
    2.5.6. In summary: benefaction 58
  2.6. The interpretative framework for the collection: benefaction or patronage?............58
    2.6.1. Patronage and benefaction: the same social exchange relationship 59
        2.6.1.1. Patronage in the Ancient Greek World 59
            Dionysius and the origin of patronage 60
            The ideological basis of Dionysius' views of patronage...........................61
        2.6.1.2. Patronage and benefaction in the Empire...62
    2.6.2. Patronage and benefaction: distinct relationships 63
        2.6.2.1. Romans benefactors in the Greek East..63
        2.6.2.2. Roman patrons in the Greek East 64
        2.6.2.3. Greek scepticism 66
    2.6.3. Conclusion: Patronage and benefaction: two different, but related, forms
        of social exchange..66
  2.7. A model of social exchange as interpretative framework for the collection...............69
    2.7.1. The impact of benefit exchange in ancient social relationships.........................69
    2.7.2. Social-exchange and the collection..70

Chapter 3: Galatians 2, 1-10: the Nature of the Reciprocal Relationship between Paul and the Jerusalem Community 73
  3.1. Introduction 73
  3.2. Jerusalem holds the key...74
    3.2.1. Galatians 2,1-10: Jerusalem's role in the collection 75
        3.2.1.1. The chronological framework of the collection and Galatians: A
            hypothesis 75
    3.2.2. The structure of Galatians 2,1-10 78
    3.2.3. Paul as apostle and slave of Christ in Galatians 2..81
        3.2.3.1. An encomium..82
    3.2.4. The Jerusalem meeting 83
        3.2.4.1. The position of Jerusalem in the earliest Christian movement....................85
        3.2.4.2. The agreement at the Jerusalem meeting (Gal 2,7-10) 86
        3.2.4.3. Do not forget the poor (Gal 2,10)...88
        3.2.4.4. The Jerusalem meeting from the perspective of benefit-exchange 90
    3.2.5. Benefactors or beneficiaries? The Antiochene collection..................................91
    3.2.6. Benefit exchange in Ancient Jewish Society 93
        3.2.6.1. The unique face of Jewish benefaction 93
        3.2.6.2. Characteristics of Jewish benefit exchange..95
        3.2.6.3. Differences between Greek and Jewish benefaction 97
    3.2.7. Benefit exchange and the Jerusalem leadership...99
    3.2.8. The Jerusalem leadership as benefactors at the meeting.................................100
    3.2.9. Paul as would-be benefactor of Jerusalem..102
    3.2.10. A command or a request? 103

3.2.11. The Jerusalem leadership's strategy at the meeting 104
3.2.12. The socio-economical situation in Jerusalem 107
   3.2.12.1. The impact of famines on Ancient Judea 107
   3.2.12.2. The Jerusalem Church and the poor 111
3.3. Conclusion 113

Chapter 4: Beneficiaries of Jerusalem: Paul's Interpretative Framework for the Collection 116

4.1. Introduction 116
4.2. From two to one: Galatians 2,11-14 and Paul's independent collection effort 116
4.3. Paul's renewed commitment to the reciprocal relationship with Jerusalem 121
4.4. Paul's missionary program and the collection 124
4.5. Beneficiaries of Jerusalem 126
   4.5.1. Paul as broker of the heavenly patrons 126
4.6. Romans 15,25-27: the Pauline communities as beneficiaries in the reciprocal relationship with Jerusalem 128
   4.6.1. The collection as an expression of the reciprocal relationship between the Pauline communities and Jerusalem 128
4.7. Corinthians 8,1-6: religious reciprocity and the collection 134
   4.7.1. The literary integrity of 2 Corinthians 134
   4.7.2. The collection as χάρις 135
   4.7.3. The response of the Macedonians to the benefactions of God 136
4.8. Religious reciprocity and the framework of the collection 138
4.9. 2 Corinthians 8,13-15: balanced reciprocity and the collection 140
   4.9.1. The chiastic structure 140
   4.9.2. Material and spiritual reciprocity between Jerusalem and the Pauline communities 140
4.10. 2 Corinthians 9, 11-15: the collection and Jerusalem's response of gratitude 144
   4.10.1. The structure of 2 Corinthians 9,11-15 144
   4.10.2. Jerusalem's gratitude for the overflowing grace of God 145
   4.10.3. The collection and the principle of socio-religious approval .. 149
4.11. Conclusion 150
   4.11.1. The collection as an exchange relationship 150
   4.11.2. Theological conceptualisations of the collection 152

Chapter 5: Managing the Collection Effort in Corinth 155

5.1. Introduction 155
5.2. 1 Corinthians 16,1-4 and the organisation of the collection in Corinth 156
   5.2.1. The 'poetic sequence' and 'referential sequence' of 1 Corinthians 16,1-4 156
5.3. The apostolic directives for a successful collection effort in 1 Corinthians 16,1-4 ... 158
5.4. Paul's autocratic leadership style and the organisation of the collection 162
5.5. The crisis in Corinth and the new intra-textual relationship between Paul and the Corinthian believers 164
   5.5.1. The situation between 1 Corinthians 16 and 2 Corinthians 1-9 164
5.6. Paul's textual strategies in 2 Corinthians 8-9 166
5.7. Paul's patriarchal role in 2 Corinthians 8-9 167
   5.7.1. The 'potestas' of the paterfamilias 169
   5.7.2. 'Pietas' and the family 170
   5.7.3. Reciprocity between parents and children 171
   5.7.4. Metaphorical use of familial terms 171
   5.7.5. Summary 172

5.8. 2 Corinthians 8-9: Salvaging the collection... 173
   5.8.1. 2 Corinthians 8,1-6: An agonistic exemplum 173
5.9. 2 Corinthians 8,7-9: The Christ-event as basis for the Corinthian collection............ 176
   5.9.1. Testing the spiritual integrity of the Corinthians 176
5.10. 2 Corinthians 8,10-12: The nature of the contributions of the Corinthians 180
   5.10.1. Overview of the structure 180
   5.10.2. Instructions for the conduct of the beneficiaries... 180
5.11. 2 Corinthians 8,10-15: The deliberate tension between rivalry and realism............ 183
5.12. 2 Corinthians 8,16-24: Paul's commendation of Titus and his helpers 184
   5.12.1. The Letter of Recommendation 184
   5.12.2. 2 Corinthians 8:16-17: Affirmation of the integrity of Titus 185
   5.12.3. 2 Corinthians 8,18-22: Commendation of the envoys, and reconfirmation
           of Paul's loyalty to group norms... 186
   5.12.4. 2 Corinthians 8,23-24: The authorisation of the 'apostolic trio,' and Paul's
           appeal to the Corinthians 189
5.13. 2 Corinthians 9,1-5: Motivation for the sending of the delegation to Corinth......... 189
   5.13.1. Overview of the structure 189
   5.13.2. Paul's boasting... 190
5.14. 2 Corinthians 9,6-10: God's gracious gifts lead to generosity................................. 193
   5.14.1. Overview of the structure 193
   5.14.2. The metaphorical use of agrarian imagery... 193
5.15. Conclusion.. 198
   5.15.1. Paul's persuasive strategies and the collection in the Corinthian
           correspondence 198
   5.15.2. Theological conceptualisation of the collection in 2 Corinthians 8-9............ 200

Chapter 6: Success and Failure? The Delivery of the Collection in Jerusalem 204
6.1. Success at last!.. 204
6.2. Romans 15: Preparing for the delivery of the collection 206
   6.2.1. A New ideological angle of incidence on the collection..................................... 206
   6.2.2. Securing the bond of unity... 207
   6.2.3. Paul as 'diakonos' of the sacred ministry to Jerusalem 208
   6.2.4. Redefining 'success'... 209
6.3. Paul in Jerusalem 210
   6.3.1. New nationalistic sentiments in the Jerusalem Church.. 213
   6.3.2. The compromise 213

Chapter 7: Conclusion.. 216
7.1. The interpretative framework for the collection 216
7.2. The 'performative' functions of Paul's theological reflection on the collection 216
7.3. Paul's reinterpretation of the basic principles of benefit exchange 217
7.4. The completion of the collection 218
Bibliography... 221
Index of Modern Authors... 236
Index of Passages... 240
   Ancient Texts 240
   Early Jewish Texts... 241
   Early Christian texts 242
   Biblical texts.. 242
Index of Subjects 246

Abbreviations

AGJU	Arbeiten zur Geschichte des antiken Judentums und des Urchristentums
AncB	Anchor Bible
AJP	American Journal of Philology
AncSoc	Ancient Society
ANRW	H. Temporini – W. Haase (eds.) Aufstieg und Niedergang der römischen Welt. Geschichte und Kultur im Spiegel der neueren Forschung. Berlin – New York.
AThANT	Abhandlungen zur Theologie des Alten und Neuen Testaments
AthD	Acta Theologica Danica
AUSS	Andrews University Seminary Studies
BBB	Bonner Biblische Beiträge
Bib	Biblica
	Biblical Interpretation
BNTC	Black's New Testament Commentaries
BU	Biblische Untersuchungen
BZ	Biblische Zeitschrift
CBQ	Catholic Biblical Quarterly
CQ	Classical Quarterly
EHS.T	Europäische Hochschulschriften. Reihe 23, Theologie
EKK	Evangelisch-Katholischer Kommentar
EpRe	Epworth Review
EQ	Evangelical Quarterly
EvTh	Evangelische Theologie
ExpT	Expository Times
FzB	Forschung zur Bibel
FRLANT	Forschungen zur Religion und Literatur des Alten und Neuen Testaments
GaR	Greece and Rome
GTA	Göttinger Theologische Arbeiten
HNT	Handbuch zum Neuen Testament
HSCP	Harvard Studies in Classical Philology
HThK	Herder's Theologischer Kommentar
HTR	Harvard Theological Review
HUCA	Hebrew Union College Annual
ICC	International Critical Commentary
Interp.	Interpretation
JBL	Journal of Biblical Literature
JRS	Journal of Roman Studies

JSNT	Journal for the Study of the New Testament
JSNTS	Journal for the Study of the New Testament, Supplement Series
JSOTS	Journal for the Study of the Old Testament, Supplement Series
JThS	Journal of Theological Studies
KEK	Kritisch-Exegetischer Kommentar
KThS	Kohlhammer Studienbücher Theologie
LCL	Loeb Classical Library
MSSNTS	Monograph Series. Society for New Testament Studies
NICNT	New International Commentary on the New Testament
NIGTC	New International Greek Testament Commentary
Neotest.	Neotestamentica
NTA	Neutestamentliche Abhandlungen
NTD	Neues Testament Deutsch
NTS	New Testament Studies
NT.S	Novum Testamentum. Supplements
ÖTK	Ökumenischer Taschenbuchkommentar zum Neuen Testament
Rexp	Review and Expositor
RNT	Regensburger Neues Testament
SBL.DS	Society of Biblical Literature Dissertation Series
SBLSBS	Society of Biblical Literature Sources for Biblical Study
SBS	Stuttgarter Bibelstudien
SKK	Stuttgarter kleiner Kommentar
ThHK	Theologischer Handkommentar zum Neuen Testament
ThZ	Theologische Zeitschrift
TynBul	Tyndale Bulletin
UTB	Uni-Taschenbücher
VF	Verkündigung und Forschung
WBC	Word Biblical Commentary
WMANT	Wissenschaftliche Monographien zum Alten und Neuen Testament
WUNT	Wissenschaftliche Untersuchungen zum Neuen Testament
ZNW	Zeitschrift für neutestamentliche Wissenschaft
ZPE	Zeitschrift für Papyrologie und Epigraphik

Chapter 1

Introduction

The Current Communis Opinio on Paul's Collection

New Testament scholars frequently emphasise the importance of Paul's collection for Jerusalem (hence: *'the collection'*). In particular: the theological motives of the different parties involved in the collection, as well as the chronological framework of this project have presented themselves as important topics for discussion.[1] Although scholars have always been aware of the caritative functions of the collection, and have frequently stressed the importance thereof, most have, in the end, opted for a strictly 'theological' understanding of this imaginative project. As a matter of fact, according to the present scholarly consensus, Paul understood the collection as a means by which to achieve some 'higher theological aims,' as the following quotations indicate:

> The real significance of the collection is not the money as such or the amount of help it will bring, but the demonstration of unity between Jews and Gentiles within the Church.[2]

> ... sie [the collection] - war mehr als eine Hilfsleistung für die Armen der Urgemeinde.[3]

> The collection was not merely a means of alleviating want; it was also a recognition of Jerusalem's special status as the mother church of the new Israel, an acknowledgement on the part of the Gentile Church of their indebtedness to Jerusalem as the origin of spiritual blessing (Rom 15,27).[4]

---

[1] The importance of the collection is reflected in almost all monographs dealing with the chronological framework of Paul's ministry. Cf. Suhl, *Paulus und seine Briefe*; Lüdemann, *Paulus, der Heidenapostel I*; Hyldahl, *Die Paulinische Chronologie*; and Riesner, *Die Frühzeit des Apostels Paulus*.
[2] Holmberg, *Paul and Power*, 38.
[3] Eckert, "Die Kollekte des Paulus für Jerusalem", 66.
[4] Fung, *The Epistle to the Galatians*, 102-103.

> Auch muß vornhinein gesagt werden, daß es nicht genügt, die Sammlung nur als Hilfsaktion für in materieller Not befindliche Glaubensbrüder und -schwestern anzusehen.[5]

It is not difficult to see why the collection has frequently been related to, and explained, in terms of theological factors. Even a superficial reading of Paul's references to the collection, dispersed throughout his four so-called 'main-letters' (e.g. 1 Cor 16,1-4; 2 Cor 8-9; Gal 2,10; Rom 15,25-31),[6] indicates that this was no 'ordinary' fund raising project. The collection had far-reaching implications for all the parties involved. But what functions did the collection actually fulfil within the early Christian movement? Was it a visible means to give expression to the unity between Jewish and Gentile Christians?[7] Or was it a conscious effort on the part of the apostle to emphasise the legitimate position of Gentile Christianity *"als Frucht am Baum im Weingarten Israel?"*[8] Or should one rather, together with Johannes Munck, understand the collection from the perspective of Paul's final journey to Jerusalem in the company of a contingent of non-Jewish Christians as part of a 'provocative' missionary strategy to fill the Jews with envy at the very sight of Gentiles bringing a monetary offering into the Holy City?[9] Does Dieter Georgi's modified version of Munck's thesis perhaps uncover the *traditionsgeschichtlichen Hintergrund* of the collection with his view that Paul, in line with [den] *Zeichenhandlungen der alttestamentlichen Propheten*, understood this project as an eschatological demonstration for Jerusalem? Is he correct when he assumes that

---

[5] Gnilka, "Die Kollekte der paulinischen Gemeinden für Jerusalem", 301-2.

[6] According to Trobisch, *Die Paulusbriefe und die Anfänge der christlichen Publizistik*, 103, Paul's collection, which is only referred to in his four main letters, was decisive in grouping these letters together in the early Christian canon. In his own words: "der Spendenaufruf für Jerusalem verbindet alle vier Briefe: Der Galaterbrief erklärt, wie es zu dieser Aktion gekommen ist. Am Ende des 1. Korintherbriefes beschreibt Paulus, wie diese Kollekte in den Gemeinden in Galatien wie in Korinth organisiert werden sollte. Im 2. Korintherbrief bildet dieser 'Dienst an den Heiligen' (2 Kor 9,1) das zentrale Thema des Spendenaufrufes in 2 Kor 8-9. Und der erfolgreiche Abschluß dieses Projektes ist Röm 15,26 vermeldet."

[7] In this regard Hainz, *Koinonia*, 152, understands the collection "als eine Konkretion bzw. als Ausdruck und Beweis der zwischen Jerusalem und den heidenchristlichen Kirchen bestehenden 'Gemeinschaft'." Brändle, "Geld und Gnade (zu II Kor 8,9)", 270, also shares the same view: "Eindeutig scheint mir, daß die Kollekte für Paulus in erster Linie die Zusammengehörigkeit der heidenchristlichen Gemeinden mit der Muttergemeinde in Jerusalem repräsentieren sollte."

[8] Bartsch, "Wenn ich ihnen diese Frucht versiegelt habe", 107.

[9] Munck, *Paulus und die Heilsgeschichte*, 298-302. According to Munck it was Paul's "...Absicht, die Juden zu erretten, indem er sie auf die Heiden eifersüchtig macht, die in grosser Zahl das Evangelium annehmen." As the deliverer of the collection, he therefore acted like a 'Moses-like' figure who aimed at bringing the unbelieving Jews to repentance.

the collection was intended to visibly remind the Jews of the pilgrimage of the nations to Jerusalem?[10] Or should one rather follow some of the new notions, such as Klaus Berger's understanding of the collection as an act of almsgiving on the part of Gentile Christians to the poor in Jerusalem as a substitute for their own circumcision?[11] Or Furnish's promising suggestion that Paul's churches probably understood their gifts to Jerusalem as an act of patronage, which placed the Judean believers under obligation to them as client congregations?[12] Perhaps it may be more sound to interpret the collection as an undertaking which had diverse significance for the respective participants,[13] and which simultaneously fulfilled different theological functions within the various socio-historical contexts in the early church?

1.1. Uniting body and soul again

Despite some new opinions concerning the collection, the views of Munck and Georgi have provided the conceptual framework for the current understanding of the collection.[14] It appears as if they did 'solve' the most puzzling questions related to the collection to the satisfaction of the majority of scholars. That this would be the case is illustrated by similar understanding regarding the collection being found repeatedly in academic publications that directly or indirectly deal with this project.[15] Recent research has not

---

[10] Georgi, *Der Armen zu gedenken*, 84-85.

[11] Berger, "Almosen für Israel", 180-203.

[12] Furnish, *2 Corinthians*, 413.

[13] So, e.g., Nickle, *The Collection*, 100-143, who understands the collection as an act of Christian charity, as well as a visible expression of the unity of the church. At the same time, the collection also fulfils an important eschatological function in terms of Paul's own apostolic ministry and the position of Israel in the '*Heilsgeschichte*'. See in this regard also McKnight, "The collection".

[14] Witherington, *Conflict and Community*, 423, is of the opinion that the studies of Georgi and Nickle have had the most impact on scholars' understanding of the collection, but that the work by Georgi has been more influential.

[15] In the most recent commentaries the significance of the collection is, to a large extent, still interpreted in terms of the views developed by Munck and Georgi (cf. e.g., Wolff, *Der zweite Brief des Paulus an die Korinther,* and Barnett, *The Second Epistle to the Corinthians*). In many recent works on Paul's theology, the authors do not even bother to address the collection issue in any detail (e.g., Barrett, *Paul*, and Lohse, *Paulus*). Even more puzzling is the fact that biblical scholars, who make use of sociological theories to interpret the social framework of Paul's ministry, do not pay much attention to the collection either. One would have at least expected these researchers, in their attempts to explain the 'social dynamics' of Pauline Christianity, to deal with the impact of social factors on Paul's conceptualisation of this project in a much more constructive manner than what the present case is (e.g., MacDonald, *The Pauline Churches*). Research articles also do not offer much that is new on the collection (cf. e.g., Legrand,

really broken much new ground. Most scholars still proceed from the assumption that Paul understood the collection mainly as an 'eschatological provocation' to Jerusalem, and as a symbol of unity between the early Christians. Although (some of) these interpretations might be correct, they do not distinguish clearly between various interpretations of the collection by Paul and by Jerusalem respectively. Scholars focus mainly on Paul's theological understanding of the collection, while ignoring the basic interpretative framework of meaning, which he attached to this project, and which also constituted his various theological reflections in this regard.

To a large extent, Paul and the other parties involved in the collection project are portrayed as a group of intellectuals who developed complex cognitive interpretations in service of some higher theological ideals. The fact that they were people of flesh and blood, who formulated solutions to specific problems they faced within the confines and constrains of their own life-world(s), has largely been ignored. The most recent example of such a consistently theological interpretation of the collection, with little consideration for the socio-historical and ideological frameworks, within which this project was undertaken and within which it attained specific meaning(s), is presented in the study of Beckheuer. According to him, Paul's eschatological interpretation of Trito-Isaiah led him to develop a *Rettungsgeschichte für Heiden und Juden,* which articulated the collection during all its phases.[16] Even when Paul dealt with practical questions related to the organisation of the collection, he did it *in der Sprache der theologischen Reflexion* (1 Cor 16,1-4).[17]

"That We Remember the Poor"). The short study by Reumann, "Contributions of the Philippian Community to Paul and to Earliest Christianity", at least addresses the possible involvement of the Philippians in the collection, while a technical discussion on the background of certain concepts used by Paul when dealing with the collection is presented by Ascough, "The Completion of a Religious Duty". A ray of hope toward a more satisfactory interpretation is, however, to be found in a materialist analysis of the collection by Horrell, "Paul's Collection: Resources for a Materialist Theology". According to Horrell, Paul's use of theological language in terms of the collection should not lead us to 'over-spiritualise' his concerns, since his main concern was essentially and unavoidably material, namely the collection and redistribution of money. Horrell correctly states that the so-called 'spiritual' and 'material' dichotomy in terms of the collection is a false and "ultimately unsustainable distinction ... The spiritual and material, the social and theological, are here inextricably intertwined" (p. 79).

[16] Beckheuer, *Paulus und Jerusalem. Kollekte und Mission im theologischen Denken des Heidenapostels,* 81.

[17] Beckheuer, *Paulus und Jerusalem,* 271. His interpretation of 2 Cor 9,5f. where the collection is understood as a blessing to the people of Jerusalem along the lines of Is 65, 9, reflects his own theological pre-occupation: "Dieser religiöse Sinnhorizont aus TriJes verdeutlicht dem Heidenapostel die Gewißheit der Segensfülle, die er auf das Kollektenunternehmen bezieht. So wie bei TriJes der Übergang von der früheren Gerichtsprophetie zur Heilsverheißung vollzieht, so verkündigt Paulus im Zusammenhang mit der

The theoretical question to be addressed in this study is whether this strong emphasis on the 'theology of the collection' does not restrict a more holistic understanding of this project. A more encompassing approach that focuses on the consistent interplay of all the relevant social and theological factors related to the collection is long overdue. Since the collection formed a central facet of Paul's apostolic ministry, and also determined his apostolic self-understanding and social status[18] within the early Christian movement, present 'scholarly consensus', needs to be challenged by new perspectives that will again unite the 'body and soul' of early Christianity.

Ideologies, conventions and processes inherent to the social environment within which the early Christians found themselves largely determined their understanding of reality. These factors also instilled meaning to the collection, from its 'theological conception' to its organisation and the eventual delivery thereof. Paul's theological reflection on this project carried with it particular values and beliefs from his environment. His theological views also informed and transformed some of these beliefs and values. Therefore, the *socio-historical context* of the collection cannot merely be viewed as 'background information', as a sort of a vantage point from which to proceed to the 'actual theological understanding' of this project. It should rather be seen as the interpretative framework, as both decor and foreground within which symbols, beliefs, perceptions, and social forms of interaction of Paul and the other role players in the collection took shape and attained specific socio-religious meanings.

In the light of the lacunae in present research, and the theoretical questions posed, the aim of this study is the investigation of the interaction between various social and theological facets concerning the collection. In other words, the collection will be approached as a venture by Paul to help solve the poverty of the believers in Judea, and in so doing, to give concrete expression to his role as 'benefactor' of the believers in Jerusalem. At the same time, the interaction between Paul and the leadership of the Jerusalem community, who viewed themselves as benefactors within the early Christian movement, will also be analysed.

Organisation der Sammlung den gnädigen handelnden Gott, der mit seinem geschichtlichen Eingreifen durch Jesus Christus den Übergang vom Unheil zum Heil demonstriert."

[18] 'Status' is used in this study to indicate social standing of individuals within their respective groups and within society. Status thus functions as a social position. But status also functions as a value, since one's status is invariably assessed in terms of what others perceive one's position to be worth. Cf. in this regard also the views of Kidd, *Wealth and Beneficence in the Pastoral Epistles*, 50-55, and Malina & Neyrey, "Conflict in Luke-Acts", 97-124.

1.2. Hypotheses and aims of the investigation

The following hypotheses will be tested in this study:

A. The collection is to be understood in terms of the social convention of *benefit exchange*. Reciprocity was at the heart of all forms of benevolence in the ancient Graeco-Roman world. The bestowal of gifts initiated the establishment of long-term relationships that involved mutual obligations and clear status differentials between the transactors.

1. Paul interpreted the request from the leadership of the Jerusalem church at the Jerusalem meeting, not to forget the poor (Gal 2,10), in terms of the principles inherent to reciprocal relationships within the Graeco-Roman world. In this relationship the Jerusalem leadership functioned as the initial *benefactors*, since they, by recognising Paul's Law-free gospel, indebted him to them.

2. In response to their benefaction to Paul, the Jerusalem church 'requested' from him and Barnabas, as representatives of the Christian community in Antioch, and as *beneficiaries* in this reciprocal relationship, to address the needs of the socially destitute in Jerusalem (Gal 2,10). By this 'request' the Jerusalem leadership publicly acknowledged that Paul (and Barnabas) had access to material means, which were not routinely available to them.

B. In order to fulfil his obligations towards Jerusalem, but also because the church in Antioch did not live up to their responsibilities in this regard, Paul took it upon himself to organise a collection in the Christian communities in Galatia, Achaia and Macedonia (and Asia?) under his control. Throughout the project these Christian communities, under Paul's control, were included as *beneficiaries* in the reciprocal relationship between him and the Jerusalem church.

1. In terms of the so-called 'coherence-contingency'[19] scheme of Paul's hermeneutic, he used the 'stable, constant elements' which underlay the 'ideological' basis of his gospel to persuade his communities to participate in the collection. He also employed new strategies and theological motives, which were necessitated by specific situations that he had to deal with, in order to reveal the 'true' nature of the collection. In this regard, Paul constantly emphasised the religious nature of this project, which involved his communities in a reciprocal relationship not only with Jerusalem, but also with God. Although the theological principles basic to Paul's convictional framework, such as the impact of God's grace and the Christ-event on the lives of believers, played a central role in his understanding of the collection, he also intertwined his thinking with praxis. In other words, by

---

[19] Cf. in this regard Beker, "Recasting Pauline Theology: The Coherence-Contingency Scheme as Interpretative Model", 15-24.

allowing the contingent situation of the moment to constantly shape his own understanding of the collection, Paul took care not to 'fossilise' his understanding of this project into a static system of thought.

2. Paul utilised specific rhetorical strategies and 'contextual theologies' in the course of the collection project, not only to ensure the completion of this project, but also to secure his future role as benefactor of Jerusalem. In other words, these 'theological motives' also functioned to support the apostle's socio-religious position and status within the early Christian movement. From Paul's point of view, his ability to realise the initial expectations of the Jerusalem church to provide in the needs of their poor, was the basis of his socio-religious credibility within the parameters of the early Christian movement. In order to ensure the completion of the collection, Paul offered various contextual (re)interpretations of the nature, function and advantages of this project for all parties involved by constantly relating it to the basic framework of benefit exchange.

C. The conflicting ideologies of Paul and Jerusalem threatened the eventual acceptance of the collection. A negative response to the collection would imply an abrupt end to the reciprocal relationship between Pauline Christianity and the Jerusalem church, as the two most important 'interest groups' within the early Christian movement. In anticipation of a possible rejection of the collection, Paul presented a new ideological angle to the collection at a late stage in this project (Rom 15,25ff), over against his previous theological reflection that focussed on securing the successful completion of this project (cf. 1 Cor 16,1-4; 2 Cor 8-9; Gal 2,10).

1. Paul's expectation of a negative response to the collection by Jerusalem compelled him to reinterpret his own obligation, as well as that of his communities, towards the Jerusalem church (Rom 15,25ff). He did this by shifting the emphasis away from the generally accepted views on reciprocity ('gifts must be rewarded with counter gifts'), to giving according to the principles of selfless service, and the fulfilling of one's responsibilities, irrespective of the response on the side of the recipients. Paul thus turned the collection into an 'eleventh hour success' from his own communities' point of view.

2. Although Luke is not well informed on the Pauline collection, he offers a brief overview of Paul's final visit to Jerusalem to deliver the collection (Acts 21,17ff.). From the available information it may be inferred that Paul and James devised an emergency solution to ensure the eventual acceptance of the collection by the Jerusalem church. However, the capture of Paul in the Temple brought an abrupt end to this imaginative project, at least from the perspective of his early Christian biographers. Nevertheless, we are left with a picture of the provisional acceptance of the collection by the Jerusalem church, with Paul briefly acting as their

benefactor, by using money from the collection to pay for the Nazarene vows of some of their members.

In summary: the basic objective of this investigation is to come to terms with the Pauline collection from the perspective of *social exchange*.[20] Within the parameters of this investigation, we shall firstly focus on various forms of social exchange within the ancient Graeco-Roman world, in order to determine the basic interpretative framework for the collection. Thereafter, the respective theological understandings of these principles by the major role players involved in this project, namely Paul, the Jerusalem church, and the Pauline communities, will be analysed.

1.3. Theory underlying a 'holistic' understanding of the collection

A comprehensive picture of the collection demands consideration of two theoretical aspects namely: (a) the various ideologies/theologies of the early Christian movement, which, in turn, should be analysed in terms of (b) the larger 'social and ideological scripts' prevalent in the Graeco-Roman and Jewish worlds during the first century CE. It is not sufficient to study the collection in isolation, or merely to decipher the *traditions-geschichtliche* background(s) of the various role players. Ideologies do not take shape or develop separately from their contemporary social and historical realities, but they do so in interaction with, and in response to particular social processes and beliefs.

1.3.1. Ideological factors and the collection

Ideology gives verbal, visual and symbolic expression to, and at the same time also defines the collective beliefs and behaviour of particular groups. This is done by means of the articulation of specific forms of conduct, the conceptualisation and legitimisation of specific values and practices, the integration of social phenomena and symbolic realities in encompassing systems of meaning. Obviously, the ideas, concepts, beliefs and traditions espoused and promoted by a group are those "which are most compatible with the self-interests of its members and/or their leaders."[21] The self-interests of individuals and groups often generate ideas which, when

---

[20] In this study, social exchange, as opposed to institutionalised forms of economic exchange, refers to the reciprocal relationships that are established and/or maintained between parties involved in an exchange of services and/or gifts.

[21] Elliott, *What is Social-Scientific Criticism?*, 52.

organised and employed, "explain and justify these self-interests, [and so] constitute an ideology."[22]

Ideology, in its function of maintaining, protecting and promoting sectional, or personal interests, can easily be misappropriated to sustain and legitimise asymmetric relations of power between respective partners, but also between group members and outsiders who hold on to conflicting interpretations of reality. Anthony Giddens,[23] identifies three principal modes of ideological function, namely: the representation of sectional interests as universal interests, the denial of contradictions, and reification, where a situation or historical state of affairs is represented as natural, permanent and eternal.

In this study, the ideologies of the early Christian movement are approached with reference to the beliefs, practices, norms and values of the various individuals and communities involved in the collection.[24] These ideologies provide the theological basis and the concomitant conceptual framework(s) for the practical '*Gestalt*' of the collection during its various phases.[25]

The ideologies of the various early Christian groups functioned as the binding force, the cement, that kept them together and gave them a distinct social identity and a shared consciousness of their special religious status

---

[22] Elliott, *What is Social-Scientific Criticism?*, 52. Cf. also the views of Thompson, *Studies in the Theory of Ideology*, 4, and Eagleton, *Ideology*, 43. Eagleton, who refers to at least six ways of defining ideology (pp 28-31), points out that ideology cannot be studied without understanding the social contexts; the various forms of discourse, and the ways in which concepts are used in the communication process by the various persons and groups involved (p. 223).

[23] Giddens, *Central Problems in Social Theory*, 6; 193ff. understands ideology in terms of "the capability of dominant groups or classes to make their own sectional interests appear to others as universal ones." The theoretical insights of this eminent social theorist have been applied to the field of the New Testament by Horrell, *The Social Ethos of the Corinthian Correspondence*.

[24] Theology is 'religious ideology', that is, a religious interpretation of reality. When reality is understood from the perspective of metaphysical intervention, ideology refers to all the beliefs and values, as well as to the language structures that are produced to verbalise and to reflect upon these symbolic realities.

[25] Obviously, the 'ideological' point of departure of the researcher determines his/her approach to any investigation of ideology in the New Testament. There is clearly no such thing as a neutral (objective) approach to this 'ideological' concept: ideology! Cf. also the views of Searle, *The Construction of Social Reality*, 7-13. The various theoretical paradigms presently operative within the field of New Testament research are no safeguards against personal prejudices on the part of researchers. All approaches, be it the trusted historical-critical methods, or new literary or social-scientific approaches, are by their very nature perspectives. They have a certain innate distorting quality since they approach the New Testament from a preconception of what is to be looked for. But then again, whoever looks for nothing finds nothing.

before God. But these ideologies did not remain abstract ideas and idealistic thought-structures. They were embedded and visibly expressed in specific socio-religious structures, practices, and stereotyped patterns of interaction.[26] At the same time, the believers also utilised a common body of verbal signs, that is, a 'verbal repertoire', to give expression to their beliefs, and to signify the various phenomena they encountered. The verbal repertoire of the various early Christian communities thus, not only served as 'storehouses' of their acquired knowledge,[27] but also as 'expressions' and further substantiation of their ideologies.[28] However, the various religious statements that they produced were more than mere expressions and confirmations of their social and symbolic realities. In fact, it was part of a dynamic, ongoing process of establishing, maintaining, and at times, adjusting or completely altering, specific meanings and practices.

In order to come to terms with the ideological factors involved in the collection, we must, on a lower level of abstraction, take cognisance of the various 'theologies' of the major role players in the collection. These include: *Paul*, the protagonist responsible for the organisation; theological conceptualisation and practical execution of the collection; the *churches* in Galatia, Macedonia and Achaia involved in the actual 'Sammlung,' as well as the views of the ever-changing *leadership* of the church in Jerusalem.[29] However, there are a number of impediments: Firstly, the New Testament only presents us with the basic outline of the collection from which we must try to construct the views of the various parties involved. Secondly, this information stems mainly from Paul's letters. In order to construct an idea of the views of Jerusalem and that of the churches responsible for the collection, we are dependent on a few indicators in his letters, such as the ways in which these role players are addressed; references to their respective statusses (and possible variations in this regard); the forms and contents of the intra-textual discourses; reflections on their beliefs; etc. At best, this remains a precarious undertaking, since Paul and the other parties

---

[26] The early Christian communities constructed their own life-worlds in which all forms of interaction and behaviour were shaped by socially constructed norms, to give meaning and social shape to their existence. Cf. in this regard the views of Berger & Luckmann, *The Social Construction of Reality*, 13, on people's 'world-building' activities.

[27] In this role, language usually routinises and stabilises social interaction - Luckmann, *Life-world and Social Realities*, 79.

[28] The ideology/ies of a group permeates all its texts. It determines and directs the structure and contents of all forms of oral and written communication.

[29] The ever-changing face of the leadership of the Jerusalem church is reflected in various texts in the New Testament. They are known as: *die Zwölf* (Apg 6,2), *die Apostel* (15,4), *die Geltenden* (Gal 2, 26) bzw. die sog. *Säulenapostel* (2,9), *die Herrenbrüder* (1 Kor 9,5) *und die Ältesten* (Apg 15,4)' - cf. Lang, "Paulus und seine Gegner in Korinth und in Galatien", 420.

in the collection did not always share the same views on the nature and functions of this project.

On the basis of the asymmetric distribution of power, which Paul perceived to exist between himself and the other role players in terms of the collection, he claimed the right to exercise influence over the formulation and reproduction of the symbolic order that defined and shaped the nature and identity of this project.[30] Paul's own interests have thus shaped the content, as well as the intended effect of his discourse about the collection. As a matter of fact, in his efforts to advance his own agendas and sustain his basis of power in the early church, the rhetoric applied in his letters by addressing matters pertaining to the collection, functioned as social modes of control. Thus, Paul at times fell prey to 'ideological manipulation' in order to promote his own interests. Therefore, one should be careful not to merely accept his 'theologising' at face value.

1.3.2. The ideological and social frameworks for Paul's collection

Dominant ideologies, practices and institutions, from the Graeco-Roman and Jewish environments, shaped the various role-players' understanding of the collection, by providing the vocabulary, symbols, social frameworks and analogies for this undertaking. In particular, the principles of reciprocity that were embedded and reflected in benefit exchange relationships provided the *basic interpretative framework* for the collection. However, as mentioned above, the ancient sources at our disposal are not always very informative, leaving us with only scant information from which to construct a coherent picture of such diverse facets as the social peculiarities of the conventions of *euergetism* and patronage. Thus, one has to resort to the use of comparative material from better documented societies, such as peasant communities, together with some hypotheses and academic guesswork(!), to come to an understanding of the nature and 'mechanics' of these social exchange relationships.

We also have to take into consideration that the available material on ancient reciprocal relationships, such as friendship, benefaction and patronage, mainly reflects on the sectional interests of the privileged groups, who had access to wealth, power and honour within Graeco-Roman society.[31] Most people within this predominantly agrarian society

---

[30] Giddens, *New Rules of Sociological Method*, 110, states that "what passes for social reality stands in immediate relation to the distribution of power." However, the fact that the other parties involved in the collection did not always share Paul's perception of the collection and his basis of power, implies that a discrepancy existed between his *perception* of his own power with regards to the collection and his *actual authority* in the early church.

[31] Most members of the Roman Empire were peasants. According to Garnsey and Woolf, "Patronage of the Rural Poor in the Roman World", 154, up to 80% of the pop-

were poor and illiterate. While being involved in a never-ending struggle to maintain honour and to stay above a subsistence level, the primary concerns of these people were not to write literature or to leave any inscriptions and monuments behind, but rather to obtain bare essentials of life, such as food, shelter and clothing. Obviously, a number of other factors also caused these extreme low levels of literacy and consequent lack of literary sources, such as the expense and scarcity of writing materials, weak public education systems, and the predominant 'oral consciousness' of the time.[32] Meir Bar-Ilan illustrates this 'oral mindset' concerning the position of Jewish children during the first century CE clearly:

> [I]n a traditional society, knowing how to read was not a necessity; neither for economic reasons, nor for intellectual ones.... Why should a farmer send his son to learn how to read when it entails a waste of working time (= money)? Why should he himself learn how to read if this culture is based on an oral tradition (though not with a written Torah)? According to the Torah, there is no need to read or write, except for writing the Mezuzah, Teflin, and the Torah itself. However, for these purposes there was always a scribe, so a Jew in antiquity could fulfil the commandments of the Torah while being illiterate.[33]

Another difficulty facing the study of ideological and cultural scripts of the 'Umwelt' of the early Christians, is related to the question whether it is a legitimate procedure to use the available documents to construct a picture of the ideological agendas of authors and readers, as well as the contours of the world/s in which they lived. In other words, may one use these texts as 'windows', which allows access into the preliterary stages or historical backgrounds of the texts in question? Would this not be merely a subjective interpretation of the documents at one's disposal, since these are literary products beyond which one can no longer proceed? Would such a construct not merely be an image of oneself in the texts; only finding what one wants to find there?

The literary critic Murray Krieger's dated, but still useful, differentiation between texts as 'windows' and 'mirrors' could prove a helpful way out of this *impasse*.[34] One should follow his suggestion by regarding the

---

ulation were occupied on the land. They were largely ignored by the urban elite who controlled Graeco-Roman society since they were considered to be unworthy of attention. Cf. also the informative study of Hanson and Oakman, *Palestine in the time of Jesus*.

[32] Cf. in this regard Svenbro, *Phrasikleia*, who traces the evolution of reading in Greek antiquity through its various stages.

[33] Bar-Ilan, "Illiteracy in the Land of Israel in the First Centuries C.E.", 55.

[34] Krieger, *A Window to Criticism*, 3-4. A number of biblical scholars have applied these concepts to come to terms with the nature of the New Testament texts. Cf., e.g., Donahue, "Windows and Mirrors: The Setting of Mark's Gospel". Schneiders, *The Revelatory Text*, 113, relates these concepts to her own reinterpretation of Paul Ricoeur's not-

texts at one's disposal as both mirrors and windows. In other words, they reflect important facets of the socio-historical contexts in which they were produced.³⁵ At the same time, however, they also function as a self-contained system of signs that generate meaning and engage the readers in the reading process. Thus, without naively accepting that textual references to the Pauline collection refer directly to extra-textual realities, one could, nevertheless, (through a careful analysis of the various indicators) gain valuable information on the ideological scripts operative in the world behind the texts.

Historical factors relevant to the understanding of the collection have to be taken into consideration, such as the chronology of this project, *traditionsgeschichtliche* backgrounds, possible historical analogies from the environment, etc. Nevertheless, one is faced with a serious shortage of information in this regard. In terms of primary sources, one only has the remarks in Paul's letters from which to construct the basic historical framework for the collection. However, it is not the focus of this study to get embroiled in the labyrinth of intriguing debates concerning aspects, such as the *chronological framework* of the collection, or the relationship between Acts and Paul's letters. The aim of this study is not so much to provide 'new' solutions to historic issues of this nature, but rather to understand the collection from a new interpretative framework in terms of the reciprocal interaction between the major role players, as well as in terms of the various ideological interpretations that they attached to this project.

Due to the shortage of historical information regarding the collection, it is unfortunately not possible to 'reconstruct' the full picture of what actually took place.³⁶ But this should not deter one from historical scrutiny of the available material, since I contend that these texts, not only reflect the interests of the persons and groups by whom they were produced, but also

---

ion of "the world behind the text" ("the text as window"), "the world of the text" ("the text as mirror"), and "the world in front of the text", which deals with transformative potential of the text for present readers.

³⁵ To view ancient texts merely as autosemantic units that can be studied without taking notice of the values and conventions operative in the society in which their authors and readers lived, and which decisively influenced the form and contents of these documents, leads to a one-sided, biased view. As a matter of fact, the social contexts in which all utterances are made and in which texts are produced, place restraints on the linguistic choices of all speakers/ authors.

³⁶ The very nature of ancient historical sources also places constraints on our understanding of the phenomena and processes under investigation, since these sources only present us with their own culturally conditioned interpretations of the relevant facts, not with *bruta facta*. We could, therefore, at best, only *construct possible scenarios* in this regard. Reconstructions of the historical facts/situations in question (in positivistic sense) are out of the question.

present us with explicit (and implicit) encodements of conditions external to the texts in question. In other words, the meanings communicated by these texts are determined (and constrained) by the socio-historical locations of the authors and their communities. Therefore, with the aid of: (a) the available knowledge concerning the institutions, events and historical practices (that is, diachronical developments and causal relationships) during the periods under investigation; (b) the nature of the available historical sources (world views, ideologies, social codes, referential possibilities, etc.), and (c) the various tools of historical criticism, we could construct a basic picture of the historical contexts within which the texts in question were produced.

1.4. The larger picture: using models

The data in the documents and inscriptions related to the socio-historical framework(s) of the collection provides us with important information about the key actors, events and the social processes. What these sources *do not deal with*, however, are causal factors in terms of the functioning and dynamics of ancient Graeco-Roman and Jewish societies. In other words, the 'how, why and what' of these societies are not always explicitly spelled out. This includes: the network of political, social and economic conditions in the Graeco-Roman world(s) in which the systems of benefaction and patronage were generated and fostered; the impact of these social exchange relationships on society in general and on the conceptualisation and organisation of the collection in particular; the persons and groups who benefited from these relationships; the belief-systems that ideologically legitimated the Pauline collection; possible contradictions and social conflicts with (representatives of) other belief-systems; the nature of societal competition the collection may have fostered; socio-economic impacts of this undertaking on the early Christian movement in the short-term and in the long-term, etc.[37] In order to move beyond a 'historical description' of the phenomena, or beyond a technical examination of particular historical fragments,[38] to an explanation of the various factors, ideologies and social forces involved in the collection, certain cognitive models could facilitate the ordering, analysis and explanations related to

---

[37] Cf. in this regard the theoretical perspectives of Elliott, "Patronage and Clientage", 147.

[38] Bloch, *The Historian's Craft*, 155, is correct when he states: "... the knowledge of fragments, studied by turns, each for its own sake, will never produce the knowledge of the whole; it will not even produce that of the fragments themselves."

this complex welter of material.³⁹ In other words, one needs to make use of consciously structured 'instruments' to form a coherent picture of the collection, which will not only explain the relationship between the social phenomena in question, but which will also allow for categorisation, comparison and synthesis of the (elements of) social and historical data. This will also facilitate the drawing of general inferences about their salient, recurrent social features.⁴⁰

Theories of gift exchange in pre-industrial agrarian societies, together with important information on various forms of reciprocity in the ancient Graeco-Roman world, will be used in this study to construct an appropriate working model of ancient social exchange relations (cf. Chapter 2). This model, which should not only reflect, but also explain salient features of the premises, procedures and understanding of reciprocal relations within these societies, will also serve as a 'heuristical' tool, to come to terms with the social patterns of interaction between the main actors involved in the collection. Following my basic hypothesis, that specific social dependency relations were incited by: (a) the command/request of the Jerusalem leadership to remember the poor, and (b) Paul's acceptance of this responsibility, this model should reveal and explain the relationship between relevant social phenomena. In order to come to terms with these facets, an approach will be followed throughout this study that is neither exclusively inductive (that is, from material to hypothesis) nor exclusively deductive

---

³⁹ According to Carney, *The Shape of the Past. Models and Antiquity*, 8, a model "...acts as a link between theories and observations. A model will employ one or more theories to provide a simplified (or an experimental or a generalised or an explanatory) framework which can be brought to bear on some pertinent data." Malina, "The Social Sciences and Biblical Interpretation", 231, suggests that a model is "an abstract simplified representation of some real world object, event, or interaction constructed for the purpose of understanding, control or prediction."

⁴⁰ According to Elliott, *What is Social-Scientific Criticism*, 44, models "... provide the means for seeking, analysing, and explaining repeated behaviours, social roles, institutions, patterns of stratification, modes of social interaction and conflict, and correlation between beliefs and behaviour, social organisation, and worldviews."

(from model to material), but will include both. This will involve a reciprocal movement between the material and - when certain factors are not explicit in the material under analysis - explanatory hypotheses and conjectures, to provide an appropriate model for this project.

Should the study of the collection be approached from the conceptual framework of ancient social exchange relationships, new vistas will, hopefully, open up, and new insights will emerge in terms of the nature and socio-religious functions of this project. This study responds to this particular challenge.

Chapter 2

Benefactor or Patron? Social Exchange in the Graeco-Roman World as the Interpretative Framework for the Collection

2.1. Introduction

... μόνον τῶν πτωχῶν ἵνα μνημονεύωμεν. According to Paul, this request/command of Peter (Gal 2,10) led to the commencement of his collection for Jerusalem, a project that took up much of his time and energy during his missionary activities in the eastern provinces of the Roman Empire in the mid-fifties. A few years after this request/command was made to him at the so-called 'Jerusalem council' (48 CE), Paul organised an imaginative project in the Christian communities founded by him.

As indicated in Chapter 1, various theological constructions are offered by scholars to explain the motivations for, and nature of this project. But the question still remains, whether an adequate understanding of the collection has been arrived at by the various theological endeavours? One clearly needs larger 'cognitive maps' in order to understand the interplay of the various socio-cultural and theological factors relevant to the collection. Thus, it is necessary to find an *appropriate and adequate model* to structure and interpret the available information on the collection, as well as to draw conclusions about the distinct, recurrent features of the larger social frameworks within which this project took place. This necessitates an overview of 'goods-exchange', based on information from comparative clan-based societies, which will provide some general principles underlying reciprocal relations in those societies. Secondly, an analysis and evaluation of information from the ancient Graeco-Roman world, which deals with the social exchange of gifts and services, will facilitate the design of a working model for the interpretation of the collection. The study of two repeated patterns of *social exchange*,[1] within which recip-

---

[1] Peterman, *Paul's Gift from Philippi*, 3, uses the term 'social reciprocity' to refer to the convention that operates in certain societies which dictates that when "...a person (or persons) is the recipient of goods in the form of a favour or a gift, the receiver is oblig-

rocal interactions between individuals and groups were conceptualised and concretised, namely *benefaction* and *patronage*, should provide a basic picture of exchange that will elucidate the collection, in terms of its basic processes and salient features. Within this conceptual framework, the 'theologies' and various forms of interaction of the major role players in the collection will be investigated in the course of the investigation (Chapters 3-7). Such a model of social exchange, which is historically embedded in specific reciprocal relationships in the ancient Mediterranean world, should not only articulate the hypotheses expressed in Chapter One, but should also clarify the collection from a new angle.

2.2. Gift-exchange and social relations in primitive societies

Man is a reciprocal being, *homo reciprocus*; whether in so-called 'primitive societies' where the exchange of gifts leads to the establishment of long-term relationships between the transactors; or in modern economic transactions where commodity-exchange establishes a relation between the goods transacted. In archaic societies in particular, social exchange was a general convention that functioned on the various levels of society, between groups and individuals. Cicero, for example writes that if obligations are incurred between two parties, an adequate response is required: "[F]or no duty is more imperative than that of proving one's gratitude."[2] And Seneca does not hesitate to point out that reciprocal interchange constitutes the *chief bond* that holds people together in society.[3]

---

ated to respond to the giver with goodwill and to return a counter-gift or favour in proportion to the goods received." Stegemann & Stegemann, *Urchristliche Sozialgeschichte. Die Anfänge im Judentum und die Christusgemeinden in der mediterranen Welt*, 1995, 43, in their analysis of various forms of ancient reciprocity, identify four forms, namely: (a) *Familiäre Reziprozität*, with its emphasis on the household and the clan, and brotherly love as social form of expresssion; (b) *Ausgeglichene Reziprozität* or reciprocity between people of equal status, such as friends and neighbours, with hospitality, benefactions and friendship as social forms of expression; (c) *Generelle Reziprozität*, or reciprocity between socially unequals, such as between patrons and clients, or rich and poor, with patronage, almsgiving, religious service, and discipleship as social forms of expression, and (d) *Negative Reziprozität* with strangers and enemies, and hospitality and love as social forms of expression.

[2] *De Officiis* 1.47. Cf. the English translation by Miller, *Cicero, De Officiis*, 1975 (LCL).

[3] *De Beneficiis* I.4.2: "De beneficiis dicendum est et ordinanda res, quae maxime humanam societatem adligat." In the present study, the text in Basore, *Seneca, Moral Essays. Vol III: De Beneficiis*, will be followed.

In the modern day there is still no such thing as a 'free meal', or, for that matter, a 'free-gift coupon', as Mary Douglas[4] tells us. Contrary to the sceptic views of cultural relativists, mutual obligations still continue hand in hand with various forms of exchange (together with differentiation of status and power, albeit in more complex and disguised forms) in var-ious forms of social interaction today.[5] Although the obligations imposed on participants in the reciprocal process might vary in time and space in relation to their status, we could speak of a universal norm of reciprocity based on, at least, the minimal demand that people must reward those who have helped them.[6] Westermack[7] accurately captures this universal imp-ortance of reciprocity: "...to requite a benefit, or to be grateful to him who bestows it, is probably everywhere, at least under certain circumstances, regarded as a duty."

2.2.1. Marcel Mauss

Although significant research has been undertaken on social exchange within various cultural contexts, no other work has captured the imagination of scholars in recent years to such an extent as has the French anthropologist Marcel Mauss' monograph on the exchange of gifts in primitive societies, originally published in 1925.[8] In terms of his ethnographic investigations of, amongst others, the potlatch of the Haïda and Tlingit Indian tribes in North America, Mauss found that within these 'total systems' of services and counter-services, every exchange (of which the economic transactions is but one element) forms part of the larger reciprocal system, "including banquets, rituals, military services, women, children, dances, festivals and fairs,"[9]. In other words, these exchanges do

---

[4] Cf. Douglas' foreword to the new translation by Halls of Mauss, *The Gift. The Form and Reason for Exchange in Archaic Societies*, London: Routledge, which is aptly called "No free gift".

[5] Cf. e.g., Blau, *Exchange in Power and Social Life*, 88-114; Becker, *Reciprocity*, 73ff., and Cook, *Social Network Theory*.

[6] Gouldner, "The Norm of Reciprocity: A Preliminary Statement", 161-178; esp. 171, identifies a second demand, namely that people should not injure those who have helped them. However, this aspect is already implied in, and basic to the first minimal demand.

[7] Quoted in Gouldner, *Reciprocity*, 161.

[8] Although the book of Mauss at first did not attract much attention, the well-known work of Claude Lévi-Strauss, *Les Structures Elémentaires de la Parenté*, in which he is very much indebted to Mauss' ideas, served to put the latter's interpretation of gifts and reciprocal obligations very much in the spotlight. In his introduction to Pearce's English translation of the work of Paul Veyne, *Bread and Circuses*, Oswyn Murray (xv) states that Mauss also provided the basic theory for Veyne's monumental analysis. Cf. also the use of Mauss by Saller, *Personal Patronage under the Early Empire*, 72, and Marshall, *Enmity in Corinth*, 1-3.

[9] Mauss, *The Gift*, 5.

not only involve the individual honour of the giver and recipient, but also that of other members in the same community.[10]

In terms of his views on the 'inalienability of things as gifts' that create an indissoluble bond with the original owner, Mauss is of the opinion that " ... gift exchange is an exchange of inalienable things between persons who are in a state of reciprocal dependence."[11] In other words, over against modern forms of commodity exchange (which involves a correlation between the objects exchanged in terms of the economic realities of purchase and sale), gift exchange (which establishes relations between the subjects involved) does not involve 'price-tags'. For Mauss gifts and returns are clearly not substitutes for exchange in primitive societies. They rather replace our system of sale and purchase,[12] having more or less the same function as economic exchange has in advanced societies, although in terms of different presuppositions and laws. For example: gifts do not only establish and secure the continuation of social relations in these societies by creating debts that have to be repaid, but they also demarcate the various, stereotypical social roles of the parties involved, while, at the same time, serving as the basis for social and political organisation. The *'gift economy'* is thus a 'debt economy'.

2.2.2. C.A. Gregory's model of gift-exchange in clan-based societies

In his investigation of the gift economies of Papua New Guinea, based on theoretical insights from Marx, Straffa, Mauss and Levi-Strauss, Gregory draws an important distinction between objects of exchange in clan- and class-based economies.[13] According to Gregory, in clan-based societies objects of exchange often assume the 'non-alienated forms of the gifts', with reproduction becoming gift-reproduction. Secondly, in class-based societies processes dominate, while *personification* processes dominate in clan-based societies. This implies that different values are respectively

---

[10] Basically, the system is quite simple: "...just the rule that every gift has to be returned in some specified way sets up a perpetual cycle of exchanges within and between generations. In some cases the specified return is of equal value, producing a stable system of statuses; in others it must exceed the value of the earlier gift, producing an escalating contest for honour. The catalogue of transfers that map all the obligations between its members can describe the whole society. The cycling gift system is the society" - Douglas, *The Gift*, viii-ix.

[11] As rephrased in Gregory, *Gifts and Commodities*, 19.

[12] Mauss, *The Gift*, 36.

[13] In his discussion on the differences between class- and clan-based societies, Gregory, *Gifts and Commodities*, 36-40, refers to the distribution of land, which, according to him is relatively unequal in class-based societies, but more equal in clan-based societies. In order to derive these bipolar oppositions between clan and class, Gregory also mentions other factors, such as the production and exchange of food, the existence of subgroups and social classes within societies, etc.

attached to people and to objects in these societies. In contrast to the strong emphasis on reciprocity between the objects transacted in commodity-based societies, clan-based societies rather focus on *social relations* between the transactors.[14]

In clan-based societies gifts are inalienable objects. They form part of the collective possessions of the clan.[15] The strong bonds between things and persons are often expressed in the personification of gifts, which are regarded by their producers as an extension of their person. Thus, when somebody gives a gift to another person, s/he still retains ownership thereof, since it his/her inalienable property.

In the exchange between individuals, a gift-debt relationship is established between giver and receiver. When the recipient simultaneously gives a gift in return, both parties are mutually indebted to each other. The only way in which these gift-debts, incurred by the reciprocal transactions in one exchange, can be cancelled, is by reversing the whole exchange-process in terms of specified gifts of the same sort. Although gift-exchange usually takes place simultaneously, thus incurring mutual debts, it may also take place at different points in time. Reciprocal obligations will differ from concurrent forms of gift-exchange.

Gift exchange creates an unequal relationship of domination between the parties involved. In this regard, the giver attains some superiority. His/her basic aim is not to maximise net income, but rather net giving; in other words, to acquire a large following of people ('gift debtors'), outside his family circle who are obliged to him.[16] What a gift transactor desires, are the personal relationships that the exchange of gifts creates, and not the objects themselves. The gifts of 'high rank' Particularly important. Since all gifts are ranked into hierarchies, this implies that the person giving gifts of 'higher rank' has the superior position in an exchange relationship.[17]

---

[14] Any form of direct, one-to-one exchange in a clan-based society presupposes a state of reciprocal dependence between the transactors. In this regard a continuum of dependency relationships determines the nature of gift-exchanges. An individual in a clan-based society of the ideal type, is surrounded by "...a series of concentric circles each representing the ever widening co-membership spheres to which he belongs" (Gregory, *Gifts and Commodities*, 42). Those close to the centre form intimate personal relations, such as fellow clansmen; while those closer to the periphery, from tribesmen to strangers, tend towards commodity exchange. Intra-clan exchange tends to be non-competitive, while inter-clan exchange tends to be competitive.

[15] In other words, this distinction between alienability and inalienability is "...just another way of talking about the presence or absence of private property" - Gregory, *Gifts and Commodities*, 44.

[16] Gregory, *Gifts and Commodities*, 51.

[17] Malinowski, *Argonauts of the Western Pacific*, 86-87, points out that in primitive societies the individual who owns things is expected "...to share it, to distribute it, to be its trustee and dispenser. And the higher the rank the greater the obligation."

2.3. The social embededness of exchange in the Graeco-Roman world

In our brief overview of comparative material from clan-based societies to determine the processes involved in gift-exchange, it has become clear that: (a) any form of gift-exchange produces mutual obligations between the parties involved; as well as (b) clear status demarcations, with the giver in the superior position. Refusal to fulfil the roles associated with the basic principle of *balanced reciprocity* (that is, returning the same kind of gifts, or gifts of equal value for those received), distorts the basic fibre of society. Any refusal to accept or reciprocate gifts, leads to loss of credit, honour and trust, and ultimately, exclusion from further exchanges and a decline in social status, "... particularly as a person's reputation as one who does not honour his obligations spreads in the community."[18] According to Levi-Strauss,[19] the bestowal of gifts often functions as a deliberate means to establish domination. In the *agonistic contests of gift-giving,* which often characterise social interaction in clan-based societies, the person who cannot match the gifts bestowed upon him/her, becomes obliged to the giver, thus losing his/her own prestige, rank, authority, and privileges to his/her benefactor.

On the basis of these observations we may now venture into the next phase of study, namely the investigation of *patronage* and *benefaction* as two basic forms of social exchange from ancient Mediterranean world. These two forms of reciprocity will be used as an explanatory framework to comprehend social interaction within the context of the Pauline communities.[20] In other words: this data could facilitate a basic model of social exchange that will elucidate the nature of the collection.

---

[18] Blau, *Exchange in Power*, 108.

[19] Lévi-Strauss, "The Principle of Reciprocity", 85.

[20] Cf. Chow, *Patronage and Power*, who understands social interactions within the Corinthian community in terms of Roman patronage. On his part, Winter, *Seek the Welfare of the City*, uses the principles inherent in ancient benefaction to come to terms with Paul. Another form of social interaction marked by reciprocal interchange, namely friendship, which will be briefly dealt with in terms of 'client-friendships' with patrons, will not be addressed at length in this study, because the collection is not conceptualised in these terms by Paul. Kinship relations, another form of social reciprocity, will be dealt with in terms of Paul's patriarchal role in his intra-textual interaction with the Corinthians in 2 Cor 8-9, in terms of the contingent nature of his hermeneutic and his efforts to salvage the collection, when it ran the risk of drawing to an abrupt halt (cf. Chapter 5).

2.4. Patronage: a system of social control

> Die römische Patronatsrechts- und Sozialbeziehung, bzw. das Klientelwesen ist die grundlegende Rechts- und Sozialbeziehung zwischen sozial, rechtlich, materiell oder in anderer Hinsicht Ungleichen im römischen Kulturkreis.[21]

This quotation summarises the sentiments of recent research on patronage,[22] one of the most important forms of social exchange in the ancient Roman world that can be described as a pervasive, voluntary form of interaction between socially disproportionate individuals, as well as between socially disproportionate individuals and groups involved in a reciprocal exchange of material goods and services.[23] Earlier researchers were hesitant to ascribe such a central position to patronage in Rome. This was probably due to the popular view that this system became insignificant during the early Empire with its centralised authority, only to reappear much later in the Empire in the form of rural patronage. But this theory has lost most of its appeal. According to the present *communis opinio*, patronage presents us with one of the most enduring socio-political systems in the Roman world, which not only successfully weathered the storms of the Republic, but also provided the framework for the ideologies and power structures in Imperial Rome. However, scholars are not unanimous about the exact nature of this system that influenced interaction between individuals and groups on all levels, and which was embedded in the language[24] and phys-

---

[21] Bormann, *Philippi. Stadt und Christengemeinde zur Zeit des Paulus*, 187.

[22] Cf. e.g. Shelton, *As the Romans did*, 13-14: "The patronage system was one of the most deep-rooted and pervasive aspects of ancient Roman society."

[23] Because of the complexity and variability of patron-client relations, and due to different presuppositions, models and methods used by researchers, various descriptions of patron-client relations have been offered in this regard. According to Badian, *Foreign Clientelae*, 10; "... *clientela* is not (in origin or development) a simple development, but at all times a name for a bundle of relationships united by the element of a permanent (or at least long-term) *fides*, to which corresponds the *officium* of the client who receives its *beneficia*." Saller, *Personal Patronage*, 1, again observes that patronage firstly involves: "... the reciprocal exchange of goods and services. Secondly, to distinguish it from a commercial transaction in the marketplace, the relation must be a personal one of some duration. Thirdly, it must be asymmetrical, in the sense that the two parties are of unequal status and offer different kinds of goods and services in the exchange - a quality which sets patronage off from friendship between equals." With minor adaptations, the definition of Saller has found wide acceptance amongst researchers. Cf. e.g., Krause, *Spätantike Patronatsformen im Westen des Römischen Reiches*, 4-5, and Millett, *Patronage and its Avoidance in Classical Athens*, 16.

[24] Saller, *Personal Patronage*, 7-40, offers a good overview of the language structures and terms relating to patronage, such as *amicus, officium, beneficium* and *gratia*.

ical structures[25] of the Roman world. This is mainly due to the fact that the historical sources do not present us with pure, ideal types of patronage.

2.4.1. Patronage before the principate

According to Drummond,[26] patronage during the time of the middle to the late Republic, indicated a dependant relationship between two parties, in which the difference in power and status was acknowledged. Furthermore, it was essentially a personal, voluntary relationship, which could be understood from the perspective of *fides*. This implied that certain individuals were in the protection of more powerful superiors, which involved a variety of reciprocal *officia* (that is, obligations in terms of both parties involved). Patronage was not confined to specific forms of aid, but found expression in a number of mutual services that were not regulated by formal ceremonies or prescribed by legislation.

Many concrete forms of social exchange in late Republican Rome could be understood in terms of patron-client bonds, the 'classic' form being that between landlords and tenants/peasant farmers, where the former were responsible for providing land and protection, and the latter for delivering basic services and honouring their patrons in public. Many landless peasants entered into long-term relationships with their social superiors by cultivating plots of land owned by the latter. Another very common form of interaction between socially disproportionate individuals was that between Roman patricians and their freedmen.[27] This *patronus-libertus* relationship was formed through *manumissio*, which was usually granted to slaves who had accumulated wealth, or as a reward for faithful service to their masters. After they had otained their freedom, freedmen received Roman citizenship. However, they remained in the *potestas* of their former masters and still had to perform a stated number of days' work for them.[28] This also applied to their children, since this form of patronage

---

[25] The numerous inscriptions related to patronage are proof of the immense impact of this ideology on Roman society. Even Roman architecture could be understood from this perspective. According to Wiseman, "Pete nobiles amicos. Poets and Patrons in Late Republican Rome", 28-49, and Wallace-Hadrill, "Patronage in Roman Society: From Republic to Empire", 63-64, the physical structures of upper-class Roman houses also serve as a reflection on the centrality of patronage in Roman society.

[26] Cf. Drummond, "Early Roman Clientes", 101-103.

[27] See the discussion of *manumission* in Badian, *Clientage*, 2-4, and Eisenstadt & Roniger, *Patrons, Clients and Friends*, 53-55. Wallace-Hadrill, "Patronage", 76, however, points to a number of differences between die *patronus-libertus* relationship and the *patronus-cliens* relationship, such as the fact that the former was not voluntary; the freedman had no choice as to accept his former master as his patron, and the obligations of service and deference were enforceable by law.

[28] See the thorough overview of the nature of relations between patrons and freedmen in Spain under Roman rule by Curchin, "Social Relations in Central Spain", 75-90, as

was hereditary. In theory, *clientela* continued until the patron and/or freedmen's families had died out.

Socio-political factors also gave rise to various other social dependency relationships between superiors and inferiors in the Roman Republic, particularly between Rome and its occupied territories.[29] Instead of opting for a democratic model of government, Rome chose to attach new territories to the central government through the channel of patronage. According to the treaties which determined the positions of these territories (in terms of direct Roman government over non-citizen subjects, or as free cities bound to Rome, or as self-governing *coloniae* and *municipia*), personal contact between the Senate and these 'client territories' was at all times necessary. One of the ways this was made possible, was through personal contacts between envoys from these territories and specific Roman aristocrats and military commanders, with whom many cities formed patron relations.[30]

The quick growth of the Empire contributed to internal corruption and strife between the great oligarchs of Rome. Especially, in the second century BCE, when the political struggle became more intense with the Senate's iron grip over the State, a fierce contest took place for the small number of high offices in Rome. The votes of the clients were, therefore, of the utmost importance to ensure access to political positions, which, from the perspective of these oligarchs, was an important way of ensuring their own *dignitas;* their prestige in the political arena.

The freedom of choice on the part of clients, which allowed them to withhold their loyalty (and their vote) and even transferring their allegiance to some other patron/s, still left them without any significant political power. The nobility were unwilling to admit *plebeians* into high office and real power.[31] However, the reforms of Gaius Marius (155-86 BCE), who was consul from 104-100, had far-reaching consequences, not only for the history of the Late Republic in general, but also for patron-client relations in particular. His bold move to recruit the landless poor (*capite censi*) and the marginalised from Rome and other territories, gave rise to a new form of patron-client bonds. These unpropertied citizens, who now flocked into the army, viewed their commanders as patrons and showed 'clientele alleg-

---

well as the discussion of *manumissio* in the Roman world and in early Christianity by Harrill, *The Manumission of Slaves in Early Christianity*, esp. Chapter 1.

[29] Cf. Badian, *Clientelae*, 4-7.

[30] Cf. Badian, *Clientelae*, 154ff., and Quaß, *Die Honoratiorenschicht in den Städten des Griechischen Ostens*, 138-90.

[31] In contrast to the fourth century where social tensions between the social classes in Roman society were solved through the Licinian-Sextian laws, second century rulers were not interested in solving the plight of the socially underprivileged. Various attempts to reform the socio-political system, such as the efforts of the brothers Gracchi (133-121 BCE), were fruitless and led to open conflict.

iance' to them, even after they were established as veterans in various Roman colonies with grants of land.

At the end of the Republic, characterised by its violent conflict between the *populares*, the reformist politicians and their followers, and the *optimates*, those who supported the oligarchy, the landless increasingly turned their backs upon their previous aristocratic patrons, and rallied behind these new powerful leaders who personally controlled large fortunes. Through the military support and personal loyalty of these '*Heeresclientelen*' a number of powerful individuals succeeded in gaining control over central political institutions, which obviously placed traditional patterns of patronage under strain.[32]

2.4.2. Patronage in the early empire

2.4.2.1. The princeps as patron

The emperor could be described as the all-powerful patron in the Roman world, who had access to, and control over, significant material and other resources, such as land, money, status, honour, etc. As holder of *imperium proconsulare* the *princeps*, not only governed all senatorial provinces and acted as commander-in chief of the army, but, through his possession of the *tribunicia potestas*, he was also in the position to introduce any new legislation in the name of the interests of the people of the Roman Empire. Possessing the highest *dignitas* and *auctoritas* in society, the emperor lay claim to titles such as *Imperator Caesar Augustus*, and also controlled the imperial property (*patrimonium Augusti*), as well as his own private property (*res privata*), which made him the wealthiest man in the Empire.[33]

It was expected of the emperor, as 'patron' of the army and the *populus Romanus*, to constantly bestow benefits upon his subjects. In this regard, patronage played an important role in securing high offices. *Amicitia principum*, friendship with the emperor, was a sure way of gaining access to senatorial magistracies and other honourable positions. Numerous examples exist of personal clients/friends of the emperors who gained high

---

[32] See Alföldy, *The Social History of Rome*, 93.

[33] Octavius Augustus serves as a clear-cut example of the emperor as 'super-patron' of the state. After inheriting the military *Heeresclientel* from his (step)father, Julius Caesar, he moved swiftly to enlarge his clientele in order to include, not only the army (as military clientele), but also all inhabitants of the Empire (as political clientele). In this regard Augustus' acceptance of the honorary title *pater patriae* in 2 BCE was intended to incorporate all subjects under his 'paternal protection'. Augustus presented himself as the *defensor plebis*, the champion of the ordinary people. In his *Res Gestae*, published posthumously, he in fact boasts about his enormous benefactions, claiming to have given large amounts of money, as well as grain and entertainment to the people, amounting to something like 600 million *cesterces*.

offices, as well as money, immunities and other sought after privileges. These positions were distributed as *ad hominem* favours to friends without being 'restrained' by modern principles of impartiality, fairness, and equality. At the same time, the imperial *donativa* distributed to the soldiers, served to keep them loyal to the emperor - as one big family under the care of their 'imperial father'. Money (*congiaria*) was also distributed from time to time to the plebs, particularly when a new emperor appeared on the scene.

The reciprocity ethic was also relevant to relations between emperor and population. The emperor forever placed the *populus* in debt to himself. Obviously, as Seneca states in his *De Beneficiis* (V.4.2) they were not in the position to repay these benefactions in kind, but this did not exempt them from the obligation to show their *gratia* through loyalty and public displays of respect.

A vexing question is whether the emperors, in the process of bestowing benefits upon their subjects, actually monopolised the system of patronage, in the sense of becoming universal patrons? In other words, was it still possible for other powerful individuals also to function as patrons in the *Imperium Romanum*? "No," says Veyne:[34] "Rome had no *patronus* other than the Emperor, *pater patriae*... . The Emperor was the sole *euergetes* and the sole *patronus* of his city." Recent research, however, tends to emphasise the continued relevance of patronage in the Principate. Garnsey and Saller,[35] for example, are of the opinion that patron-client relations continued, but in different forms. The emperors distributed their material benefits as personal favours to their clients so as not to undermine the "incentive for personal gratitude on the part of the subjects."

The available information seems to support the latter view that the emperor did not usurp all patron resources. Senators and heads of powerful families still remained important figures, who were called upon by younger ambitious aristocrats and other hopeful clients during the customary

---

[34] Veyne, *Bread and Circuses*, 388-9. He cites a number of examples to support his view, such as the fact that the emperor reserved the right to erect public monuments and provide extraordinary festivals and shows only for himself. He also quotes Dio Cassius, who tells us that most public banquets (which patrons usually held for their clients) were abolished or limited in terms of their extravagance, and curbs placed on the amounts that *praetors* could spend from their private means on festivals. Cf. in this regard also Bleicken, *Verfassungs-und Sozialgeschichte des Römischen Kaiserreiches*, 57.

[35] Garnsey & Saller, *The Roman Empire*, 150. See also Bormann, *Philippi*, 193 and Wallace-Hadrill, "Patronage", 79-84. Wallace-Hadrill notes that the emperor did in fact function as universal patron, but immediately adds that we should not understand the universal patronage of the *princeps* in an exclusivistic sense. The emperor did not discourage other forms of patronage. As a matter of fact, it was actively encouraged, especially in occupied territories.

morning salutations. In terms of the description of patronage as a pervasive, *voluntary* form of interaction between socially disproportionate individuals and groups, one could, therefore, assume that individuals and communities in the Principate still had the right to choose their own patrons, even in Rome.[36]

2.4.2.2. Brokerage: Pliny the Younger as an example of a 'middle order' patron

According to the anthropologist Jeremy Boissevain,[37] we should distinguish between two categories of patronal resources. The first would be resources such as land and wealth that are directly controlled by the patron (the so-called 'first order resources'). The second would be strategic contacts with other people who control such resources directly or who have access to such persons ('second order resources'). The first group of people is patrons, while the second group is brokers. In societies where central government does not exercise direct control over all of its occupied territory, or where the people do not have direct access to those who control basic necessities, brokers serve to mediate between these parties. Due to their contact with both the patrons and clients, brokers are in a position to channel material benefits from patrons to clients. And they also present an ideal opportunity for patrons to broaden their clientele (and honour).

Although brokerage also functioned in patron-client relations during the Republic,[38] it was particularly important during the Principate to secure access to the benefactions of the emperor. Contact with the *familia* or the *amici Caesaris* (such as the *equites,* senators and other people who stood in close relationships with the emperor) was of particular importance in this regard. The letters of *Pliny the Younger* (61/2-113 CE) serve as interesting examples of this kind of reciprocal relation with the emperor.[39] Pliny, for example in a letter to a friend, Apollinaris (*Ep.* II.9.2), tells how he succeeded in securing the support of Emperor Trajan for Sextus Erucius

---

[36] See Nicols' review of Wallace-Hadrill (ed.) "Patronage in Ancient Society", 129-135. He goes too far when he remarks that Augustus and his successors should be seen as figures who stood above this system and who where not constrained by the expectations associated therewith. The fact that emperors, such as Claudius and Galba, were murdered because of their delaying payment of the *donativum* to their soldiers, makes this clear.

[37] Cf. Boissevain, *Friends of Friends*, 147-148.

[38] Saller, *Personal Patronage*, 74-78, in particular uses Boissevain's notion of brokerage to come to terms with the nature of patronage under the emperors. However, he does not leave enough room for brokerage in the time of the Republic. Cf. the important contribution in this regard by Dixon, "A Family Business: Women's Role in Patronage and Politics at Rome 80-44 BC", 91-112.

[39] Cf. Sherwin-White, *The Letters of Pliny the Younger.*

in his candidature for the *quaestorship*. In another letter he requests from the emperor a praetorship for a friend of his, Attius Sura (*Ep.* X.12).

As client-friend of the emperor, Pliny responded personally to Trajan's benefactions by frequently expressing his own gratitude to him. These imperial benefits enabled Pliny to maintain his position as patron, and his *dignitas* among his own clientele, which included friends and specific communities. For example, after the emperor transferred Caelius Clemens to Pliny's staff in Bithynia (*Ep.* X.51), the latter expressed his gratitude to the emperor by saying that he did not dare to return '*gratiam parem*', try as he might.

As a powerful patron himself, Pliny was often in the position to bestow benefactions upon his friends without direct intervention of the emperor. In a letter to Firmus (*Ep.* I.19) he offers the latter a sum of 300 000 *cesterces* to add to his existing 100 000 cesterces so that he could qualify for the equestrian order. Pliny motivates this bestowal of generosity by referring to the friendship of his mother, his uncle and himself with the father of Firmus, which placed him under the obligation to help Firmus. However, at the same time, the reference to this long friendship between them, is used to insure that Firmus will not forget the benefit bestowed upon him.

2.4.2.3. Patronage and friendship

A group of people, who frequently found their way to the doors of powerful individuals and families, were the protégés, or the 'inferior- or client-friends' (*amicitiae inferiores*), who fell somewhere between the category of friends on equal terms and that of patrons and clients proper. The term *patronus* is seldom used in Roman literature in the (post-Augustan) Principate.[40] Likewise, the term '*cliens*' is not freely used in terms of people of inferior status involved in exchange relationships. The reason for this should probably be sought in the connotations of social inferiority and degradation connoted by these terms, which authors such as Seneca, Tacitus and Pliny the Younger, tried to avoid in their references to interaction with people lower on the social scale.

The language of friendship was better suited to describe relations between socially disproportionate individuals involved in exchange relationships, since "... the word *amicus* was sufficiently ambiguous to encompass both social equals and unequals."[41] Seneca (*Ben.* VI.34.2-3) refers to the

---

[40] Whenever the term *patronus* is used, it does not refer to 'influential protectors', but rather to advocates, patrons of communities and ex-masters of freedmen - Garnsey & Saller, *Roman Empire*, 152-154.

[41] Saller, *Personal Patronage*, 11. This idea is also expressed, although in terms of different categories, by Edlund, "Invisible Bonds: Clients and Patrons through the Eyes of Polybius", 132: "To a Roman 'friendship' could take many forms: there were the personal friends (*familiares*), political friends (*amici*), and the friendship between patrons and

division of friends into three groups.[42] This entailed classifying their followers in terms of their respective social statuses and stipulating how each of these groups should be received at the houses of patrons. The first group, the *'amicos primos'*, should be received *'in secretum'* (in privacy); the second group, the ordinary or 'second-class' friends (*'habuerunt secundos'*), *cum pluribus*. In other words, these lesser friends or protégés were to be received as *groups* during the customary morning salutations. The last group, the clients proper (*numquam veros*, the 'never-true-friends'), were to be received *universos*, which implied that this group was made up of the poor plebs who thronged to the houses of the patrons before sunrise in the mornings, where they awaited some monetary handouts. According to Martial, many rich patrons had a hundred or more of these clients. As a matter of fact, "In der Kaiserzeit wurde ein großer Klientenstamm zur Prestigesache. Als politische Waffe konnten die Klienten nicht mehr eingesetzt werden."[43]

The second group of friends, the so-called client-friends or protégés, included a wide spectrum of people, who needed the support of powerful patrons to secure specific benefits for themselves in return for their loyalty. Once again, the letters of Pliny the Younger present us with valuable information on these relationships that were generally described as *'amicitiae'*, as if between equals. Pliny himself was very much aware of the social distinction between different classes of friends, as he shows in a letter to Praesens (*Ep.* VII.3), where the latter is encouraged to return to the city with its "*dignitas, honor, amicitiae tam superiores quam minores.*"

Pliny constantly uses friendship terminology to refer to relations between himself and his superior friends and protégés. An interesting example of the first type of friendship (*'amicos primos'*) is reflected in his response to a letter of Gallus, reminding him of his duty to defend Corellia, the daughter of a late patron of his, Q. Corellius Rufus (*Ep.* IV.17). Pliny then recalls how he, as an ambitious young politician who wanted to further his own career, was assisted by Corellius Rufus. As a matter of fact, the latter treated him with the same respect that he would have shown any equal (*Ep.* IV.17.6). Therefore, on the grounds of this long-term responsibility to protect his friend's family and reputation even after his death,

---

clients based on *fides* in the sense of trust and absolute loyalty." According to Osiek & Balch, *Families in the New Testament World*, 50, this language of friendship, as it was used in the patronage system, actually reveals how significant power exchanges were brokered through personal relationships.

[42] Seneca obviously did not agree with this practice. According to him, friendship consisted of bringing a friend to an equal level as oneself (*Ben.* II,15,1).

[43] Prell, *Armut im antiken Rom. Von den Gracchen bis Kaiser Diokletian*, 260.

Pliny was now prepared to defend Corellia, so as to honourably fulfil the responsibilities that this reciprocal relationship placed upon him.

Contact with influential persons and families, who could further one's career or secure benefits that were not easily attainable, such as legal aid, property, money,[44] protection,[45] etc., continued to be of importance throughout the Principate. Literary clients, such as philosophers, poets and authors, also frequently courted well-to-do individuals. Some poets were fortunate enough to attract the attention of powerful patrons, such as the tragedian Varus, who received a million cesterces from Augustus. Philodemus of Gadara, the first century BCE Epicurean house-philosopher, was also on the receiving end of a reciprocal relationship with a very influential patron, Calpurnius Piso, the father-in-law of Julius Caesar.[46] Most of these literary clients, however, were involved in a never-ending search to find patrons, who would support them financially, in return for the pleasure their works and witty company provided. The patrons would open their houses to public recitations and also provide the necessary funds for the publication of these works.[47] Many of the financially able, therefore, had to yield to the pressure of masses of hopeful clients who gathered outside the doors of patrons' houses at the customary morning salutations.

2.4.2.4. Patronage of communities

Continuing with Pliny, one knows that his clientele did not only include his friends, but also a number of cities such as Tifernum Tiberinum in Etruria, Comum, and Firmum in Picenum. As would be expected, he did not hesitate to recall his own benefactions to them, as is recorded in a letter to a family member (*Ep.* IV.1.4-5) where he refers to the fact that Tifernum Tiberinum had elected him as their patron when he was still a young

---

[44] Seneca (*Ben.* I.2.4) says that a benefactor should help one person with money, another by standing surety for him, another through using his influence, another through advice, and yet another with helpful maxims.

[45] Martial, for example, had to seek the help of some of his influential 'friends' to protect him, when a number of poems falsely attributed to him were distributed in which insulting attacks on some powerful public figures were made (*Epigrams* 7.72).

[46] In his work *On Household Management* (23.22-36), Philodemus says that the best way to earn a living is by sharing philosophical discourse with the rich. According to Clarke, "Poets and Patrons at Rome", 46-54, it was a favourite pastime of poets to court the emperors. Martial succeeded in securing important honours for himself, such as an honorary equestrian tribunate, so that his complaints about his own socially inferior position as client of some powerful patrons should not to be taken too seriously - cf. Holzberg, *Martial*, 69.

[47] The investigation of White, "The Friends of Martial, Statius and Pliny and the Dispersal of Patronage", 265-300, points to the fact that no well-defined group of patrons, predisposed to encourage and subsidise writers, actually existed in Rome.

man.⁴⁸ According to Pliny they responded to him like grateful clients should: to them his arrival in the city is like a feast and his departure a reason for sadness. At the same time it brings great joy to the city to honour him. Obviously, in terms of the reciprocity ethic, Pliny had to respond with a benefit to express his gratitude for these bestowals of honour. This he did, in order not to bring shame to their friendship with him, by erecting a temple for them at his own cost.⁴⁹

In an analysis of Pliny's patronage of communities, John Nicols⁵⁰ distinguishes between formal patronage and informal forms of patronage, pointing out that the title '*patronatus*' was conferred upon individuals who possessed the necessary qualifications to become official patrons of specific cities by a *decretum* of the municipal senate. This formalisation of patronal relationships, which according to the so-called *tabulae patronatus* was also hereditary,⁵¹ was in most instances dependant upon the status and origin of the prospective patrons. Therefore, Pliny's wealth was probably reason enough for the people of Tifernum to officially select him as their patron, thus providing a tempting incentive to him to bestow benefits upon them. Informally, a number of benefactors who did not possess the status of patron, nevertheless, conferred benefactions on communities, thus unofficially acting out the role of patrons.⁵²

2.4.2.5. Patronage and collegia

Numerous inscriptions testify to the importance of the role of patrons in the Roman *collegia*, the voluntary private associations for local urban *plebeians* of various vocations such as handworkers, fruit and vegetable

---

⁴⁸ This election of Pliny as patron at young age was probably prompted by the fact that he inherited a large estate near this city from Pliny the Elder. In order to secure the younger Pliny's goodwill and influence, the inhabitants quickly elected him as their patron - cf. Nicols, "Pliny and the Patronage of Communities", 368-369. Cf. also the discussion of the benefactions bestowed by Pliny on his home town, Comum, in Duncan-Jones, *The Economy of the Roman Empire*, 29ff.

⁴⁹ In another letter (*Ep.* V.19), where Pliny writes a letter of recommendation on behalf of his freedman, Zosimus, to Paulinus, he openly boasts about the manner in which his own people (that is, members of his *familia* and his clients) honour him.

⁵⁰ Nicols, *Pliny*, 365ff.

⁵¹ Nicols, *Pliny*, 369, n 18, quotes the customary formula that regulated the hereditary nature of patronage over communities: "... sibi liberis posterisque suis in fidem clientelamque suam recepit."

⁵² Nicols, *Pliny*, 384-5, in terms of the "official patronage over communities" observes that: "... *patronatus* had by extension, become a title or dignity which communities conferred as an *actio gratiarum*. ... And because the conferral of the title was closely connected to the ideas of benefaction, gratitude and obligation, the community could use the honour to encourage or reward benefactors just as the benefactor could expect his prestige and *dignitas* to be enhanced by the community."

traders, fishermen, bakers, firemen, etc. Members of these associations met regularly in their *schola* or official 'clubhouses' under the protection of deities such as Minerva (handworkers), Vesta (bakers), Mercurius (businessmen), Ceres (the *mensores frumentarii*), etc. According to Liebenam[53] the most important characteristics of these *collegia* were:

> 1) der bleibende Zweck, zu dessen Erfüllung die Genossenschaft durch den freien Willen der Mitglieder gegründet ist,
> 2) die Unabhängigkeit des Bestandes vom Wechsel der Mitglieder,
> 3) regelmässige Zusammenkünfte zur Beratung von Vereinsangelegenheiten sowie zu
> 4) gemeinsamen Opfern, Festen und Mahlzeiten,
> 5) die gemeinschaftliche Kasse und die Sonderung der Rechte der Gesamtheit und der Einzelnen.

The *collegia* provided important services to its members, such as social support, banquets, and decent burials for the members after their death. Associations organised themselves along the existing hierarchical structures of Roman society. The titles of their governing bodies, their patron deities, their issuing of decrees and appointing of patrons, etc., were indicative of "a typically Roman appreciation for rank and the authority of office."[54] Why? Probably because this imitation of the institutions of power provided their members access to (analogous) forms of prestige and honour within the boundaries of the *collegia*, which they could not otherwise experience in their hierarchically structured world.[55]

The available inscriptions show that influential individuals from the aristocratic Roman orders, the senators and equestrians, were often chosen by *collegia* as their patrons.[56] It was the responsibility of the patrons to perform important services, such as paying for the feasts of their *collegia*, providing buildings and decorations, donating money, and, importantly, using their political influence to the advantage of the associations. At the same time, members and officials of the associations, who performed outstanding services, such as building or renovating clubhouses at their own cost, were frequently appointed as patrons (and allowed such 'luxuries' as double portions of food at banquets).[57] In response to their

---

[53] Liebenam, *Zur Geschichte und Organisation des römischen Vereinswesens*. 180. Cf. also the important overview of associations in the Graeco-Roman world in Klauck, *Die religiöse Umwelt des Urchristentums* I, 49-57.

[54] Garnsey & Saller, *Roman Empire*. 157. Cf. also Liebenam, *Organisation* (n233), 178, and Prell, *Armut im antiken Rom*, 258-260.

[55] See in this regard also the views of MacMullen, *Roman Social Relations*, 75-76.

[56] Examples exist of powerful individuals who were named as *patroni* of all the influential associations in the city, such as Sentius Felix in Ostia, or even of associations in different cities - cf. Liebenam, *Organisation*, 212-220.

[57] Numerous women were also members of *collegia*, specifically in the funerary clubs. Some of them were even elected as patrons in a number of instances. In an interesting

benefactions, patrons were honoured with statues, crowns, inscriptions (for which many of them also provided the funds!), and with titles, such as πάτρων, προστάτης, and εὐεργέτης.

Sacral *collegia* that organised themselves around certain deities were very popular. Although oriental cults were viewed with much suspicion by the emperors, the Jews in the Diaspora were allowed to meet in their synagogues. In terms of its general characteristics and operation, some Jewish synagogue groups were quite similar to that of *collegia*.[58] Literary evidence exists of patrons, including some female patrons, who made contributions to the synagogues in the form of furnishings and building materials The members of the Jewish communities commemorated these benefits by sometimes recording these persons in inscriptions, and honouring others by giving them golden crowns, and seats of honour in the synagogues.[59]

2.4.2.6. Plebs and patrons: patron-client relations from the 'bottom' and from the 'top'

Patronage was the basic form of interaction between people of different social statuses in the Roman world. The majority of people were not so fortunate as to form 'face-to-face' client-friendships with patrons. They had to compete with large groups of other hopeful clients for the goodwill and material support of the relatively small group of influential individuals to meet their basic needs.[60] In the hope of receiving material rewards in return for their public loyalty and support, these clients flocked in huge numbers to the houses of their patrons every morning (Seneca, *Ben*. VI.34. 2-4).[61] Their 'clientele responsibilities' entailed attending the morning

---

inscription from about 224 CE we read how the *quinquennales* of the *fabri* of Volsinii honoured Ancharia Lupercha, the wife of the patron of their *collegium*, Laberius Gallus, an equestrian, by co-opting her as a patroness, and by placing a bronze statue of her next to that of her husband in their meeting house - Gardner & Wiedemann, *The Roman Household*, 179.

[58] Cf. in this regard Collins, "Money, Sex and Power", 7-22, 11-13, as well as White, *Building God's House in the Roman World*, 77-85, and Rajak, "Benefactors in the Graeco-Jewish Diaspora", 305-319.

[59] H.-J. Klauck, *Die religiöse Umwelt des Urchristentums*, 57-58, is sceptical as to whether Judaism (and early Christianity) could be placed on the same level as private cultic associations.

[60] Martial (*Epigrams* 3.8) writes that an immigrant to Rome's only hope of earning a living was to compose verses, plead in the courts, or to perform the *officia clientum* for these great houses.

[61] The clients who flocked to the houses of patrons in the mornings (cf. also Pliny, *Ep*. III.12.2) were often frustrated by the fact that they showed up too late for the hand-outs, or that the patrons were absent, or that they did not receive any material 'rewards' for

salutations, accompanying their patrons in public, applauding their speeches and recitals, etc. In return for their services they could expect some monetary handouts, the *'sportulae'* or daily wages, which according to Martial (*Epigrams* 1.59; 3.7) amounted to about one hundred *quadrantes* (roughly six *cesterces*), or gifts such as clothes, invitations to dinners, land, etc. Nevertheless, for most clients these *'sportulae'*, if they were fortunate enough to get it, were not enough to secure a proper livelihood, because it was not intended as alimony for the less privileged. At the same time it was not distributed on a regular basis.[62] These monetary distributions rather fulfilled a socio-political function.[63] Furthermore, patrons sometimes refused to hand out *sportulae*,[64] or when they did, they gave it to specific clients at the expense of others. This gave rise to constant competition among clients for the available benefactions. Martial and Juvenal, amongst others, reflect on some of the hardships that clients had to suffer at the hands of arrogant patrons. Martial tells how he lost out on the daily handout, because he failed to address one of his patrons, Caecillianus, with the necessary title of respect (*Epigrams* 6.88). Juvenal in his *Fifth Satire*, tells of the insults that a client, Trebius, had to endure at a dinner of his patron, Virro. Assuming that the invitation was the 'reward' for his services (such as attending the *salutationes* 'at an hour when the stars are fading'), a big shock awaited Trebius at the dinner table. Viro offered him 'the third place on the lowest couch,'[65] as well as bad wine and food, while he himself ate and drank only the very best.

While Juvenal and Martial recalled some of the humiliations suffered by clients, at the same time one also hears of the frustrations on the part of

---

their efforts. Therefore, clients sometimes bribed servants to get in, or waited for their patrons on the street (Juvenal; *Sat.* 3.189). Seneca (*Ben.* VI.33.9-34.5) chastises those patrons who refer to the long lines of people who gather in front of their doors as 'friends': "... to stand in long queues to greet your 'friends' is a disgrace, since friendship is not to be found in a reception hall, but in the heart."

[62] In *Epigrams* 5,22 Martial refers to a frustrating encounter with a patron, Paulus. Going through a lot of trouble to get to his patron's house, he hears from the *ianitor* that Paulus is not at home. To this he responds with a warning that he will bring an end to his clientship if Paulus continues to be absent when he calls.

[63] In order to secure a big clientele, as well as their own social standing or *dignitas*, patrons constantly had to distribute tangible benefits to their clients. As Osiek & Balch, *Families*, 52, correctly remark, the terminology used to refer to exchanges between patrons and clients, such *beneficium*, *meritum* and *gratia*, created the expectation of reciprocal, but not exact, exchange.

[64] Cf. e.g. Juvenal's anger (*Sat.* VII.1-97) at a patron who refuses monetary support for the poet on the excuse that he himself also wrote excellent poetry.

[65] Seating arrangements were important indications of the guests' honour and status in Roman society as Chow, *Patronage and Power*, 74, correctly notes.

patrons.[66] Seneca (*De Brev. Vit.* 2.4), laments the predicament of the rich (= patrons) as follows:

> To how many are riches a burden! From how many do eloquence and the daily straining to display their powers draw forth blood ... To how many does the throng of clients that crowd about them leave no free-dom! In short, run through the list of all these men from the lowest to the highest - this man desires an advocate, this one answers the call, that one is on trial, that one defends him, that one gives sentence; no one asserts his claim to himself, everyone is wasted for the sake of another. Ask about the men whose names are known by heart, and you will see that these are the marks that distinguish them: A cultivates B and B cultivates C; no one is his own master.

In spite of all the frustrations, abuse and humiliations individuals endured, the system of patronage remained one of the basic forms of social interaction in the Principate.[67]

2.4.3. Patronage: a summary

In this section we looked at patronage in terms of its historical development in the Roman Republic and the Empire. It has become clear that patronage found expression in a number of mutual services between individuals, or between individuals and groups of unequal social status, such as: (a) landlords and tenants; (b) patricians and their freedmen; (c) members of *collegia;* (d) Rome and its occupied territories, and (e) officially appointed patrons of Roman communities. These *fides*-based relationships, with clear differentiations, in terms of status and power involving specific *officia* regarding patrons and clients, were not formally regulated by legislation, but were flexible as necessitated by the particular needs of the parties involved.

Patron-client relationships took on many shapes, ranging from long-term, even hereditary, responsibilities toward each other and each other's families, to groups of people who organised themselves in solidarity

---

[66] In this regard a well-known figure from the Graeco-Roman period also comes to our attention: The κόλαξ or flatterer, who through his excessive compliance with his patron's desires, exploited the very basis of 'friendship' between the rich and their dependants. Theophrast, in his well-known work *Characters* devotes a whole section to unmasking and ridiculing the 'shameful' but profitable behaviour of the flatterer who will even humiliate himself to the point of fulfilling the duties of a slave. Plutarch, in his treatise: "How to tell a flatterer from a friend" (*Quomondo adulator ab amico internoscatur),* also reflects on the dangers flattery holds for true friendship with its moral values of trust, sincerity, and permanence - cf. Engberg-Pedersen, "Plutarch to Prince Philopapus on How to Tell a Flatterer from a Friend", 70.

[67] In order to secure access to material benefits, clients had to exploit to the best of their ability the existing social stratification through their public displays of gratitude. On their part, the patrons were also under pressure to keep their existing clienteles happy and to win over new clients; or, as Pliny puts it in his letter to Priscus (*Ep.* II.13.9), patrons had to protect their benefactions by increasing it.

around certain powerful figures, who could further their common causes. During the Early Empire, the *princeps* usurped much of the traditional powers of the patrons. Therefore, the role of brokers became increasingly significant to secure access to the benefactions of the emperor. In order to mask the social differences between patrons and clients, the terminology of friendship was frequently used to give expression to, and regulate the relationship between patrons and clients, since it was ambiguous enough to encompass social equals and unequals.

Patronage had a strong 'political side', as expressed in the role of the emperor, and military and civilian patronage over cities and territories, as well as a more private-personalised side, as reflected in relations between patrons and their freedmen, landowners and peasants, and various forms of client-friendships. In spite of the obvious advantages of patronage within the Roman world with its strongly embedded social hierarchies, it was definitely not an ideal relationship, as can be seen in the frequent exploitation of clients on the one hand, and misuse of patrons on the other hand. However, it remained one of the basic and most enduring forms of social interaction throughout the Roman era.

2.5. Benefaction

Within the socially stratified Graeco-Roman world the exchange of services was never voluntary, but reciprocal. According to the late first century magnate, Dio Chrysostom of Prusa in Bythinia (*Oratio* 75.6), at least the following three distinct social relationships were marked by reciprocal obligations: children to parents; beneficiaries to private benefactors, and cities to their public benefactors. In the rest of this chapter our attention will be focused particularly on Dio's categories of private and public benefactors.

The views of Aristotle (384-322 BCE), as expressed in his *Nicomachean Ethics*, is a good starting point to address the ways in which the exchange of benefits became embedded in social relationships in the ancient Mediterranean world. In Book III.8-IV of this monumental work, which deals with moral virtues, Aristotle presents us with portraits of a series of personages who have been turned into types of everyday speech. Their character traits, such as courage, intelligence and generosity, are presented as the correct inner orientation for those who desire true happiness or εὐδαιμονία (Book I). These moral virtues must be learnt as part of a long process which is only "... erfolgreich abgeschlossen, wenn man zu seinen Affekten ein richtiges Verhältnis gefunden hat und infolgedessen die richtigen Ziele spontan verfolgt."[68]

2.5.1. Aristotle on 'magnificence' and benefaction

In his presentation of the ideal personality-types, Aristotle focuses on a virtue called μεγαλοπρεπεία or 'magnificence' (*NE* IV.2.1ff.), which is related to great expenditure by the nobles. Poor men can never be magnificent, since they do not have the financial means (IV.2.13). This is a privilege only reserved for the magnificent man who belongs to the class of the highborn and the famous (IV.2.14). He engages in public benefactions ·that are the greatest and the most honoured (μέγιστα καὶ ἐντιμότατα - IV.2.15). These include great expenditure in service of the gods, such as votive offerings, public buildings, sacrifices, and holding of religious offices, as well as public benefactions, such as giving banquets or building ships of war (IV.2.11). Private expenditure, such as weddings or the enter-tainment of foreign guests, is also undertaken, but then only in the interest of the general public.

Aristotle's profile of the magnificent man who bestows collective benefits upon his community or city out of his own pocket, presents us with a helpful description of *euergetism*[69] in the socially stratified Graeco-Roman world. Here the nobles, who, due to their birth and wealth controlled access to all essential services, were expected to provide various services to their cities in exchange for public bestowal of honour from the masses. In another work, *Art of Rhetoric* (1361a 28-43), Aristotle states that true wealth consists in doing good; that is, in monetary handouts, giving of scarce and costly gifts, and helping others to maintain an existence. The return on these benefits is τιμή, public honour, which may take on many forms, such as sacrifices, memorials, grants of land, public burials, seats, etc.[70] Any gift (δῶρον) therefore functions simultaneously

---

[68] Höffe, *Aristoteles*, 222.

[69] Some historians of ancient history refer to the social phenomenon of benefit exchange by its transliterated Greek name, namely '*euergetism*'. Cf. e.g., Veyne, *Bread*, 10, who credits Boulanger and Marrou for coining this concept. According to Veyne, *Bread*, 103-104, *euergetism* was "... both a spontaneous and forced activity, voluntary and constrained. Every *euergesia* is to be explained by the generosity of the *euergetēs*, who has his own motives, and by the constraints imposed upon him by the expectations of others, public opinion, the 'role' in which the *euergetēs* is caught." At the same time *euergetism* was civic, in the sense that it benefited the city or the citizens as a whole. But it was also an act of the notables, who gave benefits because they saw themselves as superior to the mass of the people (the *plebes*).

[70] The image of the rich aristocratic figure that acts as benefactor to his poor fellow-citizens has been the topic of reflection in many treatises. Cf. e.g., the krypto-oligarch, Isocrates, who in his *Aeropagiticus*, 31-35 idealises the good old days when the rich

"as 'an embodiment' of the money or the object that its recipient desires and the 'honour' that its giver loves."[71] In other words, in the ideal situation, the objects exchanged satisfy the needs of both benefactors, as lovers of honour (φιλότιμοι), and beneficiaries, as lovers of money (φιλοχρήματοι - *Rhet* 1361a43-1361b3).

Aristotle also introduces us to the so-called great-souled man, ὁ μεγαλόψυχος, in his *Nichomachean Ethics* (IV.3.1ff.), a figure that, so he tells us, is intensely concerned with the issue of honour and shame (IV. 3.17). Over against aristocratic emphasis on birth and wealth as claims to superiority and public honour (IV.3.19), the great-souled man despises people who do not possess virtue.[72] Himself being a good man (ἀγαθός), and thus in possession of moral nobility, the great-souled person has the right disposition towards wealth, poverty, and bestowal of honour. He often engages in reciprocal giving with other individuals, but he does not like to receive gifts since the latter is a mark of inferiority. Therefore, in typical agonistic fashion, he returns any services with interest so as to put the original benefactor into his debt once more. He also carefully keeps score of the benefits he has conferred, but has a bad memory for those he has received. The great-souled man is thus not different from the people who, according to Menander, even hate those who do them a good turn.[73] Typical of the great-souled man, is his reluctance to look others in the eye for any help, probably because it entails the start of another reciprocal relationship.

This great-souled figure presents us with typical attitudes toward reciprocal exchange in the Graeco-Roman world. The reluctance of people to be at the receiving end of such exchanges is clearly reflected in his behaviour, which is a far cry from Aristotle's own ideal that the one who receives a favour is to remember it, while the one who bestows it, is to forget about it (that is, he should not seek a return). According to him a true virtue is displayed in doing good, rather than in receiving some form of good (IV.1.7).

Aristotle, in his sketch of the magnificent man and the great-souled man, presents us with the profile of the two basic types of benefactors in the Graeco-Roman world, namely (a) the noble figure who engaged in collective undertakings for the common good of all his fellow citizens,[74]

---

came to the rescue of the poor by lending out money and land at moderate rentals, and providing work for others.

[71] Kidd, *Wealth and Beneficence in the Pastoral Epistles*, 113.

[72] Cf. also the discussion in this regard by Höffe, *Aristoteles*, 225.

[73] Cf. Hands, *Charities and Social Aid in Greece and Rome*, 32.

[74] This figure matches Veyne's description of *euergetism*. In his excellent analysis of benefactors in the Graeco-Roman world, Veyne only deals with collective forms of benefit-exchange, and not with the more personalised side thereof. (Cf. also Bolkestein, *Wohltätigkeit und Armenpflege im vorchristlichen Altertum*.)

and (b) the individual in the upper social strata of society who engaged in reciprocal interchanges of a more personal nature with status-equals, or near-equals.[75] This dual meaning of the term εὐεργέτης in the Graeco-Roman period is also confirmed by Spicq[76] who maintains that this word retained its banal sense, 'benefactor', but it also became a technical term for the 'benefactor-protector' of a city or a people, and, in case of the gods, the whole world. 'Benefaction' therefore refers to both these forms of social exchange in the Graeco-Roman world. We shall now firstly turn our attention to the more personalised type of benefaction by way of a discussion of Seneca's *De Beneficiis*.

2.5.2. Seneca on interpersonal benefit-exchange

2.5.2.1. The aim and structure of De Beneficiis

Lucius Annaeus Seneca,[77] the well-known first century CE Stoic philosopher, wrote his *De Beneficiis*, an ethical treatise on benefits, somewhere between 56-64 CE, but most likely during his service in Nero's court.[78] Although not his best-known, and certainly not his most outstanding work, *De Beneficiis* is the most detailed work available on benefit-exchange in the ancient Graeco-Roman world. But Seneca's insights into the exchange of benefits are not original. He forms part of a long tradition of philosophical reflection on the underlying norms and social functions of reciprocal relations, such as Plato, Xenophon, and Aristotle.

Addressed to Aebutius Liberalis, a fictive character,[79] this long treatise deals with the responsibilities or *officia* of people involved in reciprocal

---

[75] Both Seneca (*Ben.* II.17.2ff) and Plutarch (*Moralia* 582F) use the image of the throwing of a ball in order to describe the relationship between benefactor and beneficiary on interpersonal level. Seneca tells us that the ball (= the benefit) should be suited to the character of both; otherwise it should not leave the thrower's hand. Therefore, the thrower should know the 'partner' to whom he is throwing the ball. Plutarch again tells us that a person who refuses to catch a well-directed ball thrown at him and lets it fall to the ground (= the recipient who refuses to accept a gift), actually disgraces it.

[76] Spicq, "εὐεργεσία", *Theological Lexicon of the New Testament*, 107-113.

[77] Cf. the good overview of Seneca's life and work by Klauck, *Die religiöse Umwelt des Urchristentums II.*, 79-85. Cf. also the important essay of Abel, "Seneca. Leben und Leistung".

[78] According to Stevenson, "The Ideal Benefactor and the Father Analogy in Greek and Roman Thought", 425-6, *De Beneficiis* is more than a philosophical exercise: "It seems as much concerned to reconcile conflict between *potestas* and *pietas* in the Roman context and to advance the model of the good parents for the good king."

[79] Addressed as *optime Liberalis* (I.1), he is on the one hand presented as the 'good man', the role model for all involved in reciprocal relations (I.1.3). This idealistic presentation of *Liberalis* as the living proof of Seneca's exhortations and as a role model for the intended readers, points toward the fictitiousness of the addressee. But in line with Sen-

relations. Seneca states that a benefit forms a common bond which binds two people together (VI.41.2). Therefore, from his basic point of departure that "every obligation involving any two people makes an equal demand on both" (II.1.18), he addresses the question on how to give and receive benefits on *interpersonal level* (I.1.1; V.1.1). The ever-present problem inherent to social exchange, namely debtors' reluctance to return benefits, forms the framework against which Seneca's instruction should be understood. He cannot express his disapproval of this practice strongly enough (I.1.13). It is the greatest possible crime anybody can commit, surpassing tyranny, theft, adultery, etc. (I.10.4).

Aware of the serious threat that ingratitude holds for the practice of giving, receiving and returning benefits, and for the *concordiam humani generis* (IV.18.1), Seneca presents an idealistic reinterpretation of the basic tenets of this system in terms of Stoic ethical perspectives, by providing a *lex vitae*, a law of conduct, in this regard (I.4.2). But this is not conducted along the usual lines. Seneca's aim is to replace the generally accepted perception in the ancient Graeco-Roman world that one has to give with a view to receive something back,[80] with an ethic of giving as an intrinsically rewarding experience. This '*Umwertung der altrömischen Wert*' could be summarised as: "... die Verlegung des Maßtabs für Gut und Böse vom Äusseren ins Innere. Entscheidend in allen Sachlagen ist die Gesinnung...."[81] In typical Stoic fashion, Seneca emphasises the reason and intentions (*animus*) of the individual, which should be used in order to make the right selection (II.31.1). Whether he succeeds or not, is irrelevant to his happiness.[82] The mere act of the will (as a virtue) is sufficient to produce *gratus*.

According to Seneca the good man (*vir bonus*) is able to achieve these lofty ideals, since he is able to give, receive and return benefits in spite of ingratitude on the part of the recipients. This theme actually forms a ring-composition, an *inclusio*, which encompasses the entire treatise:

Theme: 'How to bestow benefits in spite of ingratitude' - I.1-13

---

eca's *admonitio*, Liberalis also functions as the "would-be wise man in need of further instruction" (cf. II.18.4). The identification of Liberalis with 'the unhappy debtor' in reciprocal relations (VI.41.1-2) confirms this perspective.

[80] Cf. Hands, *Charities and Social Aid in Greece and Rome*, 26-48.

[81] Sørensen, *Seneca. Ein Humanist an Nero's Hof*, 194.

[82] The Stoic, Diogenes of Babylon, stated in the second century BCE that the purpose of life was "... to act in accordance with good reason in the selection and rejection of the things that are in accordance with nature and rejecting what is contrary to nature continuously" - Sharples, *Stoics, Epicureans and Sceptics*. 102-3.

How? Fulfil the role of 'the good man' who pleases the gods by bestowing benefits, even on the ungrateful (I.1.9).

Body: There is only one sort of good, the *honourable* (V.5.5; 7.2.2). Since both the giving and the grateful receiving of benefits are honourable (V.5.3; IV.16.2), the good man gives, receives and returns benefits (V.12.4). A *beneficium* is a virtue in itself (IV.15). The good man therefore finds happiness in the mere act of giving benefits. Following the example of the fatherly god (II.29.4; IV.4-8; 4.17ff; VI.20-24), he does this without seeking personal gain or returns. On the other hand, the bad man cannot do good (V.13.1-3), since he does not know how to give and receive benefits. His ingratitude destroys *concordia* and *societas* (IV.18).

Conclusion: The '*Steigerung*' of ingratitude should be countered by the bestowal of new benefits. Imitation of the gods by persistent goodness, in the end, triumphs over ungratefulness (VII.26-32).

In order to assist the *vir bonus* to give concrete expression to the lofty ideals of imitating the fatherly god, and in this way reflect his own embededness in the *all* (IV.12.5),[83] he has to learn the correct principles underlying reciprocal relations, as well as the necessary diplomacy in daily interchanges.[84] In this process Seneca, the idealist, also becomes the practical philosopher who frequently resorts to casuistic reasoning on a wide spectrum of daily situations in which reciprocal interactions may take place, thus creating a dialectic tension between ideals and reality; between the possibility of viewing the bestowal of a benefit and gratitude as virtues in themselves, and the harsh reality that benefits eventually have to be reciprocated.

2.5.2.2. *The true nature of a benefit*

For Seneca a true benefit is a virtue (*virtus*). It is to be desired because of itself, not for any external advantages it may hold (IV.20.1). The visible form in which any benefit is presented, however valuable it may seem, is perishable, but the true benefit can never be destroyed (III.7.1-5; V.5.4). A true benefit is determined by the inner disposition (*animus*) of the benefactor and recipient, not by the size or value of an extrinsic gift (I.6-7), or

---

[83] Klauck, "Der Gott in dir (Ep 41,1). Autonomie des Gewissens bei Seneca und Paulus", 11-32, 20, summarises the Stoic position in this regard as follows: "Die Natur ist Gott, und Gott ist in der Natur, und der Mensch mit seiner besonderen Vernunftbegabung ist in der Lage, die Natur zu durchschauen auf ihre göttliche Gesetzmäßigkeit hin."

[84] Cf. Maurach, *Seneca. Leben und Werk*, 107.

the status of the giver. In other words, intention determines the moral character of any action.[85]

At the same time Seneca accentuates the *inalienability* of giver and gift. Using the distinction between the outward form of a benefit and the 'true benefit', he states that the latter remains unaltered in the process of giving and receiving material gifts (VI.2-3). Thus, even though a recipient may lose all outward benefits he possesses, such as his money or property, his benefit still stays intact. Any benefactor could therefore echo Mark Anthony's ironic words: *hoc habeo, quodcumque dedi* ("whatever I have given, that I still possess!"). As a matter of fact, the only way in which one can make one's material possessions one's own, is to give them away as gifts. The moment a gift is given away, it turns into a benefit.

2.5.2.3. The role of the benefactor: benefits are gifts, not loans

Seneca describes a benefit as the act of a person who derives joy from the bestowal of gifts, thus making the intention of the giver more important than what is given (I.6.1). Benefits are also to be viewed by the giver as *gifts*, not as investments (I.1.9) or loans (II.34.1). Shameful self-centred motives, such as the wealth or exalted social position of the recipient (IV.3, 1-2), should be very far removed from the benefactor's mind. Not even ungratefulness on the side of the recipient should deter a benefactor to continue with the conferral of benefits, on the same unthankful person! (VII.32.1).[86] At the same time, personal comfort and safety, as well as material means, should also be sacrificed for the sake of others, once again without looking for any returns (IV.13.5). But, when giving to a friend in need, the benefactor should be careful not to bring financial ruin upon himself (II.15.1-2).

2.5.2.4. Benefit-exchanges are not agonistic competitions

The *agonistic* ancient Mediterranean culture turned most forms of social interaction, from invitations, meals, public debates, recitals, business transactions, right up to gift-exchanges, into agonistic contests for honour. As a matter of fact, the great Greek athletic contests provided the metaphoric framework for the agonistic Graeco-Roman attitude towards life.[87]

---

[85] Cf. in this regard, Inwood, "Politics and Paradox in Seneca's *De Beneficiis*", 241-266, 259.

[86] Seneca offers an interesting motivation for the continued bestowal of benefits by saying that if one were to choose between not recovering benefits and not giving them, the first option should be taken (I.1.13), since not to give benefits only forestalls the fault of the ungrateful man.

[87] These *agonistic* motifs were often used in popular philosophical circles. According to Schwankl, "Lauft so, daß ihr gewinnt. Zur Wettkampfmetaphorik in 1 Kor 9", 177: "Der Wettkampf des Sportlers ist in den popularphilosophischen Abhandlungen (Diat-

These motifs were also related to the context of social exchange, often turning it into a competition for honour among benefactors, as well as for goods and services among prospective beneficiaries. However, Seneca would not have anything of this; at least not in terms of misusing the bestowal of gifts as a means to insult or humiliate others (I.1.8). His disgust expressed at emperor Tiberius' public humiliation of the praetorian, Marius Nepos, whose debts he paid only after adding insulting admonitions (II.7.2), or Gaius' shocking reaction to Pompeius Pennus' gratitude after he spared his life by extending his left foot to be kissed (II.12), make this very clear. Seneca's sensitivity to the social circumstances of the recipient should also be mentioned in the same breath. The person who experiences humiliating circumstances should be helped in private (II.9.1).[88] At the same time the benefactor, by being alert to the needs of his recipient, should avert the latter to have to ask him for help (II.2.1-3). He should promptly deliver the benefits he had promised. Recipients should not be kept in suspense, or forced to ask a second time (II.5.1-5). Benefits should also not be misused as opportunities to offer advice, or to level reprimands at the recipients (II.5.6).

2.5.2.5. Choose worthy recipients

Two conditions are to be met for any service to qualify as a benefit: Firstly the service rendered should have some importance, and it should be performed solely in the interest of the recipient. Benefits should not be bestowed thoughtlessly. Therefore, those who are 'worthy' of receiving gifts should be carefully sought out (I.1.2). Seneca offers a profile of the 'ideal recipient': Somebody who is upright, sincere, mindful, grateful, who does not steal, who is not greedily attached to his own, and who is kind to others (IV.11.1). If a person matching these character traits were poor and not in a position to return a benefit, this should, according to Seneca, not disqualify him (IV.10.3-4).[89]

---

riben) Sache eines jeden, der recht zu leben sucht, und veranschaulicht speziell das Ringen um die Tugend." Paul also made use of these motifs within paraenetic contexts in his letters in order to help the early Christians to maintain an own identity in a hostile environment - cf. e.g., 1 Cor 9.24-27; Gal 2.2; Phil 1,30; 2.16; 3,12-14; 1 Thess 2.2.

[88] Glorious benefits, such as military decorations or official honours however, should be given publicly (II.9.1).

[89] However, the contingent needs of everyday life force Seneca to make a few adjustments as to the 'proper' recipients (IV.11.2-3). For example, one should avoid giving benefits to somebody who is on the verge of moving to some distant country, or to a sick person who has no chance of recovering. On the other hand, benefits are to be bestowed upon the stranger who is putting into the harbour, and one who is about to embark again, or to a shipwrecked stranger.

2.5.2.6. Internalised reciprocity and social approval

In the ancient Mediterranean world, social interactions outside the family were based on the scheme of giving and returning the equivalence received. The success of these exchanges was dependent on the *fides*, the goodwill and trust of the parties involved, as Alciphron tells us: "A good deed is not unrewarded, even though the recompense for the benefaction does not appear immediately. And, over and above the hoped-for-rewards, the consciousness of a good deed done sustains men and warms their hearts..."[90] In spite of these idealistic remarks, benefit-exchange often turned into agonistic competitions between rivals. At the same time, the principle of *balanced reciprocity*, which assumes that the parties involved were to benefit equally from their social interaction, was also ignored. Those in debt did not always reciprocate, or at least not with benefits of equal value. This brought the system of benefits, which according to Seneca formed the chief bond of society, into jeopardy.

As we have seen, Seneca responds to this problem by turning the bestowal of benefits into a virtue as such, thus making it an intrinsically rewarding experience (I.1,9).[91] But would this altruistic behaviour on the part of the benefactor actually encourage benevolent behaviour along the lines suggested by Seneca? Would any relationship that was conceptualised as an exchange of rewards not come to an abrupt end when these expected reactions were not forthcoming? In any society based upon the notion that the advantageous consequences of people's good deeds are important inducements for doing them, at least some incentives are needed to encourage unselfish behaviour of this sort. The principle of *social approval* is one such an incentive, since it is one of the basic rewards sought by individuals in exchange-relations. Seneca also utilises this principle by 'adding' to his basic conception of benefits the joy, which a giver receives on account of bestowing a benefit upon a grateful recipient. This is clear from his criteria for worthy (= grateful) recipients, and his description of a benefit as something which brings joy (I.6.1; V.20.4).[92]

Although the gratefulness of the recipients cannot be coerced from them, Seneca is of the opinion that the person who has no desire to heap any burdens upon his recipients when giving a benefit, and who makes it

---

[90] Letters of Fishermen 10.5. Cf. the English translation of Alciphron by Benner & Forbes, *The Letters of Alchiphron, Aelian and Philostratus*.

[91] Although Seneca often stresses that the benefactor should forget that he bestowed a benefit (e.g., II.10.4), he later 'admits' that it is actually part of his own persuasive strategy to overstate a fact in order to convey the real value of something (VII.22.1-2).

[92] For Seneca the reward for a virtuous act lies in the act itself (IV.1.3). When the virtuous course is followed, it brings happiness (II.22.1). Even if the recipient responds negatively to such a virtuous act, this should not distract the good man from his course.

look as if he is not bestowing, but actually returning a gift, usually reaps a grateful return. Others gladly return benefits to him (V.1.4). In other words, it leads to social approval, and also to the necessary reward for the time, energy, material skills, etc. invested by the giver in the exchange.[93] In terms of the basic values underlying social exchange, such gratitude on the side of the recipient also creates an obligation to reciprocate the benefits received, thus resulting in a full-fledged mutual exchange of favours.

2.5.2.7. What benefits should be given?

Seneca identifies three hierarchical categories of benefits to be bestowed: The necessary, the useful, and the pleasurable (I.11.6). The first category includes things without which people cannot live (such as being saved from the wrath of a tyrant); secondly, those without which they ought not live (liberty, chastity, and a good conscience), and thirdly, those without which they are not willing to live (family, the household gods). Among the useful benefits is included money to provide for a reasonable living, public office, and assistance to those with high political aspirations. The third category of pleasurable benefits is the superfluities, which tend to pamper a man.[94]

2.5.2.8. Should the benefactor ask for a return?

No. One should rather lose a benefit than ask for a repayment (I.1.13). Nevertheless, Seneca places even more restrictions on the giver by stating that the recipient should not be constantly reminded of the benefits bestowed upon him. He should remember it on his own accord. To recall these in the presence of the recipient is in fact a reminder that he should repay it (II.11.1-2).

On the other hand, in terms of everyday life, Seneca has to make a few exceptions to his basic rule, by stating that one should ask for a return in a time of crisis (V.20.7), but then only if the recipient is in the financial position to make a return (V.21.3). In this regard even more tact is needed in choosing the right time to ask for a return than for its initial bestowal (V.25.3). The many recipients, who are just slow and dilatory, should also be admonished to make a return (V.22.1-3). By reminding the forgetful, a

---

[93] Blau, *Exchange in Power and Social Life*, 101, refers to three basic 'costs' that individuals usually incur in providing social rewards for others, namely 'investment cost' - that is, the time and effort needed to acquire the skills required for furnishing instrumental services; 'direct cost' - that is the subordination involved in expressing respect or manifesting compliance, and 'opportunity cost' - that is the alternative foregone by devoting time to a given exchange relation.

[94] Gifts that last, are to be preferred (I.12.1-4). The longer it lasts the longer the recipient will be grateful.

second benefit is actually bestowed upon them, since they are kept from doing wrong by not returning a benefit.

The ideal benefactor then? Well, it is he "... who gives readily, never demands any return, rejoices if a return has been made, who in all sincerity forgets what he has bestowed, and accepts a return in the spirit of one accepting a benefit" (II.17.7).

2.5.2.9. Benefits and the recipient: choose the right benefactor

According to Seneca it requires even more discernment to choose a benefactor than a recipient, because it is nothing less than grievous torture to be under obligation to somebody one objects to (II.18.3-8). Since exchange of services in ancient societies often implied the commencement of a long-term relationship between the parties involved, Seneca's admonition should not be passed over too lightly. Once an individual accepted a gift, he was placed under obligation to the benefactor, which implied mutual exchanges of gifts and counter-gifts.

The commencement of any social exchange relation was dependent upon the acceptance of the benefactor's gift. Seneca is well aware of this rule: "Obligare enim non possum nisi accipientem; liberari tantum. Si reddidi, possum."[95] Therefore, his advise is that one should reject an unwanted gift (more correctly: an unwanted relationship), and also verbally state one's position in this regard (I.11.1). This humiliation to the benefactor would bring an abrupt end to the relationship (VI.42.1). Another alternative is to immediately send back a gift in return, so as to wipe out a gift with a gift, which is nothing, less than a repulse (IV.40.5).[96]

How should one go about actually bringing one's needs to the attention of a benefactor? Seneca refers to Socrates who once tactfully said within hearing range of his friends, that he would have bought himself a coat if he had the money. A rivalry then broke out among the friends as to who would be the first to give it to him (VII.24.1).

2.5.3. Ingratitude and obligations

Social exchanges bring differentiation in power, the more so if a person commanded certain services which others need, while being independent of any services which they had control over. This imbalance of power usually establishes reciprocity in the exchange, since nobody wants to be in an inferior position, as Aristotle tells us in his discussion of the 'great-

---

[95] VII.18.2: "For I am able to place a man under obligation only if he accepts; I can be freed from obligation only if I make return."

[96] Aristotle (*NE* VIII.8.9), who discusses benefit-exchange in terms of friendship categories, states that if one had made the mistake of accepting a service from the wrong person, such a relationship should be brought to an abrupt end.

souled man' (*NE* IV.3.24). Thucydides[97] shares the same view. According to him the one who takes the initiative in an exchange, is in the stronger position. The recipient, who has now lost the edge in the relationship, has to repay this kindness, not as a favour bestowed, but as debt repaid. Seneca is well aware of this problem. Therefore, he addresses the predicament of the recipient, warning him that the hasty return of a benefit is a sign of ingratitude. It points to a person who wants to get rid of the burden of being under obligation to a benefactor (VI.35.3-5).

Instead of looking for every possible opportunity to rid oneself of one's debts, one should rather adjust oneself to the convenience of the benefactor and wait for a suitable chance to make the return (VII.19.3). A debt is not a burden, but something to be gladly accepted.[98]

Seneca's aim is to create a balanced reciprocal situation where the duties and responses of both benefactor and recipient are viewed as of equal importance. In other words, over against unilateral gifts, which entrench power differentials and often lead to exploitation, the 'normal context of exchange' should consist of an exchange of obligations where each in turn renders to the other the services that he requires (II.18.2).

2.5.3.1. Gratitude is sufficient reward, but one's debt must still be repaid

In terms of the well-known 'Stoic paradoxes', Seneca on the one hand states that a benefit bestowed upon a recipient is fully repaid by his gratitude, since the actual exchange takes place in the minds of the giver and receiver, with the latter meeting the goodwill of the benefactor with his own goodwill (II.31-32). On the other hand, a benefit is both a beneficent act, as well as the object which is given, such as money, a house, etc. A benefactor thus bestows two things on a recipient: property and goodwill. Therefore the latter is indebted in terms of two facets (VII.15.3). "One repays the true benefit with gratitude, but for the object we still owe an object" (II.35.1).[99] A similar gift to the one received should be returned. Just as Cicero (*Off.* 1.48) Seneca stresses that one's gratitude is displayed in the returned gift. This gratitude should be expressed publicly. One should actually invite the whole city to witness it, so Seneca tells us (II.23-25). Those who refuse to express it in the open, is not discreet,

---

[97] Quoted in Marshall, *Enmity in Corinth*, 10.

[98] Seneca also offers a number of reasons influencing the ungrateful reaction of a recipient (II.26-29), such as a too high an opinion of himself, causing him to interpret a benefit as a 'payment' for his services, and not as something which places him under obligation. Greed is another reason for ungratefulness, causing a person not to be satisfied with the benefits he had received (II.27.4). But jealousy is the worst problem, causing the recipient to be envious of others who had received bigger benefits from the same recipient.

[99] Cf. also Inwood, "Politics and Paradox", 261-262.

rather they are ungrateful. Also a benefit should also neither be accepted in a submissive manner, nor in a spirit of indifference. A verbal expression of gratitude in public would be a fitting response.[100]

2.5.3.2. The agonistic contest of benefit-return

Although Seneca rejects the agonistic attitude on the part of the benefactor in reciprocal giving, he does, in fact, use the image of an athletic contest when dealing with the responsibilities of the recipient. The moment a gift is accepted, the latter should become like a racer ready to leap forward; waiting for the right moment to return a gift (II.25.3). However, this does not imply that Seneca sanctioned any misuse of the bestowal of gifts as a means to insult or humiliate others (I.1.8). In this most honourable contest of conquering benefits with benefits, the debtor should not only equal the gift bestowed upon him; but his ideal should be to surpass it in deed and spirit (I.4.3-4). But, at the same time, Seneca also relates these agonistic images to the correct inner orientation of the recipient, which will enable him to match his benefactor's *animus* (V.4.1-4). In the ensuing 'battle', the person who has learnt how correctly to owe a debt cannot be outdone in benefits. Therefore, from this perspective, people of lesser means and lower social status can bestow benefits upon those who are of high status: slaves can bestow benefits upon their masters, sons upon their fathers, subjects upon kings, etc.

2.5.3.3. What kind of benefits should be returned?

As indicated earlier, benefit-exchange in the ancient Mediterranean world was not legally regulated in terms of the value of the goods that had to be returned, and the time that was allowed to elapse between the bestowal and return of benefits - although it was generally believed that benefits of equal value had to be returned within a short period of time. In Arrian's *Epictetio Dissertationes* (II.9.12), for example, it is stressed that a balance of 'giving and receiving' is to be maintained, at all times, in social exchanges. "Parity maintains not only the *status quo* of the relationship but also the status of each individual."[101] It was, therefore, expected of a recipient to return whatever was within his means to do.

Conflicts often erupted between benefactors and recipients regarding the value of the gifts offered and returned. Seneca (III.8-10) rejects the

---

[100] Seneca actually offers a few possible phrases to be used in such situations, such as the following: "I shall never be able to repay to you my gratitude, but, at any rate, I shall not cease from declaring everywhere that I am unable to repay it." These feelings of appreciation should be seen on one's face and heard from one's lips. Cf. in this regard also Mott, "The Power of Giving and Receiving: Reciprocity in Hellenistic Benevolence", 61-2, and Peterman, *Paul's Gift*, 69ff.

[101] Peterman, *Paul's Gift*, 72.

possibility that a court of law could settle this type of problem, because the measure of gratitude involved in an interchange cannot be adequately determined by a judge. At the same time, the external value of benefits, or the grandeur with which they are given, could also not be used as a means to determine their value. To award Roman citizenship; to defend someone in court; or to escort an aristocrat to the seats of honour at a public game, might be impressive, but are these really more important than bestowing less glamorous benefits, such as offering a person advice which prevents him for committing a crime, or consoling a sad person who wants to commit suicide, or sitting at the bedside of a sick person?

Seneca also refers to disputes between benefactors and recipients over the value of their gifts and return-gifts. The unhappy benefactor for example tells his recipient that he gave him a house, to which the latter replies: "Yes, but I warned you that yours was tumbling down upon your head!" Seneca aptly captures the gist of these dilemmas as follows (III.9.3-10.1):

> since benefits may be given in some form and repaid in another, it is difficult to establish their quality. Besides, for the repayment of a benefit no date is set....

The ideal situation, where both benefactor and recipient carefully selected one another, would be Seneca's solution to these conflicts; that is, where the benefactor knows that a benefit (although not specified) will eventually be returned to him. And even if it were not, he would already have received the gratitude of the recipient as sufficient reward. On his part, the recipient would return a benefit cheerfully when the benefactor wished it (VI.43.1-3).

2.5.4. The social embededness of benefit-exchanges

Apart from interpersonal benefit-exchanges between individuals of the same or different social statuses, which is his main concern, Seneca in *De Beneficiis* also focuses on social-exchanges among family members, friends, as well as patrons and clients.[102] However, neither friendship nor patronage form the interpretative framework within which benefit-exchange is understood by Seneca.[103] Admittedly, he himself

---

[102] Reference has already been made to the role of friendships, which could start, with an exchange of gifts. Although Seneca sees true friendship as something that only exists between wise men who share everything in common (VII.12.2-5), he admits that bonds of friendship are also formed through exchanges, by putting a recipient on equality with the benefactor (II.15.1). In other words, 'friendship' implies that a bestowal of benefits leads to a *fides*-relationship, which is 'affirmed' when the recipient fulfils his *officia*. The resultant mutual-exchanges, as well as the knowledge that both parties can rely on each other to fulfil their respective duties, keep friendship intact.

[103] Contra Chaumartin, quoted in Maurach, *Seneca*, 100-101, who is of the opinion that patronage forms the interpretative framework for the understanding of *De Beneficiis*.

... swam in the sea of patron-client relations; he used it to further his career and to define his position in Roman society. He knew the system of giving *beneficia* and repaying *gratia* as well as anyone living in Rome.[104]

Many examples used by Seneca in *De Beneficiis* are therefore typical of patron-client interactions, such as his references to the imperial benefactions bestowed on individuals and the *populus Romanum* (II.7.2; 25.2; III.27.4; VI.19.1-5); 'client-friendships' (VI.34-35); typical benefits bestowed by patrons (II.21.5; III.9.1-2); etc. Nevertheless, this is not to say that Seneca approved of all these patron-client relations. As a matter of fact, he offers strong criticism against the misuse of power, which often went hand in hand with many forms of patron-client relations, such as 'client friendships' (VI.34-35) between powerful Roman patrons and their large clientele, who flocked to their doors every morning during the customary morning salutations. The relationships, between the emperor and the *populus Romanus*, as well as that between other public figures and citizens, which included public bestowal of benefits, do not qualify either, even though they are undertaken for the common good of all (VI.19.1-5). *For a service to qualify as a benefit it must have been undertaken because of a specific individual, and not just bestowed on him as one of the crowd.*

2.5.5. Collective benefaction (euergetism)

2.5.5.1. Benefactors and beneficiaries in honorary inscriptions

Moving to the second type of benefactor, the noble individual who conferred collective benefits upon his community, one could approach such types of social exchange from two perspectives: from the 'top down', that is from the perspective of those who fulfilled the role of benefactors, as well as from the 'bottom-up', that is, from the perspective of people who stood at the receiving end of these benefits. In the ensuing overview, information from both these angles of incidence will be used to come to terms with *euergetism* in the Graeco-Roman world up to the time of the Empire. The most important sources of information in this regard are probably the *honorary decrees*,[105] those stereotyped public expressions of gratitude on

---

[104] Inwood, *Politics and Paradox*, 244.

[105] See the discussion of the structure of honorary decrees by Danker, "2 Peter 1: A Solemn Decree", 64-82; Danker, *Benefactor: Epigraphic Study of a Graeco-Roman and New Testament Semantic Field,* 20ff, and Quaß, *Die Honoratiorenschicht in den Städten des griechischen Ostens,* 26ff. According to Winter, *Seek the Welfare of the City,* 27, the "Greek epigraphic benefactor genre conveyed the following information: Whereas A did X and Y for our city, it is therefore resolved to honour A as follows...in order that all may see that the people appropriately honour benefactor commensurate with their benefactions." Gauthier, *Les cités grecques et leurs bienfaiteurs. Contribution a l histoire des institutions,* in his impressive analysis argues that the traditional content of these honor-

the part of the beneficiaries for the efforts of the nobles who helped them in various ways, such as providing military and monetary support, games, cheap or free grain, buildings, banquets, etc.[106] As a matter of fact, *euergetism* actually went hand-in-hand with what a number of researchers refer to as the 'epigraphic habit' since

> ...it was advantageous to donors to put their donations on public record, while, from the other side, honours could be made meaningful by being perpetuated in stone by a grateful recipient community or its representatives.[107]

For example, Lucius Gastricius Regulus, who held the offices of *aedile, prefect iure dicundo, duovir, and quinquennial duovir*, was honoured in Corinth as *agonothētē* of the Tiberea Caesarea Sebastea, the Isthmian and the Caesarean games, as well as for his introduction of poetry contests, an athletic contest for girls, his renovation of buildings and the holding of a banquet for the people of the colony, etc.[108] Another example comes from the wall of the northern portico of the agora of Priene,[109] where a number of inscriptions honour Moschion, who on at least four occasions advanced money to his city to help solve its grave financial problems. He also contributed to the cost of building a gymnasium, repaired Alexander the Great's sanctuary, assumed the priesthood of Olympian Zeus, etc.

Honorary decrees confirmed the elevated status of benefactors as belonging to the category of the nobles, the καλοὶ καὶ ἀγαθοὶ ἄνδρες. These individuals, who put the welfare of their cities before their own interests, were often commended for their outstanding moral character traits, such as καλοκἀγαθία and φιλοτιμία, and for the excellence and prestige which were already manifested by their ancestors. To have one's own people honour one's services by expressing their gratitude (χάρις) through inscriptions and/or through the erection of statues in market places or sanctuaries, was due recognition for every person involved in the 'noble search' (more correctly: in the agonistic competition[110]) for honour. In this process

---

ary inscriptions underwent certain changes during the second century BCE. The new emphasis on cultic honours and the shift away from benefaction towards patronage in late Hellenism, which turned benefactors into powerful patrons of their communities, are highlighted by him.

[106] Cf. the detailed discussion in Quaß, *Honoratiorenschicht*, 84ff.

[107] Rajak, "Benefactors in the Graeco-Jewish Diaspora", 305-319, 308. Cf. also, McMullen, "The Epigraphic Habit in the Roman Empire", 233-246, and Meyer, "Explaining the Epigraphic Habit in the Roman Empire", 74-96.

[108] As reward his son erected a monument for him in accordance with the decree of the council of the city - cf. Kent, *The Inscriptions 1926-1950*, No. 153.

[109] Cf. in this regard Hiller von Gärtringen, *Inschriften von Priene*, No 1, and Veyne, *Bread and Circuses*, 99; 106.

[110] The agonistic language of the athletic world is also used to give expression to benefactions - cf. Veyne, *Bread and Circuses*, 133. The emperor Augustus is honoured in

benefactors were also awarded eloquent titles such as σωτήρ, φιλότιμος, and εὐεργέτης. Other honours followed: special seats at public games, golden crowns, public eulogies, positions in temples - even for their families and offspring. For instance, in an inscription from Kos (241-200 BCE), the doctor Hippokrates was rewarded for his goodwill and service to his people by receiving a golden crown in the theatre of Dionysius (στεφανῶσαι δε᾽ αὐτὸν καὶ ἐν τῶι θεάτρωι τοῖς Διονυσίοις χρυσέωι στεφάνωι ἀρετῆ ἕνεκεν καὶ εὐνοίας).[111] On his part, the priest Akornion also received a golden crown at the Dionysia from the people of Dionysopolis, where he was to be crowned annually for his outstanding services as envoy and mediator on behalf of his city. At the same time a bronze likeness of him was to be erected in the best place in the agora.[112]

Individuals who were elected to public positions, such as magistracies, were expected to direct their expenditure on behalf of the community to pleasures and public works, *voluptates* and *opera publica*.[113] Numerous public benefits were, therefore, bestowed as part of the moral and legal obligations associated with the holding of public positions (the so-called *euergesia ob honorem*), and others were bestowed voluntarily, that is, when benefits were given over and above the call of duty. However, these benefits were always to be conferred on the whole community, not only on a few fortunate individuals. All citizens had to benefit from it, not only friends or family members. Benefactions were not intended as forms of public charity. As Veyne puts it: "... pagan literature is full of civic or patrician pride; this harsh climate is the climate of euergetism, which gives edifices and pleasures to the citizens rather than alms to the poor."[114]

The picture presented to us by the inscriptions, is that of a socially stratified society with the notables conferring benefits in exchange for the τιμαί of the masses, which also served as expressions of the latter's social and political allegiance. In this regard, bestowal of benefits could actually be understood as a form of 'tax' on the elites, limiting the uncontrolled

---

this fashion in the well-known decree by the province of Asia under the proconsulship of Paulus Fabius Maximus in 9 BCE to replace the existing calendar by taking the birth of Augustus (23 September) as the beginning of the new year in Asia. It is stated in this decree that Augustus' benefits surpassed all his predecessors, and that those coming after him would have no chance in improving on these (as an *agonistic* challenge to all-would-be emperors). Cf. the discussion of this decree by Danker, *Benefactor*, 215-222; Price, *Rituals and Power*, 54-58; and Klauck, *Vom Zauber des Anfangs*, 8-10.

[111] Benedum, "Arztinschriften aus Kos", 265-276. Dio Chrysostom twice refers to the στέφανοι καὶ προεδρίαι καὶ κηρύγματα (*Oratio* 66.2; 75.7) as rewards for benefactions.
[112] Danker, *Benefactor*, 77-79.
[113] Veyne, *Bread and Circuses*, 10ff.
[114] Veyne, *Bread and Circuses*, 20.

accumulation of wealth by inducing them to spend some of it on their communities.[115] Nevertheless, these financial burdens were not to be disproportionate to the expected honours, which would turn benefactions into forced public service. A symbiosis between the different social classes was only possible in a system of balanced exchange, as idealised by the philosophers. In this regard, Aristotle presents friendship as the true bond of the state (*NE* VIII.1.4). More specifically, he understands friendship in political terms,[116] as an exchange relationship between the rich and the poor where the superior party receives a larger share of honour and the inferior a larger share of material benefits (*NE* VIII.14.2-4). These friendships regulated intercourse between socially disproportionate individuals, and also formed the basis of an orderly *politeia*.

2.5.5.2. The agonistic context of benefit-exchange

Although bestowal of benefits was voluntary, immense pressure was brought to bear on benefactors to depart with their possessions.[117] The placing of inscriptions in prominent public places such as busy marketplaces or sanctuaries, or even better: offering the benefactors the choice where they wanted their statues to be erected,[118] as well as the phraseology of the inscriptions, functioned as 'payments for services rendered'. but also encouraged the agonistic attitude, prevalent among benefactors.[119] Decrees often ended with an exhortatory formula, introduced by the phrase ὅπως ἅπαντες εἰδῶσιν, (or with a ἵνα- clause) in order that all could see that the inhabitants of a specific city appropriately honour their benefactors.[120] By making it clear that they were fulfilling their reciprocal responsibilities towards their 'great sons', they also, in terms of the reciprocity ethic, provided an incentive to the same person, and also to other would-be benefactors, in order to bestow further benefits upon them. In the words of

---

[115] So Hands, *Charities and Social Aid in Greece and Rome*, 36-37, and Kidd, *Wealth and Beneficence in the Pastoral Epistles*, 114.

[116] See Schroeder, "Friendship in Aristotle", 37ff. Obviously, Aristotle also places friendship in a broader framework in *NE* VIII-IX.

[117] In a fascinating conversation between Critobulus, and the philosopher Socrates in Xenophon's *Oeconomicus* (2.1-18) this point is made clear.

[118] E.g., Pliny, *Ep.* VIII.6.14.

[119] Plutarch of Chaironeia, the first century CE middle-Platonist, confirms this in his *Moralia* (820B) when he says that the numerous ostentatious statues and portraits of benefactors in Rome only serve to arouse envy among their ranks. However, because of negative responses from the side of the masses towards nobles who are not prepared to share their wealth (822A), many of them succumb to public pressures, but with disastrous results; they bring financial ruin upon themselves. Some of them even go so far as to borrow money to pay for their expenditure, eventually ending up with shame and contempt instead of fame and honour (822DE).

[120] Cf. Larfeld, *Griechische Epigraphik*, 226.

Rajak: The honours "... were a not-too-subtle statement to the donor that he had a reputation which could only be kept up by further benefaction."[121]

The decree and letters to Iunia Theodora (a native of Patara), who resided in Corinth during 43 CE,[122] presents us with an interesting example in this regard. Because of her generous assistance to the Lycians, she is honoured by their council by making her a co-member, as well as by presenting her with a golden crown on her departure to the gods, together with an inscription on her behalf. In an accompanying letter to the magistrates of Corinth, Iunia Theodora is praised for her hospitality towards people from her '*Heimat*' who often visit Corinth. It is also stated that if she continued, and intensified(!) her benefits towards them, the council and people would also intensify their gratitude towards her (lines 30ff.).[123]

Generally, *euergetism* was a long-term reciprocal relationship between a benefactor and his/her community. Numerous inscriptions in this regard honour benefactors for continued benefactions to their communities.[124] When the community responded with the necessary public gratitude in the form of an inscription, a statue, or other tangible shows of gratitude towards a benefactor, the latter, in terms of the principles of the reciprocity ethic, was expected to furnish new benefits.

Over against the lavish words of praise in the honorary inscriptions, moral philosophers were not so positive towards civic benefactors. Dio Chrysostom, for example, is very critical of their hunger for public recognition (*Oratio* 66.2-6).[125] For this philosopher, true inner happiness cannot be secured by means of the agonistic pursuit of fame and honour. He ridicules the efforts of individuals who strive after honorary ribbons from the Assembly, which in the end cost them their fortune, while it could

---

[121] Rajak, "Graeco-Jewish Diaspora", 307. Peterman, *Paul's Gift from Philippi*, 85-6, summarises the social functions of inscriptions in terms of: (a) the important role of gratitude as a serious social obligation; (b) the role of εὐχαριστία in the inscriptions that serve as a label to describe the actions of the grateful, and (c) the importance of the ἵνα or ὅπως clauses to incite others to benefaction.

[122] Cf. Pallas; Charitondis & Venencie, "Inscriptions Lyciennes trouvées a Solômos pres de Corinthe", 496-508, and Pleket, *Epigraphica Vol II*.

[123] Cf. the 'freie Wiedergabe' of this text by Klauck, *Neutestamentliches Oberseminar. Ein Reader*, 106: "Möge das sie dazu ermuntern, ihre Hilfsleistungen für unser Volk noch zu intensivieren, denn sie weiß ja, daß wir im Gegenzug unsere herzlichen Gefühle für sie und die Zeichen unseres Dankes nicht im geringsten abmindern werden, sondern im Gegenteil alles tun werden was ihre Verdienste in ruhmvollem Licht erscheinen läßt."

[124] Cf. e.g., the inscriptions for the procurator Culleo, who was honoured by Castulo, an important city in the south of Hispania Tarraconensis, for his staggering benefits such as donations of buildings, land, and roads, as well as for his remission of large amounts owed to him by his city. - Duncan-Jones, "The Procurator as Civic Benefactor", 79-85.

[125] See in this regard, Jones, *The Roman World of Dio Chrysostom*, 110ff., and Kidd, *Wealth and Beneficence in the Pastoral Epistles*, 89-90.

have been bought at the *agora* for a few drachmas. In Dio's view the rules inherent to the 'reciprocity code' (= equivalent value in return for goods bestowed) are thus transgressed by beneficiaries who seek maximisation of gain and minimisation of cost. But to hear one's name being proclaimed by his fellow citizens, or to receive a few olive leaves, had totally blinded them to this flagrant exploitation.[126]

2.5.5.3. Bread for the hungry

Shortages of basic food supplies, especially grain, were a constant problem that faced people throughout the Graeco-Roman period.[127] A number of reasons could be cited, such as: wars, which often led to pillaging and burning of crops;[128] the locality of numerous cities far removed from sea ports - which was crucial to transport of grain;[129] political manipulation of markets, such as stockpiling grain for export which denied local consumers access to their staple food, and natural crop failures that were brought about by insufficient or excessive rainfall, or damage to crops by pests.[130] These problems were so severe that Polybius (36.17) related the depopulation of Greece to natural disasters, such as disease and destruction of crops by bad weather.[131] Shortages of food and the constant efforts to alleviate these problems by private benefactors, became a permanent feature of society.[132] The same holds true for the officially appointed σιτῶναι or grain commissioners, the σιτοφύλακες (grain wardens), and the ἀγορανόμοι, that is, private individuals who were given the responsibility of buying grain for their cities. Inscriptions frequently honour these *agoranomoi* for their interest free loans to their cities, but even more so for "...die von ihnen bewerkstelligten Verkäufe von Lebensmitteln zu (unter das gültige Marktniveau) gesenkten Preisen."[133]

---

[126] To rectify this situation, Plutarch suggests a totally different approach whereby benefits should be given unexpectedly by a donor, without bargaining for something else. At the same time it should also be related to an occasion, which is connected with the worship of the gods, which would lead the people to piety and worship (*Moralia* 822B).

[127] We know from the available information that the Roman economy was largely underdeveloped, affecting many of people, mostly peasant farmers, who lived on or near subsistence level – cf. Garnsey & Saller, *The Roman Empire*, 43.

[128] Cf. Quaß, *Die Honoratiorenschicht in den Städten des Griechischen Ostens*, 231-234.

[129] Rickman, *The Corn Supply of Ancient Rome*, 16.

[130] The difference between food shortages and famines is not that easy to define. Usually, the term λιμός is used by ancient authors to denote situations where people died because of a total lack of food over an extended period of time, whereas σιτοδεία is used to denote food shortages over a shorter period of time.

[131] Cf. Also Jameson, "Famine in the Greek World", 6.

[132] Cf. Garnsey, *Famine and Food Supply in the Graeco-Roman World*, 15.

[133] Quaß, *Die Honoratiorenschicht in den Städten des Griechischen Ostens*, 250.

As is to be expected, pressures were often brought to bear upon rich nobles to assist their communities in times of severe food shortages. Due to weak infrastructures in the cities, grotesque scenes, such as consumption of strange foods, even cannibalism, as well as riots and plundering often accompanied these crises. Well-known in this regard is the address of Dio to the angry crowd of Prusa intent on raiding his barns and threatening to stone him during a grain shortage (*Oratio* 46). At this time the grain-price was higher than normal, causing the inhabitants to blame Dio and other rich nobles for the state of affairs. He responds by referring to the benefactions he and his ancestors had already conferred (46.2-3; 9), and by claiming his innocence regarding the present shortage. He also informs the angry crowd that he did not lock his grain up in order to conveniently increase the price, because his farms did not even produce enough grain for his own needs (46.8). Dio then offers to assist them in the buying of grain, but at the same time also threatens to leave the city (46.12-13), which would imply one less benefactor for Prusa.[134]

In spite of munificent forms of assistance by nobles to their communities, generally, most of them used their benefactions to increase their own honour and not so much to alleviate the needs of others.[135] Therefore, they frequently indulged in the more popular and glamorous benefits such as games, monetary handouts, and festivals. Whenever poor people received material assistance in ancient Graeco-Roman society, it should be understood within the framework of collective benefactions, which were bestowed on communities as a whole, and not on specific individuals. The general atmosphere of *euergetism* in the Graeco-Roman world is very different from the early Christian world of Tertullian a few centuries later, when he writes in his *Apologetica* (39,7) that, instead of engaging in *euergesia*, Christians rather give to the poor, the orphans and the old people. The situation in the Roman period was not different either.

> Eine Armenpolitik existierte somit nicht... Ansätze altruistischen Handelns sind bei den Römern zwar sichtbar, jedoch erkannte erst die Spätantike die Armen als soziale Kategorie, die der Hilfe anderer bedarf. Es war das Christentum, das den Armen ihren Platz innerhalb der Gesellschaft einräumte.[136]

---

[134] See Jones, *The Roman World of Dio Chrysostom*, 24; Quaß, *Die Honoratiorenschicht in den Städten des Griechischen Ostens*, 253-255.

[135] Assistance to the poor was clearly not a moral obligation for the well to do. When the emperors or benefactors distributed money or other forms of material assistance, it was usually handed out to the whole community, regardless of the financial positions of the various recipients. The distribution of free grain in Rome, or selling of grain under current market prices by the state, was an advantage to the privileged citizens who were fortunate enough to receive it. But as Veyne, *Bread and Circuses*, 244, correctly remarks: "... a few bushels of free corn every month did not suffice to keep anyone alive."

[136] Prell, *Armut im antiken Rom*, 296.

However, this is another story to which we shall return in Chapter 3.

2.5.6. In summary: benefaction

In the Greek world it was expected of the nobles to perform services to their cities at their own expense through the bestowal of benefits, while the recipients had to respond with public honour such as statues, inscriptions, golden crowns, special seats in the theatres, etc. These positive public responses in turn placed the benefactor-protectors under pressure to confer new benefits. Within the agonistic Graeco-Roman culture with its competition between benefactors and beneficiaries to permanently place each other in debt through huge gifts that could not be reciprocated, benefits were not bestowed out of humanitarian concerns, but rather to increase the benefactors' honour. Public benefits were always collective; they were intended for the community as a whole, irrespective of the financial situation of the various individuals involved.

At the same time, reciprocal exchanges of a more personal nature took place between individuals and small groups throughout the Graeco-Roman world. Any bestowal of a benefit signalled the start of a long-term reciprocal relationship with specific obligations, linked to the role of both benefactor and beneficiary. While the former was dependent upon the positive response of his/her beneficiary to his/her gifts, it was expected of the latter to show in turn his/her gratitude by making an adequate return.

2.6. The interpretative framework for the collection: benefaction or patronage?

In our discussion thus far we have dealt with benefaction on personal and collective levels in the Graeco-Roman world, as well as with patronage in the Roman Republic and the Principate. The question presenting itself, is whether benefaction and patronage refer to the same form of social exchange between socially disproportionate individuals and/or groups, or rather to two distinct relationships? Differently phrased, do we have similar exchange relationships within the ancient Greek and Roman cultures, which were linguistically expressed in numerous modes, and forms within various socio-historical contexts?

In spite of divergent theoretical angles of incidence to patronage and benefaction, the majority of scholars would answer in the affirmative to this question. These concepts are used more or less interchangeably in academic disciplines at present, that is, as references to the same kind of relationship between socially unequal individuals (or groups) in which an exchange of resources take place.

2.6.1. Patronage and benefaction: the same social exchange relationship

2.6.1.1. Patronage in the Ancient Greek World

'Patron-and-client language' is almost entirely absent from ancient Greek texts to our disposal. But Wallace-Hadrill[137] has dismissed this impediment with the following argument: "If there is an objective exchange of goods and services whereby political support is given in exchange for material benefits, one can properly speak of patronage even if the Greeks didn't have a word for it." Paul Millett[138], following Saller's definition of patronage, also finds it inconceivable that reciprocal exchange of services between individuals did not take place in the Greek world. He explains the absence of information on patronage in terms of the enduring Athenian democracy. The great bulk of surviving literary evidence about Greek social life comes from this atypical *polis*, where: "... the democratic ideology, with its emphasis on political equality, was hostile to the idea of personal patronage, which depended on the exploitation of inequalities of wealth and status."[139] Therefore, deliberate and effective steps were taken to eliminate patronage in Athens. However, in other places, such as in Hesiod's peasant village, Ascra, in Boetia, (c. 700), as well as in Attica during the time of Solon (c. 600) reciprocal interchanges did in fact take place between people of similar or different social status. At the same time Millett also relates the well-known figures of the *kolax*, the *parasitos*, and the *philos* to specific forms of reciprocal interaction in the Greek world, which in turn, fits in with his understanding of patronage.

Gruen[140] is also of the opinion that patronage is not a typical Roman institution. According to him, Rome only acknowledged the Graeco-Roman act of patronage by reinterpreting it to fulfil its own specific needs. Veyne, in turn, who distinguishes between Greek *euergetism* and the benefactions of the Roman nobles,[141] understands *euergetism* as a union of

---

[137] Wallace-Hadrill, *Patronage in Ancient Society*, 65-66. See also Finley, *Politics in the Ancient World*, 41.

[138] Milett, "Patronage and its Avoidance in Classical Athens", 15ff.

[139] Milett, "Patronage and its Avoidance in Classical Athens", 17.

[140] Gruen, *The Hellenistic World and the Coming of Rome I*, 182ff.

[141] Veyne, *Bread and Circuses*, 86, 121, draws a distinction between the *euergetism* of the Greek dignitaries and that of the Roman nobles in Republican Rome. Although in the municipal towns of the Empire this difference was not that big, in Rome it was a totally different story. Here the population saw the senators as statesmen. The Roman crowds therefore did not besiege their homes (something which happened from time to time in Greek cities) to force benefactions from them – (p. 202). The Roman senators were serious politicians, possessing real power, which implied that they did not have to cultivate their superiority through gratuities *ob honorem*. Other than the *largesses ob honorem* of

patronage, symbolic largesses of the officials, and funerary liberalities in the Greek world.

Thus far the views of some researchers. However, what about ancient literary information? Do we, in fact, possess any historical material that addresses the origins of Roman patronage? Yes, there is at least one interesting text in this regard, the *Antiquitates Romanae* of Dionysius of Halicarnassus, who came to Rome around 30-29 BCE, at the time when Augustus brought an end to the civil war in the middle of the 187th Olympiad.[142] This well-known historian and teacher of rhetoric presents us with the basic determinants of the relationship between patrons and clients, which, according to him, were to be found in the Greek world.

Dionysius and the origin of patronage

In the Roman Antiquities, Dionysius deals with the Roman history up until the time of the first Punic war. In I.9-11 he also sketches the 'original' pattern of patronage, by focusing on the following aspects:

1) *The founder*. Romulus, the founder of Rome (753 BCE), is also named as the founder of patronage (II.9.1).

2) *How?* Romulus supposedly divided the population of Rome into two classes with separate functions assigned to the aristocracy (οἱ εὐπατρίδας) and the plebeians (οἱ δημοτικοί). While the patricians devoted themselves to tasks related to the management and control of the primary social institutions, namely religion, politics and the legal system, the plebeians were to engage themselves in agriculture, cattle breeding and trading (II.9.1).

3) *Why?* The aim of Romulus' patronage was to create a society where harmony would reign by renaming and (re)structuring the nature and content of social interaction between the poor and the rich (II.9.1). Over against negative 'labels' used by the Thessalonians and Athenians to denote the socially inferior position of the clients (II.9.2), Romulus protected the rights and dignity of the lowly and the poor by giving the relationship between them and the rich a new name: πατρωνεία, and by turning this relation into a philanthropic and political comradeship (II.9.3).[143]

---

the officials in Greek cities, such as providing games for the people, Roman *aediles*, in fact, had to produce games. It was one of their functions.

[142] Cary, *The Roman Antiquities of Dionysius of Halicarnassus*, vii.

[143] Polybius, who also wrote a history of Rome between 220-67 BCE, avoided, as far as possible, the use of transliterated Latin words, especially in his descriptions of *patrocinium*. Unlike him, Dionysius did not hesitate to use the Latin equivalent πατρωνεία. According to Edlund, "Invisible Bonds", 129-136, 132, Plutarch (*Romulus* XIII.5) went one step further by using "... the transliterated terms πάτρωνας and κλίεντας which he equates with προστάτης and πελάτας respectively."

4) *Regulations governing interaction between patrons and clients*: The reciprocal responsibilities of patrons and clients toward one another in terms of public and private matters, are spelled out. Patrons, as the 'senior partners' within these relationships, had to expound the law to their clients; take care of them in financial matters; etc. (II.10.1). On their part clients had to provide financial assistance to their patrons by providing dowries for their daughters; pay their patrons' losses in private suit; etc. (II.10.2).

5) *A legal relationship:* Any breach of these rules by patron or client was punishable (II.10.3).

6) *A hereditary relationship:* Patron-client relations continued from generation to generation (II.10.4). In order to 'normalise' status-differentials between patrons and clients, Dionysius relates Romulus' structuring of the responsibilities of patrons and clients to the primary social institution in the Graeco-Roman world, namely kinship (II.10.1; 2; 4).[144]

7) *Results: A*ccording to Dionysius, Romulus' system of patronage was highly successful on interpersonal level (II.10.4). He expresses this in typical agonistic language when he says that it gave rise to a 'competition of goodwill' between patrons and clients. However, Romulus' patronage also succeeded on political level, since patron relations were also extended to other cities and colonies, and for more than six hundred years put an end to violent internal conflict in Rome (II.11.1-3).

The ideological basis of Dionysius' views of patronage

Does Dionysius' narration of the founding of patronage provide one with an answer to the presence of patronage in the ancient Greek world? Unfortunately not. Bormann captures the present scholarly opinion in this regard: "Die Darstellung, die Dionys vom Patronat gibt, ist weder für die Gründungszeit Roms, noch für seine eigene Gegenwart eine historisch exakte Beschreibung der Verhältnisse."[145] To name but a few problems: Dionysius' remark that the regulations which underlay patron-client relations were enforceable by law, does not have a solid historical basis;[146] so too his assertion that individual clients aligned themselves only to one

---

[144] Although patronage and kinship are two clearly distinguishable forms of relationships, Dionysius uses kinship language to 'mask' the social statuses of patrons and clients with more ingratiating concepts. He identifies the patron's role with that of the *paterfamilias;* and that of the client with that of a loyal member of the *familia*, which implies a lifelong hierarchical relationship built on *pietas* and respect - cf. Joubert, "Managing the Household", 214-5.

[145] Bormann, *Philippi*, 202. See also Benner, *Die Politik des P. Claudius Pulcher*, 21-22.

[146] Most historians today are of the opinion that patronage was always a moral relationship, entered into voluntarily. So e.g., Garnsey & Woolf, "Patronage of the Rural Poor in the Roman World", 154.

patron.[147] Touloumakos sounds the death knell to Dionysius' ambitious description of the origins of patronage: "Name und Inhalt - so Dionys - fehlten dagegen bei den Griechen völlig."[148]

In spite of his idealistic description of patronage, Dionysius' work is not without value. It presents us with important insights into the ideological manipulation of this institution by those who were in the position to shape the knowledge associated with the dominant symbols and structures in ancient Roman society in such a way that these legitimised their own sectional interests. Dionysius, influenced by a growing idealisation of early patronage during the time of Augustus,[149] harks back to the 'good old days' when harmony existed between rich patrons and their clients, and also between Rome and its allies. The only alternative to this 'noble' form of social control would be an abusive and exploitative social system (as reflected in history in the oppressive behaviour of the Athenians and the Thessalonians towards their clients). Dionysius thus presents his readers with only two options: oppression of the poor by the powerful, or acceptance of the patron-client system initiated by Romulus. But in both options social control over the poor and the lowly is taken for granted. The only question that needs to be answered, is which form of social domination is *morally* the correct one; to this Dionysius obviously provides an unequivocal answer.

2.6.1.2. Patronage and benefaction in the Empire

John Nicols,[150] in his analysis of formal and informal patronage of communities, also deals with the relationship between *patronatus* and benefaction. Following the likes of Gelzer and Badian, he is of the opinion that both patronage and *euergetism* are *fides*-based relationships. Caesar was apparently the first to distinguish between benefactors in general and a subgroup of benefactors, who bore the formal title of *patronatus*, but both relationships continued to be based upon *fides* (and not on *ius*) and bene-

---

[147] Martial names at least four patrons of his, namely Postumus, Gallus, Decian and Maximus – cf. Prell, *Armut im antiken Rom*, 261.

[148] Touloumakos, "Zum römischen Gemeindepatronat im griechischen Osten", 312.

[149] Dionysius draws an implicit link between the figures of Romulus and Augustus. The latter probably functioned as the physical embodiment of the lost ideals of Romulus in his role as *pater patriae*, (that is, the universal patron) of the *populus Romanus*. In other words, Augustus functioned as the person who would once again restore the institution of patronage as a source of social and political stability in the empire after it fell in disrepute at the end of the republican era. Bleicken, *Verfassungs-und Sozialgeschichte des Römischen Kaiserreiches*, 47 expresses it very clearly: "Als weiterer Ehrentitel tritt i. J. 2 v.Chr. schließlich noch *pater patriae* hinzu, durch den Augustus nicht nur als sorgender Vater der Römer, sonden vor allem als Neubegründer Roms und damit als zweiter Romulus hingestellt werden sollte."

[150] Nicols, "Pliny and the Patronage of Communities", 365ff.

factors and *patroni* continued to perform the same services.¹⁵¹ Therefore, he concludes that patronage (of communities) and benefaction in the ancient Roman world are actually one and the same social relationship, the difference being one of *form* rather of *substance*.

Most biblical scholars also share the view that patronage and benefaction are the same exchange relationship. Moxnes,¹⁵² for example, following the theoretical insights of Blok, and Eisenstadt and Roniger, uses patronage and *benefaction* as synonyms. More precisely, he describes *benefaction* as "another predominant form of patronage in antiquity," similar to that of the emperor, but on a smaller scale. Therefore, Moxnes, in his discussion of Luke's view of God and of Jesus, interchangeably refers to God as 'benefactor and patron', 'exclusive patron', 'benefactor-patron', and 'benefactor'.¹⁵³ However, when patronage and benefaction are approached on a lower level of abstraction within Graeco-Roman contexts, a number of differences between them become apparent, which, I believe, should be taken into consideration in this kind of research.

2.6.2. Patronage and benefaction: distinct relationships

2.6.2.1. Romans benefactors in the Greek East

As the Romans increasingly became the dominant force in the East, the Greeks reacted to their new rulers in typical Graeco-Roman fashion by referring to them in honorary decrees such as: ‛Ρωμαῖοι οἱ κοινοὶ εὐεργέται.¹⁵⁴ This phrase, which was often used to honour Greek leaders, started appearing in inscriptions related to Romans from the second and first century BCE from as far afield as Athens, Cyrene and Asia Minor.¹⁵⁵ However, to say that the Roman occupiers were merely fitted to the long

---

¹⁵¹ Nicols, "Pliny and the Patronage of Communities", 380.

¹⁵² Moxnes, "Patron-Client Relations and the New Community in Luke-Acts", 242ff. Mitchell, "Greet the Friends", 247, n79, criticises Moxnes for not distinguishing between patronage, benefaction and friendship.

¹⁵³ Moxnes, "Patron-Client Relations and the New Community in Luke-Acts", 252-8. The same views are also expressed by Russell, "The Idle in 2 Thess 3:6-12: an Eschatological or a Social Problem?" 105-119; Winter, *Seek the Welfare of the City*, 41ff.; and Vyhmeister, "The Rich Man in James 2", 265-283.

¹⁵⁴ Cf. Erskine, "The Romans as Common Benefactors", 70, n3, who points out that this epithet appears in 16 inscriptions in the first two centuries BCE in references to the Romans in the Greek East, although they are not the main subject in these inscriptions. In most of these decrees the honorandi(s) acted as an intermediary/ies between Rome and his/their city.

¹⁵⁵ According to Erskine, "The Romans as Common Benefactors", 71-3, the ideology of royal beneficence was pervasive in Greek society. The Greek cities considered their king as benefactor, while he himself considered himself to be a duty in order to fulfil this role. At the same time local ruler cults also used the term *euergetes* as an epithet.

tradition of Greek *euergetism* would be an underestimation of the complexities of the Greek response to their new masters. The Romans were not just described as benefactors, "... they were a particular form of benefactor, *common benefactors,*"[156] who conferred their own set of benefits upon their subordinates.

Why did Greek cities refer to the Romans as Ῥωμαῖοι οἱ κοινοὶ εὐεργέται until the end of the first century BCE? Probably because this expression constituted part of their efforts to come to terms with the crisis caused by the replacement of traditional reciprocal interactions between Greek benefactors and beneficiaries by Rome as the new superpower. The Roman occupiers were obviously very different from the Greek leaders, and also quickly usurped their power. In the eyes of the Greeks, the Romans became universal benefactors, and were soon honoured in a new way as *common benefactors*. On their part the Romans themselves "... would not have shared in the euergetistic ideology of the Greek world in the same way that the kings and local élite did."[157] Thus a specific understanding of the 'new reality' that the Romans brought with them, found expression in this epithet.

2.6.2.2. Roman patrons in the Greek East

It is not until after the Third Macedonian War (c. 170 BCE) that the term 'patron' came to be used as a reference to Roman officials in Greek honorary inscriptions.[158] Contact with Roman nobles, and later with the emperor himself, was of the utmost importance for Greek cities, in terms of gaining monetary and military assistance, tax exemptions, specific civic rights (such as the much sought after status of *civitas libera*), etc. Therefore, official embassies from Greek cities soon became a common sight in Rome, and the object for numerous honorary decrees 'back home'.[159] According to Quaß:

> Aufgrund der weltbeherrschenden Stellung der römischen Nobilität mußten allerdings 'Freundschaften' zu griechischen Stadtpolitikern notwendig den Charakter von Klientelverhältnissen annehmen. Solche Freundschaften unterlagen damit m.M. den gleichen Normen und Bewertungen, wie sie innerhalb der römischen Gesellschaft für Freundschafts- und Klientelverhältnisse galten.[160]

---

[156] Erskine, "The Romans as Common Benefactors", 73.

[157] Erskine, "The Romans as Common Benefactors", 83.

[158] So Touloumakos, "Zum römischen Gemeindepatronat im griechischen Osten", 305.

[159] Rich individuals usually established embassies on behalf of their cities by personally financing these visits to Rome.

[160] Quaß, *Die Honoratiorenschicht in den Städten des Griechischen Ostens*, 189-90.

Apart from the Roman understanding of contacts with Greek cities in typical patron-client terms, early initiatives of the Roman Senate to appoint patrons to certain cities also contributed to the introduction of the system of patronage to the Greek East. The Greek communities, who through their numerous contacts with the Romans came to know the system of patronage quite well, responded by also honouring their Roman benefactors as patrons.[161] But the impact of patronage in the Greek East should not be overestimated. Honorary inscriptions for the Romans were more often reflected in typical Greek phraseology. According to Touloumakos:[162]

> Die übliche (allgemeine) Bezeichnung für die Römer in den griechischen Quellen ist, wie für einzelne, 'Wohltäter' bzw. 'gemeinsame Wohltäter' (εὐεργέται, κοινοὶ εὐεργέται), oder 'Retter und Wohläter' (σωτῆρες καὶ εὐεργέται); manchmal werden sie auch als 'Freunde und Bundesgenossen' (φίλοι καὶ σύμμαχοι) oder, ebenso wie bestimmte römische Befehlshaber und maßgebliche Politiker in Rom, die 'Mächtigen' (ἡγούμενοι) genannt.

Even Greek terminology to denote the system of patronage was not used that frequently: "Der römische Patron von Privatpersonen oder Städtern wird in den Urkunden (Weihinschriften)...nicht *prostates* genannt; sein Verhältnis zu diesen wie jenen heißt πατρωνεία ... nicht προστασία...."[163]
Perhaps this is too strong. We do actually possess some evidence where προστασία is used in the sense of *patrocinium*. For example, in an inscription for Marcus Antonius Promachus in Corinth[164] he is called τὸν φίλο[ν] καὶ π[ρο]στάτην, which is clearly equivalent to the Latin *amicum et patronum*. Although this does not imply that προστασία in all instances was understood as a reference to patronage, Greek authors also used it in this way at times.[165] But Touloumakos is correct when he says: "Bezeichnenderweise hat jedoch der Patronat, als Sache und Begriff, im griechischen Osten keine allzu große Verbreitung gefunden."[166] From the

---

[161] Cf., e.g., the inscription from the people of Cyrene honouring C. Claudius (c.92 BCE), quoted in Rawson, "The Eastern Clientelae of Clodius and the Claudii", 230. Here Claudius is referred to as patron and benefactor, an occurrence that became more prominent after the first century CE. Roman emperors and their functionaries are also a few times referred to as 'patrons,' or as 'patrons and benefactors' - Touloumakos, "Zum römischen Gemeindepatronat im griechischen Osten", 320, n54; 322, n57-9.

[162] Touloumakos, "Zum römischen Gemeindepatronat im griechischen Osten", 318-9.

[163] Touloumakos, "Zum römischen Gemeindepatronat im griechischen Osten", 316. The term *patroneia* is seldom used in inscriptions. He finds only three inscriptions, amongst others the honorary decree from Kolophon.

[164] Kent, *Inscriptions*, no 265.

[165] Polybius would be a good example in this regard. Cf. Edlund, "Invisible Bonds", 129-136.

[166] Touloumakos, "Zum römischen Gemeindepatronat im griechischen Osten", 316-7.

above-mentioned examples we may conclude that the Greeks in general did not understand the Roman rule over them as *patrocinium* (as the Romans themselves did). Therefore Roman officials' patronage over Greek cities was not understood by the latter in a hereditary sense.[167] The Romans were rather seen, and duly honoured, as powerful benefactors; less frequently as patrons. In other words, the Greeks used well-known concepts from their 'traditional verbal repertoire', and reinterpreted them to honour the Romans, and not so much the typical Roman forms, which were, in turn, more frequently used in Western parts of the Empire.

We also have some indications that the Romans themselves understood patronage as a specific Roman relationship. Cicero (*Verr.* II.2.154), for example, tells us that C. Verres expected of his Greek subordinates to honour him in an inscription, not only with the *Roman title of patron*, but also as saviour, because he was not satisfied merely with the Roman title.

2.6.2.3. Greek scepticism

Although the language of the Greek honorary decrees praises the Romans as common benefactors, we also hear a few critical voices among the ranks of Greek authors against the system of patronage. Polybius (30,18), for example, although definitely not anti-Roman, reacted very negatively to the behaviour of King Prysias II of Bythinia, who once received a Roman embassy in the clothes of a freedman, thus turning the relationship with his Roman hosts into a typical *patronus-libertus* relationship. This king even agreed to do everything within his power to please them, just as an obedient freedman would do towards his patron and former master.

On his part, Lucian (*Nigr* 22f) ridicules the typical patron-client relations that were to be found in the heart of the Empire, namely in Rome. In narrating the views of Nigrinius after his return from a visit to Rome, we hear how ridiculous the latter finds the activities of those that throng to the houses of the rich (patrons) and wait upon their mercy. These people (the clients) actually have to get up in the middle of the night, walk through the city on foot and then gather at the doors of the rich together with big crowds of other hopefuls. Nigrinius, so Lucian tells us, finds these people, and their shameful behaviour, even more vulgar than the rich Romans (patrons) who are blinded by these flatterers.

2.6.3. Conclusion: Patronage and benefaction: two different, but related, forms of social exchange

Contrary to the consensus among many scholars that patronage and benefaction refer to the same social form of social exchange in the Graeco-

---

[167] Cf. Nicols, "Pliny and the Patronage of Communities", 369, for the hereditary nature of this form of Roman patronage.

Roman world, the available historical data, in my opinion, presents us with a different picture, that is, with two different, but related, forms of social interchange. In other words, in both these relationships we have an exchange of goods and services that creates a social relationship between the parties involved, but the contents of the goods exchanged and the nature of the ensuing social relationships are different.

In our analysis of euergetism we have dealt with civic benefaction in the Graeco-Roman world, as well with as interpersonal or private benefaction in the Greek and the Roman world. In terms of Roman patronage we have focused on the following forms: landlords and peasant farmers, the *patronus-libertus* relationship, patronage of communities, the role of the emperor, client-friendships, brokerage, and the clienteles of individual Roman patrons.

Our discussion has provided us with a general picture of patronage and benefaction in terms of the reciprocal nature of these relations, as well as the social bonds that were established and/or strengthened by these interactions. However, on a lower level of abstraction, that is, on the level of the specific historical 'Gestalten' of patronage and benefaction as it functioned in the Greek and Roman worlds, we did find specific forms of patronage that were unique to the Roman world in terms of their *structure and content*, such as the relationship between patrons and freedmen, or that between the emperor and the people of Rome. Official patronage of communities, where the title 'patron' was conferred upon individuals who possessed the necessary 'qualifications', as determined by the *leges Ursonensis* and *Malacitana*, also took on a distinctively Roman shape, both in terms of *form and content*, as did the formation of large clienteles who gathered at the doors of Roman nobles during customary morning salutations. Regarding its *social nature*, Roman patronage also differed from benefaction, particularly in terms of status differentials between patrons and clients, which were emphasised further by social exchanges. Patrons remained in the superior position, even if they failed to reciprocate their clients' public bestowals of loyalty and honour. Return gifts from clients did not place patrons in a submissive position.[168]

---

[168] The harsh realities of Roman life frequently led to exploitation of clients. Although clients could theoretically end a relationship in such instances, this was easier said than done. Competition among large groups of would-be clients for the benefactions of a relatively small group of Roman patrons was intense, making it difficult to find new patrons. Socio-economic realities, therefore, forced many clients to bear with public humiliation and failure to reciprocate on the part of their patrons, in the hope of receiving at least some material rewards along the way for their clientele services. At the same time patronal 'rewards' for the services rendered by clients became more or less fixed during the middle of the first century CE. It is accepted by a number of scholars that by the time

Turning to Greek benefaction, we also find a number of characteristics, which justify distinguishing it from patronage. In terms of civic benefaction the available evidence shows that benefits were always furnished on all citizens of a specific community, and not on a few fortunate individuals (as was often the case in patronal relationships, such as the *amici caesaris*, or those who were client-friends of influential brokers). The basic characteristic of euergetism was its *collective nature*. However, in the case of benefactions between individuals (and small groups) of equal or near-equal social status, the social relationship between individuals was instituted and kept in tact *by face-to-face exchanges* of services and counter services.

In comparison to Roman patronage, status differentials between benefactor and beneficiary/ies in collective and interpersonal benefaction were not 'entrenched' by benefit-exchanges. Recipients of public benefits, for example, seldom took on a submissive role (as was often the case with clients of powerful patrons). On the contrary, in decrees they frequently state how they proudly fulfilled their obligations toward their benefactors, thus placing the latter in their debt once more. This does not imply, however, that benefactors' social status, as belonging to the class of the aristocrats, changed when beneficiaries paid their debts of honour. Benefaction was, after all, acts of the notables who furnished gifts and services, because they saw themselves as superior to the masses.[169] However, in order to maintain their public honour, as well as their role and status as benefactors that went hand in hand therewith, they had to confer further benefits on their communities. In interpersonal benefit-exchanges it was somewhat different. In these face-to-face interactions, the change in the role and status of the interlocutors from benefactor to beneficiary, and vice-versa, was clearly more accentuated.

Contra some researchers' views that the difference between benefaction and patronage is one of form rather than of substance, it appears that there are in fact substantial differences between these relationships in terms of their nature, structure and content, which merit understanding these as two distinct forms of social exchange. Of course, this does not imply that there were no overlapping functions between these, or that certain forms of social interchange could not have been understood in terms of both benefaction and patronage by various parties (such as the patronage of the emperor that was also interpreted in *euergetistic* terms by the Greeks),[170] but in general, during the first century CE, Roman patron-

---

of Trajan the daily *sportula* of six *cesterces* was "*als Standardtarif eingebürgert*" - Prell, *Armut im antiken Rom*, 262.

[169] Veyne, *Bread and Circuses*, 104.

[170] Hendrix, "Benefactor/Patron Networks in the Urban Environment: Evidence from Thessalonica", 39-58, 55, states that both benefactor-beneficiary and patron-client net-

age coexisted alongside other forms of exchange, such as 'kinship and friendship relations',[171] and 'charity and euergetism'.[172] It is only during the late Empire, with Roman ideologies firmly embedded, that one could probably speak of patronage as a universal phenomenon, usurping all the functions of the civic benefactor, but this theme falls outside the scope of our investigation.[173]

2.7. A model of social exchange as interpretative framework for the collection

2.7.1. The impact of benefit exchange in ancient social relationships

One of the basic social processes that governed the interaction among individuals and groups in ancient societies was the drive to reward gifts with gifts (and, in negative terms, to return evil with evil). In this regard the following two principles, basic to most archaic forms of interchange, took shape at an early stage:

a) An individual, who supplied a rewarding service to another, placed him/her under obligation.

b) In order to discharge this obligation, the latter had to confer a benefit on the first, in turn.

These exchanges then led to the constitution of specific, institutionalised forms of exchange that fulfilled two primary functions, namely to create bonds between individuals and groups, and also to establish super-ordination. For example, apart from *euergetism* and patronage, diverse forms of friendship were formed between individuals outside the parameters of the *familia* or the *oikos* in which either or both these functions were institutionalised, such as guest-friendships, friendships between socially disproportionate individuals, friendships between status equals, ritualised friendships, etc.[174] Interpersonal benefaction, as one of the basic social relationships based upon the exchange of services, also endured throughout antiquity in various cultural contexts. As a matter of fact, it was probably the one truly universal form of social exchange present in the ancient

---

works established and at the same time also reinforced the mutual status of the individuals and groups involved in these exchange relationships.

[171] So Saller, *Personal Patronage under the Early Empire*, 23.

[172] So Garnsey & Woolf, "Patronage of the Rural Poor in the Roman World", 154.

[173] On patronage in the late empire see Krause, *Spätantike Patronatsformen im Westen des Römischen Reiches*.

[174] Cf. e.g., Herman, *Ritualised Friendship and the Greek City*; Fitzgerald, "Friendship in the Greek World Prior to Aristotle", 13-34.

Greek world, the Roman world, and also within ancient Jewish society (cf. Chapter 3).

As indicated earlier, Seneca provides us with a gold mine of information in his *De Beneficiis* on the nature and functions of 'face-to-face' exchanges between individuals and groups. Unfortunately, scholars, in general, do not take Seneca's benefit exchange to be a social relationship proper, and usually interpret his views in terms of relationships such as φιλία/*amicitia*.[175] But he clearly understood the exchange of benefits in terms of an independent social relationship brought about by the exchange of services between individuals. Obviously, as Seneca tells us, these exchanges could also take place within the parameters of other exchange relationships, such as friendship or patronage. But his main concern is with benefit-exchange as a specific reciprocal relationship between individuals.

Because of the comprehensiveness of his discussion, and because of the widespread occurrence of this form of social exchange throughout the ancient Graeco-Roman world, Seneca's interpretation of benefit-exchange provides us with a basic framework that helps us to come to terms with the Pauline collection. In our interaction with the primary material relevant to the collection (Chapters 3-7), we shall have to determine whether the available data fits our postulated framework of benefit exchange; or whether it should be modified by omission or commission in order to reduce the risk of forcing the issue. At the same time, the impact of other forms of social exchange on the collection such as *euergetism* and patronage, have to be taken into account. As Chow[176] and Bormann[177] have pointed out, patronage also sheds light upon specific social interactions referred to, or implied in Paul's letters. We should therefore be sensitive to the nature of the material under investigation, as well as to the level of abstraction at which it is approached in our analysis.

2.7.2. Social-exchange and the collection

Seneca in his *De Beneficiis* provides us with a helpful conceptual framework for the understanding of reciprocal relations, that is, for benefit exchange on interpersonal level in ancient Mediterranean societies. In this regard the *basic processes* inherent to interpersonal benefit exchange as described by him could be summarised as follows:

a. An individual renders a rewarding service to another person/ small group.

---

[175] Cf. in this regard the efforts of Marshall, *Enmity in Corinth*, and White, "Morality Between Two worlds: A Paradigm of Friendship in Philippians", 201-215. Unfortunately, they do not leave enough room for Seneca's own perspectives on benefit exchange, as Bornmann, *Philippi*, 171, correctly points out.

[176] Chow, *Patronage and Power*.

[177] Bormann, *Philippi*.

b. The person/ small group, to whom the service is rendered, accepts the service.

c. The recipient is obliged to the person who rendered the service.

d. The recipient discharges his/her obligation by rendering a service to the first in turn.

e. The original benefactor is placed under obligation by the return service to react with a second service.

Although the concern of these exchange relations is mostly with the exchange of extrinsic benefits, the significance of the 'extrinsic' goods given and returned, cannot be understood in isolation from the *social relationships* which is formed and/or maintained by means of benefit-exchanges. From this perspective the following basic model of benefit exchange could be constructed:

Phase 1
Scenario A:
An individual (or group) in need of specific services makes his/her needs known to a person/group who is perceived as being in the position to provide the services required. The latter, (i) either responds negatively, thereby ending the relationship, or (ii) responds positively, thereby confirming the expectations about his ability to deliver the services in question. In terms of status-demarcations, the superiority of the benefactor in the exchange-relationship is also confirmed.

Scenario B:
An individual makes a claim (that is, without any prior requests from a person/group in need of specific services) in terms of the establishment of a relationship with another individual (or group) through the rendering of particular services.

Phase 2:
The extrinsic service is delivered. In terms of Phase 1; Scenario A, this serves as visible confirmation of the benefactor's honour, and confirms his/her superiority in the exchange-relationship. In terms of Phase 1; Scenario B, the giver makes a claim to superiority in a subsequent relationship.

Phase 3:
The recipient (i) either refuses the services offered, thereby abruptly ending the relationship, or (ii) accepts it, thereby establishing a hierarchical interpersonal relationship characterised by stereotypical role-expectations and *officia*.

Phase 4:
When the service is accepted, the recipient becomes obliged to the benefactor for the duration of this phase of the relationship. This phase is

characterised by a distinct power differential between the benefactor and recipient.

Phase 5:
The recipient (i) either refuses to return a service, which leads to further submission, hostilities, or a total break in the relationship, or (ii) returns a service.

Phase 6:
The return service is offered to the benefactor, thus confirming the recipient's honourable fulfilment of his *officia*.

Phase 7:
The benefactor (i) either rejects the service offered, which leads to conflict or a break-off in the relationship, or (ii) accepts the service, thus reversing the hierarchical positions of the interlocutors: the benefactor is now placed under the obligation to respond with a new service to the recipient, who attains the superior position.

Phase 8 etc.:
The whole process (from Phase 2 onward) is repeated.

With the help of this conceptual model we can now approach the collection in Chapters 3-7.

Chapter 3

Galatians 2, 1-10: the Nature of the Reciprocal Relationship between Paul and the Jerusalem Community

3.1. Introduction

Present research on the collection is interested mainly in the various theological angles of incidence to the collection by Paul and on Jerusalem, and not so much in the primary framework of the meaning, within which the apostle situated this project, and at which level his churches were also persuaded to become involved in the collection.[1] It is one thing to say that the apostle gave this project "a more theological interpretation as an acknowledgement of Jerusalem's actual importance in God's election- and salvation-history,"[2] or to speculate about the meaning of the collection after its delivery in Jerusalem as "... der konkrete Akt, der die Gleichheit und damit die Gemeinschaft zwischen der gebenden und empfangenden Urgemeinde herstellt ...,"[3] but it is an altogether different matter to ask regarding the *basic framework of meaning* behind the various theological conceptualisations of the collection. In this regard, a distinction should be made between the primary level of meaning (that is, the basic interpretative framework), and the secondary levels of meaning (the ideological conceptualisations), within which the collection took shape and attained specific meanings for the various parties involved. Most scholars uncritically advance from the presumption that the secondary level of theological

---

[1] Meeks, *The First Urban Christians. The Social World of the Apostle Paul*, 110, points to the complaints of Klaus Berger and Bengt Holmberg that not enough attention is being paid to the way in which the Pauline communities understood the collection. But, alas, they themselves do not move beyond theological constructions in this regard. A welcome exception in this regard is Betz, *2 Corinthians 8 & 9*, 47-48, who identifies what he calls the "theological substructure" of the collection in 2 Cor 8,5. This entails the following aspects: "(1) the connection between the divine gift of salvation and the human response of self-sacrifice; (2) the connection between the charitable giving expected of Christians and God's beneficence; (3) the common ancient understanding of the nature and function of gifts; (4) the connection of gift-giving with the cult."

[2] Holmberg, *Paul and Power*, 30.

[3] Bartsch, "Wenn ich ihnen diese Frucht versiegelt habe", 106.

reflection also functioned as the basic framework, within which the Pauline communities were persuaded to become involved in this project. However, Paul moved to this secondary level of reflection only when he wanted to place the collection within a broader framework of meaning, or when it encountered specific difficulties.

Benefit exchange provided the interpretative framework within which Paul placed the collection. Since his communities were well versed in the basic principles and obligations inherent to gift exchange that permeated most forms of social interaction in the Graeco-Roman world, this social exchange relationship was the obvious choice, by means of which to come to terms with the nature and organisation of the collection. The magnitude of the collection project within the orbit of Paul's communities, but also the limited resources at the apostle's disposal, necessitated a basic coherent framework of meaning that was shared by all his communities alike, and which did not require any further cognitive legitimisation. Benefit exchange in this regard provided an ideal platform for Paul's theological conceptualisations of the collection.[4]

3.2. Jerusalem holds the key

In order to come to terms with the interpretative framework of the collection, the ideological position of the Jerusalem church, as one of the main parties involved in this project, must be addressed first of all. A number of questions automatically present themselves as objects of investigation in this regard. Did the church in Jerusalem, for example, demand a form of monetary support from Paul and his churches on the basis of their superior position in the early Christian movement? Did they bestow specific benefits on Paul, which morally obliged him to them? Or did Paul out of his own free will undertake this project to address the economical hardships that stared the believers in Jerusalem in the face, and in this process inaugurate a reciprocal relationship with the former?

The answers to these questions are bound up with our understanding of the role of the church in Jerusalem, the would-be recipients of the collection, but also the apparent inaugurators of this project. However, as Ludger Schenke correctly states, any effort to address the theological views or

---

[4] Paul frequently borrowed concepts related to the collection from the field of bene-fit exchange. E.g., his use of the term χάρις in 2 Cor 8-9 in particular, not only serves as a *terminus technicus* for God's salvation in Christ, but also as a reference to the gift-exchange between the Gentile churches and Jerusalem. A number of other terms employed by him, such as δωρεά (2 Cor 9,15); ἁπλότης (2 Cor 8,2; 9,11), δίδωμι (2 Cor 8,5; 10, 16; 9:9) and εὐλογία (2 Cor 9:5-6), also form part of the semantic word-field of gift giving.

historical developments in the Jerusalem church is a risky undertaking.[5] Due to the fact that we are only left with scanty bits of information at our disposal, on Jerusalem's views, beliefs, and practices in the early Christian sources, it is not easy to come to terms with these believers' position in terms of the collection and their relationship with Paul and the communities under his supervision. But we should not be too pessimistic, since a careful analysis of the data encoded in Paul's letters may provide us with some important clues.

Our starting point is Galatians 2,1-10, Paul's version of the meeting between the delegation from Antioch and the leadership of the believers in Jerusalem. Here the request/command not to forget the poor was put to Paul, which determined the nature of all further interactions between him, his communities and Jerusalem. An analysis of the socio-historical context of letter of Galatians, the intra-textual roles of the interlocutors, and the ideological factors operative in terms of Paul's interpretation of the meeting with the Jerusalem leadership, could offer us some valuable, and less speculative, results, and, hopefully, the correct key to also unlock the collection from Jerusalem's perspectives.

3.2.1. Galatians 2,1-10: Jerusalem's role in the collection

3.2.1.1. The chronological framework of the collection and Galatians: A hypothesis

It would not be far from the truth to say that Galatians 2,1-10 is one of the most frequently discussed texts from the Pauline corpus. This text is also important, for our purposes, since it offers valuable information on the position of the Jerusalem believers in the early Christian movement at the time of the Jerusalem meeting, where the contours of the collection presumably took shape.[6] In order to come to terms with this intriguing text, the socio-historical context of the letter to the Galatians must be taken into consideration since it forms the décor, the interpretative frame of reference, for Paul's intra-textual remarks. However, as any New Testament scholar would know, this is no simple task. Questions, such as whether Galatians was written before the Corinthian epistles, or whether the former was written to the believers in South or North-Galatia, are still heavily debated issues in academic circles.[7]

---

[5] Schenke, *Die Urgemeinde*, 9.

[6] According to Schlier, *Der Brief an die Galater*, 80-81, Jerusalem was at this stage *"der geschichtliche und moralische Vorort der Kirche."*

[7] Cf. in this regard discussions of the various arguments in terms of the so-called 'Landschaftshypothese' and the 'Provinzhypothese' in, e.g., Borse, *Der Standort des Galaterbriefes*; Mussner, *Der Galaterbrief*; and Borse, *Der Brief an die Galater*.

Recently Breytenbach[8] has presented a forceful argument for the 'Provinzhypothese' based on an investigation of the communicative context of the letter, the nature of the population in South Galatia, and the history of the development of early Christianity in this region. Nevertheless, as he rightly admits, it only remains a hypothesis, albeit a hypothesis that, according to him, explains most of the historical problems related to the recipients of the letter. This view, also defended in recent publications by the likes of Dunn[9] and Riesner,[10] is of course not accepted by adherents of the North-Galatian theory, who generally date the letter after Paul's (second) visit to the believers in Galatia, somewhere in the mid fifties. They also share the viewpoint that Paul's understanding of the gospel in Galatians points to a later stage of theological reflection, closely resembling the thought of 2 Corinthians and Romans. Adherents of the North Galatian theory therefore usually agree that Galatians was written a year or two before Romans, and just after the completion of the Corinthian correspondence, or at least, parts thereof,[11] whereas adherents of the South-Galatian theory usually opt for an earlier date, between CE 50-51.[12]

Since the above mentioned historical and chronological issues do not fall within the main focus of this study, a few preliminary remarks regarding the basic chronology of the collection and Paul's letter to Galatia should suffice. Without becoming too entangled in the labyrinth of arguments in this regard, the following working hypothesis will also be used as the *basic chronological framework* within which the collection will be interpreted in the course of this study:

(a) Three years after his calling, and for the first time after his conversion, Paul went to Jerusalem to meet with Cephas (Gal 1,18). After this meeting Paul returned to the regions of Syria and Cilicia (Gal 1,21).

(b) Paul visited Jerusalem for a second time fourteen years later (CE 48). This visit was prompted by the presence of the ψευδαδέλφοι in the church in Antioch, who insisted that the believers must be circumcised (Gal 2,4). In response, Paul, Barnabas and Titus went to Jerusalem to resolve this issue. This led to a private meeting between them and the

---

[8] Breytenbach, *Paulus und Barnabas*, 99-112.

[9] Dunn, *The Epistle to the Galatians*, 5ff.

[10] Riesner, *Die Frühzeit des Apostels Paulus*, 258-9. See in this regard also Scott, *Paul and the Nations*, 24-26, and Oegema, *Für Israel und die Völker*, 33-34, also opt for the 'Provinzhypothese' but, at the same time, choose a later date than usually accepted among adherents of this hypothesis, that is during the mid-fifties, after 1 Corinthians, and during, or even after the period in which 2 Corinthians was written.

[11] E.g., Mußner, *Der Galaterbrief*, 10-11. See, however, Betz, *Galatians*, 5, 12, who, in spite of espousing the North Galatian hypothesis, opts for an early date for the letter.

[12] So, Dunn, *The Theology of Paul's Letter to the Galatians*, 16. Bruce, *The Epistle to the Galatians*, 43ff. opts for an even earlier date, at c. 48, from Antioch before the Jerusalem Meeting.

leaders of the church in Jerusalem, (the so-called 'Jerusalem meeting'), which resulted in the request/command that Paul should not forget the poor in Jerusalem (Gal 2,10).

(c) The incident in Antioch between Paul, Peter and Barnabas, concerning table fellowship between Jews and Gentile Christians, took place some time after the Jerusalem meeting at the time of Peter's visit to Antioch (CE 48/9? - cf. Gal 2:11-14).

(d) After the Antioch incident, Paul started an independent missionary program in Galatia, Asia, Macedonia and Achaia (ca. CE 49-56/7). He spent about eighteen months (50-52) in Corinth, and three years (52/3-55) in the city of Ephesus. Paul also devoted much time to organising the collection in the churches in these areas, and wrote a number of letters that also dealt with this project, such as 1 Corinthians (ca. 55 from Ephesus), Galatians (ca. 55/6 from Macedonia), the *Letter of Reconciliation* (that is, the present 2 Cor 1-9 from Macedonia - c. CE 56), and Romans (56/7 from Corinth).

(e) The collection journey to Jerusalem followed at the beginning of 57. Paul refers to this approaching visit to Jerusalem to deliver the collection in Romans 15:25-27. Unfortunately, we are left in the dark as to the eventual response of the believers in Jerusalem. Galatians fits into this structure at section (d); that is, as a letter, probably written to believers in North Galatia from Macedonia, just after the so-called *Letter of Tears* was sent off to Corinth (that is, the present 2 Cor 10-13).[13] Paul visited the Galatians for the first time after his meeting with the leaders of the church in Jerusalem (Acts 16,6), and after the conflict in Antioch. This incident led to Paul's withdrawal from the church in Antioch and to the start of an independent missionary program. After visiting the believers in Galatia for a second time, during which time Paul also probably organised the collection (Gal 4,13-15; [Acts 18,23]), he moved to Ephesus. Shortly after the successful completion of the collection in Galatia, a group of 'wandering missionaries', who had ties with factions in the church of Antioch and Jerusalem, and who opted for a strictly Jewish way of life, visited the believers in Galatia. Viewing themselves as followers of the Messiah, Jesus, they impressed on the Galatians to keep Jewish rituals. They under-

---

[13] Cf. also the views of Borse, *Der Brief an die Galater*, 12ff, and Rohde, *Der Galaterbrief*, 10ff., who place Galatians between 2 Cor A (that is, 2 Cor 1-9), and 2 Cor B (2 Cor 10-13). A number of scholars, such as Schnelle, *Gerechtigkeit und Christusgegenwart*, 54; Eckstein, *Verheißung und Gesetz*, 252, n13, and Söding, "Zur Chronologie der paulinischen Briefe", 1991:57-58; 1997:3ff, however, opt for an even later date, after the solving of the Corinthian crisis from Macedonia or even Achaia.

mined Paul's claims of being an apostle, as well as his 'liberal' views regarding the Mosaic Law and the continued relevance of Jewish rituals.[14]

In response, Paul wrote the letter to the Galatians shortly after having completed 1 Corinthians, and the so-called *Letter of Tears* (2 Cor 10-13), but before the *Letter of Reconciliation* (2 Cor 1-9). The argument of some scholars, that Galatians was written before 1 Corinthians because the collection is not dealt with in any detail in Galatians 2,10, (which supposedly serves as an indication that this project has not even been initiated in Galatia at the time of writing),[15] actually provides a strong argument for the opposite view. Firstly, the (present subjunctive) form of the verb μνημονεύω in Galatians 2,10 points to the fact that Paul had already been involved in the collection for a long period of time before Galatians was written.[16] Secondly, this cursory reference to the collection does not only indicate that the project was well-known among the Galatians, but also that it was already successfully completed.[17]

3.2.2. The structure of Galatians 2,1-10

Rhetorical analyses have dominated investigations of Paul's letters in recent years. The approach of Kennedy, who approaches Paul's letters as speeches,[18] and the approach of Betz, who asserts the epistolary integrity of Paul's letters while giving special consideration to their rhetorical features, have been particularly influential approaches regarding rhetorical analysis.[19] However, I am of the opinion that recent rhetorical analyses of Paul's letters in general, and Galatians in particular,[20] have not conc-

---

[14] See the informative overviews of Paul's opponents in Galatia by Lategan, "Levels of Reader Instruction in the Text of Galatians", 171-184; Söding, "Die Gegner des Apostels Paulus in Galatien", 132ff; and Wehr, *Petrus und Paulus*, 34-37.

[15] Cf. e.g., Bornkamm, *Paulus*, 329ff; Georgi, *Der Armen zu gedenken*, 30ff; and Hyldahl, *Die Paulinische Chronologie*, 64-75; Witherington, *The Paul Quest*, 316.

[16] So Söding, "Zur Chronologie der paulinischen Briefe", 26.

[17] So also Becker, "Der Brief an die Galater", 37. Contrary to Taylor, *Paul, Antioch and Jerusalem*, 116-122, who is of the opinion that the reference in Gal 2,10 cannot simply be reduced to the collection, because μνημονεύω refers to an obligation that was placed on the shoulders of the church in Antioch, I would argue, together with the majority of scholars, that Paul did in fact make a cryptic reference to the collection here because of the Galatians' familiarity with this project.

[18] Kennedy's major work in this regard is: *New Testament Interpretation through Rhetorical Criticism*.

[19] Cf. in this regard Betz, *Galatians*, as well as his: *2 Corinthians 8 & 9*. The works of Betz and Kennedy served as a catalyst for numerous rhetorical analyses on New Testament material, also on Paul's other letters. See e.g., Jewett, *The Thessalonian Correspondence*; Mitchell, *Paul and the Rhetoric of Reconciliation;* and Hughes, "Rhetorical Criticism and the Corinthian Correspondence", 336-350.

[20] Cf., e.g., the rhetorical analyses of Hester, "The Rhetorical Structure of Galatians, 223-33; Longenecker, *Galatians*, c-cxix; Bachmann, *Sünder oder Übertreter: Studien zur*

lusively proven that these letters were structured as rhetorical speeches (surrounded by epistolary prescripts and conclusions); at most they can be analysed merely in terms of specific rhetorical structures.[21] Paul's letters offer slender support for the supposition that he possessed any formal knowledge of, or training in the theory and practice of current forms of Graeco-Roman rhetoric.[22]

Although numerous rhetorical features are found in ancient letters, they were not conceptualised in terms of, or analysed in strict rhetorical terms by ancient authors. In the extant rhetorical handbooks from antiquity, there is no established relationship between rhetorical forms and epistolarity.[23] Within the range of multi-facetted functions of ancient letters (official, magic, poetic, private, or religious letters), their authors did, for instance, apply rhetorical features in their invention of arguments to validate specific theses, as well as in their selection of certain *topoi*, or the arrangement of their subject matter according to standard epistolary conventions (that is, the letter-opening, body, and closing), and style (such as antitheses, *homoeoteleuton*, chiasmus, parenthesis, ellipsis, etc.). Nevertheless, these rhetorical conventions were not used in a systematic, 'handbook-like' manner. The similarities between the rhetorical and epistolary genres should thus rather be understood as the result of 'universal principles of argumentation', and not so much in terms of the development of these in a formal, methodological manner by the epistolary theorists.[24]

We may assume that Paul's letters lack the formal, full-blown rhetorical conventions of his day although he did share the culturally-embedded means of argumentation that formed part of the social framework of generally transmitted knowledge within the Graeco-Roman world. In other words, Paul did not systematically apply formal rhetorical categories in his intra-textual argumentation, but he was well aware of the basic functions of rhetoric, since it formed part and parcel of the culture within which he found himself.[25]

Argumentation in Gal 2,15ff, and Hübner, *Biblische Theologie des Neuen Testaments*, 57ff.

[21] Boers, also expresses this view in *The Justification of the Gentiles*, 45.

[22] In this regard I share the views of Porter, "Paul of Tarsus and his Letters", 567; Klauck, *Die antike Briefliteratur und das Neue Testament*, 179-180; and Kern, *Rhetoric and Galatians*, 203-230.

[23] In the words of Malherbe, *Ancient Epistolary Theorists*, 2, "... epistolary theory ... is absent from the earliest extant rhetorical handbooks, and it only gradually made its way into the genre." Cf. in this regard also S.E. Porter, "Paul of Tarsus and his Letters", 566.

[24] Reed, "The Epistle", 191.

[25] Paul was born a Roman citizen and grew up in the elite category of Graeco-Roman society – Witherington, *The Paul Quest*, 94. The apostle apparently received his childhood education in Jerusalem. Here, he not only learned to read and write in Greek and Hebrew

In view of the above mentioned remarks, we may proceed to an analysis of the basic communicative structure of Galatians 2,1-10 in order to consider Paul's understanding of his own position as well as that of Jerusalem at the time of their meeting.[26] I do not propose to address all the exegetical problems in the text, but rather to confine myself to a brief explication of the persuasive nature of the text, as well as to the roles of the author and intended readers within the textual world.

Galatians 2, 1-10, as an independent pericope,[27] is embedded within a larger section (Gal 1,11-2,21) in which Paul defends his own apostleship. After first of all stressing his divine appointment as apostle in the salutation of the letter (1,1-5), Paul leaves out the *capitatio benevolentiae*, typical of most of his letters (e.g. Rom 1,8ff; 1 Cor 1,4ff.; 1 Thess 1,2ff.), and instead opts for an ironical rebuke of his readers in 1,6-10. This is then followed by an autobiographical overview of his own calling as apostle (1,11-24), and the Jerusalem meeting (2,1-10).

Galatians 2,1-10 consists of an *introduction* (vv. 1-2a), where the reason for Paul's second visit to Jerusalem after his conversion is provided, and the *main section* (vv. 2b-10), where the aim, contents and outcome of his meeting with the leadership of the church in Jerusalem is spelled out:

Paul's second visit to Jerusalem (vv. 1-2a)
    The delegation: Paul, Barnabas, Titus (v. 1)
    Paul's reason: κατὰ ἀποκάλυψιν (v. 2a)

The apostolic meeting (vv. 2b-10)
    a. *Aim* (v.2b)· καὶ ἀνεθέμην αὐτοῖς τὸ εὐαγγέλιον
        ὃ κηρύσσω ἐν τοῖς ἔθνεσιν
        κατ' ἰδίαν δὲ τοῖς δοκοῦσιν
        μή πως εἰς κενὸν τρέχω ἢ ἔδραμον.
    b. *Defence of Christian freedom over against the Jewish intruders* (vv. 3-5)
        (i). Verse 3 (parenthesis): Titus was not forced to be circumcised
        (ii). Vv. 4-5: Paul resisted those who threatened the Gospel
    c. *The contents of the Jerusalem Meeting* (vv. 6-10)
        (i) The result: ἐμοὶ γὰρ οἱ δοκοῦντες οὐδὲν προσανέθεντο (v. 6d)

(perhaps also Aramaic), but was also taught the Hebrew Scriptures – see also Hengel, *The Pre-Christian Paul*, 54-60.

[26] Since Paul is involved in a strong defence of his own apostleship and his belief systems in response to the teaching of his opponents, here in the Letter to the Galatians, one has to bear in mind that this is a text with strong apologetic-polemic traits - so Stuhlmacher, *Das Paulinische Evangelium*, 85, and Oepke, *Der Brief des Paulus an die Galater*, 28.

[27] Cf. in regard to the structure analysis of Gal 1,10-2,21 by Niebuhr, *Heidenapostel aus Israel*, 56ff.

(ii) Reason:
    (a) ἰδόντες ὅτι πεπίστευμαι τὸ εὐαγγέλιον τῆς ἀκροβυστίας καθὼς Πέτρος τῆς περιτομῆς... (vv. 7-8).
    (b) γνόντες τὴν χάριν τὴν δοθεῖσάν μοι (v. 9a)
(iii) Response of the στῦλοι:
    (a) δεξιὰς ἔδωκαν ἐμοὶ καὶ Βαρναβᾷ κοινωνίας,
    (b) ἵνα ἡμεῖς εἰς τὰ ἔθνη, αὐτοὶ δὲ εἰς τὴν περιτομήν (v. 9b-c)·
(iv) The command/request to Paul (v. 10): μόνον τῶν πτωχῶν ἵνα μνημονεύωμεν.

3.2.3. Paul as apostle and slave of Christ in Galatians 2

Paul presents himself to the Galatians as an apostle appointed by God, thus providing divine legitimisation to his own mission and to his views in the rest of the letter. At the same time he is also the exemplary slave of Christ (Gal 1,10), who is fully obedient to his Lord and Master.[28]

The readers (ὑμεῖς), contrary to Paul's usual positive presentation in the introductory section of his letters, are presented as actually turning away (1,6) from the grace of Christ to another gospel. According to Dunn[29] this is a poignant irony, in view of the Galatians' fascination with the teaching of the Jewish intruders. But, at the same time, as part of Paul's strategy not to place too much explicit pressure on the readers, the blame for this state of affairs is placed squarely on the shoulders of the accursed Jewish intruders in their midst, only referred to as τινές (1,7-8).[30]

Paul's strong identification with God (as indicated by his emphasis of the divine origins of his apostleship throughout the first two chapters) is his strongest trump card in the discourse. Within the Pauline symbolic universe (which he assumes is still shared by the intended readers, in spite of their sympathy for the intruders), the problem of the church's possible 'ideological exodus' is addressed by constantly bringing their relationship with God into play. Thus, the implication for them is clear: rejection of

---

[28] As Christ's slave, Paul's behaviour is held up as a model to be emulated by the readers - so Dodd, "Christ's Slave, People Pleasers and Galatians 1.10", 90-104.

[29] Dunn, *The Epistle to the Galatians*, 39-40. The same type of language is also to be found in 2 Maccabees, where the apostasy of some Jews from the covenant faith during the Maccabean crisis is described.

[30] The use of τινές and τίς as references to enemies of the 'true gospel' is typical of early Christian vilification-strategies. Instead of referring to them by name, they are usually presented as *incognito*, shady figures, not worthy of being mentioned by name. Cf. in this regard, the discussions of specific examples of early Christian vilification by Du Toit, "Vilification as a Pragmatic Device in Early Christian Epistolography", 402-414; Joubert, "Persuasion in the Letter of Jude", 75-87, and Thurén, "Hey Jude! Asking for the Original Situation and Message of a Catholic Epistle", 451-65.

Paul's authority as God's official emissary entails seriously endangering their own faith relationship with God. Niebuhr[31] summarises Paul's aims in this regard as follows:

> Die autobiographischen Ausführungen in Gal 1f haben demnach die Funktion, angesichts in Galatien aktueller Auseinandersetzungen um das paulinische Apostolat, hervorgerufen durch eingedrungene Beschneidungsagitatoren, die Leser des Galaterbriefs mittels einer Selbstrechtfertigung dazu zu bringen, sich für die Position des Paulus zu entscheiden.

3.2.3.1. An encomium

According to Misch[32], the aim of autobiographical writing in antiquity was to "... depict an ideal standard of culture or a definite type of character, cast into the form of a self-portrait." In this regard, Malina & Neyrey[33] offer a helpful interpretative framework to understand Paul's self-portrait in Galatians along the lines of the ancient *encomium* or speech of praise. In the composition of an *encomium,* the following four categor-ies of the person in question were usually taken into consideration: (a) origin and birth (*eugeneia*); (b) nurture and training (*anastrophē*); (c) acc-omplishments and deeds (*epitedeumata kai praxeis*), and (d) comparison of the subject with others (*synkrisis*). In Galatians 1-2, Paul provides imp-ortant information about his birth (1,15), his life and education under God (1,17bff), his accomplishments (2,1-10),[34] and a brief comparison with others (2,11-14).

Apart from spiritual virtues, the encomiast usually also narrated his deeds of fortune, such as his fame, fortune and the like.[35] Paul does the same by emphasising his own fame within the early Christian movement, which spread rapidly after he became a follower of Christ (1,23-24). His reputation was further enhanced by his first meeting with Cephas and James (1,18-19), and the personal meeting with the Jerusalem leaders, who were regarded as the most important figures in the circle of Jesus' disciples (2,2). By appearing in their company and by being treated as an equal to Cephas (2,7-9), Paul's own reputation was also established within early Christian circles. The extension of their right hand of fellowship to him,

---

[31] Niebuhr, *Heidenapostel aus Israel*, 10. Cf. also the views on Paul's apostleship in Haacker, *Paulus*, 115-122.

[32] Misch, quoted in Dodd, "Christ's Slave, People Pleasers and Galatians 1.10", 96. See also the form-critical analysis of the autobiographical section in Gal 1-2 in the light of ancient conventions of biography by Lyons, *Pauline Autobiography*.

[33] Malina & Neyrey, *Portraits of Paul,* 23ff.

[34] E.g., Paul highlights some of his virtues in Gal 1-2, such as his obedience to God's revelation (2,1), his loyalty to the gospel as reflected in his staunch defence of its prin-ciples in Jerusalem, and his courage by not yielding to the false brothers (2,2.5).

[35] Malina & Neyrey, *Portraits of Paul*, 46-47.

served as public acknowledgement of his new role and status. Therefore he did not hesitate to proudly parade his legitimisation by them (2,9).

In Galatians 1-2 Paul describes his own 'career' in terms of commonplace categories provided by the typical ancient speech of praise, for the organising of information about a person. In this way he presents himself to his readers as an eminently honourable person, since he has "... high-ranking associates; he enjoys considerable good fortune through God's benefactions; he possesses an excellent reputation, which has been publicly acknowledged by the elite of the group."[36] Paul's self-presentation in Galatians also underlines the fact that his divine appointment as apostle did not remain a private matter. On the contrary, it has been publicly recognised and confirmed through his exemplary behaviour.

3.2.4. The Jerusalem meeting

Thus far we have dealt with literary aspects related to Paul's intra-textual presentation of himself and his intended readers. However, our aim is to move to the world behind the text, that is, to the situation at the Jerusalem meeting. Without entering into a long discussion as to the extra-referential capabilities of texts, I am of the opinion that Galatians does in fact offer important historical information regarding: (a) the situation at the time the letter was written (that is, the 'contextual world'),[37] and (b) the historical reality/ies referred to and reflected on in the text (the 'historical world'). Information relating to the historical world is used in the text only as far as it is relevant to the contextual world, as well as from the ideological perspectives of the author. Therefore, when dealing with references to the historical world, Paul's ideological position in Galatians 2, 1-10, and his rhetorical strategy of oscillating between his own independence (in terms of the crisis situation in the contextual world) and Jerusalem's superior position (in terms of the state of affairs in the historical world), has to be taken into consideration. Since it is my contention that sufficient references to Paul's historical world are embedded within the intra-textual world of Galatians, so as to allow for a basic construction of the *situation* at the Jerusalem meeting, we could advance to the next stage, which would, hopefully, bring us into contact with information on the *world behind the text*.

Paul spells out the historical reason for the Jerusalem meeting. According to him the presence of Judean Christians in Antioch, who tried to impose specific rituals, related to Torah observance on Gentile believers, impelled Antioch to seek the help of the leadership of Jerusalem. The

---

[36] Malina Neyrey, *Portraits of Paul*, 48.

[37] This term is borrowed from Petersen, *Rediscovering Paul*, 8, who refers to the intratextual world created in letters as the narrative world "... from which any real-world history must be reconstructed."

latter held the primary position in the early Christian movement at that stage. These ψευδαδελφοι, as Paul refers to the intruders in Galatians 2,4, also posed a serious threat to Antioch's missionary endeavours.[38] Although Paul went to Jerusalem as an official representative of the church of Antioch, he was more than just a local church leader. Paul's apostolic awareness and his missionary endeavours predated his involvement with the church in Antioch. He thus fulfilled two roles at the meeting: He officially represented the Antiochene church, but at the same time, within the contours of his role as missionary to the Gentiles, he also presented the interests of a wider group of Christian communities that took shape as a result of his earlier work. Therefore, one should add another factor, apart from the immediate problems facing the church of Antioch that necessitated this visit to Jerusalem, namely, Paul's own position and the contents of the gospel that he proclaimed - that had to be sanctioned officially. He needed the 'blessing' of the Jerusalem authorities in this regard, so as to continue unhindered with his own work, and to secure unity within the early Christian movement.

Behind Paul's ostentatious reason for his visit to Jerusalem in Galatians 2,2, namely the heavenly disclosure that compelled him to go there, he could not hide his more basic fear regarding the presentation of his gospel before the church authorities for their consideration. This is expressed in his use of *agonistic* motifs in 2,2: μή πως εἰς κενὸν τρέχω ἢ ἔδραμον.[39] The success or failure of Paul's missionary endeavours was closely linked to the approval of the church leaders in Jerusalem. Given the fact that Paul had taken particular care to ensure his own independence from Jerusalem thus far in Galatians, this rather surprising remark in 2,2 has sparked some lively discussion under scholars. On the one hand, many scholars maintain, together with Hainz,[40] that Paul was not seeking:

---

[38] At the same time the presence of these people pointed "... auf die Verschärfung der theologischen Situation in Jerusalem hin, wo sich inzwischen eine radikal gesetzesstrenge Faktion gebildet hatte," and who also stood very critical of the *'beschneidungsfreie Heidenmission.'* - Hengel, *Zur urchristlichen Geschichtsschreibung*, 95. These 'false brothers' most probably had ties with Jerusalem. Therefore, their views at this stage found *'positive Resonanz'* in large sections of the Jerusalem church - Wehnert, *Die Reinheit des christlichen Gottesvolkes aus Juden und Heiden*, 118.

[39] The metaphor of a race is often used by Paul in his letters (e.g., 1 Cor 9,24-26; Gal 5,7; Phil 2,16), which carries within itself a note of commitment, discipline, exercise, and striving towards a specific goal - cf. Also Schwankl, "Lauft so, daß ihr gewinnt. Zur Wettkampfmetaphorik in 1 Kor 9", 174-191; and Papathomas, "Das agonistische Motiv 1 Kor 9.24ff", 223-241.

[40] Hainz, "Gemeinschaft (κοινωνία) zwischen Paulus und Jerusalem (Gal 2,9f.)", 73, and Boers, *The Justification of the Gentiles*, 61, who share the opinion that Paul did not go to Jerusalem to seek a judgement about the correctness of his gospel. Rather, he was

> ... eine Legitimierung durch Jerusalemer Autoritäten; er machte diese nicht zu Richtern über sich und sein Evangelium, vielmehr wollte er sich selbst und mehr noch seine Gegner überzeugen von der sachlichen Übereinstimmung zwischen seinem und ihrem Evangelium. Was er suchte, war eine Demonstration der Einheit der Kirche.

On the other hand, one cannot overlook the fact that throughout Galatians 2,1-10 the authority of the Jerusalem leadership is assumed; even explicitly acknowledged. This confronts us with the question whether the Jerusalem leadership was the superior party at the meeting?

3.2.4.1. The position of Jerusalem in the earliest Christian movement

At the time of Paul's visit to Jerusalem in the company of the other delegates from Antioch, Jerusalem was the centre of the early Christian movement. It was the headquarters of the disciples, the eyewitnesses of the ministry of the earthly Jesus. From here all missionary work was supervised (cf. Acts 8,12). Due to its principal position as the historical and religious centre during the early stages of the early Christian mission (that is, before the independent Pauline mission led to the formation of Christian communities throughout the Graeco-Roman world), it was the only natural thing to do for the church in Antioch to send a delegation to Jerusalem, requesting their assistance to help solve the problems encountered with the presence of the Torah-observing believers in Antioch. For Paul, as one of the leaders of Antioch, this also implied laying before the leaders of Jerusalem the contents of the gospel that he preached among the Gentiles (καὶ ἀνεθέμην αὐτοῖς τὸ εὐαγγέλιον ὅ κηρύσσω ἐν τοῖς ἔθνεσιν).[41]

The argument in Galatians 2, 1-10 is like a pendulum, swinging between Paul's independence from Jerusalem, on the one hand, to the acknowledgement of their superior position, on the other. However, not even Paul's determined efforts at stressing his own apostolic status could hide the fact that Jerusalem's leadership was the superior party at the start of the meeting. They are referred to as οἱ δοκοῦντες in verses 2,6 and 9, that is, '*die führenden Häupter der Gemeinde*'.[42] In verse 9 the δοκοῦντες are identified, and duly honoured with a further title: στῦλοι. Paul tells us who they are: James, Cephas and John. Together the three of them formed the

---

concerned about the unity of the church that would have been brought into jeopardy if Jerusalem rejected his gospel.

[41] The verb ἀνατίθημι is carefully chosen by Paul so as not to create the impression that he went to Jerusalem in a submissive role so as to get an authoritative ruling from the Jerusalem leadership on his Torah-free gospel. In Acts 25,14 this verb has the meaning of setting forth one's cause. In Gal 2,2 it could be translated as setting forth one's case with a request for counsel (or decision). According to Paul the reason for his visit was linked to his fears that the presence of the 'false brothers' in Antioch would nullify his years of hard work.

[42] Mußner, *Der Galaterbrief*, 104-5, n25.

'men of high repute' and the 'pillars', that is, the inner circle within the Jerusalem church.[43] These honorary titles symbolised the honour and social standing of the Jerusalem leadership among the earliest followers of Jesus.[44] At the same time, as part of Paul's intratextual rhetorical strategies, these references to the Jerusalem leadership served as an important sign to his readers of his close ties with, and respect for the leadership of Jerusalem. The fact that they accepted his gospel thus renders the accusations of his opponents in Galatia regarding his law-free gospel invalid.

3.2.4.2. The agreement at the Jerusalem meeting (Gal 2,7-10)

According to Dinkler,[45] Paul, in his version of the Jerusalem meeting in verse 7(f.), has made use of the written protocol that was used in the meeting, which was published simultaneously in Aramaic and Greek. Lüdemann[46] in turn, is of the opinion that the decision of the meeting is only presented in 2,9, while verse 7-8 reflects on a tradition from the time before the meeting in Jerusalem. This tradition dates back to the earlier meeting between Peter and Paul.[47] Although it is historically possible that

---

[43] In the LXX the στῦλοι are used in reference to the pillars of the tabernacle and the temple. Following Barrett's metaphorical understanding of this image, Dunn, *The Epistle to the Galatians,* 109-10, is of the opinion that Jerusalem regarded James, Peter and John as the pillars of the eschatological temple of God's new people.

[44] In spite of all the respect with which the δοκοῦντες were treated, Paul, on the rhetorical level of the text, also emphasises another principle operative in this regard, namely, the judgement of God (v. 6c), thus implying that people's public status does not matter to God. He shows no partiality (θεὸς ἀνθρώπου οὐ λαμβάνει- cf. also Deut 10, 17; Sir 35,12; Rom 2,11). Paul, as his official representative, shares the same divine point of view. Therefore he could 'legitimately' relativise the high social position of the Jerusalem leaders. Although embracing the agreement reached in Jerusalem, as well as their positive reaction, Paul openly strikes a critical note in verse 6, by deliberately distancing himself from them. Dunn, *The Epistle to the Galatians,* 103, rightly calls the composition of this verse a spectacular balancing act. On the one hand, Paul admits how important a positive decision of the side of the Jerusalem leadership was to him. He actually needed the full weight of their support behind him to secure the future of his own missionary program. But, at the same time, Paul wanted to make it very clear that he did not recognise Jerusalem's authority over himself and his missionary work.

[45] Dinkler, "Der Brief an die Galater", 175-183.

[46] Lüdemann, *Paulus, der Heidenapostel I,* 93. At the same time Lüdemann doubts whether Paul's apostolic status was ever reviewed or approved at the meeting due to the absence of any indications in this regard.

[47] This view is also shared by Kim, "The 'Mystery' of Rom 11.25-6 Once More", 412-429. He is of the opinion that Gal 2,7-8 reflects the agreement reached by Peter and Paul at their previous meeting in AD 34/5. At the Jerusalem meeting it was endorsed, but also modified in view of the fact that Peter was no longer *the* representative of Jewish mission, but only one of three, headed by James. At this meeting the earlier 'informal' division of mission fields between Peter and Paul was elevated to the level of a formal contract.

Peter and Paul came to some sort of an earlier agreement in Jerusalem, it is doubtful whether Galatians 2,7-10 refers to any prior meeting in this regard. Paul's use of a parallelism between the participles in verse 7 (ἰδόντες) and verse 9 (γνόντες), and the compositional unity of these verses do not leave much room to come to any conclusion other than that Galatians 2,7-8 refers to the proceedings of the present meeting between Antioch and the 'pillar-apostles'.[48]

In verse 6-10 the contents of the Jerusalem meeting are summarised. Paul starts off with the most important news, which forms the pivotal point of this pericope:[49] ἐμοὶ γὰρ οἱ δοκοῦντες οὐδὲν προσανέθεντο (v. 6d). The Jerusalem leadership thus affirmed the gospel as preached by Paul and the other delegates in Antioch, and imposed no further obligations on them, such as circumcision or other Jewish legal observances. Paul also gives the reason for their decision: They recognised the grace that God had bestowed on him (v. 9a). In other words, they did not merely take note of his missionary work as a *fait accompli*; they actually came to terms with the true state of affairs, namely that his claims of being called by God was true. Obviously, from Paul's ideological perspective they could come to no other conclusion, apart from compromising their own position as the 'pillars' of God's new people. The Jerusalem leadership simply had to acknowledge the fact that the very same God, who had appointed Peter to work among the circumcised, also appointed Paul to work among the uncircumcised (vv. 7-8).[50]

The 'official' agreement reached at the meeting: ἵνα ἡμεῖς εἰς τὰ ἔθνη, αὐτοὶ δὲ εἰς τὴν περιτομήν (v. 9), should not be understood in terms of a strictly ethnical/geographical division of missionary responsibilities, since the Graeco-Roman world was not that clearly divided between 'Jews and Gentiles'. It is not as if unity in the early church could only be secured *'durch eine gewisse Trennung'*.[51] On the contrary, this decision actually prevented the 'downgrading' of non-Jewish Christianity to a mere addition to the Jerusalem church, or to the development of a totally independent form of Christianity in the Graeco-Roman world.[52] What the agreement did imply, was that Paul would accept responsibility

---

[48] So also McLean, "Galatians 2.7-9 and the Recognition of Paul's Apostolic Status at the Jerusalem Meeting", 67-76.

[49] So, also Oepke, *Der Brief des Paulus an die Galater*, 77.

[50] This view is also expressed by Gnilka, *Paulus von Tarsus*, 96.

[51] Georgi, *Der Armen zu gedenken*, 22. Wehnert, *Die Reinheit des christlichen Gottesvolkes aus Juden und Heiden*, 119, is also negative in his evaluation of the outcome of the meeting: "So deutet bereits die Tatsache der Unterscheidung zweier verschiedener Arbeitsbereiche in v.7-9 die Existenz zweier letztlich unvereinbarer theol. Konzeptionen an, die nur ein Nebeneinander und kein Miteinander im Handeln zuließen."

[52] So Becker, "Der Brief an die Galater", 36.

for the Gentile mission, while Jerusalem would represent the interests of Jewish believers and further missionary efforts among the Jewish people in Judea. In other words, the leadership of the two most prominent interest groups in the early church agreed that they would accept responsibility for the proclamation of the one gospel within their respective constituencies. The right hand of κοινωνία (v. 9) formally sealed this agreement.

3.2.4.3. Do not forget the poor (Gal 2,10)

The only request/command put to Paul at the meeting is stated in verse 10: μόνον τῶν πτωχῶν ἵνα μνημονεύωμεν. This verse obviously raises a number of issues: Should we, for example, after Paul's insistence in verse 6d that no additional demands were made on him by Jerusalem, understand this as a concession?[53] More specifically, does the term μόνον express a reservation as to the agreement referred to in verses 7-9, or does this adverb function as a type of postscript? According to Legrand[54] it is difficult to avoid the impression that this verse points to the fact "... that a restriction, or at least a condition, was attached by the Assembly." However, since the content of the agreement was formally concluded by means of a handshake (v. 9), verse 10 then rather functions as a command/request that followed after the 'formal' procedures, as the grammatical structure also indicates.

The meaning of the verb μνημονεύω has also given rise to some discussion. Questions such as whether the present subjunctive form of the verb implies a continuous action in the present or in the future, has produced various answers, of which Georgi's solution is still the most convincing. According to him, Paul's choice of the specific '*Aktionsart*' of the verb points to the fact "... daß er hier von einem *ständigen* Handeln sprechen will."[55] In other words, the 'remembering' (as a reference to the collection) was an ongoing activity. At the same time μνημονεύω has been interpreted from various theological perspectives.[56] However, word-studies of this nature are often based on theological presuppositions that are not supported by the textual context. The danger of overloading words with theological meaning and superimposing a specific ideological frame-work of understanding on the text then lurks just around the corner.

---

[53] Betz, *Galatians*, 101, understands this as an inconsistency on the part of Paul which is downplayed by him, thus implying that this request was supplementary, and also unrelated to the main debate as well as to the present Galatian crisis.

[54] Legrand, "That We Remember the Poor' (Gal 2:10)", 162.

[55] Georgi, *Der Armen zu gedenken*, 28.

[56] Beckheuer, *Paulus und Jerusalem*, 75-77 understands this term through the perspective of Trito-Isaiah concerning the eschatological salvation of Israel, as well as in light of the sacrificial tributes of Ex. 30,11-16.

Verse 10b has also attracted much attention, specifically the sudden change of person from verse 10a to verse 10b, where the verb σπουδάζειν is used only with reference to Paul. It could best be explained in light of the fact that verse 10a refers to the command/request put to both Paul and Barnabas at the time of the meeting, while the eagerness in verse 10b refers to Paul's collection after he had parted with Barnabas. At the same time the aorist ἐσπούδασα·

> ... steht mit folgendem Infinitiv Aorist ποιῆσαι und drückt aus, daß der in dem Relativsatz beschriebene Eifer angelaufen war und noch in vollem Gang ist.[57]

Hall, in turn, suggests that the aorist tense of the verb ἐσπούδασα provides "... conclusive evidence that Paul was concerned with famine relief at the time of the visit described in that letter."[58] More specifically, he relates this visit of Paul to Jerusalem to the famine-relief visit after the so-called Antiochene collection referred to in Acts 11,27-30. This is incorrect. Galatians 2,10b rather refers to the situation at the time when Galatians was written, as the change from the first person plural in 10a to the first person singular in 10b indicates. In verse 10b, as a form of commentary on the narrative, Paul thus tells the Galatians that he had eagerly devoted himself to the collection after the Jerusalem meeting.

The most frequently discussed issue in verse 10 undoubtedly deals with the meaning of the enigmatic term πτωχός, emphatically placed at the beginning of the sentence before the verb. Well-known in this regard is Karl Holl's thesis that the term πτωχός was a synonym for the 'official' title of the believers in Jerusalem: οἱ ἅγιοι.[59] The three basic viewpoints regarding Paul's understanding of the term πτωχός could be summarised as follows:

(a) The term πτωχός is used as an honorary title for the Jerusalem believers along the lines of the so-called *anawīm* Jewish piety.[60]

(b) πτωχός, as used by Paul in Galatians 2,10 and Romans 15,27, refers to the material poverty of the Jerusalem church.[61]

---

[57] Beckheuer, *Paulus und Jerusalem*, 86.

[58] Hall, "St. Paul and Famine Relief: A Study in Galatians 2,10", 309-311. However, he erroneously insists that the aorist should only indicate a completed activity.

[59] Holl, "Der Kirchenbegriff des Paulus in seinem Verhältnis zu der Urgemeinde", 58ff. See in this regard also the two informative studies of Keck, "The Poor among the Saints in the New Testament", 100-129, and: Keck, "The Poor among the Saints in Jewish Christianity and Qumran", 54-78.

[60] E.g., Schlier, *Der Brief an die Galater*, 80; Georgi, *Der Armen zu gedenken*, 23; Käsemann, *An die Römer*, 383; Betz, *Galatians*, 102.

[61] E.g., Gewalt, "Neutestamentliche Exegese und Soziologie", 87-99; Berger, "Almosen für Israel", 181; Lüdemann, *Paulus, der Heidenapostel I*, 108ff.; Eckert, "Die Kollekte des Paulus für Jerusalem", 71.

(c) Paul uses πτωχός both as a reference to the materially poor, as well as in terms of the Jewish *'anawīm* piety.[62]

Without entering into a long debate, it would suffice to say that number (c) probably comes closest to summarising the respective views of Paul and Jerusalem in terms of their understanding of the 'poor'. Although certain members of the Jerusalem church probably used the term πτωχός as an honorary self-designation, during the mid-forties to fifties, it also served as an indication of their socio-economic position from Paul's perspective.[63] Paul actually uses another term, οἱ ἅγιοι, as a designation of the Jerusalem believers (cf. 1 Cor 16,1. 2 Cor 8,4; 9,1.12).[64]

3.2.4.4. The Jerusalem meeting from the perspective of benefit-exchange

Reciprocity was basic to most forms of social interaction in the ancient Graeco-Roman world (cf. Chapter 2). Determined by the principle of balanced reciprocity (that is, returning the same sort of gifts, or gifts of equal value for those received), any exchange of gifts or services went hand in hand with specific obligations on the part of benefactors and beneficiaries, with the former always ending up in the superior position. Refusal to return services led to the loss of public honour, and ultimately, to the exclusion from further social exchanges.

Galatians 2,1-10 could also be understood from the perspective of benefit exchange, since the interaction between the parties at the Jerusalem meeting is also described in terms of the principles of social reciprocity. Since Paul, as a *Hellenistic Jew*, was not only well versed in the basic tenets of Judaism, but also in typical Greek practices,[65] Graeco-Roman notions of benefaction were quite familiar to him.[66] However, before

---

[62] E.g., Matera, *Galatians*, 78, and Legrand, "That We Remember the Poor",168.

[63] This is confirmed in Rom 15,26 where the partitive genitive, τοὺς πτωχοὺς τῶν ἁγίων ἐν Ἱερουσαλήμ, points to the material poverty of the believers in Jerusalem.

[64] So, Klauck, *2. Korintherbrief*, 67, and Gnilka, "Die Kollekte der paulinischen Gemeinden für Jerusalem", 310-311.

[65] According to Becker, *Paulus*, 58: "Es gibt also mehrere Indizien, die zusammen doch den Eindruck verstärken, daß Paulus eine höhere Allgemeinbildung genossen hatte, die für den Hellenismus offen war ... Paulus selbst zeigt im Spiegel seiner Briefe, wie er doch einen guten Anteil hellenistischer Bildung mitbekam. Nur so ist es auch erklärlich, daß er als ehemaliger Jude sich konsequent auf die Gründung heidenchristlicher Gemeinden einließ und doch wohl ganz gut mit der hellenistischen Sozialisation und Herkunft seiner Gemeindeglieder umgehen konnte."

[66] Probably already during his childhood in Tarsus (Acts 9,11.30), and thereafter in Jerusalem (Acts 22,3), Paul came to know the basic principles inherent to Graeco-Roman social exchange. Although he was raised within a strict Jewish family, the impact of social reciprocity made it felt in all forms of social interaction between the inhabitants of both these cities. Hengel, *The Pre-Christian Paul*, 54-60, points out that first century

engaging ourselves in these aspects in Galatians 2, the question as to whether Paul and Barnabas also brought a collection from Antioch to the mother church, as Luke presumes (cf. Acts 11,27ff.), needs to be addressed. This question is important in order to determine which roles the participants fulfilled at the Jerusalem meeting.

3.2.5. Benefactors or beneficiaries? The Antiochene collection

The meeting between the delegation from Antioch and the Jerusalem leadership formed part of a long-standing reciprocal relationship. Luke, in particular, gives a specific form to this relationship in Acts 11,19-30, as his reference to Antioch's collection for Jerusalem indicates.[67] This visible expression of solidarity was undertaken in view of a worldwide famine that threatened the Jerusalem church, and which was delivered to them by Barnabas and Paul.

The historical reliability of Acts 11,27-30 has been the topic of numerous debates. Also, this issue is of importance for our present purposes, because of its bearing on the specific nature of the reciprocal relationship between Jerusalem and Antioch. If Luke's version of an Antioch collection is historically reliable, and if it is true that:

> ... die Kollektenreise ursprünglich mit der Reise zum Apostelkonzil identisch war, und daß Lukas die eine Reise, die zwei Anlässe hatte, die Kollekte und den Streit um die beschneidungsfreie Heiden-mission (vgl. 15,1), in zwei Reisen zerlegte,[68]

then we might assume that the delegation from Antioch would have been welcomed as benefactors at the start of the Jerusalem meeting, with Jerusalem as the beneficiaries. In terms of the principles inherent to benefit exchange, this would have placed the latter under obligation to show their own gratitude with a return service of some sort, since the receiving of benefit was always considered as a debt that had to be repaid (Seneca, *Ben.* II.23.2).

Ever since F. C. Baur's sharp criticism of Luke's prejudiced view of the church as "... ein sehr schwaches und unklares Bild, das für die geschichtliche Betrachtung wenig sicheres darbietet...."[69] scholars have been

---

Jerusalem was an almost Hellenistic city in many respects, which must have been quite attractive to Greek speaking Jews from the Diaspora, such as Paul's family.

[67] In Acts 11, 19-26 we read of the grounding of the Christian community in Antioch by the so-called Hellenists who fled from Jerusalem during the persecution (Acts 8,1ff).They also proclaimed the gospel to Gentiles in the Syrian capital (11,19-21). Luke tells us that Jerusalem sent Barnabas to Antioch to consolidate the activities in the newly founded Christian community (11,22-24). After becoming the leading figure here, Barnabas also brought Paul to Antioch (11,23-26) - cf. Lüdemann, *Das frühe Christentum nach den Traditionen der Apostelgeschichte*, 139-140.

[68] Pesch, *Die Apostelgeschichte*, 356.

[69] Baur, *Geschichte der christlichen Kirche. I.*

divided into two camps on this issue. Without getting involved in this intricate debate, I take, as my point of departure, the view of Martin Dibelius, who in his form-critical investigations of Acts came to the conclusion that "... die geschichtliche Zuverlässigkeit der Apostelgeschichte aber ist von Fall zu Fall zu ermessen, jeweils nach dem Material, das Lukas verarbeitet hat."[70]

A comparison between Luke's version of the Antiochene collection in Acts 11,27-30, and Galatians 1-2, throws a shadow of doubt over the historicity of the former account, in spite of various scholarly efforts to reconcile the obvious discrepancies. For example, Luke's mention of a visit by Paul and Barnabas to Jerusalem before the Jerusalem meeting recorded in Galatians 2 is in stark contrast to Paul's autobiographical information in this regard.[71] At the same time, not a word is said in Galatians about a famine which posed a serious threat to the believers in Judea; let alone a collection that was taken to Jerusalem by Paul and Barnabas either at this meeting with the δοκοῦντες, or perhaps sometime earlier.[72] These discrepancies between Luke and Paul point to the fact that Acts 11,27-30 is a Lukan composition of various independent traditions at his disposal.[73] Luke clearly knew about the meeting between Paul and Barnabas and the Jerusalem authorities. At the same time he also had some basic information on the collection at his disposal in terms of:

(a) the organisers: Paul and Barnabas;[74]

(b) the recipients: Jerusalem;

(c) the delivery of the collection by Paul in Jerusalem (Acts 24,17), and

(d) the basic terminology (that is, the *terminus technicus*) that was used by Paul to refer to his collection, namely the concept διακονία (cf. Acts 11,29; 12,25; 2 Cor 8,4.19-20; 9,1; Rom 15,25.31).

Luke connected these and other independent traditions into a new unit in Acts 11,27-30 in order to conform to the principles of narrative smoothness. At the same time, in his efforts to communicate the 'true meaning' of

---

[70] Dibelius, *Aufsätze zur Apostelgeschichte*, 9.

[71] Cf. also Schenke, *Die Urgemeinde*, 322.

[72] Witherington, *The Acts of the Apostles*, 373, who accepts the historical reliability of the Lukan account of the Antioch collection, dates it to about 48 CE. On their part, Hengel & Schwemer, *Paul between Damascus and Antioch.*, 243, are of the opinion that this collection would have taken place in about 42 CE. Cf. also the discussion of the nature of the Lukan community in Botha, "Community and Conviction in Luke-Acts", 145-165.

[73] See also Weiser, *Die Apostelgeschichte I*, 275f.; Roloff, *Die Apostelgeschichte*, 182f.

[74] Luke's high regard for Barnabas is evident from the positive presentation of the latter throughout Acts (cf. 4,36-37; 9,7; 11,26.30; 12,25; 13,1-14,28; 15,1-39). Luke also knew (from his Antiochene sources?) that Barnabas was well-known and honoured for his beneficence in early Christian circles (cf. Acts 4,36-7) - Tannehill, *The Narrative Unity of Luke-Acts*, 148.

the narrated events to his intended audience, Luke grouped his own reconstruction of the Antioch collection together with other material on Antioch (11,19-26),[75] thus actually misplacing it. What should have been part of Paul's final visit to Jerusalem to deliver the collection, in the end became two separate collection efforts.

In view of the above mentioned remarks, a collection by the believers from Antioch before the Jerusalem meeting seems highly unlikely. Paul's silence in this regard lends further support to our views. Had such a collection actually taken place, Paul would have referred to it within his *encomium* in Galatians 1-2, since it would have served as a very tangible achievement on his part within the early Christian movement, and a clear signal to the readers regarding his long-standing loyalty to Jerusalem. Such a selfless deed of service to believers in the mother church would have provided proof of his outstanding moral qualities. At the same time, within the agonistic context at the start of the Jerusalem meeting (cf. Gal 2,2), any mention of Jerusalem's acceptance of the collection would have tipped the scales in Paul's favour during the conflict with his adversaries, as well as within his the relationship with Jerusalem, since the acceptance of a gift always indicated the commencement of a long-term relationship between the parties involved, with the obligation shifting to the beneficiaries.

3.2.6. Benefit exchange in Ancient Jewish Society

3.2.6.1. The unique face of Jewish benefaction

Although we have dealt at length with the social matrix of benefit exchange in the Graeco-Roman world in Chapter 2, as the primary context within which the collection was undertaken in the Pauline communities, the question has not yet been addressed as to whether the same principles were operative in ancient Jewish society. This question is relevant to the Jerusalem leadership's understanding of the nature of their relationship with Paul. Did they, for example, interpret the recognition of Paul's apostleship along the lines of benefit exchange? And did they in this process place Paul in their debt? Our first inclination would be to respond negatively to these questions, since, contrary to euergetisic practices in the Graeco-Roman world, public bestowal of honour in the form of statues, golden crowns, honorary decrees, etc., were forbidden in the Jewish world. Josephus (*Contra Apionem* II.217), for example, tells us that those who lived according to Jewish laws could not expect material rewards such as silver, gold, crowns of wild olive or parsley. Within Jewish society people

---

[75] The reference to Paul and Barnabas' return to Antioch in 12,25 was probably placed at the end of the persecution of Peter in Chapter 12 to create the impression that Antioch assisted Jerusalem not only on material level, but that they actually also pro-vided support during the dark hours of persecution - so also Pesch, *Apostelgeschichte*, 370-371.

also did not rise to high religious offices on account of their personal wealth, as was the case in Graeco-Roman society (*CA* II.185-6). The only public honour that the Jews were allowed to bestow along the lines of Graeco-Roman *euergetism* was the daily sacrifice in the temple for the imperial Roman family on behalf of all Jews (*CA* II.74-78). Other public displays of gratitude, such as the erection of statues for benefactors (*CA* II. 74f), or costly funerals and monuments for their dead, were forbidden (*CA* II.205).

In the Diaspora, where the systems of *euergetism* and patronage were operative, relatively few examples exist of Jewish participation in civic *euergetism* or patron-client relations. Indeed various scholars have drawn our attention to the presence of Jewish honorary inscriptions in Palestine and the Diaspora.[76] But Rajak[77] correctly points out that - although Jews were not outside the framework of *euergetism*, and, although they at times honoured Greek and Roman officials along typical *euergetistic* lines, - the absence in Jewish epigraphy "... of virtually all the language in which the transactions of euergetism can be conducted" cannot be an accident. "To enter the Jewish world, as a sympathizer or proselyte, would have been to learn a new dialect of a familiar language."

Although some traits of civic *euergetism* were present in ancient Jewish society during the first century CE, solid evidence for the presence of patronage only appears in Rabbinic literature from about the mid-third century CE.[78] *In Y. Berachot* 9,1 for example, we read of a client who, when visiting his patron, asked the patron's servant to inform the patron, that he was waiting at the gate of the court. The behaviour of this patron is then contrasted with that of God, who not only allows petitioners into his presence, but also immediately answers those who plead their case before him.

Although civic *euergetism* and patronage, as it functioned within the Graeco-Roman world, did not play a significant role in Jewish society, this does not imply that benefit-exchange were totally absent. On the contrary; gift exchange and the subsequent reciprocal relationships between benefactors and beneficiaries formed an important facet of ancient Israelite society, but then in particular forms, as the following examples show.[79]

---

[76] E.g., Lifshitz, quoted in Collins, "Money, Sex and Power", 7-22, has collected no less than 102 Jewish inscriptions concerning benefactions related to synagogues, while Rajak, "Benefactors in the Graeco-Jewish Diaspora", 310ff., in turn, analysed a number of Latin and Greek inscriptions in this regard in the Jewish Diaspora.

[77] Rajak, "Benefactors in the Graeco-Jewish Diaspora", 319.

[78] Cf. in this regard, Sperber, "Patronage in Amoraic Palestine (c. 220-400)".

[79] I am indebted to the views of Bolkestein, *Wohltätigkeit und Armenpflege im vorchristlichen Altertum*, and, in particular, to Peterman, *Paul's Gift from Philippi*, 22-50 who offer more fully documented evidence from a variety of Jewish texts, which, for obvious reasons, need not be repeated again in full.

In Genesis 33, it is told how Jacob presents a large gift to his brother Esau in order to win his favour. In spite of their differing views of the relationship (Jacob operates from the perspective of a vasal greeting his lord,[80] whereas Esau probably views the relationship with Jacob in kinship terms), the gift is accepted, and the reciprocal relationship restored, because of Jacob's insistence. Exodus 2,15ff., in turn, refers to Moses' assistance to the seven daughters of Reuel at a well in Midian. On their return to their father's house, and on hearing how Moses had helped them, he asked them why they did not invite him to a meal. They then went back and brought him to Reuel. In his interpretation of this text, Philo (*Mos.* 1,58) states that Reuel reprimanded his daughters because of their ingratitude for the benefit that Moses had bestowed upon them. He then sent them back to invite Moses to a meal in order to repay the favour. Moses, in turn, responded by staying with Reuel and eventually marrying one of his daughters.

A more clear-cut example of benefit-exchange is recorded in 1 Samuel 25, which deals with David's interaction with Nabal during his sojourn in the wilderness. After giving unsolicited protection to his shepherds (= the benefit from the benefactor), David sent a delegation to Nabal (vv. 4-8), informing him about the nature of his benefactions and then requesting provisions for his soldiers (= the request for a return gift from the side of the benefactor). However, Nabal refused (vv 10-11) and responded with slander (= rejection of the benefactor and the reciprocal relationship). In response to this public humiliation David vowed to kill all in Natan's household in order to restore his own honour (vv. 12; 22). Fortunately, Nabal's wife, Abigail, prevented this slaughter by delivering a large gift to David, while begging him not to kill all in her household because of her husband's ingratitude (vv. 23-31).

3.2.6.2. Characteristics of Jewish benefit exchange

Numerous examples in the Bible deal with the exchange of gifts or services in ancient Israel (e.g., Jud 8, 5-9.35; 2 Sam 14,22; 2 Kings 4,8-17; 2 Chron 20,10-1; etc.). In order to form a clearer picture of the characteristics of these exchange relationships, the following two aspects must be taken into consideration:

(a) *The position of the destitute*: The socially underprivileged, such as the poor, widows, slaves, strangers, etc., played a significant role within ancient Israel's ethos, particularly from around the second half of the seventh century BCE (cf. Deut 15,1-18; 24,17-22). As part of ancient Israel's strong emphasis on "die Verankerung der religiösen Gesetzgebung

---

[80] So Westermann, *Genesis 12-36*, 524.

im Alltagsleben,"[81] these groups became the focal point of Israel's of almsgiving and care. This religious duty of giving to the poor often involved reciprocity. In Deut 15,8, for example, it is supposed that the gifts bestowed on the poor are to be considered as loans that must be returned.[82]

(b) *The importance of divine reward for giving*: God was viewed as the implicit object of people's almsgiving, particularly in wisdom circles. In Proverbs 19,17, for example, the wise man who is helping the poor is presented as making a loan to Jahwe. Within this context it is not the poor, but God who functions as the beneficiary since he is placed in debt to the wise man.[83] That the poor were not in a position to reciprocate the benefits they received from their benefactors, posed a threat to the very nature of social exchange. But this stumbling block was overcome by the idea of Jahwe's personal intervention in reciprocal relations. As the one who sides with the downcast, he would personally reward their benefactors.

Within the ambit of Diaspora Judaism, with its strong emphasis on almsgiving and prayer, as well as its strict dietary-, marriage- and Sabbath laws as socio-religious identity markers, the impact of Graeco-Roman social exchange relationships is also evident.[84] However, the matter of divine reward for good deeds remained a prominent theme, as the book of Tobit shows.[85] Amidst Tobit's blindness he is rewarded for his righteous deeds (which included the giving of alms) in the form of a goat, which his wife received as extra payment for her work (2,11-14).[86] When Tobit

---

[81] Bultmann, *Der Fremde im antiken Juda.*, 37.

[82] The poor in this situation refers not only to people who were materially disadvantaged, but also to people who lost their inherited social status – cf. Bultmann, *Der Fremde im antiken Juda*, 82.

[83] These ideas presuppose another well-known concept that Jahwe is on the side of the poor and the oppressed (e.g., Ps 103,6; 146,7-9).

[84] Admittedly Diaspora Judaism was not an unitary movement with a set of neatly worked out dogmas, rituals, symbols, etc. - so Overman, "The Diaspora in the Modern Study of Ancient Judaism", 63-78. On the other hand, there existed a number of identity markers to socially mark Jewish identity for those both inside and outside their communities - so Rutgers, *The Hidden heritage of Diaspora Judaism*, 31-42. According to Segal, *Paul the Convert*, 193, 194-195, "for the Jewish community as a whole, the special laws, not conversion experiences, functioned to raise Jewish commitment and ensure Jewish survival as a nationality and religious group in the Diaspora."

[85] Cf. Marböck, *Gottes Weisheit unter uns. Zur Theologie des Buches Sirach*, 20.

[86] Moore, *Judaism in the First Centuries of the Christian Era*, 172-173, points out that the Jews distinguished between works of loving kindness and alms. Alms were shown to the poor and the living, while the former was shown to both rich and poor, as well as to the living and the dead. Alms was also undertaken with the help of money, while deeds of loving kindness included money as well as any other possible means of assistance to others. Strack & Billerbeck, *Das Evangelium nach Matthäus erläutert aus Talmud und Midrasch*, 538, point to the instructions by some rabbis that almsgiving had to be

responds in disbelief to this large gift, his wife reminds him of the fact that good works in the end do bring a return (2,14). Later in the book the 'theological' effect of alms-giving is spelledced out even more clearly: ἐλεημοσύνη ἐκ θανάτου ῥύεται, καὶ αὐτὴ ἀποκαθαίρει πᾶσαν ἁμαρτίαν (12,9; cf. also 4,10f.). In other words, God's response to the righteous man who gives alms is not only limited to material returns, but also to returns on a religious level. As a matter of fact, taking care of the needs of the destitute is considered as such a big benefit, that God replicates the benefactor with the most precious gift he himself possesses, namely salvation. This cultic interpretation of ethical behaviour is also shared by Jesus ben Sirach. He stresses (in 3,14) that alms or good deeds towards one's father (ἐλεημοσύνη) atones for sins. This also holds true for almsgiving in general (3,30), since good deeds towards one's neighbour, specifically to the poor (29,8-13), lead to salvation from death.[87]

3.2.6.3. Differences between Greek and Jewish benefaction

The above mentioned examples point to the presence of gift-exchange in the Jewish world. However, clear-cut examples of benefit exchange in Jewish texts are not as manifest as one would have expected.[88] In contrast to Graeco-Roman texts, where the nature and contents of reciprocal relationships such as friendship, patronage and *euergetism* receive much attention, conscious reflection on social exchange relations is much more restricted in ancient Jewish sources.

At the same time, these reciprocal relations in ancient Israel and in the Diaspora did not take on the same appearance as in Graeco-Roman society. The notion of the noble individual, who was engaged in collective undertakings for the common good of his fellow citizens, typical of the Greek world, did not feature prominently within Jewish society. Reciprocal interchanges of a more personal nature between fellow Israelites would probably be the closest parallel between typical Israelite and Graeco-Roman forms of benefaction, although the responsibilities and statuses of benefactors and beneficiaries in Jewish reciprocal relationships were not

---

undertaken in secret by, amongst others, placing money anonymously in the special chest that was put in the temple for this purpose.

[87] Marböck, *Gottes Weisheit unter uns*, 176-184 correctly notes that the atoning function of good deeds should also be understood in conjunction with Sirach's strong emphasis on prayer and obedience to the law.

[88] See also Peterman, *Paul's Gift from Philippi*, 42, who, likewise, does not find sufficient examples of social reciprocity in the Old Testament and other Jewish texts "... that clearly depict the operation of social reciprocity." However, the fact that this phenomenon is not referred to in detail in Jewish texts, could be explained by factors such as the context-dependent nature of these documents, as well as the fact that reciprocity formed such a basic part of their value system and social stock of knowledge that it did not need to be repeated in full in every single instance.

that clearly demarcated. But, the biggest difference in this regard would be the objects of benefaction. Over against the Graeco-Roman world, where assistance to the poor was not understood as a moral obligation (cf. Chapter 2), the socially destitute played a significant role within reciprocal interactions in the Jewish world. Bolkestein[89] tells us that the major motivation for the bestowal of benefits in the Roman world were related to the joy of giving; the expectation of an adequate return; the striving for honour; and political ambition.[90] In the Greek East the same principles applied. When material assistance was provided by benefactors (such as assistance in the form of grain or food), it was usually handed out to all inhabitants of a city or community regardless of the financial position of the recipients. Garnsey and Saller correctly note that the ideology of Graeco-Roman *euergetism* was civic, not humanitarian – "... very few euergetists would have described what they were doing as poor relief."[91] But, according to Klauck:[92]

> Anders sah es im Judentum aus. Trotz mancher Datierungsprobleme, die uns die Quellenbelege aufgeben, kann man inngesamt doch festhalten, daß die jüdische Armenpflege für den Bereich der vor- und außerchristlichen Antike vorbildlich war.

In Jewish society material care for the poor in the form of almsgiving was not only important on a social level, but also on a religious level, since the giving of alms was nothing less than entering into a reciprocal relationship with Jahwe who would personally reward the benefactors.

On the other hand, close a resemblance exists between the Graeco-Roman forms of interpersonal benefaction and that in Hellenistic-Judaism. Although Josephus and Philo (*De Decal.* I.4-7) rejected the practices of civic *euergetism* with its public bestowal of honours, such as golden crowns and purple robes, they, on the other hand, were very much at home with typical Graeco-Roman principles of personal benefaction. Philo, for example, in *De Virtue*, 82-84, when dealing with the question of loans, states that the best way to lend out money is to give without restriction to those in need (μάλιστα μὲν χαρίζεσθαι τοῖς δεομένοις), since a gift is in a sense a loan (καὶ ἡ χάρις τρόπον τινὰ δάνειον ἐστιν) that will gladly be repaid by the recipient when times are better. In *Cherubim* 122-123, Philo compares the bestowal of benefits with commercial transactions where the benefactors fulfil the role of sellers, since they place their beneficiaries in debt. Within such a context it is not only the 'sellers' that

---

[89] Bolkestein, *Wohltätigkeit und Armenpflege im vorchristlichen Altertum*, 317ff.

[90] In this regard, the recipients of state grain in Rome, during the time of Julius Caesar, were actually a privileged group of about 150 000 people, and not necessarily in want of earthly goods - Garnsey, *Famine and Food Supply in the Graeco-Roman World*, 211ff.

[91] Garnsey & Saller, *The Roman Empire*, 101.

[92] Klauck, "Die Armut der Jünger in der Sicht des Lukas", 160-195, esp. 170.

look for a repayment on their benefits, but the recipients also try to make a return, thus turning the bestowal of gifts into a sale.[93]

3.2.7. Benefit exchange and the Jerusalem leadership

In view of the above mentioned remarks, the question whether the leadership of the church in Jerusalem understood their recognition of Paul's ministry as a benefit, which obliged him to show his gratitude with a return service, may be answered affirmatively. The basic principles of benefit exchange were also known in the Jewish world, although the strong emphasis on almsgiving (ἐλεημοσύνη) gave it a distinct shape. Due to the fact that the three 'δοκοῦντες' were originally from Galilee,[94] we may assume that they were also informed as to the functioning of Graeco-Roman forms of benefit exchange. Greek influence in Galilee was still very evident during the first century CE. In Lower Galilee alone, around 40 percent of ancient inscriptions that were found until the present are in Greek. Furthermore, the cosmopolitan urban centres, as well as the examples of Greek buildings, art, gymnasiums and stadiums (such as in Tiberias), and the continued presence of the Herodian dynasty, all point to the strong influence of Hellenism in this region.[95]

If we may then summarise the basic ideological position of the 'δοκοῦντες' at the Jerusalem meeting, in view of the above mentioned Jewish perspectives on benefaction, they were of the opinion that:

(a) Any positive response from their side as the senior party to Paul and Antioch would place the latter in their debt;

(b) The needs of the materially poor in their midst had to be addressed as part of the early Christians' religious duties. This responsibility also included fellow believers that were not part of the Jerusalem community;

---

[93] Cf. also Peterman, *Paul's Gift from Philippi*, 47.

[94] They formed part of the disciple group who earlier accompanied Jesus on his travels in Galilee. He avoided the urbanised centres in Galilee during his public ministry, limiting himself only to the small villages and towns spread out through the countryside. The majority of these people were peasant farmers, who adhered strictly to the Torah and were affected only minimally by the impact of Hellenism. As a matter of fact, these villages often saw themselves under threat from local pagans and the influences of Hellenism. We could actually speak about a long-standing and widespread reaction against the culture of the urban-based rulers in this regard - cf. e.g., Horsley, *Archaeology, History, and Society in Galilee*, Chapter 5. But this does not imply that the principles inherent to Graeco-Roman social exchange were totally unknown in these parts of Galilee, as the episode of the Centurion in Capernaum clearly illustrates (Lk 7,1-10).

[95] It is still a bone of contention among scholars as to whether all of Galilee was Hellenised, or only Lower Galilee. Cf. in this regard, e.g., Freyne, *Galilee from Alexander the Great to Hadrian*, 144, and Meyers, "Galilean Regionalism: A Reappraisal", 125-131.

(c) By helping the poor in Jerusalem, these believers would be placed in a reciprocal relationship with God who would personally reward them. The Jerusalem leadership therefore had a moral right to expect a material response from Paul and Barnabas at the conclusion of the meeting (Gal 2,10b).

3.2.8. The Jerusalem leadership as benefactors at the meeting

The 'δοκοῦντες' were in the position to 'officially' determine the nature of Paul's gospel at the meeting in Jerusalem. Their decision, whether we interpret it as an authoritative instruction (as the Jerusalem leadership probably understood their own ruling), or as a directive (as Paul interpreted their decision), was crucial to the immediate future of Paul. Any refusal on the part of Jerusalem to recognise the contents of Paul's message, in spite of his own insistence that he had received it independently from them by means of a heavenly revelation, would bring public humiliation on him among the followers of the risen Jesus.

Jerusalem reacted positively to Paul's gospel as he tells us in Galatians 2,6-10. From the perspective of benefit-exchange, the Jerusalem leadership actually fulfilled the role of *benefactors* by recognising what had been true beforehand, namely that Paul was appointed by God to proclaim the gospel. Their giving the right hand of κοινωνία to Paul (and Barnabas), 'officially' confirmed this fact, as well as the legitimacy of Antioch's gospel. But how should this handshake that sealed the agreement at the meeting be interpreted? Was it a sign of Jerusalem's supremacy, or at least an indication of Paul's recognition of their superior position?[96] A brief look at some examples from Jewish texts may provide us with some clues. In 2 Kings 10,15, for example, we read how Jehu, in the process of eliminating the priests of Baal, came across Jonadab, the son of Recheb and, after determining his integrity, asked him to extend his hand to him as a symbol of the new-found comradeship between them. In Ezra 10,19 we read how all those who married non-Israelite women, as a sign of commitment, gave their hand that they would send them away. In 1 and 2 Maccabees the 'giving of the (right) hand' functions as the symbolic conclusion of peace treaties; a form of welcoming; a pledge; a formal assurance between socially equals, or between superiors and inferiors; etc. (cf. 1 Macc 6,58; 11,50.62; 13,45.50; 2 Macc 11,26). Josephus also offers a number of examples in this regard, such as king Artabanus' extension of his right hand (τὴν δεξιὰν ἐδίδου) as a sign of assurance to the inhabitants of the land that a treaty was concluded, ("because no one would ever prove false when he had given his right hand"- *Ant*. 18.328-9). Any breach of an

---

[96] Schlier, *Der Brief an die Galater*, 79, and Betz, *Galatians*, 100, both share the view that this symbolic gesture does not automatically point to Jerusalem's supremacy.

agreement after the extension of the right hand was viewed in a very serious light. Even Jahwe announced his judgement on those breaking their word after symbolically committing themselves to him in this manner (e.g. Ezek 17,18).

From the above mentioned examples it is clear that the extension of a right hand within ancient Jewish society functioned as a symbol of goodwill, peace (after the ending of hostilities), friendship and mutual commitment to an agreement. In short, it symbolised the beginning, renewal or strengthening of a relationship between individuals and groups. Often, the initiative in the extension of the right hand was taken by the superior party in the relationship, thus symbolising a bestowal of honour upon the inferior party (usually also in conjunction with some tangible benefits).

Paul's use of the term κοινωνία in 2,9 provides some further contextual indications as to how we could understand this symbolic gesture by the leadership of Jerusalem. Firstly, according to Sampley,[97] it points to the consensual *societas* between Paul and Barnabas and the pillars, James, Peter and John. But, at the same time, this handshake symbolised more than a personal arrangement or transaction. It actually signified the conclusion of an agreement between the representatives of the two most prominent interest groups in the early Christian movement, while, at the same time, also expressing the commitment of both sides to honour the reciprocal responsibilities agreed upon. Their common goal would thus be to accept responsibility for the advancement of the one gospel of Jesus Christ within their respective 'constituencies'.

Secondly, the fact that the superior party took the initiative in extending the right hand of fellowship, until that stage of the meeting, served as a visible confirmation of the benefit they had bestowed on Paul, namely the 'official' recognition of his apostleship. By recognising his right to proclaim the very same gospel among the Gentiles that Peter proclaimed among the circumcised, they did in fact, from Paul's own understanding of the meeting, place him on the same socio-religious level with themselves as the leaders, the inner circle, within the early Christian movement. Paul was thus now officially considered as an equal partner, an apostle appointed by God, and as the leader responsible for the organisation and co-ordination of the Gentile mission (although from his ideological perspective, Jerusalem indeed only confirmed the existing state of affairs).[98]

---

[97] Sampley, *Pauline Partnership in Christ*, 26-32.

[98] Although Paul does not explicitly state that his apostleship was recognised by Jerusalem, the latter's actions, such as their apprehension of the outward signs of his divine commission (v. 7), as well their recognition of the grace that God had given him to establish churches (v. 9), are clear indications of their acceptance of his divine appointment as apostle. In this regard Schlier, *Der Brief an die Galater*, 78, states that the use of

3.2.9. Paul as would-be benefactor of Jerusalem

Jerusalem's benefit raised Paul's socio-religious status within the early Christian movement from that of a local church leader to that of apostle, one of the select few who were divinely appointed to stand at the head of the proclamation of the gospel in the early Christian movement. At the same time, the Jerusalem leadership's benefit was also extended to Antioch, which placed Paul, in his role as apostle and as representative of Antioch (together with Barnabas), in Jerusalem's debt. It was now expected of him to show his gratitude by responding with an equally impressive service in order not to remain under permanent obligation to them. And, as Paul tells us, Jerusalem did not hesitate to communicate their needs to him and Barnabas in this regard: μόνον τῶν πτωχῶν ἵνα μνημονεύωμεν (Gal 2,10a).

Within the agonistic context of ancient benefit exchange, with its obvious differentiation in power between the parties involved, reciprocity in the exchange was established by the fact that individuals disliked to remain at the receiving end of such relationships. However, Paul and Barnabas showed no signs of unwillingness to respond to Jerusalem's command/request, even though this implied that they would become indebted to Jerusalem until the collection was delivered. There is a close parallel in this regard between Paul and Seneca in terms of the latter's ideals for benefit-exchange (cf. Chapter 2).[99] Paul's reaction according to Galatians 2,10b, where the responsibility for the collection switched from Antioch to him alone (cf. the change from the first person plural to singular), makes this evident: ὃ καὶ ἐσπούδασα αὐτὸ τοῦτο ποιῆσαι. By mentioning the enthusiasm and eagerness with which he accepted this request, Paul presents himself as *the ideal beneficiary* in terms of:

(a) *The positive response to his benefactors*. Seneca tells us that a benefit should be viewed as a gift from a friend, not as a heavy burden from which the beneficiary must free himself at the earliest possible opportunity. A recipient should not think of himself as a debtor, but as somebody who is bound to his benefactor through the common bond created by the benefit (VI.41.1-2). Paul's use of κοινωνία to explain the true meaning of Jerusalem's handshake (verse 9) expresses more or less the same idea. The emphasis for him is not so much on the debt he incur-

---

χάρις in verse 9 actually refers to the '*Apostelgnade*'; that is, to God's appointment of Paul as apostle. McLean, "Galatians 2.7-9 and the Recognition of Paul's Apostolic Status at the Jerusalem Meeting", 75, also points out that Paul's appeal to the decision of the Jerusalem leadership would not make any sense within the polemical-apologetic framework of Galatians if they did not in fact recognise his apostleship.

[99] It is no wonder that a tradition developed in the early church of a supposed correspondence between Paul and Seneca - cf. Malherbe, "Seneca on Paul as Letter Writer", 414-421.

red, but rather on the subsequent relationship between him and Jerusalem. As a typical collectivist, group-oriented person, Paul saw it as his mission to labour for the well being and solidarity of the early Christian movement, which included both Jewish and Gentile believers. Therefore he avidly accepted responsibility for the needy believers in Jerusalem, which he believed would serve as an important visible expression of the fellowship between them.

(b) *The public display of gratitude.* According to Seneca an expression of gratitude should not be a private matter. Those who refuse to express it in the open are not discrete, but ungrateful. A benefit should also not be accepted submissively, or in a spirit of indifference (II.23-25). In this regard Paul does not hesitate to talk openly about the benefit conferred upon him by Jerusalem (Gal 2,1-10). As a matter of fact, his use of the verb σπουδάζειν in verse 10b points to the enthusiasm with which he personally embraced the opportunity to be of service to Jerusalem.

(c) *Responding with a return-service.* In the ideal exchange relation, a benefactor always bestows two things upon a recipient: a *tangible benefit* of some sort, as well as *goodwill*. Therefore the latter owes two things in response: gratitude and a material service (Seneca, *Ben.* II.35.1; VII.15.3). According to the principle of balanced reciprocity, gratitude without an adequate material return was not enough. True gratitude had to lead to, and was only fully displayed once the return had been made (Cicero, *Off.* 1.48). Paul's use of the aorist form of the verb in verse 10b, which indicates that he had already been involved in the collection for some time when the letter to the Galatians was written, confirms this image. As an honourable person he was thus presently doing everything in his ability to realise his positive response to Jerusalem's command/request (as the Galatian believers who had already completed this project knew all too well).

3.2.10. A command or a request?

"Hatten die 'Säulen', wenn sie die Kollekte initiierten, eine Forderung gestellt? Oder eine Bitte geäußert?"[100] In other words, should the verbal response of the Jerusalem leadership: 'μόνον τῶν πτωχῶν ἵνα μνημονεύωμεν' (Gal 2,10) be understood as a *command* issued by the superior party to the submissive representatives from Antioch, or as a request to them? The answer to this question depends on the fact whether verse 10a is to be seen as part of the agreement reached in Jerusalem, or to be seen as Jerusalem's reaction to Paul's positive response to their command/request, at the close of the meeting. If this formed part of the formal agreement, then we must take 2,10(a) as a reference to one of the formal

---

[100] Gnilka, "Die Kollekte der paulinischen Gemeinden für Jerusalem", 303.

stipulations to which Paul consented.[101] But when 2,10(a) is understood as a response from Jerusalem that was expressed to Paul only after the symbo-lic handshake and after his positive response to the benefit that was besto-wed upon him, it must be understood as a request, but then as a request from the benefactors to the beneficiary within the parameters of a recip-rocal relationship.

The contents of Galatians 2,1-10 favour the second option. As we have seen, Paul makes it evident that the main issue on the agenda in Jerusalem was the validity of his gospel (2,2). This issue was successfully resolved through Jerusalem's recognition of his proclamation (2,6-9). As a matter of fact, no other obligation was placed upon his shoulders (2,6d). Verse 10(a) therefore does not refer to the contents of the agreement in terms of a com-promise or a supplementary demand. This view is supported by the Greek construction, since the ἵνα conjunction in verse 10 introduces a new thou-ght that is not dependent on the previous δεξιὰς ἔδωκεν. Paul takes care to place this request at the end of his report of the meeting in order to clearly separate the request regarding the care for the poor, from the previously mentioned agreement in verses 7-9. Therefore we may conclude that the contents of verse 10(a), did not form part of a legally binding contract to which Paul (and Barnabas) agreed, but rather a request to which he con-sented and which, within the principles inherent to benefit exchange, placed a *moral obligation* on him to deliver the promised services. Alth-ough Paul committed himself to the collection as one of the official repre-sentatives of Antioch, he also understood the request of the Jerusalem leadership as a personal request to him in his capacity as an apostle of the Gentiles.

As an honourable person who was prepared to put the welfare of his group before his own, Paul knew how to pay his debts; not only to God, but also to his benefactors, even if it meant becoming involved in a time-consuming collection that would place him in debt to Jerusalem for a long period of time. However, at the same time Paul also knew that the delivery of the collection would publicly confirm his status as an apostle and also his role as benefactor of Jerusalem. He therefore placed the collection on his agenda soon after the Jerusalem meeting and the incident in Antioch.

3.2.11. The Jerusalem leadership's strategy at the meeting

It is not easy to decide from Paul's remark in 2,2 to whom he presented the content of his gospel in Jerusalem: To the whole church, as implied by his use of αὐτοῖς in verse 2(b), or only to the δοκοῦντες, as implied by the

---

[101] Both Betz, *Galatians*, 101, and Dunn, *The Epistle to the Galatians*, 112 understand verse 10a as an additional request, which formed part of the official meeting to which Paul agreed. But if this did in fact form part of the formal meeting, 2,10a would have functioned as a legal obligation placed on the shoulders of Paul and Antioch.

expression in verse 2b: κατ' ἰδίαν δὲ τοῖς δοκοῦσιν? In other words, did Paul and Barnabas have two separate meetings, one in public with a representative group from the church in Jerusalem, and another in private with James, Peter and John? Although the Greek may be constructed as to refer to two separate meetings, or to a single meeting with the δοκοῦντες, the particle δὲ in 2,2c seems to indicate a distinction between the two engagements, thus favouring the interpretation of two separate meetings. Although it is not possible to come to a final conclusion, the decisive meeting was the one held with James, Cephas and John. They were the leading figures whose acceptance of Paul's gospel was crucial to the future of his missionary work and to unity in the early church.

Paul mentions that he and the leaders met in private. Why? Was it because of the fact that the larger meeting of the church referred Paul's case to a smaller, private meeting of the leaders, where some members of the traditionalist faction in the church (2,4) interfered in order to ensure that their concerns were safeguarded?[102] Or was it a reversed version of the ancient system of deliberating with the group as a whole before the leading members met privately when some issue of general importance had to be addressed?[103]

Two further options may be considered. The first one would be that the meeting took place *in private* as an expression of the close friendship between Paul, Barnabas and the δοκοῦντες, or more correctly, as a form of patron-friendship. In Chapter 2 Seneca's division of wealthy patrons' friends into three groups has been referred to (*Ben.* VI.33.3-34.5). According to him the first group, the so-called *amicos primos*, or close friends of the patron, who were mostly of the same social status as he, were to be received *in secretum* (in privacy). The second group, the protégés, were to be received in groups during the customary morning salutations, while the last group formed part of the crowd, who in the early mornings had to wait outside for some monetary handouts. The private meeting between the leaders of Jerusalem and Antioch could be interpreted in the light of the patron-friendship, because both Paul and Barnabas had a long-standing personal relationship with the leadership of Jerusalem, as the Book of Acts and Paul's remarks in Galatians 1,18-19 make clear. This would imply that the Jerusalem leaders invited their 'client-friends' to a private meeting as a symbol of the close ties with them, and perhaps also in anticipation of the positive outcome of the meeting. However, the absence of friendship terminology in Galatians 2, as well as the fact that patronage around the first century was still very much a Roman phenomenon, renders it improbable that Paul understood the Jerusalem meeting in these terms.

---

[102] So Dunn, *The Epistle to the Galatians*, 93.
[103] So Mußner, *Der Galaterbrief*, 104, n23.

Another, more feasible, view in terms of the available information in Galatians 2, would be that a private meeting was decided upon by Jerusalem as part of their strategy to deal with socio-economic crisis in their midst, as well as with the successful new Christian movement under the Gentiles. The deteriorating economic situation in their city (cf. below) compelled the church leaders to look at other Christian communities that fell under their supervision for help. However, at first this must have been a rather embarrassing idea. The fact that the Jerusalem leadership could not solve the financial problems of their own community, in spite of their determined efforts posed a potential threat to their own status in the early church. They therefore opted for a private meeting with the leaders of Antioch. Such a meeting provided a safeguard against public conflict or humiliation for them if their strategy at the meeting failed to produce the necessary results, namely, to secure their own position in the early church and, at the same time, obtain help from the outside to assist the poor in their midst.

But, how could Jerusalem's turning to Antioch (who at the initial stages of the meeting formed the inferior party) be reconciled with their attempts to maintain their own authority under the believers? A private meeting could at best only alleviate some immediate tension. The only 'permanent' solution, and the only honourable strategy in this regard for the Jerusalem leadership, was to enter into a *benefit exchange relationship* with Paul and Antioch. They did not possess the authority to unilaterally coerce a collection from Antioch. However, by acting out the role of their benefactors through their recognition of Paul's gospel and Antioch's right to continue with its missionary program among the Gentiles, they could secure their own position as apostles and benefactors in the early church. On the basis of the bestowal of these benefits, they could, without fear of losing their own esteem under their followers, legitimately request a specific return-benefit from their beneficiaries. The basic idea that eventually gave rise to the collection project thus originated in Jerusalem, although the conceptualisation and structuring of this project was largely Paul's work.

The Jerusalem leadership gave a clear indication as to what they deemed would be a sufficient response to their benefit: the care for their poor in the form of a monetary gift. In terms of their strategy at the meeting, they were well aware of the fact that, apart from the financial relief such a project would bring, it would also have far reaching implications for the unity of the Christian movement. But, on the other hand, although Paul in particular was raised to the level of the would-be benefactor of Jerusalem through his positive response to their request, the leadership of Jerusalem also knew that any caritative project of this nature would keep Paul (and Barnabas) in their debt for a long time. As a matter of fact, one may speculate whether it was not part of a deliberate strategy on their part to 'overwhelm' Paul with benefits in order to keep him (and through him, also his Gentile churches) in semi-permanent submission. Within the ancient agonistic context of gift exchange, where the normal expectation was that the debtor should not only equal the gift bestowed upon him, but that he/she should actually surpass it in order not to remain in debt to his benefactor, it would not have been an uncommon strategy to 'out-give' one's beneficiaries. On the other hand, Jerusalem's strategy may also be viewed from a positive perspective. Instead of using their benefits as a means of crushing Paul into permanent submission, they rather saw it as an opportunity to create a bond of fellowship with the Christian communities founded by Paul. Benefactors were always interested in the number of new relationships that an exchange of gifts created. The more 'gift-debtors' benefactors had, the higher their own social standing and prestige. Therefore, the Jerusalem authorities did not hesitate to bestow the necessary benefits on Paul. This was a safe way of ensuring that knowledge about their own position in the early Christian movement would become known to non-Jewish believers.

The nature of Jerusalem's strategies leads us to another question, namely as to why the '*dokountes*' requested a collection from Paul and Barnabas? Were they at this stage really in financial difficulty as indicated above? This question merits our attention in the following section.

3.2.12. The socio-economical situation in Jerusalem

3.2.12.1. The impact of famines on Ancient Judea

Lenski[104] paints a grim picture of social stratification in agrarian societies, such as that of Roman Judea of the first century CE. According to him only two percent of the population in these societies belonged to the ruling elite, while about eight percent comprised the so-called service class in the cities, and the remaining ninety percent lived in villages and worked on the land to support the first two classes. Recent research supports this picture.[105] Ben-David[106] reckons that during this time, more than seventy percent of the Jewish peasant farmers and day labourers in and around the

---

[104] Lenski, *Power and Privilege*, 284.

[105] See in this regard, e.g., Dommershausen, *Die Umwelt Jesu*, 95; Oakman, *Jesus and the Economic Questions of his Day*, Ch.1-2, and Sanders, *Judaism: Practice and Belief*, Ch.9.

[106] Ben-David, *Talmudische Ökonomie*, 458. He is of the opinion that the average farmer in Palestine only had about 150 denarii to take care of taxes and the needs of his family, usually with about four to five members - p. 298. Stegemann & Stegemann, *Urchristliche Sozialgeschichte*, 89, come more or less to the same conclusion. According to them, the average net income per head during the first century was about 40 denarii.

cities lived beneath the subsistence level, which was about 200 denarii per year. Schenke[107] summarises the major reasons for this depressing social situation in Judea as follows:

> Die Neugründungen der Städte, die Repräsentationsbauten, der luxuriöse orientalische Lebensstil an den Fürstenhöfen, die offene und unverschämte Bereicherungssucht der römischen Prokuratoren und hohen Beamten führten zu einer Steigerung der Steuerlast, die unerträglich wurde. Sie lag durchschnittlich mindestens bei 30 - 40 Prozent. Dazu kamen die religiösen Steuern: die Zehntabgabe zur Unterhaltung des Tempelpersonals, die jährliche Tempelsteuer und die Verpflichtung, jährlich einen weiteren 'Zehnt' in Jerusalem beim Paschafest zu verzehren.

As a typical pre-industrial city, Jerusalem was largely dependent on the surrounding villages and on trade with neighbouring territories to provide for its basic needs.[108] In spite of its weak infrastructures, people from all over Palestine and the Diaspora flocked to Jerusalem because of its importance as the religious capital of the Jewish people.[109] However, the cumulative impact of the staggering state and religious taxes, the under-developed economy, the unstable political situation in Judea, and catastrophes such as food shortages and famines, had a severe effect on the inhabitants of the city.[110] The Christian community in Jerusalem did not escape these harsh conditions either, as Luke indicates in his reference to a worldwide famine during the reign of Claudius (cf. Acts 11,27-30).[111] However, Luke's view that the entire *imperium Romanum* was affected by this famine should probably be understood in terms of the numerous local

---

[107] Schenke, *Die Urgemeinde*, 38.

[108] Due to the absence of strong fountains in the proximity of the city, water supply was also a constant problem. Josephus (*BJ* 5.410) tells us that in times of food shortage and famine, water was sold to the inhabitants of Jerusalem in measured units.

[109] Jerusalem probably also attracted a large number of peasant farmers, who became day labourers in the city to avoid the high taxes since inhabitants of cities during the reign of Herod the Great paid much less tax than farmers. According to Oppenheimer, *The Am Ha-Aretz*, 71, farmers had to pay about 23 percent of their annual income in taxes in this time.

[110] Jewish citizens had to pay two types of tax to the Romans, namely the *tributum soli* (a land tax), and the *tributum capitis* (personal tax) - Millar, *The Roman Empire and its Neighbours*, 92ff., as well as numerous indirect forms of tax, collected on the value of products or merchandise, by the ever-present tax-collectors. These taxes ranged anything from between 2-25 percent. These taxes were so depressing that many people, according to Josephus (*Ant.* 18.90), saw this as the main reason for the Jewish-Roman war.

[111] In spite of the prophet Agabus' prophecy (Acts 11,28) that ὅλην τὴν οἰκουμένην would be hit by this famine, no historical proof exists of such a worldwide catastrophe. The closest we could come to a crisis of this nature are references to a series of local food shortages during the reign of Claudius. Riesner, *Die Frühzeit des Apostels Paulus*, 113-116, finds proof of no less than twelve '*lokale Hungersnöte*' between the winter of 40/1 in Rome and the famine in Asia-Minor in 57 CE.

food shortages/famines during this time in Egypt, Syria, Greece, and also in Judea.[112]

Josephus (*Ant.* 20.51) also refers to a big famine in Judea (τὸν μέγαν λιμὸν) during the procuratorships of Cuspius Fadius (44-?46) and Tiberius Alexander (?46-48).[113] This famine in Judea, which could be dated somewhere between 44-46 CE, was probably followed a few years later by yet another famine (Josephus, *Ant.* 3.320).[114] Josephus tells us that it took place during the highpriesthood of Ismael ben Phiabi, who, according to Schwartz,[115] was appointed in this position in 49 CE.[116] Although it is difficult to pinpoint the exact dates of these famines, referred to by Luke and Josephus, we may deduce that during the years 44-49 the people of Jerusalem were hard hit by one or two very severe food shortages.

Food crises normally led to steep increases in grain prices that made it almost impossible for the poor to buy grain. In this regard Josephus (*Ant.* 3.320) reports that the price of grain was thirteen times higher than normal during the famine of about 49 CE. Even worse: Outright starvation and

---

[112] Cf. Garnsey, *Famine and Food Supply in the Graeco-Roman World*, 21, who states that between 45-47 CE numerous food crises affected all of these territories.

[113] The date of this famine is dependent on the text-critical choice between ἐπὶ τούτου or ἐπὶ τούτοις in the available texts of *Ant.* 20. Together with the majority of resear-chers we opt for the latter possibility that would then place this catastrophe somewhere between 44-48 CE. Perhaps Josephus' reference to Queen Helena of Adiabene's bene-faction, where she sent large quantities of figs from Cyprus and grain from Egypt to the people of Judea (*Ant.* 20.51-53), could help date this famine even more accurately. We know from information in the Tebtunis papyrii that Egypt experienced very high grain prices due to crop failures in the spring of 45 CE. This would imply that there would only have been excess grain in Egypt at the earliest during the spring of 46. On the other hand, Ogg, *The Odessey of Paul*, 52-53, has indicated that the high grain prices in Egypt in 45 CE might have been in anticipation of the expected crop failures in 46. But Josephus' reference to the fact that Queen Helena's beneficial activities had already started during the procuratorship of Cuspius Fadus (*Ant.* 20.2), would favour an earlier date for the famine, somewhere between 44-46 CE.

[114] It is also possible to date the reference to the famine in *Ant.* 20.51 not before the crop failure in Egypt in 45 CE, but after it, to between 46-48. If this were correct, Josephus' reference to a famine during the time when Ismael ben Phiabi was highpriest (*Ant.* 3.320), would then refer to one and the same prolonged famine.

[115] Schwartz, "Ishmael ben Phiabi and the Chronology of Provincia Judaea", 177-220.

[116] The well-known thesis of Jeremias, "Sabbatjahr und neutestamentliche Chronologie", 98-103, that the famine, which he dates to about 48 CE, was worsened by the Sabbatical year of 47/8, is still a topic of discussion - cf. e.g., Hengel, *Zur urchristlichen Geschichtsschreibung*, 94f., and Wehnert, *Die Reinheit des christlichen Gottesvolkes aus Juden und Heiden*, 264. If Jeremias is correct, this implies that there would have been no harvests in Judea before the spring of 49 CE. However, Wacholder, "The Calendar of Sabbatical Cycles during the Second Temple and the Early Rabbinic period", 153-196, has pointed out, on the basis of new calculations, that this Sabbatical year did not take place in 47/8 but in 48/9.

death was the fate of large numbers of Judeans (cf. Josephus, *Ant.* 20.51). Plagues and epidemic diseases usually also went hand in hand with food crises such as these, because, as the mid-second century physician and philosopher Galen[117] tells us, many people during these times only had recourse to unfamiliar foodstuffs such as twigs, shoots of trees, bulbs, cooked fresh grass and roots of indigestible plants. Rabbi Johanan, in his reconstruction of the diet of the Israelites during the seven-year famine recorded in 2 Kings 8, even refers to occurrences of cannibalism.[118] Although historical evidence on mortality rates during famines in Judea is not available,[119] we may assume that, due to the weak economic infrastructures, these food crises were life threatening to thousands of people.

Famines also led to social dislocation, such as large-scale emigration, the selling of children, suicides, and riots against the rulers as one of the last resorts of utterly desperate people.[120] In this regard, we know of two official forms of support to the poor from the Jewish authorities that were probably operative as early as the first century CE. In the Mishnah tract, *Peah* 8,7, reference is made to the *quppah*, a fund to which Jewish people had to contribute to every Friday when two officially appointed people collected the money, which was divided afterwards among the poor by a committee of three, in the form of food, money and clothes. Only people who did not have enough food left for at least fourteen meals were helped from the *quppah*. The *tamchui* was a fund from which food such as bread, beans and wine was provided to strangers and the poor on a daily basis; that is, to people who did not have enough food left for at least two meals.[121] Because of a lack of sufficient historical evidence as to the existence of such organised charity in Jerusalem in the New Testament period, a number of scholars reject an early dating.[122] On the other hand,

---

[117] Quoted in Garnsey & Saller, *Roman Empire*, 97.

[118] See Garnsey, *Famine and Food Supply in the Graeco-Roman World*, 29.

[119] The early Christian historian, Eusebius (*Hist. Eccl.* 9.8) offers a very graphic description of a famine in Palestine in 312-313 CE under Maximin. Due to a severe drought and a war, countless people died in the cities and even more in the villages. Plagues and hunger wiped out almost the whole population. This led to people eating strange, even poisonous foods, and many women turning to shameful behaviour such as begging in public.

[120] Garnsey, "Famine in Rome", 60. "... 'Hungry people do not listen to reason,' Seneca was to complain, and his nephew, Lucan the poet, said, 'the grain supply provides the mainsprings of hatred and popularity. Hunger alone sets cities free, and reverence is purchased when rulers feed the lazy mob: a hungry population knows no fear'..." - quoted by Winter, "Acts and Food Shortages", 71.

[121] See Shurden, *The Christian Response to Poverty in the New Testament Era*, 73.

[122] E.g. Seccombe, "Was there Organized Charity in Jerusalem before the Christians", 140-143.

many scholars are of the opinion that such a practice did not only exist at an early stage in Jerusalem, but that it actually provided the basic framework for the Christians' own system of care for the poor.[123] Luke's vague knowledge of such a system, as reflected in his narration of the appointment of the seven helpers in Acts 6, 1-7, supports the idea that a system of this nature was already operative during the first century CE.[124]

3.2.12.2. The Jerusalem Church and the poor

The Jerusalem community did not escape the severe consequences of the famines in Judea during 44-49 CE. Although they probably also, at the initial stages of the church, took part in the official Jewish poverty care for the poor, the apostles soon started an independent form of poverty care to address the needs of their own members. Luke refers to the so-called *Gütergemeinschaft* of the Jerusalem Christians in the summaries in Acts, according to which the members who had possessions sold them and distributed the money amongst the poor. In the second summary (4,32-35) Luke comes closer to the actual situation in Jerusalem by saying that believers placed the proceeds at the apostles' feet who then distributed them under the needy. This points to the presence of a 'gemeinsamer Kasse',[125] a common fund under the auspices of the apostles at a relative early stage in the Jerusalem community, which was used to assist the believers, who, because of famines and the depressing social conditions, could not provide for their own livelihood. However, this community of goods was probably voluntary and not strictly regulated by the apostles. Private property still continued in the Jerusalem community.

In spite of Luke's idealistic interpretation of the Jerusalem community in terms of *hellenistischen Sozialutopien*,[126] we may also state:

> ... daß es die in den beiden Summarien von Lukas beschriebene soziale Solidargemeinschaft in der Urgemeinde tatsächlich gegeben hat, auch wenn sie nach

---

[123] So Jeremias, *Jerusalem zur Zeit Jesu*, 147; Haenchen, *Die Apostelgeschichte*, 255, 424. Over against this viewpoint, Walter, "Apostelgeschichte 6,1 und die Anfänge der Urgemeinde in Jerusalem", 370-393, rejects an independent form of poverty care among the Jerusalem Christians, because, as one of the "lose Gruppierungen innerhalb der jüdischen Tempelkultgemeinde Jerusalems" (p. 376), they still shared in the official Jewish poverty support.

[124] See also Lüdemann, *Das frühe Christentum nach den Traditionen der Apostelgeschichte*, 80-82.

[125] So Klauck, "Armut", 171. According to Capper, "Reciprocity and the ethic of Acts", 499-518, this community of goods functioned primarily through meal-fellowship.

[126] Klauck, "Gütergemeinschaft", 93. Horn, *Glaube und Handeln in der Theologie des Lukas*, 43, also links Luke's reference in Acts 4,34: οὐδὲ γὰρ ἐνδεής τις ἦν ἐν αὐτοῖς to the fulfilment of the promise in Deut 15,4. According to Horn, Luke combined both these Jewish and Greek traditions so as to present the Jerusalem church "in ihren Anfängen als die Verwirklichung im Schnittpunkt sowohl jüd. als auch griech. Hoffnungen."

Form und Organisation nicht einfachhin dem idealen Typos folgt, den Lukas darstellt.[127]

This community of goods was based on a 'charismatisch-enthusiastischen Grundlage',[128] which, on the one hand, implied a spontaneous sharing of material means along the principles as spelled out by Jesus. On the other hand, the Jerusalem Christians' actions were also determined by their fervent expectation of an imminent *parousia* of the resurrected Christ.

Luke's reference to the appointment of the seven helpers from the ranks of the Hellenists in Acts 6,1-7 to take over the responsibility for the care of the poor, in spite of his obvious efforts to conceal the theological differences between the Hebrews and the Hellenists in the Jerusalem community, also reflects the socio-economic hardships of believers during the early years of the Jerusalem church, particularly those who came from the Diaspora. Due to the Hellenists' more critical stance toward the temple cult, they were probably not received with open arms at the official Jewish poverty support, while their Christian community also began discriminating against them. Their public protest to this state of affairs eventually led to the appointment of a number of men from their midst to take care of the poor.[129] This appointment probably represents a second, more organised phase of assistance to the poor in the Jerusalem community. The economic hardships that believers had to face during the mid-forties, together with the ideological differences between the different factions in the community, forced the apostles to appoint helpers to accept full-time responsibility for the poor.[130]

Within the Jerusalem community poverty was not idealised; it was a daily reality that stared believers in the face. When one does not know where one's next meal would come from or where one's family would find clothes or shelter, a term such as πτωχός quickly looses its connotations as an honorary title or a reference to the community's exalted position within the early Christian movement. This expression from the mid-forties and fifties pointed to the concrete situation in Jerusalem; that is, to the mater-

---

[127] Schenke, *Die Urgemeinde*, 92.

[128] Klauck, "Gütergemeinschaft", 97.

[129] Food shortages often led to public unrest or riots. E.g., Tacitus (*Annals* 6,13) refers to a huge riot in Rome during 32 CE about the excessive grain prices.

[130] Hengel, *Eigentum und Reichtum in der frühen Kirche*, 41-42, bases the material neglect in the Jerusalem community in Acts 6,1-7 on the fervent eschatological expectations of the believers that caused them to throw all forms of economical organisation overboard. However, if my presupposition is correct that Acts 6,1-7 also provides a historical glimpse into the socio-economical situation in Jerusalem during the mid-forties, this eschatological enthusiasm (which was rife from the initial stages of the church, that is from about 33/4 CE) was quickly tempered by the harsh realities of believers starving, falling ill (and dying?) because of malnutrition and severe food shortages.

ially poor in their midst and to the rest of the community's solidarity with their unfortunate predicament. However, this is not to say that the ideology inherent to the so-called *anawīm* poverty (where the spiritually poor are synonymous with 'the pious' or 'the saints') did not also impact on the Jerusalem community's self-understanding. What better hope could there be for poverty-stricken believers staring hunger in the face, than to hear that they were the special objects of Jahwe's favour? But this spiritual understanding was always secondary to the material conditions of many believers in the Jerusalem community; this is also apparent from the request of the Jerusalem leadership to Paul in Galatians 2,10b.[131]

The poor had to be supported. This was part of the early Christians' ethical responsibilities as spelled out in the love command of Jesus. Therefore when they were at the end of their own abilities in this regard, Jerusalem turned to other Christians outside of Jerusalem for help. Perhaps the material assistance from Queen Helena, a proselyte of Adiabene in Mesopotamia, a few years earlier to the people of Jerusalem (Josephus, *Ant.* 20.51-53), provided an important analogy for the Jerusalem leadership.[132] After she had personally experienced the severity of the famine during her visit to Jerusalem, she bought large quantities of figs and grain and sent them to the inhabitants of the city. The Jerusalem church leadership could therefore, during the phase of particular economic hardship experienced in about 48 CE (at which time Paul and the delegation from Antioch also visited Jerusalem), not only request his assistance, but also present him with a concrete example of material benefaction from a Gentile benefactor to the people of Jerusalem.

3.3. Conclusion

The stakes were very high for Paul at the meeting with the 'pillar apostles' in Jerusalem. Rejection of his gospel would have had serious consequences for the visible unity of the early Christian movement. At the same time, it

---

[131] In this regard Klauck, "Gütergemeinschaft", 98, states: "Die Jerusalemer Gemeinde verarmte bald, was mitbedingt wurde durch wirtschaftliche Schwierigkeiten der Stadt und mehrfache Hungersnöte. Paulus veranstaltet für sie sein Kollektenwerk. Er nennt die Jerusalemer Christen zweimal 'die Armen' (Rom 15,26; Gal 2,10). Ob das eine Selbst-bezeichnung der Urgemeinde war, kann dahingestellt bleiben. Ihre tatsächliche Lage ist damit jedenfalls umschrieben." On his part Witherington, *The Acts of the Apostles*, 212-213, is of the opinion that the status of the Jerusalem Christians ranged from reasonably high to low social status; with the numbers of the well-to-do being significant enough to make available their large houses as meeting-places for the believers.

[132] Barnett, *Second Epistle to the Corinthians*, 397, n30, also views the assistance of Helena as a possible analogy for the collection.

would have jeopardised Paul's divine commission to build churches. However, Jerusalem's own future, or rather that of its economically deprived believers, was also linked to the successful outcome of this meeting. Jerusalem's function entailed more than just 'officially' recognising the theological views and missionary practices of Antioch's delegation. In exchange for their benefactions, that is, their recognition of the 'law-free' gospel in Antioch and Paul's apostleship, they requested material assistance from Paul for the poor in their midst. It is quite possible that the weak socio-economical situation in Jerusalem also impacted on their rather lenient attitude toward Paul's 'circumcision-free' Gentile mission. Due to the severity of the food shortages in Jerusalem during the mid to late forties, the leadership of the mother church, because of their own '*Naherwartung*' and lack of proper organisation in terms of the redistribution of possessions among their members, was now faced with a poverty-stricken community. The only solution in this situation was to turn to believers outside Jerusalem for help. In this regard the benefaction of Queen Helena of Adiabene to the people of Jerusalem from between 44-46 CE probably provided them with a helpful analogy.

The meeting between Paul and the leaders of the church in Jerusalem was not a modern-day theological meeting where an intellectual exchange of ideas took place. Jerusalem was part and parcel of the ancient eastern Mediterranean world where most people were illiterate, living from the hand to the mouth and often not knowing where their next meal would come from. Therefore, the leaders of the church in Jerusalem, realising the potential which Paul's missionary work showed in terms of alleviating the plight of their poor, and at the same time knowing that they were in the superior position within the relationship as benefactors to him and Antioch, did not hesitate to indicate to him how to repay his debt of gratitude.

In terms of the model of benefit exchange drawn up in Chapter 2, I could briefly summarise the basic processes at work, in the reciprocal relationship between Paul and the Jerusalem leadership as described in Galatians 2,1-10:

(a) The 'pillar-apostles' rendered a rewarding service to Paul and Antioch, which in terms of the status-demarcations within the reciprocal relationship, served as a claim to their own superior position as benefactors of Paul and Antioch.

(b) Paul gratefully accepted the benefit bestowed upon him, thus confirming Jerusalem's position as benefactor. At the same time Paul, in his position as beneficiary, now became obliged to Jerusalem.

(c) In return, the *dokountes*, who were in need of specific services (= material assistance) made their needs known to Paul in particular, who was perceived as being in the position to provide these services. The latter responded positively, thereby confirming the public expectations about his ability to deliver the ministrations in question.

(d) From then on the pressure was solely on Paul, the would-be benefactor of Jerusalem, to make good his promises, by delivering the collection to Jerusalem in order to secure his own honour.

Chapter 4

Beneficiaries of Jerusalem: Paul's Interpretative Framework for the Collection

4.1. Introduction

The need for a concrete project to address the needs of the poor in the Jerusalem church took shape at the Jerusalem meeting. This project was conceptualised within the parameters of the reciprocal relationship between the leadership of the Jerusalem community and the leadership of the believers in Antioch. However, soon after this meeting a crisis in Antioch threatened the future of such a project, before it had even begun.

In this chapter I shall endeavour to come to terms with this crisis in Antioch, which caused Paul to start an own missionary program, as well as to organise an independent collection for Jerusalem. The apostle's efforts to incorporate the Christian communities in Galatia, Macedonia and Achaia in the reciprocal relationship with Jerusalem, will also be analysed in terms of the interpretative framework of the collection.

4.2. From two to one: Galatians 2,11-14 and Paul's independent collection effort

Paul changes the first person plural in Galatians 2,10a to the first person singular in verse 10b, thereby indicating that the responsibility for the collection shifted from Antioch to himself. Although Antioch was included in the original request at the Jerusalem meeting, Paul took it upon himself in his capacity as apostle of the Gentiles to organise this project.[1]

---

[1] So also Gnilka, "Die Kollekte der paulinischen Gemeinden für Jerusalem", 302. The view of Murphy-O'Connor, *Paul - A Critical Life*, 145, that Paul, in his position as 'a mere agent of Antioch' at the Jerusalem meeting, had no personal responsibility for the collection, but that after he had broken his ties with Antioch his conscience bothered him so much that he started the collection, ignores the nature of the collection as the concrete conceptualisation of Paul's obligations within the framework of the reciprocal relationship between himself, his communities and the Jerusalem church.

The reason for this can best be explained from the perspective of the incident in Antioch (Gal 2,11-14), which took place some months after the Jerusalem meeting. We know the outline of this conflict: In Antioch Paul publicly distanced himself from Cephas and Barnabas, because of their refusal to eat with Gentile believers for fear of the men who came from James (2,12).[2]

Paul gives no indication as to how long after the Jerusalem meeting this incident in Antioch took place; neither does he explain the reason for Peter and the men from James' visit to the believers in Antioch. One is also left in the dark regarding the response of Peter, Barnabas and the community in Antioch to Paul's public criticism of Peter's behaviour. What we do know, however, is that the 'truth of the gospel' (Gal 5,14) was again in danger in Antioch. Once more, it was up to Paul to 'defend' the gospel, just as he had done earlier (2,4-5). But this time he had to defend it against none other than Peter, Barnabas and the Jewish Christians whose actions had now brought them very close to that of the ψευδαδελφοί (2,4).[3] Whereas before Paul had to resist false *teaching* in Antioch, he now had to take a stand against the *behaviour* of his apostolic colleague, Peter, as well as against his own community. The mistake of Peter in Paul's eyes is clearly spelled out in v. 12: ἀφώριζεν ἑαυτόν.[4] Before this drastic step, Peter, in expression of his ἐθνικῶς ζῆν (v. 14), apparently participated fully in the life of the church in Antioch for a period of time. Here Peter had table-fellowship with Gentile Christians, who did not observe the dietary prescriptions of the Law.[5] But with the arrival of the men from James,[6] he

---

[2] The 'men from James', that is, Jewish Christians from Jerusalem, should not be equated with Paul's opponents in Galatians as Watson, *Paul, Judaism and the Gentiles*, 59ff., does. They were an official delegation appointed by James. It was their task to secure Jerusalem's role as benefactors of Antioch, as well as the ideologies of the dominant orthodox faction of the Jerusalem church. Cf also Umbach, *In Christus getauft*, 85-87.

[3] So Wehr, *Petrus und Paulus*, 60.

[4] According to Betz, *Galatians*, 108, and Wehnert, *Die Reinheit des christlichen Gottesvolkes aus Juden und Heiden*, 124, this is a technical Jewish term that describes the cultic separation from the 'unclean', thus implying Peter's return to a strictly Jewish way of life after previously following the correct path (by eating with the Gentiles). Cf. also Böttger, "Paulus und Petrus in Antiochien. Zum Verständnis von Galater 2,11-21", 80; Merklein, "Nicht aus Werken des Gesetzes...", 303.

[5] The imperfect form of the verb συνήσθιεν in v. 12 indicates that it was part of Peter's customary behaviour to eat with Gentile Christians.

[6] Paul only refers to these men as τινές (2,12). Within early Christian vilification strategies such vague references to one's opponents formed part of the deliberate negative portrayal of them as *incognito* figures - cf. Joubert, "Persuasion in the Letter of Jude", 82.

suddenly began to obey Jewish dietary laws again.[7] Peter's behaviour was 'contagious'. Soon afterwards the Jewish Christians and Barnabas (v. 13) followed suit. In Paul's view the hypocrisy of these people entailed more than the mere refusal to have table fellowship with the Gentile believers. It implied a rejection of the principles of the gospel that also promised salvation for Gentiles without conforming to the Jewish way of life (v. 14). This behaviour of Peter and the others was nothing less than a breach of the agreement reached in Jerusalem. Peter's change from earlier compliance in Jerusalem with the contents of this agreement (2,9),[8] caused Paul to interpret this change of conduct, as a self-contradiction. The same also held true for Barnabas and the Jewish Christians in Antioch.

Why did the men from James have such an impact on the behaviour of Peter and Barnabas? Was it because they were officially sent there by James to investigate rumours about Peter's table fellowship with the Gentiles? Or did they come to Antioch to observe the general situation in the community after the Jerusalem meeting? Perhaps the following hypothesis would make sense of the context of Galatians. 1-2: After the solving of the conflict regarding the circumcision of Gentile believers at the Jerusalem meeting, James sent a delegation to Antioch. This formed part of his strategy to establish Jerusalem's position as benefactor of Antioch and, in this process, also secure the ideologies of the orthodox faction in the Jerusalem church. These envoys had to reaffirm Jerusalem's authority and at the same time 'judaize' the Gentile believers.[9] At the same time they had to dissolve the boundary lines which Paul had painstakingly drawn between the Christ-followers in Galatia and the Jews in terms of his refusal to let Christians be circumcised, or to participate in the Jewish festive calendar and dietary practices.

Although James was heading the *dokountes* at the Jerusalem meeting,[10] his views with regard to the validity of Jewish customs and laws were

---

[7] Although Judaism was not an unitary, monolithic movement, food and purity laws were important identity markers of the various Jewish groups and factions. E.g., in 1 and 2 Maccabees obedience to food laws serve as an important proof of individuals' loyalty to God, while the main characters in the books of Daniel; Tobit and Judith are also praised for their refusal to eat Gentile food. See the discussion of Jewish meals in Bolyki, *Jesu Tischgemeinschaften*, 193ff.

[8] To live like a Jew basically implied adhering to the Jewish rituals and customs that formed the core of the contention within the polemical context of the letter to the Galatians, such as dietary laws and circumcision, whereas living like a Gentile implied not following these customs.

[9] Cf. also Dunn, *The Theology of Galatians*, 125-146, esp. 133. He correctly notes that Paul could not agree that the 'works of the Law' should be made a requirement of faith.

[10] This is clear from the fact that the name of James is mentioned first in 2,9, followed by that of Cephas and John. In Paul's reference to his earlier visit to Jerusalem, recorded

tempered by Peter and John's sympathies for Paul's law-free gospel. But after Peter's departure to Antioch, James apparently succumbed to pressure from the dominant orthodox faction in Jerusalem to assert the Jerusalem community's authority in Antioch. To these Torah-abiding Jewish believers the earlier request to Paul and Barnabas to take care of the poor in Jerusalem (2,10a) could have been interpreted by Antioch as a sign of weakness or incompetence to solve their own problems. Therefore, Antioch had to be informed about the 'true state of affairs' concerning the benefits that Jerusalem had bestowed upon them. The nature of the agreement between the *dokountes* and the leaders of Antioch also had to be explained from their side; particularly the fact that the Law and Jewish customs were not abolished at the meeting.[11] In this process the superior position of the Jerusalem church in the reciprocal relationship with Antioch had to be reconfirmed.

Upon the arrival of this delegation from James, Peter immediately broke off his table-fellowship with the non-Jewish believers in the house-churches, with Barnabas and the Jewish believers in Antioch emulating his behaviour soon afterwards. Peter probably took this step because his credibility as a missionary among Jewish people in the Diaspora would have been seriously compromised had the news reached Jerusalem that he persisted in such practices. Since this delegation officially represented James, the leader of the Jerusalem church, their very presence placed Peter under pressure to conform with the 'covenantal nomism'[12] of Jerusalem in order to save his own honour.

---

in 1,18-19, Cephas is mentioned first, before James. Peter, the original leader of the apostles in Jerusalem, probably left the city during Herod Agrippa's persecution of the church (44 CE). At this time James, the brother of Jesus took over the leadership until his martyrdom in 62. During Peter's visits to Jerusalem, he was welcomed as one of the inner circle, the 'dokountes', but James still remained at the head of the Jerusalem church. See also Witherington, *Grace in Galatia*, 341-355.

[11] Although James probably did not demand of Gentile Christians to be circumcised, he did expect of them to conform to specific Jewish customs in order to normalise contact between Jews and Gentiles - Wehnert, *Die Reinheit des christlichen Gottesvolkes*, 127.

[12] According to Dunn, *The Theology of Galatians*, 126, following E. P. Sanders, the term 'covenantal nomism' serves as a characterisation of Jewish self-understanding as it comes to expression consistently (though not uniformly) within ancient Jewish religious texts. In this regard their knowledge that God had made a special covenant with the patriarchs and had given them the Law as an integral part of this covenant, created in them a strong sense of special privilege over, and separateness from other people, which was also signified by circumcision and food laws. At the same time the 'works of the Law' (that is, the praxis which the Law laid on Jewish people) was very important, also within the dominant faction in the Jerusalem church as represented by the delegation from James. Paul's obvious concern was with the impact of this covenantal nomism on the believers in Galatia, since, to him it stood in direct opposition to faith in Christ. In the

In order to understand Peter's 'inconsistent' behaviour in Antioch, we must remember that he was a typical ancient Mediterranean person. In terms of Levy-Bruhl's concept of the 'primitive mentality',[13] Peter, as a 'corporate personality', did not perceive himself as an *individual* in the modern sense of the word, but believed himself to be embedded in a larger group, namely the Jerusalem church (as his primary, or 'in-group'), as well as in other Christian communities (as secondary groups). In other words, he was not 'simply co-dependent, but totally dependent' in his self-awareness.[14] Therefore, in order to save his reputation, Peter, the typical collectivist, did not hesitate to show where his loyalties lay. "He had to make a public decision, and he opted for his Jewish roots."[15] Peter's crossing back over into the realm of the Jewish way of life served as an important symbolic gesture. It publicly lent support to Jewish suspicions of those located on Paul's law-free side of the gospel.[16] Therefore, it did not take much convincing for Barnabas and the Jewish Christians to follow suit. As group-oriented people themselves, the mere fact that a person of such high social status as Peter was prepared to adhere to the values embodied by the official delegation from Jerusalem was sufficient reason to imitate his behaviour. What about the Gentile Christians in Antioch? Although Paul does not say anything about their response, we may assume that they were also convinced by the example of their leader, Barnabas, and of course by Peter, to adapt their eating customs by, temporarily at least, adhering to Jewish dietary laws.[17]

Peter probably did not break off all forms of contact with Gentile believers in Antioch. He motivated his sudden change in behaviour towards the Gentile Christians by explaining that their food did not meet the requirements of Jewish dietary laws. Peter obviously did not want to offend the

---

words of Dunn (p. 129): "... to regard the Law (covenantal nomism) as the outworking of faith is retrogressive, a stepping back from the freedom of the children of God into immature childhood and slavery (3,23-4,11; 6,12-13)."

[13] Lévy-Bruhl, *How Natives Think*.

[14] See also the analysis of typical ancient Mediterranean personalities by Malina & Neyrey, *Portraits of Paul*, 12ff.

[15] Murphy-O'Connor, *Paul - A Critical Life*, 152.

[16] Esler, "Making and Breaking an Agreement Mediterranean Style", 285-314, understands Peter's crossing back again to a Jewish lifestyle as part of a long-term goal of placing the Gentiles under pressure to accept circumcision as well.

[17] The various Jewish groups and factions during the first century were not uniform in their understanding and application of dietary laws. Although we do not know how ordinary Jews observed these laws in the first century, it seems as if the most extreme groups excluded all forms of social intercourse with the Gentiles, while more moderate groups only focused on the food that was consumed, and not so much on the racial origins of the companions eating with them – cf Gaston, "Paul and the Law in Galatians 2-3", 127-154.

official delegation from Jerusalem by participation in such meals in their presence.[18]

To Paul, the issue at stake was not the distinction in purity between Gentiles and Jews, but the unity of all followers of Christ. Because he could not accept any distinctions among believers on ideological grounds, Paul rebuked Peter in public. As a matter of fact, his strong reaction to Peter's behaviour in verse 14 indicates that he knew exactly how offensive Peter's view of the Law was for Gentile Christians. But not even this public reprimand could salvage the situation. Peter's response, which Paul for obvious reasons does not refer to,[19] apparently persuaded the believers in Antioch to side with Peter. If they had been persuaded to side with Paul, he would most definitely have mentioned it within this context.[20] In this challenge-riposte situation,[21] Paul's viewpoint was rejected; leaving him publicly humiliated.

From Paul's perspective the heart of the gospel was compromised by the hypocrisy of Peter who influenced the believers in Antioch to follow suit. However, the reaction of the other major role players in Antioch placed a serious question mark over his position as a missionary and apostle in the eyes of Antioch and Jerusalem. Since the believers in Antioch publicly sided with Peter and Barnabas, Paul's reputation as teacher, leader and apostle in Antioch was jeopardised. Therefore, after this serious loss of public reputation, the only option left for Paul was to sever his ties with the church of Antioch and Barnabas, and start an independent missionary program.[22]

4.3. Paul's renewed commitment to the reciprocal relationship with Jerusalem

In the years after the conflict in Antioch, Paul became involved in a missionary program that led to the founding of numerous Christian comm-

---

[18] Peter probably also requested that the Gentile Christians observe specific purity regulations for the sake of the unity of the church - Wehr, *Petrus und Paulus*, 73.

[19] "Daraus darf man wohl vorsichtig schließen, daß die Argumentation des Petrus Paulus in seiner galatischen Auseinandersetzung wenig hilfreich erschien und ihm vielleicht sogar geschadet hätte" - Wehr, *Petrus und Paulus*, 68.

[20] So also Becker, *Paulus*, 106.

[21] Within the agnostic context of the Graeco-Roman world, public criticism of the behaviour of other individuals of the same social status was usually viewed as a challenge to their honour that called for a riposte. Failing to answer such a challenge infrequently signalled loss of status and honour - Neyrey, *Honor and Shame in the Gospel of Matthew*, 14-34.

[22] So also, e.g., Georgi, *Der Armen zu gedenken*, 31-32; Becker, *Paulus*, 102.

unities throughout the eastern parts of the Roman Empire. During this time the apostle developed a coherent theological structure to give expression to his own views of God's salvation in Christ. Within this theological structure, which he constantly modified within contingent missionary contexts in which he found himself, the position of the Jews continued to play a prominent role. To Paul the church was a divine creation. His Spirit assembled Jews and Gentiles into a new eschatological family of believers.

Paul constantly sought ways of giving visible expression to this newfound *koinonia* in his churches with their marked social differences between believers, as well as the ethnical differences between Jewish and Gentile Christians. At the same time, he took care not turn the Christian communities under his supervision into an independent movement that existed in isolation from, or in opposition to, the Jerusalem church. The latter represented the vital link with the people of Israel, a link that could not be severed apart from jeopardising Gentile Christianity's position within the 'new people of God'.

Paul rejected any forced segregation between believers, whether in Antioch about issues such as Jewish dietary laws, or in the 'ethnically-mixed' churches under his supervision, or between the latter churches and Jerusalem. According to him, all existing boundaries between Jews and Gentiles were dissolved by the Christ-event. The followers of Christ had attained a new identity within the new family of God, and it was Paul's responsibility to communicate this knowledge to his communities, but also to change the attitudes of Jewish and Gentile believers towards each other. Paul, therefore, had no other option but to renew his commitments to the Jerusalem church. Specifically, his conviction that he was appointed by God to proclaim the gospel that was intended for both Jews and Gentiles (Gal 3,28), compelled him to fulfil his obligations in terms of the reciprocal relationship between himself and the church in Jerusalem, as it materialised during the earlier meeting with the 'pillar-apostles'.

How soon after the conflict in Antioch do we find any indications of a renewed commitment on the side of Paul to the reciprocal relationship with Jerusalem? According to Beckheuer,[23] his views did not change until after the writing of 1 Thessalonians 2,14(ff.), and Galatians 4,21(ff.). Israel is still presented in a very negative light in these letters. However, this view is only partially correct. We may assume that Paul was probably more critical of the possibility of Israel's salvation shortly after the Antioch incident, than during the later phases of his ministry. But, as Lohse[24] correctly notes, Paul's criticism in 1 Thessalonians 2,14 "… ist nicht von einer grundsätzlichen Abneigung gegen Juden verursacht." It would therefore be an

---

[23] Beckheuer, *Paulus und Jerusalem*, 96.
[24] Lohse, *Paulus*, 218.

oversimplification to interpret Romans 11,25f. as if Paul's views on Israel underwent a radical transformation (that is, from 'total damnation to universal salvation'). The μυστήριον (Rom 11,25), which Paul reveals to his Roman readers, is clearly related to the πλήρωμα τῶν ἐθνῶν, who had to be saved. Only in this way (καὶ οὕτως - Rom 11,26), will all of Israel; that is, the 'true Israelites' who are children of God and children of his promises; or as Dunn puts it: "... the Israel defined primarily by God's 'election' and 'call' (11,28-29),"[25] experience salvation. In other words, the elect in Israel, according to Paul would shortly be shown mercy, in the same way as his communities who had believed in God's promises have already experienced divine mercy (Rom 11,28.30-31).

Paul's reference to the unfaithful in Judea in Romans 15,31 indicates that, even at the time when Romans was written, he still had reservations about the salvation of Israel outside the framework of a specific faith relationship with God. On the other hand, his own conciliatory stance towards the Jerusalem church, which, in terms of the development in his own thinking,[26] also impacted on his more open-ended view of the relationship between Israel and the church in Romans, had its roots in the early phases of his independent ministry. For example, in 1 Thessalonians, Paul's earliest extant letter, he refers to the suffering that the Thessalonians had to endure, by comparing their situation to that of the churches of God in Judea (1 Thess. 2,14). As a matter of fact, the Thessalonians are presented as imitators of the Jerusalem church who remained faithful in spite of the persecution they experienced at the hands of their fellow Judeans. One could not have asked for a more positive presentation of the Jerusalem believers so soon after the incident, than what we have here in 1 Thessalonians 2,14(ff.). They are mentioned in the same breath with Jesus and God's special messengers (including Paul) in an early Christian *topos* of the suffering of the just at the hands of unfaithful.

Paul's positive presentation of the believers in Judea in 1 Thessalonians is also extended to the figure of Peter, although in a somewhat more restrained manner. After the conflict in Antioch the ways of these two apostles parted, but in 1 Corinthians 9,5 Peter is referred to again, together with the brothers of the Lord (including James), the apostles, and their wives, but this time in a neutral way. Even when Paul deals with the various factions in Corinth, including the group that strongly identified with Peter (1 Cor 1,12; 3,22), we do not hear any negative remarks from

---

[25] Dunn, *The Theology of Paul the Apostle*, 527.
[26] Söding, "Der Erste Thessalonicherbrief und die frühe paulinische Evangeliumsverkündigung", 31-56, offers a good overview of Paul's seminal theological thought in 1 Thessalonians as opposed to the more developed theological views in his main epistles.

him, from which we may carefully deduce that "Paulus läßt im 1. Kor keine persönliche Reserve mehr gegenüber Petrus erkennen."[27]

Within the first two years after the incident in Antioch, we have literary proof of Paul's conciliatory stance towards the believers in Judea. He apparently also buried the hatchet in the issue over Jewish dietary laws with Peter. Paul also recommitted himself to his obligations to take care of the poor in Jerusalem. This responsibility weighed heavily on him ever since the severance of his ties with Antioch; the more so because Antioch, who was also supposed to participate in this project to alleviate Jerusalem's needs, apparently did not get a collection drive off the ground. Although Paul accepted co-responsibility for the collection in Jerusalem as one of the official representatives of Antioch, he also committed his personal honour as apostle of the Gentiles when he responding positively to the request of the Jerusalem leadership.[28] Paul did not understand the meeting in Jerusalem and the decisions reached there merely as an agreement between two churches. According to him it was a meeting between representatives of the two most prominent interest groups in the early Christian movement.

In spite of the public humiliation that Paul had to endure in Antioch, the driving force behind his imaginative collection project was his own integrity regarding his reciprocal commitment to Jerusalem, as well as his conviction about the unity of the new people of God. At the same time this project provided the ideal opportunity for him to reclaim his own honour in the eyes of Jerusalem, albeit in a provocative, even controversial, manner.

4.4. Paul's missionary program and the collection

Our information about the organisation of the collection in Paul's communities is limited. We only possess some basic material about the involvement of the Christian communities in Achaia and Galatia in the collection (1 Cor 16,1-4; 2 Cor 8-9). We also know from 2 Corinthians 8-9 and Romans 15,25 that the churches in Macedonia were involved in the collection. The rest of the history of this project is hard to recover in any detail. When did Paul, for example, start organising the collection, and which churches were involved? It is difficult to imagine that he would not have involved the believers in Ephesus in this project during his stay of three years in their city. Is his silence about them in his letters an indication that the collection project failed there? Should we assume the same for

---

[27] Becker, *Paulus*, 107.

[28] Paul's apostolic awareness, as well as his ministry among Jews and Gentiles, predates his association with Antioch - Lohse, *Paulus*, 58ff.

other Asian cities such as Troas (Acts 16,6-11; 20,5-12), Assos (Acts 20, 13-14) and Miletus (Acts 20,15-38) - all places with Christian communities apparently also founded by Paul? And what about cities such as Iconium, Lystra and Derbe in the Roman province of Galatia, with which Paul apparently also had contact according to the Book of Acts? Unfortunately, we are left with the Lukan framework of Paul's so-called missionary journeys in Acts, as well as some bits of information from Paul's own letters, from which to form a picture of the basic organisation of the collection.[29]

Soon after the conflict in Antioch, Paul fervently set out on a new missionary course. In terms of the theory of cognitive dissonance, it seems as if he now wanted to restore his own honour and prove to Jerusalem the 'correctness' of his law-free gospel at all costs, by canvassing new recruits to join his Christian movement throughout the Graeco-Roman world. A high number of conversion occurrences would not only reinforce group cohesion within his communities, but also serve as proof of his divine commission to build churches before men and God alike (cf. 1 Cor 9,16; Phil 2,16).[30] More importantly, the sheer fact that numerous people had accepted his gospel, would have functioned as a powerful means to secure his own ideological position over against that of Jerusalem, within the parameters of the early Christian movement.

The first years, ca 49-53 CE, brought Paul to different cities in Macedonia, such as to Philippi (Acts 16,12ff.), Apollonia, Thessalonica (Acts 17,1), and Beroea (Acts 17,10ff.), as well as to the province of Achaia, with its well-known cities of Athens (Acts 17,15ff.) and Corinth (Acts 18,1ff.). Here in Corinth Paul stayed for eighteen months during the years 50-52, in which time he not only had to appear before the proconsul Gallio,[31] but also had to face a severe food shortages in the city.[32] Paul also

---

[29] Although Luke presents us with a systematic account of Paul's travels, much of this is the result of his own ordering of the sequence of events so as to emphasise the central role of Jerusalem, and later on, that of Rome. However, Luke's drastic ideological reinterpretation of the events in the early church throws the accuracy of his chronology, as well as the integrity of some of his narratives, into doubt. Therefore, this information about Paul's missionary travels must be used cautiously.

[30] Segal, *Paul the Convert*, 268, is of the opinion that not only cognitive dissonance, but also specific apocalyptic sentiments within the Pauline movement served to secure internal cohesion and raise their morale.

[31] Riesner, *Die Frühzeit des Apostels Paulus*, 180-189, in view of his interpretation of the Gallio-inscription, dates the proconsulship of Gallio at the very latest to 51/52. This would imply that he accepted this position on 1 July 51 and ended his duties on 30 June 52.

[32] Winter, "Secular and Christian Responses to Corinthian Famines", 86-106, and Gill, "Achaia", 433-454, both mention Tacitus' reference to a shortage of grain and a famine, and Suetonius' referal to a scarcity of grain due to a prolonged drought in Corinth during 51 CE.

visited Galatia twice during this time (Acts 16,6; 18,23), and then set up residence for three years in Ephesus (52/3-55 CE). The apostle's mission was clearly focused on cities in the Roman Empire. More specifically:

> ...in seiner großen Zeit betreibt Paulus nicht nur Städtemission, sondern, mehr noch, Zentrumsmission. Er sucht nicht beliebige Städte aus, sondern mit Vorliebe Hauptorte von Provinzen.[33]

During Paul's second visit to the Galatians, hinted at in Galatians 4,13-15, which probably took place just before his move to Ephesus around 52 CE, he started the collection in all earnestness. The apostle had already founded a significant number of Christian communities throughout the eastern parts of the Empire, and had an effective network of helpers in place to assist him in taking care of these communities. But, not even his full-time responsibilities in terms of addressing the problems and needs of these young Christian communities could dissociate Paul from his reciprocal responsibilities towards Jerusalem. With the same fervour and dedication with which he proclaimed the gospel over large territories within the space of a few short years, he also started organising the collection during 52 CE in the Christian communities, which he founded during these four years.

4.5. Beneficiaries of Jerusalem

4.5.1. Paul as broker of the heavenly patrons

In order to establish the basic interpretative framework of the collection, one needs to take Paul's basic role and function into account, as the driving force behind the collection process. This could facilitate a better understanding of the various interrelated facets of benefit exchange inherent in his basic understanding of the collection, as well as of the way in which he presented this project to his communities.

Paul's 'official' role in his interaction with the communities under his supervision is well known: he is the ἀπόστολος χριστοῦ Ἰησοῦ, whereas all believers under his supervision formed part of the ἐκκλησία of God (e.g., 1 Cor 1,1-2; 2 Cor 1,1; 1 Thess. 1,1). As apostle Paul was in the superior position in the interaction with his churches, because he had access to divine knowledge and mysteries that were unavailable to them. His functions as apostle could actually be compared to the role of the 'broker' within patron-client relationships. Since the principles inherent to Roman

---

[33] Klauck, "Die Hausgemeinde", 14-15.

patronage were well-known to believers in his communities,[34] Paul presented himself from this perspective as a broker-figure, who had access to the invisible world of God, Christ and the Spirit - the heavenly patrons - who controlled all 'first order resources' in the cosmos, such as life and death, land, nature, material resources, etc.[35] Not only could he claim that he saw the face of Christ in a divine revelation (2 Cor 4,6); that he undertook a heavenly journey (2 Cor 12,1-5); performed miracles (2 Cor 12,12), possessed information about God that was not routinely transmitted to 'ordinary people' (1 Cor 2,1.7; 4,1), but also he could claim that he was personally appointed by God as apostle (Gal 1). Paul's altered state-of-consciousness experiences convinced him that he was designated with supernatural authority. While all other leadership positions within his churches were of a local nature, Paul's own authority (in terms of his own claims) derived from outside his communities, namely from God. Therefore, he could legitimately claim the right to reveal God's plan of salvation.

Paul expected the believers under his supervision to accept his authority as God's official messenger (2 Cor 5,20). The message of God's salvation in Christ, and the privileged position of its official messenger, were closely interrelated. In Paul's view, his position and honour as apostle, as well as the content of his teaching, could not be separated without seriously endangering the very nature of the gospel itself (cf. Gal 1-2; 2 Cor 10-13). Invariably, rejection of his authority also led to believers accepting a different gospel.

As apostle, Paul was not only ordained with the necessary authority to mediate God's salvation, but also to involve the communities under his

---

[34] Patronage did play an important role in cities such as Corinth and Philippi during the first century CE. This fact is substantiated in two recent studies. Firstly, Chow, *Patronage and Power*, 38-82, has offered abundant literary proof of the fact that patronage served as an important way in which social relationships were organised in Roman Corinth. This is evident, from the patronal role assigned to the emperor, as well as the impact of patronage on the roles of Roman officials and local notables, and the various forms of interaction within free associations, the lawcourts, etc. Secondly, Bormann, *Philippi*, Ch 2-3, on the basis of his investigation concerning the impact of Roman institutions on the city of Philippi has concluded that: "In Philippi sind die wesentlichen Variationen des Klientelwesens bzw. des Patronatsverhältnisses bekannt und von Bedeutung" (p. 199). Both scholars, on the basis of their historical investigations, also address specific forms of interaction in the churches of Corinth and Philippi from the perspectives of patronage. In terms of our own remarks about Paul's role as broker, we are therefore on solid ground when we state that his readers were well acquainted with patronage. But, at the same time, due to the overlap of the principles inherent to interpersonal benefaction in the Hellenistic and Roman worlds (Ch 2), the believers in Achaia and Macedonia were also well versed in the latter form of reciprocity.

[35] Cf. Malina, "Patron and Client", 12, and Joubert, "Managing the Household", 216.

supervision in the collection. By situating the collection within the framework of his own apostolic authority and his function as broker of God's benefactions, Paul could legitimately demand of his communities to participate in this undertaking to alleviate Jerusalem's material needs. Thus the collection formed part of their religious responsibilities. Not only did it give expression to their own repayment of their debt of gratitude to God for his benefactions, but it also expressed gratitude to Jerusalem for the spiritual benefits they received from there.

4.6. Romans 15,25-27: the Pauline communities as beneficiaries in the reciprocal relationship with Jerusalem

4.6.1. The collection as an expression of the reciprocal relationship between the Pauline communities and Jerusalem

After grappling with difficult theological issues such as justification through faith (Rom 3,21ff.), and the special position of Israel in God's plan of salvation (Rom 9-11), Paul (in Rom 15,22-33) deals with his own itinerary.[36] In verse 28 he informs the Roman believers that on his way to Spain, he intends to pay them a visit. But first of all he has to deliver the collection to the poor among the saints in Jerusalem. Paul here actually offers us his last written reflections on the collection.

Paul states in verse 25 the reason for his visit to Jerusalem, namely to minister to the saints; that is, to deliver the collection.[37] His expression: ἡ διακονία (ἡ εἰς) τοὺς ἁγίους may be understood as a '*terminus technicus*' for the collection (cf. also 1 Cor 16,15; 2 Cor 8,4),[38] thus reflecting the nature of this project as a *concrete service* to fellow believers within the framework of reciprocal responsibilities to one another. The collection is understood as an undertaking intended to address the *welfare* of the ἅγιοι (cf. 1 Cor 16,1; 2 Cor 8,4; 9,1.12, where this self-designation of the Jerusalem church is also used by Paul).[39] This is approached in line with

---

[36] The letter to the Romans was written around 56/7 from Corinth after the collection had been completed in the various Pauline communities.

[37] See Cranfield, *A Critical and Exegetical Commentary on the Epistle to the Romans*. Vol. II, 770f.; Wilckens, *Der Brief an die Römer*, 126. Collins, *Diakonia*, 220, in line with his own understanding of 'diakonia' within the semantic area of an 'errand,' states that Paul is acting as 'courier' of his churches.

[38] So also Betz, *2 Corinthians 8 & 9*, 90, and Zeilinger, *Krieg und Friede in Korinth*, 397.

[39] Moo, *The Epistle to the Romans*, 902, from this perspective understands the collection as a ministry of love on the part of Gentile Christianity to their fellow Jewish believers, who were experiencing poverty.

the apostle's emphasis on social virtues and behaviour, which is for the common good of others within the group, even if entailing personal inconvenience and sacrifice (cf. Rom 12,9-21; Phil 2,1-11).

The reason for Paul's visit to Jerusalem is given further elaboration in his reference to the involvement of the Christian communities in Macedonia and Achaia in the collection (v. 26).[40] His emphasis of the voluntary nature of their participation, as the use of εὐδοκεῖν in verse 26 and verse 27 indicates, underlines the fact that neither Paul nor his communities understood this project as a form of 'religious tax' or as a legal obligation to church in Jerusalem. Although the Pauline communities are presented as acting out of their own free will, this does not imply that Paul did not have to persuade (and at times even manipulate) them to commit themselves to the collection, or that he himself did not personally direct the organisation of this project during all its stages. Rather these references imply that Paul (in line with the ideals inherent to the role of beneficiaries in reciprocal relations), interpreted their involvement in the collection as a *free moral decision* which they exercised within the parameters of a particular reciprocal relationship, and not as an undertaking that was unilaterally forced upon them, over which they had no control.

The expression κοινωνίαν τινὰ ποιήσασθα in verse 26 serves as a further indication of the fact that the Macedonians and the Achaians did not falter to fulfil their responsibilities towards Jerusalem. Their behaviour was in response to the spiritual gifts that they received before from the mother church (v. 27: ἐκοινώνησαν), which at the same time served as the starting point of the *reciprocal relationship* between them and Jerusalem. According to Paul, neither the physical distance between these two groups, or the cultural differences between them stood in the way of sharing their common life in Christ.[41] But this κοινωνία did not remain a purely spiritual

---

[40] Contra Lüdemann, *Paulus, der Heidenapostel I*, 117ff. the absence of any reference to the Galatian collection does not imply that it failed there, but rather that it was completed earlier, while the Macedonians and the Achaians had only recently completed their efforts. On the other hand, the conflict between Paul and the Galatians, which had given rise to his letter to them after they had already completed their collection, is perhaps another reason why Paul is silent about their collection effort.

[41] Although Hainz, "Koinonia bei Paulus", 375-392, understands the collection as "Zeichen eines lebendigen Gemeinschaftsbewußtseins," (p. 380) between Paul's communities and Jerusalem, he does not place it within the framework of benefit exchange. His criticism of Bormann's efforts to relate the gift from the side of the Philippians to Paul to the 'Benifizialwesen' (*Philippi*), reflects his scepticism regarding the formative impact of this Graeco-Roman convention on Paul's thought in general (cf. 382ff.). Hainz rather opts for a strictly theological interpretation of the 'koinonia' motif in terms of the collection. He is correct when he emphasises the necessity of addressing the theological meanings which Paul and other believers attached to these terms. But if he had taken cognisance of primary material on benefit exchange in the ancient Graeco-Roman world,

fellowship. It found concrete expression in the initial gifts bestowed from the side of Jerusalem ('the benefactors') upon Macedonia and Achaia ('the beneficiaries'), as well as in the subsequent collection. Schnackenburg[42] captures the nature of this 'koinonia' between Gentile and Jewish believers well:

> Abgesehen von anderen Aspekten dieser Hilfsaktion, die dem Apostel persönlich am Herzen lag, ist es für den Koinonia-Gedanken beachtlich, daß er nicht bloß im spirituellen Bereich bleibt, sondern menschliche, leibhaftige Beziehungen mit umschließt. Ekklesiale Gemeinschaft kann sich nicht auf eine Glaubens- oder Gesinnungsgemeinschaft beschränken, sondern drängt auf konkrete Verwirklichung bis hin zum Teilen materieller Güter.

The material assistance by the Gentile churches to Jerusalem is also highlighted in Paul's emphasis of the poverty of a section of the Jerusalem believers (οἱ πτωχοὶ τῶν ἁγίων τῶν ἐν Ἰερουσαλήμ- v. 26). In spite of the insistence of some scholars that we should interpret this expression ep-exegetically ('the poor; these are, the saints', or 'the poor saints'),[43] Paul could hardly "... have expected or intended his readers to take the phrase other than its most natural sense in the Greek...,"[44] namely, as a partitive genitive. Πτωχοὶ is thus not a synonym for ἅγιοι, but an indication of the materially poor in the church in Jerusalem.

Although munificent forms of assistance occurred sporadically in ancient Graeco-Roman society (cf. Chapter 2), in general benefactors used their benefactions to increase their own honour and not to alleviate the material needs of others. As a matter of fact, during the first century the poor were not viewed as a separate category needing special assistance.[45] However, within the Jewish world the socially destitute always occupied an important position. Therefore, Paul did not hesitate to include the plight of the Jerusalem believers in his theological motivations for the collection (cf. also 2 Cor 8,13-15; Gal 2,10). For Jewish believers within his culturally mixed communities in Macedonia and Achaia this would probably have been a sufficient reason to become involved in the collection. They would also have understood their own monetary contributions in this regard as a gift that would be reciprocated in one way or another by God. But this ideological framework was not (fully) shared by Gentiles within the

---

he would have noticed that benefits were usually bestowed on others to enhance the honour of the benefactors and not so much to address the physical needs of the recipients.

[42] Schnackenburg, "Die Einheit der Kirche und der koinonia-Gedanken", 71.

[43] E.g., Schlier, *Der Brief an die Galater*, 80; Schmithals, *Der Römerbrief*, 537.

[44] Dunn, *Romans 9-16*, 875. So, also Wilckens, *Der Brief an die Römer, 3*, 125f.; Moo, *The Epistle to the Romans*, 904.

[45] Prell, *Armut im antiken Rom*, 296.

orbit of Paul's communities.⁴⁶ Although much of Paul's activities involved the 'translation' and mediation of ideologies, *topoi* and practices embedded in the authoritative narratives and rituals of Israel to his Gentile believers,⁴⁷ he at the same time, as part of his missionary hermeneutic, also strongly identified with positive Graeco-Roman values and practices. In terms of the collection, this implied the utilisation of principles inherent in Graeco-Roman benefit exchange, which provided the basic interpretative framework for this project.

Our view that Paul's reference to the predicament of the poor in Jerusalem did not serve as the basic motivation to involve his churches in the collection, is further supported by the remarks in verse 27. Here Paul shifts his attention explicitly to the *reciprocal nature* of the relationship between Jerusalem and his communities. He stresses that, although his communities contributed voluntarily to the collection, they were also under a *moral obligation* to Jerusalem because of the spiritual gifts (τὰ πνευματικά) which they received from them (cf. Paul's use of ὀφειλέτης and ὀφείλω, which expresses the idea of being obligated because of a benefit received⁴⁸). It is not immediately clear what τὰ πνευματικά means. Are these 'spiritual gifts' the same as the πνευματικά of 1 Corinthians 14,1? Or is this a reference to the salvation, which flowed forth from the Jews in Jerusalem?⁴⁹

Perhaps we would not be too far off the mark when we understand τὰ

---

⁴⁶ Berger, "Almosen für Israel", 196, correctly notes that the 'Notlage' of the believers in Judea does not sufficiently explain the function of the collection, but he mistakingly assumes that the material expression of gratitude on the part of Paul's churches for the spiritual benefits from Jerusalem functions a secondary interpretation of the collection.

⁴⁷ Cf. Söding, "Apostel der Heiden", 193.

⁴⁸ According to Nickle, *The Collection*, 120, Paul uses the term 'debtors' here as "... an expression for the responsibility of voluntary reciprocal sharing which to him was the essence of the communal relationship in the Christian fellowship."

⁴⁹ So, e.g., Gaston, "Israel's Misstep in the Eyes of Paul", 259f., regarding the πνευματικά within the framework of his cultic-liturgical interpretation of the collection in Rom 15, also deserves mention. He understands this concept against the background of Rom 15,14-21, and in particular, verse 16 with its strong cultic overtones. Here Paul, the λειτουργὸς Χριστοῦ, in his priestly ministry, presents himself as breaking down the boundaries between the cultic and profane, as well as between Jew and Gentile, thus enabling his communities to fulfil a cultic role in their service (= the collection) to the Jews in Jerusalem. But all of this is the result of the εὐαγγέλιον τοῦ θεοῦ (15,16) that originated in Jerusalem (15,19). The collection is, therefore, also intended as a gift of gratitude to Jerusalem for their spiritual gifts that enabled the Gentiles to fully participate in God's salvation.

πνευματικά in an encompassing sense as a reference to the gospel tradition, together with all the spiritual blessings that originated in Jerusalem.[50] To put it more concretely: From the earliest phases of the early Christian movement, the Jerusalem church took centre stage as the domicile of the apostles, the eyewitnesses of the ministry of Jesus. But even more relevant to the situation of the Pauline communities: In Jerusalem the pillar-apostles, under the leadership of James, earlier recognised Paul as apostle, which enabled him to continue with his missionary activities. Since this missionary program in turn resulted in the founding of these communities involved in the collection, they were thus also indebted to Jerusalem. In terms of contemporary views of individuals' stereotyped roles within their groups (also in terms of sharing their group's basic values and beliefs), the benefits which Jerusalem bestowed on Paul was therefore interpreted by him as also obligating the churches under his supervision. Therefore, their basic motivation for becoming involved in the collection was not in the first instance the economic plight of believers in Jerusalem, but rather *the repayment of their own debts* to the mother church. Paul of course predetermined the way in which they had to settle these debts, namely by way of a collection for the socially destitute members of the Jerusalem church.

Paul refers to the necessity of a *material response* (σαρκικά) on the side of Gentile Christianity as a legitimate reply to the important *spiritual gifts* they had received from Jerusalem. However, one should not downplay these material gifts against Jerusalem's spiritual benefits as, for example, Cranfield does. He overstates this πνεῦμα/σάρξ antithesis when he says that Paul regarded the collection:

> ... as being in no way an equivalent to that which the Jerusalem church had rendered to the Gentiles: material succour, however, lovingly and generously supplied, could never repay the debt owed by the Gentile churches.[51]

Cranfield does not only misunderstand the nature of ancient social exchange, but he also ignores the meanings which the major parties involved in the collection, attached to this project. According to Galatians 2, the 'pillar-apostles' at the Jerusalem meeting did in fact understand their own request for material assistance from Paul as a sufficient response to their prior benefactions, as did Paul. Furthermore, Paul, here in Romans 15,27, also gives a 'cultic interpretation' to the collection, as his use of the verb λειτουργεῖν indicates, thus turning the collection into a provocative spiri-

---

[50] In the words of Schmithals, *Der Römerbrief*, 537, all Gentile Christians shared in "... den geistlichen Gaben des Evangeliums (v. 16ff.; vgl 1 Kor 15,1ff.) und an den die Botschaft begleitenden Gnadengaben (v. 18f.; 12,6ff.), die von Jerusalem aus in die Welt strömen."

[51] Cranfield, *A Critical and Exegetical Commentary on the Epistle to the Romans*, 774.

tual act.⁵² While he understands his own ministry as a priestly service under the Gentiles (Rom 15,16), the collection in turn functions as the Gentile Church's priestly service to the Jewish believers.⁵³ Just as the result of his work among the Gentiles was an acceptable sacrifice (ἡ προσφορὰ τῶν ἐθνῶν εὐπρόσδεκτος), the collection could also be acceptable (εὐπρόσδεκτος) as a 'sacrifice' to the Jerusalem church through the assistance of the prayers of the Roman believers (15,31). Through this deliberate conceptualisation of the collection as a *sacred ministry*,⁵⁴ Paul underlines the fact that care for the poor does not fall outside the 'spiritual' responsibilities of his communities. On the contrary, their bond with the risen Christ and their 'koinonia' with Jerusalem found concrete expression in the collection.

Perhaps it should also be noted that Paul, in his final written theological reflection on the collection, stresses that this is ultimately *his* project (ἡ διακονία μου - v. 31). Even though his communities took part in the collection, in the end it was he who saw it through, and who was now on his way to deliver this 'fruit' in Jerusalem as apostle and 'would-be' benefactor of the mother church (15,28).⁵⁵

In summary: According to Romans 15,25(ff.), the collection was a caritative project, but, at the same time, a project that was embedded within the reciprocal relationship marked by mutual obligations between himself, his churches, and Jerusalem. It was not a philanthropic undertaking, since charitable acts outside the framework of reciprocity did not exist in the ancient Mediterranean world. Within the context of Romans

---

⁵² This is in line with Paul's own understanding of Isaiah 61,6 and 66,20 which probably formed the background of the remarks in Rom 15,16. Specifically, "... nahm er aber eine Transformation von jüdischen Kategorien vor und fügte kultische Unterscheidungen ein: Er spiritualisiert nicht einfach nur die Sprache TriJes, sondern formte sie auf die eschatologische Erfüllung hin um" - Beckheuer, *Paulus und Jerusalem*, 223). In this regard Paul also took the risk of bringing this liturgical sacrifice (= the collection) to Jerusalem. His request to the Romans to pray that his διακονία would be acceptable to the Jewish Christians (15,31), points to the dangers involved in challenging the age-old boundaries between Jews and Gentiles.

⁵³ In the Greek world, λειτουργία was mainly used in reference to the public services rendered by the nobles in support of civil events. In the LXX it indicates the cultic service of the priests and the Levites. λειτουργία is used in the New Testament either in terms of sacrifices, or in terms of Paul's collection for the poor, whereby the gift takes on an eschatological character as the fulfilment of the true Christian service to God.

⁵⁴ Dunn, *Romans 9-16*, 876. See also the views of Nanos, *The Mystery of Romans*. 207-209.

⁵⁵ Paul understands 'fruit' in this context metaphorically as a service that is the result of spiritual maturation (cf. also Gal 5,22; Phil 1,11.22; 1 Cor 9,7; Rom 1,13; 6,21-22) - Ascough, "The Completion of a Religious Duty", 588.

15, the collection functioned as the repayment of a moral debt within the context of Paul's communities in the relationship with their benefactors in the Jerusalem church. Specifically, in response to Jerusalem's prior spiritual gifts to them, Paul's communities reciprocated with a material gift that would address the needs of the poor in Jerusalem. This gift also fulfilled the basic requirements in terms of the principle of *balanced reciprocity*. In other words, both parties within this reciprocal relationship agreed that this material response was sufficient 'repayment' for the bestowal of spiritual gifts from Jerusalem's side.

4.7. 2 Corinthians 8,1-6: religious reciprocity and the collection

4.7.1. The literary integrity of 2 Corinthians

2 Corinthians 8-9 now demands our attention in order to come to terms with other aspects of benefit exchange inherent in Paul's conceptualisation of the collection. However, before engaging in an analysis of relevant sections in these chapters, the problems related to the literary integrity of 2 Corinthians, and the various *Teilungshypothesen* proposed by researchers in this regard,[56] must be addressed.

I am of the opinion that the present 2 Corinthians is a composite of two originally distinct letters, Chapters 1-9, and Chapters 10-13.[57] The apparent discrepancies in terms of contents between these two sections warrant viewing them as two separate letters. However, as to the order in which these letters were written, I share the view of Klauck[58] that:

> ... der Tränenbrief ist im wesentlichen in Kap. 10-13 aufbewahrt. Der Versöhnungsbrief umfaßt Kap. 1-9, enthält also auch die Apologie und beide Kollektenkapitel.

The various arguments for separating 2 Corinthians 8 and 9, as belonging to two different letters (Betz[59]), or as two chapters written in reverse order

---

[56] Cf. in this regard the useful overviews of these theories in Betz, *2 Corinthians 8 & 9*, 3-36, and Söding, "Zur Chronologie der paulinischen Briefe", 7-12.

[57] So also, e.g., Barrett, *A Commentary on the Second Epistle to the Corinthians*, 9ff., and Furnish, *2 Corinthians*, 35ff. Furnish correctly notes that, although there is neither manuscript nor patristic support for partitioning 2 Corinthians into two different letters, this fact at the most implies that 2 Corinthians never circulated "... except in its canonical form, and that any redactional combination of originally separate letters must have taken place before the circulation of any one of them" (p. 36).

[58] Klauck, *2. Korintherbrief*, 9.

[59] Betz, *2 Corinthians 8 & 9*. On the basis of his rhetorical analysis of 2 Cor 8-9, he interprets these chapters as two distinct letters, with Chapter 8 addressed to the Corinthians as part of Paul's administrative correspondence, while Chapter 9 was written to the

(Bultmann[60]), are not convincing. Certain expressions, such as those in 9,3-5, cannot be understood without presupposing the remarks in 8,16-24. The second section of Chapter 9 (vv 6-15) also functions as a meaningful conclusion to the whole discussion, since 7,4, the *inclusio* formed by the χάρις τοῦ θεοῦ in 8,1 (the divine gifts from God) and the χάρις τῷ θεῷ in 9,15 (the reciprocal response to God's gifts) also forms an *inclusio* around the arguments in Chapters 8-9.[61] Therefore we may conclude that Chapter 10-13, as part of the so-called *Letter of Tears*, was probably written from Ephesus during 55 CE, whilst Chapter 1-9, as part of the *Letter of Reconciliation*, was written some time later from Macedonia, probably during c. AD 56.

4.7.2. The collection as χάρις

2 Corinthians 8,1-6 provides a very effective introduction to the issue of the collection in Corinth, after this project came to an abrupt halt in response to the negative reception of 1 Corinthians. Paul here refers to the exemplary behaviour of the Macedonian believers (in Philippi, Beroea and Thessalonica). His elaborate narration of their successful effort at the beginning of the *topos* of the collection forms part of a particular intratextual strategy in 2 Corinthians 8-9 that will be dealt with in more detail in the following chapter.

The *Stichwort* χάρις plays a prominent role in Chapter 8-9 (cf. 8,1.4.6. 7.9.16.19; 9,8.15). As a matter of fact, these chapters illustrate the concrete working of God's χάρις in the lives of all parties involved in the collec-

---

Achaians (9,2-5a), and which deals with their role in the resumption and conclusion of the collection. Cf. also Lang, *Die Briefe an die Korinther*, 13f.

[60] Bultmann, *Der zweite Brief an die Korinther*, 258, is of the opinion that Chapter 9 was written before Chapter 8 because 9,1 (περὶ μὲν γὰρ τῆς διακονίας τῆς εἰς τοὺς ἁγίους κτλ) would not make sense after everything that was written about the collection in Chapter 8. At this time the readers must have known about which διακονία Paul was talking, so that any further explanations would have been left out had these chapters followed on each other.

[61] Wolff, *Der zweite Brief des Paulus an die Korinther*, 163, provides a number of reasons why 2 Cor 8 and 9 belong together: "Das zeigen die engen Verbindungen mit Kapitel 8,4: der sich gleicherweise auf 8,24 wie auf 9,3 beziehende Übergang μὲν γὰρ und der anaphorische Artikel in 9,1; die Wendung 'die Unterstützung für die Heiligen' in 9,1 wie in 8,4; die Erwähnung der 'Bereitschaft' der Korinther in 9,2 wie in 8,11f.; 'seit vorigem Jahr' in 9,2 wie in 8,10; das Bitten des Titus und das Schicken der Brüder in 9,3.5 wie in 8,6.14.24; das 'Rühmen' der Korinther in 9,2-4 wie in 8,24; 9,8 klingt an 8,1f an 9,11 an 8,2, 9,13a an 8,2a (δοκιμή) und 9,13b an 8,9; 9,12-14 bringt die Konkretion zu 8,14." Cf. in this regard also Barnett, *Second Epistle to the Corinthians*, 387.

tion.⁶² In the first six verses this term is used no less than three times to refer to:

(a) the divine gift to the Macedonians 'im Sinne der ungeschuldeten Gabe'⁶³ (v. 1);

(b) the impact of this divine grace in the lives of the Macedonians, which prompted them to request of Paul whether they could share in the privilege/benefit (χάρις) of taking part in the collection (v. 4) and

(c) the nature of the collection as a 'benevolence'⁶⁴ or 'gracious service'⁶⁵ (v. 6). For Paul God's eschatological gifts do not only form the basis of his own apostolic ministry (e.g., Rom 1,5; 15,15; 1 Cor 3,10) and the Christian existence in general, but also of the collection. This active grace moves believers to commit themselves to this project, and, in turn, to each other.⁶⁶ Therefore, χάρις is nothing less than a transparency of God's goodness, and a symbol of Christian brotherly fellowship.⁶⁷

4.7.3. The response of the Macedonians to the benefactions of God

The structure of verses 1-6 indicates that God's grace, according to Paul, had an astounding effect on the Macedonians. In spite of severe testing, due to some form of affliction (v. 2ab), they were full of joy. This paradox, typical of the early Christian experience (cf. 1 Cor 7,30; 2 Cor 4,7-18; Rom 12,15), is also reflected in their socio-economical situation (v. 2cd). Their abysmal poverty overflowed in 'the wealth of their generosity'. Due to the presence of God's grace in their lives, the Macedonian believers remained steadfast in the face of severe hardship and poverty. As a matter of fact, they actively countered hardship in a public display of the highly

---

⁶² The impact of God's grace is further underlined by means of Paul's frequent use of the concepts περισσεία/περισσεύειν (cf. 8,2.7a.b; 9,8b.12), and περίσσευμα (8,14). At the same time, as Theobald, *Die überströmende Gnade*, 278, correctly notes, the semantic field of prosperity should also be related to this motif of divine grace in 2 Cor 8-9.

⁶³ Klauck, *2. Korintherbrief*, 67.

⁶⁴ So Furnish, *2 Corinthians*, 402, 416.

⁶⁵ So Martin, *2 Corinthians*, 255, and Witherington, *Conflict and Community*, 413.

⁶⁶ Well-known in this regard are the views of H. Windisch on Paul's use of χάρις in 2 Cor 8. These are summarised as follows by Zeilinger, *Krieg und Friede in Korinth*, 263: "Sie ist (1) der objektive Erweis der göttlichen Huld in Form des Heilsereignisses, (2) der dem Einzelchristen subjektiv zuteil gewordene Gnadenerweis, und (3) 'das von der göttlichen Gnade gezeugte, christliche Gnaden- oder Liebeswerk, die Auswirkung der empfangenen Gnade im Verkehr mit den Brüdern'...." F. also Dunn, *The Theology of Paul the Apostle*, 707.

⁶⁷ Paul's subtle use of χάρις here in vv. 1, 4 and 6 should be understood in a complementary sense. For example, when Paul uses χάρις in v. 6 as a metaphor for the collection, that is, as a gracious service, it at the same time points back to God's grace in v. 1 that compels believers to become actively involved in the collection (v. 4). At the same time it also points forward to the collection as a benevolence in v. 7.

regarded early Christian values of joy and generosity.[68] Their true wealth consisted in their experience of God's gifts, not in the size of their earthly possessions. To attest to the truth of what he is saying about the Macedonians' exemplary behaviour, Paul confirms with an oath that they gave to the utmost limits of their means, and even beyond it. In other words, they did not give out of surplus, "... sondern sogar noch mehr; sie haben offensichtlich sämtliche Reserven ausgeschöpft."[69] This they did of their own accord.[70] The voluntary nature of the Macedonian involvement in the collection, as well as the generous nature of their contribution, is emphasised in vv. 2-4. But their exemplary behaviour did not end there. At the same time they begged the apostle with great insistence to share in the privilege of participation in the service (διακονία) for the believers in Jerusalem, the ἅγιοι (cf. the hendiadys in v. 4c: τὴν χάριν καὶ τὴν κοινωνίαν). The nature of this project that gave rise to the Macedonians actually pleading with Paul for an opportunity to participate therein is expressed by means of the *terminus technicus*: διακονία ἡ εἰς τοὺς ἁγίους.[71] The collection was a service, more specifically a service that functioned as proof of: (a) the presence of divine grace in their lives, and (b) a symbol of the unity between the Jerusalem church and the Pauline movement.[72] This unity found concrete expression in the *participatio* of the Macedonians in the collection.

Verse 5 supplies the reason for the exemplary behaviour of the Macedonians: They dedicated themselves to the Lord,[73] that is, to Jesus Christ.[74] Paul hyperbolically states that they exceeded his expectations by becoming living sacrifices to Christ.[75] At the same time the Macedonians also gave themselves to Paul in his capacity as the official emissary of Christ. This surrender to Paul points to Macedonia's acceptance of their reciprocal obligation regarding Jerusalem. In Paul's view this was the only proper response to the divine benefits, which he had previously mediated to them. By accepting his gospel, and by also embracing his motivation for the need

---

[68] Cf. Georgi, *Der Armen zu gedenken*, 53, and Barnett, *The Second Epistle to the Corinthians*, 393.

[69] Wolff, *Der zweite Brief des Paulus an die Korinther*, 167.

[70] The term αὐθαίρετοι gives expression here to the grateful fulfillment of their obligations to Jerusalem.

[71] This expression could be translated as "... the ministry that supplies the needs of the saints" - Barnett, *The Second Epistle to the Corinthians*, 397.

[72] Cf. also Hainz, *Koinonia*, 132-141.

[73] The elliptical sentence structure: οὐ καθὼς ἠλπίσαμεν clearly lacks its sequel and needs to be supplemented by a verb such as 'they contributed,' or 'they gave'.

[74] Klauck, *2. Korintherbrief*, 67.

[75] Macedonia's behaviour was in line with Paul's views that the Christian life in its entirety (as a response to divine benefactions) should be nothing less than self-sacrifice (e.g., Rom 12,1-2; Phil 2,17).

of a collection for Jerusalem, the Macedonians actually realised God's plan (διὰ θελήματος θεοῦ).

4.8. Religious reciprocity and the framework of the collection

Behind the rhetorical strategies and theological reflections on the collection within the argumentative context of 2 Corinthians 8,1-6 (cf. also Chapter 5), some basic principles inherent to ancient *religious reciprocity* are operative. Specifically: Paul places the collection within the framework of religious reciprocity by linking it to a chain of obligations going back to:

(a) *God (8,1) and Christ (8,5) as the most important benefactors within the Pauline symbolic universe*: To Paul, God's eschatological gift of new life through Christ's sacrifice (cf. 8,9), constitutes the basis of the Christian experience. This gift places all believers in debt to him.

The reciprocal relationship between deities and humans in the ancient Mediterranean world reflects the same basic characteristics as that between human benefactors and beneficiaries.[76] Seneca (*Ben.* II.30.1-2), for example, tells us that the gift of life and the preservation thereof are the highest divine benefits. Even though the gods are not in need of anything from us, we are obliged to show our gratitude by gratefully accepting their benefits. Refusal to reciprocate divine benefits could lead to the withholding of further gifts.

Gratitude after delivery from specific crises, such as wars, diseases and personal dangers, was common to all forms of ancient religious experience. Proper responses to divine blessings were usually displayed in public through the building of temples and statues in honour of the gods, or through feasts and sacrifices. According to Philo, sacrifice was used by the earliest people as a form of thanksgiving to God (*Spec. leg.* 1,95). Apart from their orientation to the past, these sacrifices also pointed to the future as a means of securing new divine benefits:

> ... one is either giving thanks for benefits previously received or as security for those which are present or to request acquisition of good things in the future or removal of present or anticipated evils (Philo, *Spec. leg.* 1,283).[77]

---

[76] Porphyry in this regard refers to a city plagued by disease due to the departure of Asclepius and other gods, because the citizens honoured Jesus and refused the bestowal of public benefits on any other gods – cf. Mott, "The Power of Giving and Receiving", 64-67.

[77] However, Philo adds that sacrifices or buildings are not sufficient expressions of gratitude to God. Adequate honour comes through recounting his works by eulogies or song (*Plant.* 126-31).

Apart from the basic function of sacrifices as gifts to the gods (in terms of the ancient *do ut des* principle), they also functioned as specific forms of *communio* between the deities and people; as 'Sündenbockmechanismen', etc.[78]

The response of the Macedonians to divine benevolence was also in the form of self-dedication and personal sacrifice. They gave themselves fully to the Lord. Their participation in the collection served as a visible expression of their gratitude to him.

(b) *Paul as the Lord's official emissary*: In his role as broker Paul mediated divine benefactions to the Macedonians and other believers. Therefore they owed it to him to become involved in the collection.

(c) *The start of a new reciprocal relationship with Jerusalem*: By giving themselves to Paul, the Macedonians at the same time also committed themselves to the collection and to a reciprocal relationship with the Judean believers.

In summary: In 2 Corinthians 8,1-6 Paul describes the chain of religious obligations on the part of the Macedonians to 'significant others' within their symbolic universe, namely God, Christ, Paul, and Jerusalem. He uses language typical of benefit exchange to give expression to their exemplary behaviour.[79] Simultaneously, the Macedonians are described as ideal partners in the reciprocal relationship with Jerusalem because of their acceptance of Paul's motivation of the nature of the collection. They responded exactly as grateful beneficiaries should, by giving verbal expression to their gratitude and their eagerness to become involved in this reciprocal relationship. They actually turned this relationship with Jerusalem into a 'noble agonistic contest'. Not only did they joyfully embrace their role as debtors, but their generous contribution was also proof of their striving to surpass the gift from their benefactors in Jerusalem in deed and spirit.[80]

---

[78] See in this regard the overview on the nature and various functions of sacrificial cults in the ancient Graeco-Roman world by Klauck, *Die religiöse Umwelt des Urchristentums* I, 27-49.

[79] A number of terms employed by Paul in the first six verses, such as χάρις (8,1. 4.6), ἁπλότης (8,2) δίδωμι (8,1,5), and ἐπιτελέω (8,6) form part of the word-field of gift giving.

[80] Although the Macedonians and the other Pauline communities were not in the position to decide for themselves whether they wanted to become involved in the collection, the fact that their apostle did this on their behalf also morally committed them to this project. The only legitimate response from Paul's communities was in fact to enter into a reciprocal relationship with Jerusalem. Refusal to identify with their role as beneficiaries would seriously compromise their position within the Christian movement.

4.9. 2 Corinthians 8,13-15: balanced reciprocity and the collection

4.9.1. The chiastic structure

2 Corinthians 8,13-15 forms part of the apostle's efforts to persuade the Corinthians to commit themselves to the collection again. Paul in v. 13bff., as part of a larger section, 8,7-15, "die Aufforderung zum Abschluß der Kollekte,"[81] explicitly addresses the need for *balanced reciprocity* in the relationship between Corinth and Jerusalem. He does this by way of the following structure:

ἀλλ' ἐξ ἰσότητος

ἐν τῷ νῦν καιρῷ τὸ ὑμῶν περίσσευμα εἰς τὸ ἐκείνων ὑστέρημα

ἵνα καὶ τὸ ἐκείνων περίσσευμα γένηται εἰς τὸ ὑμῶν ὑστέρημα

ὅπως γένηται ἰσότης

4.9.2. Material and spiritual reciprocity between Jerusalem and the Pauline communities

The chiastic structure, as well as the repetition of the '*Stichwort*' ἰσότης (in vv. 13 and 14), highlights one of the basic principles inherent in reciprocal relationships, although wrapped in the terminology of Paul's theological reflection, namely that both parties should benefit equally from their social interaction. In verse 13, Paul stresses that the Corinthians' involvement in the collection should not lead to an exchange of places between them and Jerusalem. In other words, the Corinthians should not relieve the needs of others at the expense of their own affliction (οὐ γὰρ ἵνα ἄλλοις ἄνεσις, ὑμῖν θλῖψις). To substantiate this remark, Paul briefly reflects on the principle of equality (vv. 13b-14), before quoting a prooftext from Scripture (v. 15).

The ideal of ἰσότης was the topic of frequent discussion in Hellenistic circles. This was an important virtue within the spheres of the law, morality, and politics. Aristotle (*Pol.* 2,1), for example, did not hesitate to say that reciprocal equality is the preservative of states,[82] while Philo interpreted the term ἰσότης as a cosmic power within the framework of his own understanding of the divine logos (*Quis Rer. Div. Her.* 141-206). Follow-

---

[81] Zeilinger, *Krieg und Friede in Korinth*, 269.
[82] See Betz, *2 Corinthians 8 & 9*, 68, n.230.

ing the suggestion of Windisch that both Paul and Philo made use of a common tradition "... die Ex 16,18 mit dem ἰσότης Motiv zusammengebracht hatte," Georgi explains the repetition of ἰσότης (in vv. 13-14) in terms of speculative wisdom traditions.[83] He states:

> Man soll bei diesem Begriff wahrscheinlich die Assoziationen mitbedenken, die er in hellenistisch-jüdischer Tradition haben kann: also neben der Gleichsetzung mit Gott und neben dem charismatischen Aspekt auch die Beziehung zur δικαιοσύνη (als deren Ursprung) und die kosmische und mystische Tendenz.[84]

Therefore Paul's expression, ἐξ ἰσότητος, is more or less equivalent to ἐκ θεοῦ or ἐκ χάριτος. But, as Barrett[85] correctly points out, Georgi's speculative theory is not very convincing, because such philosophical thought is strange to Paul. At the same time the textual context does not support Georgi's thesis. At best it could be said that Paul used a 'provocative' concept from the *Umwelt* and filled it with new meaning. For his Corinthian readers this term would immediately invoke positive connotations of harmony, peace and justice. By linking the collection with these highly valued moral virtues, Paul applies the term ἰσότης to reinforce his explicitly stated view in verse 13a that this project was not intended to place the Corinthians under financial pressure. At the same time, this concept serves as a 'bridge' to effectively address the reciprocal relationship between them and Jerusalem.

In contrast to Romans 15,27, where the responsibility of the Pauline communities to repay their debt of gratitude for past benefits from Jerusalem is emphasised, in verse 14 Paul shifts his emphasis to the future; that is, to the positive acceptance and the expected return-service from the side of Jerusalem. This shift would not have come as a total surprise to his readers, since the general view in the Graeco-Roman world was that the repayment of beneficiaries' debts did not signal the end of the relationship. It inaugurated the start of a new phase where the debtors in turn became creditors, and vice-versa. Therefore, in verse 14 Paul implies that this principle of equality could be fully realised, only within the parameters of a long-term balanced reciprocal relationship, where the duties and responses of both benefactors and recipients were viewed as of equal importance. Anticipating the successful completion of the collection, Paul thus shifts the focus of his readers to the situation following Jerusalem's acceptance thereof where they would be 'promoted' to the position of benefactors.[86]

---

[83] Georgi, *Der Armen zu gedenken*, 63.
[84] Georgi, *Der Armen zu gedenken*, 64-65.
[85] Barrett, *A Commentary on the Second Epistle to the Corinthians*, 226-227.
[86] Cf. Also Hays, *The Moral Vision of the New Testament*, 465.

Contra Barrett,[87] the repetition of ἰσότης (in vv. 13b-14) is not clumsy, but part of Paul's careful rhetorical structuring of the text. Verse 13-15 actually reinforces the view that the Corinthians were not involved in a unilateral bestowal of material gifts to Jerusalem, but in a situation of balanced exchange (= ἰσότης), which did not have as its goal the entrenchment of power differentials or exploitation of any of the parties involved.

What kind of 'give-and-take' did Paul have in mind between Corinth and Jerusalem? Clearly the περίσσευμα of the Corinthians in the present time (ἐν τῷ νῦν καιρῷ) existed in their material abundance, while the ὑστέρημα of the believers in Jerusalem reflected their deficiency in this regard. But what would the future reversal, referred to in verse 14b, entail? Most probably, it pointed to some further *spiritual benefits* from Jerusalem.[88] However, a number of scholars are of the opinion that Paul had a material response from Jerusalem in mind.[89] But their economical position, on the one hand, as well as the reference in 2 Corinthians 9,12-14 to the anticipated 'spiritual response' to the collection by Jerusalem, on the other, merits understanding verse 14b in terms of the Corinthians' spiritual want that had to be addressed in future from Jerusalem's spiritual wealth.[90] Although this interpretation at first glance seems to be in contradiction with Paul's earlier reference in 8,7 to the spiritual περίσσευμα of the Corinthians, we must also consider the rhetorical function of these remarks within the larger framework of 2 Corinthians 8. As part of Paul's rhetorical strategies to involve the Corinthians in the collection after it came to a halt (which reflects an obvious deficiency in the their 'spiritual armour'), he, in line with his patriarchal-role in 2 Cor 8,7, presents them as mature believers who need not be prescribed to as before. However, in terms of the rhetorical progression in the text, Paul (from v. 11 onward) does in fact provide some explicit indications of his dissatisfaction with the Corinthians' collection effort, as his use of an imperative (v. 11: ἐπιτελέσατε), as well as this reference to their spiritual ὑστέρημα, makes clear.

---

[87] Barrett, *A Commentary on the Second Epistle to the Corinthians*, 226.

[88] According to Martin, *2 Corinthians*, 267, the expression ἐν τῷ νῦν καιρῷ refers to the present period of eschatological reality where God in his righteousness justifies the ungodly. Therefore the connecting ἵνα looks to the future age when Israel's reconciliation "... will be a vindication of God's purposes to bless the world, and that event will presage the final homecoming of the nations." However, this interpretation ignores Paul's more down-to-earth understanding of the reciprocal relationship between Jerusalem and his own communities.

[89] See Plummer, *A Critical and Exegetical Commentary on the Second Epistle of Paul to the Corinthians*, 125; Barrett, *A Commentary on the Second Epistle to the Corinthians*, 226, and Lang, *Die Briefe an die Korinther*, 320.

[90] So, e.g., Theobald, *Die überströmende Gnade*, 285-286; Betz, *2 Corinthians 8 & 9*, 69;. Wolff, *Der zweite Brief des Paulus an die Korinther*, 71; Gnilka, *Paulus von Tarsus*, 159.

According to Paul the ἰσότης between Jerusalem and Corinth was dependent on the exchange of obligations, where each in turn would render to the other the services that they required. Under the present circumstances, this involved material means. But in future these services would involve an exchange of spiritual gifts. Although Paul does not specify what kind of spiritual gifts he has in mind, we should not look much further than the suspected positive response to the collection from Jerusalem (cf. also 2 Cor 9,12-14). In other words, Jerusalem's περίσσευμα would consist '... in ihrer Freude, in ihrem Dank, in ihren Gebeten. Das alles kommt den Korinthern zugute."[91] This positive reaction from Jerusalem would not only promote Corinth to the position of benefactor in the reciprocal relationship, but on the basis of Jerusalem's prayers, also invoke God's active grace in the lives of the Corinthians that would address their spiritual deficiency. In accordance with the principles of benefit exchange, Jerusalem would thus not remain permanently in the superior position in the relationship with Corinth (as a *pars pro toto* for all Pauline communities involved in the collection). By accepting the collection they would be placed in the inferior position of beneficiaries. In this way there would also be equality, in terms of the roles and statuses of the interlocutors in the reciprocal relationship.

In verse 15 Paul provides scriptural proof for these views by freely quoting from Exodus 16,18 (LXX). This text about the gathering of the manna, according to which all Israelites in the dessert ended up with exactly the same amount of bread from heaven, is now related to the collection in order to substantiate the principle of equality, with the full authority of Scripture behind Paul. This quotation functions as 'objective proof' of Paul's views that giving will not lead to affliction on the part of the Corinthians. On the contrary, due to the religious nature of the collection, they may rest assured that God will see to it that they would be adequately reciprocated. God will personally secure the principle of equality in the exchange between Corinth and Jerusalem. At the same time this quotation in verse 15, due to its obvious connotations with the Messianic era in Jewish apocalyptic circles (e.g., *SyrBar.* 29,8; *Or. Sib.* 7,149), places the collection within the era of salvation inaugurated by the Christ-event.[92] Paul thus also understands the collection theologically as an eschatological sign; within the framework of the early Christian move-ment, the fruit of

---

[91] Klauck, *2. Korintherbrief,* 69. So also Wolff, *Der zweite Brief des Paulus an die Korinther,* 173.

[92] In the Jewish world this text stood "im Rahmen einer typologischen Parallelisierung von Wüstenzeit und Endzeit" where "... die Mannaspeisung zum Urbild einer in der messianischen Zeit neu zu erwartenden Speisung geworden ist" – Theobald, *Die überströmende Gnade,* 287.

God's grace is now shared with fellow believers in terms of possessions and spiritual gifts.[93]

In summary: In 2 Corinthians 8,13-15 Paul applies the principle of ἰσό-της to stress that both the Corinthians and Jerusalem should benefit equally from their reciprocal interaction. The Corinthians' involvement in the collection should not lead to an exchange of positions between them and Jerusalem (v. 13). To substantiate this remark, Paul reflects on the principle of 'equality' (vv. 13b-14), and applies a prooftext from Scripture (v. 15).

The following suppositions are embedded in Paul's remarks in 2 Corinthians 8,13-15:

(a) Corinth would resume their responsibilities regarding the collection;

(b) the collection would be accepted by Jerusalem, thus implying that this material gift was a sufficient response to Jerusalem's prior spiritual benefits (cf. also Rom 15,27);

(c) Paul and his communities would be promoted to benefactors of Jerusalem, and

(d) Jerusalem would reciprocate their material benefit ('the collection') in the form of new spiritual benefits to address the spiritual needs of the Corinthians, but also to ensure the continuation of this reciprocal relationship.

4.10. 2 Corinthians 9, 11-15: the collection and Jerusalem's response of gratitude

4.10.1. The structure of 2 Corinthians 9,11-15

Verses 11-15 forms the culmination of Paul's theological reflection on the collection in 2 Corinthians 8-9. Although verse 11 could be understood as a conclusion to the preceding argument (vv. 9ff.),[94] or as a repetition of the argument of verse 10, albeit in a different form,[95] we could also take it as a link between the preceding and the following verses. In particular; Paul's consistent use of the *present tense* from verse 11 onward, as well as the fact that verses 11b-14 elaborate on the impact of the collection on both recipients and benefactors alike, warrants viewing verses 11-15 as a subsection of verses 6-15, which deals with God's gracious conferring of

---

[93] Cf. also Klauck, *2. Korintherbrief*, 70, and Gnilka, *Paulus von Tarsus*, 159.
[94] So Betz, *2 Corinthians 8 & 9*, 115.
[95] So Wolff, *Der zweite Brief des Paulus an die Korinther*, 187.

gifts and the results thereof in the lives of the recipients. In verse 11 the effects of the Corinthians' generosity are addressed, in terms of the expected results of the completion of their collection, concerning Jerusalem. In verse 12, the caritative and 'spiritual' functions of this project are addressed as the reasons for Jerusalem's positive response. Verses 13-14, in turn, deal with the contents of the prayer of thanksgiving by Jerusalem, before a short prayer of thanks from Paul to God (v. 15), forms the logical conclusion to this section, and an *inclusio* with 2 Corinthians 8,1.

4.10.2. Jerusalem's gratitude for the overflowing grace of God

Paul's conviction that the same God who provides sufficient material means for all (9,10), will provide abundantly in the needs of the Corinthians, moves him to anticipate the events following the successful completion of their collection effort (in vv. 11b-14). In verse 11 the encompassing generosity of the Corinthians is addressed which, in turn, is based upon their encompassing spiritual wealth (cf. the repetition of πας). This wealth is the result of God's overflowing grace in their lives, as the *passivum divinum* (πλουτιζόμενοι) in v. 11a indicates. A close relationship exists for Paul between spiritual wealth and the sharing of material possessions with others. "Aller Reichtum gründet in Gottes Heilstat und dieser spirituelle Reichtum ermöglicht materielle Freigebigkeit aus lauterer Liebe."[96] Refusal to share one's possessions with those in need, places a question mark over the presence of God's grace in one's life.

The chain of events set in motion by the Corinthians' experience of God's grace is summarised in verse 11b, namely, the completion of the collection (which is implied in Paul's cryptic reference to the delivery of the funds to Jerusalem - κατεργάζεται δι' ἡμῶν), as well as Jerusalem's prayers of thanks to God (cf. the wordplay: εὐχαριστία - χάρις). The latter expression points to the fact that the collection is not merely the repayment of an obligation within the parameters of a particular relationship between Jerusalem and Pauline Christianity. This reciprocal relationship, at the same time, also involves God, whose active grace is present during the various stages of the project. The Jerusalem believers, who, according to Paul, are well aware of the religious nature of this gift, will therefore rightly direct their own gratitude towards God.

In verse 12a Paul further emphasises the theological nature of the collection in his reference to this project as ἡ διακονία τῆς λειτουργίας ταύτης. As in Romans 15,16ff., Paul here also uses λειτουργία in a cultic sense.[97] Διακονία and λειτουργία thus signify the true nature of the

---

[96] Zeilinger, *Krieg und Friede in Korinth*, 305.

[97] *Contra* Martin, *2 Corinthians*, 293, and Lang, *Die Briefe an die Korinther*, 325, who understand this term in its profane sense as an act of public service, the context of 2

collection as: (a) an act of selfless service to the poor members of the church in Jerusalem, as well as (b) a spiritual blessing from the gentile Christianity. These two facets are repeated in a more elaborated form in 12b and 12c, where both the financial relief (in connection with the collection as διακονία - 12b), and the spiritual purpose of the collection in terms of generating overflowing prayers to God (in connection with the collection as λειτουργία - 12c) are emphasised.

In 2 Corinthians 8-9 Paul explicitly refers to the financial relief for the first time in verse 12b, which this contribution will bring to the ἅγιοι, the believers in Jerusalem. As we have seen earlier, Paul's responsibility to provide material relief for the impoverished members of the church in Jerusalem formed the basis of the reciprocal relationship between himself and the 'pillar-apostles'. At the Jerusalem meeting he committed himself to this obligation in response to the benefits they had bestowed upon him. But Paul did not include the poverty of Jerusalem within his primary motivations for the collection. However, this does not imply that the Pauline communities were unaware of the caritative functions of the collection, but then this knowledge functioned within the framework of their reciprocal relationship with Jerusalem. In other words, the alleviation of Jerusalem's want was seen by them as the result of, and not the basic reason for, the repayment of their debt of gratitude to the mother church.

While the collection served as a concrete expression of the existing reciprocal relationship (κοινωνία) between the Pauline communities and Jerusalem, Paul conceptualised the collection as an undertaking that was intended to address Jerusalem's poverty. Therefore, the size of the contributions from his churches was of great importance to him. This is indicated in (a) Paul's reference to Macedonia's large contribution (8,2-3); (b) his *agonistic remark* in 9,4 that the Corinthians might be humiliated by the contribution of the much poorer Macedonians, but (c) also in his anticipation of the generous contribution of the Corinthians as one of the reasons for Jerusalem's thanksgiving (9,13c).

Another important function of the collection is addressed in 12c where Paul states that it will overflow in many thanksgivings to God. These overflowing prayers of thanks to God serve as manifestations of his power (cf. also 2 Cor 1,11; 4,15):

> The more thanksgiving occurs, the more grace has been bestowed and received, the greater is the testimony, and the greater the power of God. Paul's goal, therefore, was to increase the number of worshippers, for thereby the manifestation of God's power

---

Cor 9 (particularly verse 12b-c) favours the cultic understanding of λειτουργία- so Nickle, *The Collection*, 1966, 121-122; Theobald, *Die überströmende Gnade*, 299; Gnilka, "Die Kollekte der paulinischen Gemeinden für Jerusalem", 310.

would increase. Since the collection for the saints in Jerusalem served this spiritual purpose, the apostle recommended it with such incessant fervour.[98]

In spite of his sensitivity to the nature of ancient social reciprocity, Betz's surprise at Paul's use of this 'rather primitive concept of God', reflects a misunderstanding on his part of one of the characteristics of ancient reciprocal relationships, namely the constant efforts on the side of benefactors to acquire as many gift-debtors as possible. "What a gift transactor desires is the personal relationships that the exchange of gifts creates and not the gifts themselves."[99] The more people one had in one's debt, the higher was one's honour, also in ancient religion. Divine gifts did not only estab-lish and secure the continuation of relations with deities, by creating debts that had to be repaid by worshippers, but they also served as public claims to the honour of the deities. The more worshippers who were in debt to specific gods, the higher their power and status were within society.[100] Within the context of the ancient Mediterranean world, with its emphasis on repayment of debts to benefactors, deities and humans alike, it was therefore only natural that Paul would understand the thanksgiving from Jerusalem as flowing back to God. This was in fact the only legitimate response on their part, since thanksgiving was nothing less than 'sacrificial' repayments for the beneficence received. According to Paul, such debts could never be repaid in full. One remained permanently in debt to God for his eschatological benefits (cf. e.g. 1 Thess 3,9).

Paul was convinced that the collection would increase God's honour as heavenly benefactor because of the multiplication of prayers of thanksgiving. In verse 13-14 he actually constructs the contents of Jerusalem's prayers.[101] Firstly, in their praise to God (v. 13) they will acknowledge the obedience that the Pauline communities had shown in their confession of the gospel of Christ. The participation of the Corinthians in the collection is nothing less than a concrete manifestation of their faith (v 13b). Apart from the implicit pressure this statement brings to bear on the intended readers on the rhetorical level of the text to involve themselves in the

---

[98] Betz, *2 Corinthians 8 & 9*, 119.

[99] Gregory, *Gifts and Commodities*, 19.

[100] Luke's reference to the negative reaction from the silversmiths in Ephesus (Acts 19,23ff.) to Paul's missionary activities in the city serves as an example of the 'sensitivity' of the religious cults to external threats to their deities' honour. Paul's preaching in the city, according to their spokesperson, Demeter, did not only threaten these silversmiths' income, but also the reputation of the cult of Artemis, and the future of her magnificence in Asia and in the rest of the world (19,27). Cf. also Towner, "Mission Practice and Theology under Construction", 417-436.

[101] In terms of understanding vv. 13-14 as a prayer of thanksgiving consisting of an element of praise (v. 13) and an element of intercession (v. 14), I follow the insights of Betz, *2 Corinthians 8 & 9,* 120ff.

collection, it at the same time underlines the religious nature of this undertaking, since it reflects their submission to the *content of the gospel* that Paul preached to them. The collection was not an act of submission to Jerusalem, neither in Paul's eyes, nor, according to him, in the eyes of Jerusalem.[102] On the contrary, Jerusalem saw it as proof of the faith of the Pauline communities.[103]

The second reason for Jerusalem's praise to God is expressed in the fact that the delivery of the collection would serve as a visible demonstration of *koinonia* between themselves, the Corinthians, and other believers involved in this project. The acceptance of the collection would provide visible proof of the unity and equality of all believers, irrespective of their origin, as well as of their commitment to the one gospel of Christ.

In verse 14, containing the petition of Jerusalem on behalf of the Corinthians (καὶ αὐτῶν δεήσει ὑπὲρ ὑμῶν), they express their longing for the latter (ἐπιποθεῖν) because of the exceeding grace of God in their lives. Of course, Jerusalem's longing is not merely an emotional yearning to personally meet the Corinthians. Verse 14 rather refers to Jerusalem's grateful acceptance of the collection, as well as to their concomitant display of gratitude in the form of a bestowal of honour on the Pauline communities. Within the framework of Paul's theological understanding, verse 14 points to Jerusalem's recognition of the spiritual maturity of the Corinthians, due to the surpassing divine grace at work in their lives, as the reason for their (presumed) generosity to their fellow believers. Jerusalem's longing would thus be nothing less than

> ... eine Sehnsucht nach tieferer Gemeinschaft mit ihnen, um so auch selbst in verstärktem Maß an dem Reichtum der bei ihnen wirksamen Gottesgnade Anteil zu erhalten.[104]

Whereas the spiritual poverty of the Corinthians was earlier referred to in 8,13-15, Paul now, in anticipation of the successful completion of the collection, implies that the latter will serve as a clear sign of the presence of God's grace in their lives. Therefore he appropriately closes with a doxology (in v. 15).

---

[102] Contra Betz, *2 Corinthians 8 & 9*, 122ff., who interprets ὁμολογία in its legal sense as a public confirmation of the fact that the donors have entered into a contractual agreement, the substance of which was their submission to Jerusalem. This is in contradiction to the nature of benefit exchange relationships where the delivery and acceptance of a gift signalled a change in roles, status and obligations.

[103] So also Barnett, *The Second Epistle to the Corinthians*, 446.

[104] Theobald, *Die überströmende Gnade*, 301.

4.10.3. The collection and the principle of socio-religious approval

According to the principle of balanced reciprocity, the parties involved in an exchange of services were to benefit equally from their social interaction. Within the ancient Mediterranean world, with its stereotypical perceptions that the positive consequences of people's good deeds were important inducements for doing them, some incentives were needed for encouraging reciprocal behaviour. Any relationship that was conceptualised as a form of social exchange, even on the religious level, would soon cease when these expected reactions were not forthcoming. In terms of the collection this implied that the Corinthians also had to benefit personally from their involvement in the collection, and not only God! Although the general atmosphere of *euergetism* in the Graeco-Roman world was much different from the early Christian world, where the plight of the socially destitute played a prominent role, the principles inherent to benefit exchange were still not (totally) replaced by purely altruistic forms of care for the needy, particularly within Pauline circles. Veyne[105] and Prell[106] are therefore only partially correct when they state that *euergetism* was substituted for charity in the early Christian movement, since this replacement of the principles of individual self-gratification as the leading motivation for performing services to others formed part of a complex and protracted process that was probably only completed during the time of Tertullian.

The radical redefinition of philanthropy by Jesus was accepted with varying degrees of success within the various earliest Christian groups. In particular, within the orbit of the Pauline churches in the Graeco-Roman world, where the sharp dichotomy between benefaction and charity was still experienced as very real, Paul deliberately shifted the emphasis away from reward for services rendered through, amongst others, his religious interpretation of the collection. By relating the monetary gifts from his churches to their faith-relationship with God, the latter's approval of their behaviour was presented by Paul as an important incentive to the Corinthians to complete the collection.

Social approval formed one of the basic rewards sought after, by people in benefit-exchanges. Although the personal gratification to be gained by the Corinthians from bestowing a benefit that contributed to the glory of God was viewed as sufficient reward by Paul, he states (in verses 11b-14) that they were also fortunate enough to find grateful recipients in the form of the Jerusalem church. The latter knew how to direct their gratitude to God, but also to their beneficiaries. Because both benefactors and beneficiaries within this specific relationship had the same common goal, namely the honour of God, the collection was the ideal vehicle to

---

[105] Veyne, *Bread and Circuses*, 19-34
[106] Prell, *Armut im antiken Rom*, 296.

give visible expression to the κοινωνία between them. Their common faith in the one gospel of Christ united them in their thanksgiving to God.

Although the approval of Jerusalem to the collection could not be coerced from them, Paul is of the opinion that the presence of God's grace, and the (supposed) positive orientation of the Corinthians to the collection, would elicit the desired response.[107] In other words, it leads to social approval as the necessary reward for the time and money invested. At the same time, this gratitude usually also creates an obligation for the recipients to reciprocate the benefits received,[108] thus resulting in a full-fledged mutual exchange of services. According to Paul this is exactly what would happen between Jerusalem and his communities: the positive commitment of the Corinthians to the collection would lead to gratitude from Jerusalem, as well as to the latter responding with prayers of intercession (v. 14), and bestowals of honour by, amongst others, recognising their spiritual wealth.

In summary: In 2 Corinthians 9,11-15 Paul supposes the successful completion of the collection on the part of the Corinthians, as well as Jerusalem's prayers of thanksgiving for their generous contributions. However, the delivery of the collection does not merely function as the repayment of an obligation within the parameters of a particular relationship between Jerusalem and the Pauline Christianity. This reciprocal relationship involves both God, whose active grace activates both beneficiaries (to complete the collection), and benefactors (to respond with prayers and a bestowal of honour).

4.11. Conclusion

4.11.1. The collection as an exchange relationship

Paul understands the collection in terms of the interpretative framework of benefit exchange. Embedded in his theological reflection on the collection, the following aspects of social reciprocity are operative in this regard (cf. also the model of benefit exchange in Chapter 2):

(a) *The bestowal of specific benefits, and the concurrent claim in terms of the establishment of a reciprocal relationship with a selected individual or group*: This principle is presupposed in Romans 15,27, where Paul refers to the obligation of his communities to complete the collection in

---

[107] This is also what Seneca has in mind when he states that the person who has no desire to heap any burdens upon his recipients when bestowing a benefit, usually reaps a grateful return, since others gladly return benefits to him (*Ben.* V.1.4).

[108] So Blau, *Exchange in Power and Social Life*, 16.

response to the spiritual gifts (τὰ πνευματικά) Jerusalem bestowed upon them.

(b) *The acceptance of extrinsic benefits and the start of the subsequent reciprocal relationship*: Paul responded positively at the Jerusalem meeting to the benefits from the pillar-apostles (cf. Chapter 3), thereby confirming the start of a particular reciprocal relationship between them. These benefits allowed Paul to continue with his missionary work in the Roman world which, in turn, led to the founding of the respective Christian communities, which eventually became involved in the collection. According to Paul's views, his communities were also implied in the obligations inherent to the reciprocal relationship between himself and the Jerusalem church.

(c) *In terms of status-demarcations, the superiority of the benefactors in the exchange-relationship is confirmed with the beneficiaries' acceptance of their services*: This fact is underlined in Romans 15,26-27. This obligation, in terms of the apostle and his churches, was not a legally enforceable duty, but a moral responsibility that they took upon themselves within the framework of the exchange relationship with Jerusalem. Refusal to discharge these obligations could lead to loss of honour, a decline in social status, and ultimately, to exclusion from further exchanges.

(d) *The communication of the benefactors' needs to their beneficiaries, who are perceived of as being in the position to provide the services required*: In Galatians 2,10 the leaders of the Jerusalem church requested a caritative service from Paul to which he agreed, thus confirming their expectations about his ability to deliver these services.

(e) *The beneficiaries discharge their obligation by rendering a service to the benefactors*: Paul assumes the successful completion and delivery of the collection in 2 Corinthians 8,13-15. The material needs of the poor in Jerusalem will be addressed through the material sources of his churches.

(f) *The acceptance of the service obligates the original benefactors to respond with a return-service*: The roles and status differentials between the parties are reversed during the next phase of the reciprocal relationship. In this regard Paul presupposes a positive response to the collection from the side of Jerusalem. According to 2 Corinthians 9,11-14 they will show their gratitude firstly to God, but also to the Pauline communities by praying for them and by recognising their spiritual wealth.

In 2 Corinthians 8,13-15 Paul interprets Jerusalem's acceptance of the collection in terms of the *principle of balanced reciprocity* ('equality') in terms of:

(i) The parties involved: the status of both benefactors and beneficiaries will be reversed, allowing both parties the opportunity to be in superior and inferior positions during this long-term reciprocal relationship,

(ii) The exchange of gifts: material want within this relationship will be addressed by material surplus, while spiritual want will in the future be addressed by spiritual surplus.

In order to engage his communities in the social exchange between himself and Jerusalem, Paul also places this reciprocal relationship within a religious framework by linking the faith of his communities to the eschatological benefactions of God, which permanently place them in debt to him. From this perspective, the collection is presented as part of their repayment of their debt of gratitude to God (2 Cor 8,1-5). Paul also spells out the 'rewards' linked to the completion of this project (2 Cor 9,11-14): it would increase God's honour, because the recipients would offer a stream of prayers of thanksgiving to him. At the same time the latter would also intercede for Paul's communities and honour them.

The religious bond (κοινωνία) between the Pauline communities and Jerusalem, due to their sharing in the same gospel, is also emphasised by the apostle. This is not unusual, since the *social relationships* that were formed and/or maintained through the exchange of extrinsic benefits in the ancient Mediterranean world were usually considered as of more importance than the specific goods exchanged in Graeco-Roman societies. Therefore it is an easy step for Paul, in terms of his theological conceptualisation of the collection, to refer to this project as a κοινωνία, or a διακονία, so as to give expression to the service oriented, reciprocal character thereof.

4.11.2. Theological conceptualisations of the collection

Benefit exchange, as the interpretative framework for the collection, formed the basis for Paul's theological conceptualisation of this project. These two levels, although not identical, are closely connected: Paul's ideological reflection is built upon, and, at the same time, presupposes the basic framework of social reciprocity. Whenever the collection project ran into particular difficulties, such as in Galatia or in Corinth, Paul drew from the basic tenets of benefit exchange in his ideological reflection on the collection.

From the discussion of the selected texts above, it is clear that Paul places particular emphasis on the role of God's active grace in the lives of the parties involved in the collection, as well as on his own 'priestly role' in terms of the delivery of the contributions from his churches to Jerusalem. Due to his understanding of the collection from the perspective of social exchange, it is an easy step for Paul to advance to the second phase of conceptualisation of this undertaking as a χάρις, and to all further reflection on the nature of God's overflowing grace and blessings, as well as the impact thereof in the lives of the recipients (2 Cor 8-9; cf. also Chapter 5).

In similar fashion Paul also reflects on his own role and position in the collection. Particularly, in Romans 15, when the outcome of his collection-visit to Jerusalem is still in the balance, Paul strategically separates himself from the obligation of his communities, as his remarks regarding their indebtedness to Jerusalem, indicate. Theirs is the responsibility to complete the collection; his is the responsibility to address the needs of the poor (Gal 2,10), which he is at the verge of fulfilling in the form of a priestly service by personally delivering the collection to Jerusalem. Paul is no longer a mere beneficiary of Jerusalem. As the head of the collection project, from its conception to its final delivery, Paul is now on his way to present the believers in Jerusalem with a priestly blessing that would not only address their material need, but also serve as a visible sign, in the Holy City of all places, of the unity of Gentile and Jewish believers as the new eschatological people of God. At the same time, he would publicly lay claim to his hard-earned position as benefactor of Jerusalem.

The delivery of the collection would simultaneously confront Jerusalem with the dilemma of accepting contributions from the Gentiles (cf. Chapter 6), but also with Paul's law-free gospel. Because of the resistance to his views in Jerusalem, Paul is well aware of the risks involved in taking the collection there (Rom 15,30-31). But this provocative step was the only way in which to secure his own honour as apostle and benefactor of the Jerusalem church. At this stage he was not so much interested in turning the delivery of the collection into a symbolic pilgrimage of the Gentiles to the Holy City, as in challenging Jerusalem to live up to the principles inherent to the reciprocal relationship between them, by accepting the collection, and thereby also the gospel of Paul (and his communities). The delivery of the collection could thus become his big moment of glory, or his worst nightmare. Paul could walk into Jerusalem with the fruit of nearly ten years' labour, and receive the recognition and honour that was due to him, or, on the other hand, experience the humiliation of Jerusalem's rejection of the collection, and therewith, the failure of his efforts to secure unity within the early Christian movement. But the question as to whether Jerusalem did in fact respond positively to the collection will have to wait until Chapter 6, where we shall endeavour to answer this question.

Chapter 5

Managing the Collection Effort in Corinth

5.1. Introduction

Corinth was the administrative centre and the largest city of Roman Achaia since 27 CE. It was favourably situated close to the port of Lechaion, 2 kilometres to the north on the Corinthian Gulf, with one of the largest man-made harbours in the Roman world. Corinth's second port was Cenchreae, about 7 kilometres to the east on the Saronic Gulf, which, according to Strabo,[1] turned it into a prosperous city of commerce. Due to its cosmopolitan population, Corinth had a variety of pagan religions and mystery cults, such as the cults of Poseidon, Aphrodite, Cybele and Isis, and eastern religions, such as Judaism and Christianity. The presence of Christianity in Corinth was the result of Paul's missionary work. He stayed in the city for about eighteen months between 50-52 CE, during which time he proclaimed the gospel, and founded a 'mixed' church, consisting of Gentiles as the predominant group, and also some Jews.[2] He probably also organised the collection effort under the believers in the city, before he left for Galatia and Ephesus.

The Corinthian epistles present us with the most comprehensive picture of Paul's collection project. This information has been preserved mainly because of the apostle's reaction (in 2 Cor 8-9) to some issues that threatened the completion of the collection project. Ironically enough, had it not been for these problems, we would have been left almost completely in the dark as to the nature of this important project within the early Christian movement. For the most part, the collection was successfully organised and completed during, or in the aftermath of personal visits from Paul and/or his helpers to Christian communities in the territories of Galatia,

---

[1] Quoted in Engels, *Roman Corinth*, 50. Engels estimates that Roman Corinth had an urban population of 80 000 and a rural population of about 20 000 (p. 84).

[2] See the good overviews on the structure and general characteristics of the city of Corinth during the first century, as well as of the composition of the Corinthian church by Schrage, *Der Erste Brief an die Korinther*, 25-33, and Murphy-O'Connor, *St. Paul's Corinth*.

Achaia, Macedonia, and probably also to Roman Galatia and Asia, without the need for any written instructions that we know of. Therefore, the basic guidelines for the organisation of the Corinthian collection (1 Cor 16,1-4), as well as Paul's response (2 Cor 8-9) on account of this effort soon afterwards grinding to a halt, are of importance to our understanding of the 'dynamics' of the collection. The *basic organisation* and ideological conceptualisation of this project in Corinth, within the interpretative framework of social reciprocity, will therefore be addressed in the course of this chapter.

5.2. 1 Corinthians 16,1-4 and the organisation of the collection in Corinth

5.2.1. The 'poetic sequence' and 'referential sequence' of 1 Corinthians 16,1-4

Paul wrote 1 Corinthians during or about 55 CE from Ephesus to address the mounting problems within the Christian community in the city. After the negative reaction to his first letter (cf. 1 Cor 5,9), he took up his pen once more to address these and other issues, as well as to answer some questions that were put to him in writing. These questions were probably delivered in Ephesus by Stephanas, Fortunatus, and Achaicus (1 Cor 16,17). As a matter of fact, we may view 1 Corinthians as an 'Antwortbrief'.[3] This is indicated by Paul's responses to their questions by means of a typical introductory formula: περὶ δέ (cf. 1 Cor 7,1.25; 8,1; 12,1; 16,1.12).

In 1 Corinthians 16,1 Paul responds to the questions from the Corinthians regarding the collection in an *authoritarian* manner. In his role as apostle he prescribes exactly how the collection effort in Corinth should be conducted, by issuing commands (cf. e.g., the imperatives: ποιήσατε - v. 1, and τιθέτω - v. 2), and by arranging the organisation of the collection from start to finish according to the principles he had earlier laid down in the churches in Galatia.

The nature of this 'hierarchical' intra-textual interaction between Paul and his intended readers in 1 Corinthians 16 could be explained in terms of the demarcation of the *poetic sequence* of the text (that is, the sequence of events as they are narrated in the letter), and the *referential sequence* (that is, the chronological order in which these events took place). The difference between

---

[3] So Klauck, *1. Korintherbrief,* 9.

... the poetic sequence and the referential sequence disclose both formal and material peculiarities of the poetic composition. By constructing the referential sequence, we gain a basis for identifying both the actions the writer has selected for his text, and the ways in which he has related them. In this respect, comparison of the two sequences provides us with access to the writer's formal plot devices and the rhetorical strategy they serve.[4]

When the poetic sequence and the referential sequence within a particular text are identical, it points to the complete projection of the deep structure of the text on to its surface structure. When they differ, such as here in 1 Corinthians 16, it points to the rearrangement of the chronological and logical extra-textual events on the surface structure of the text, with the aim of creating an organised text-world to effectively reflect the ideological viewpoints (and persuasive strategies) of the author.

In 1 Corinthians 16,1-4 Paul rearranges the chronological events ('the referential sequence') from his perspective as *divinely appointed apostle* so as to create a deliberate, hierarchical distance between himself and his readers. Within the epistolary *praesens* of 1 Corinthians 16,[5] that is, the time frame within which both the intra-textual author and readers find themselves (which, in turn, is determined by the narrated events), the discourse takes place according to the dominant ideological perspectives of the intra-textual author. This 'praesens' is situated sometime after the completion of the collection effort in Galatia (16,1), but before the completion of the Corinthian attempt. However, due to the fact that the reception of the letter is presupposed in the intra-textual discourse, the gap between the locus of Paul and his addressees are already bridged within the text.

The structure of 1 Corinthians 16,1-4, in terms of the *referential* or chronological *sequence of events*, referred to, could be presented in the following manner:

KEY: 'C' indicates *completed events*;
    'P' indicates the *epistolary 'praesens'*;
    'F' indicates *future events*, and
    'S' indicates *supposed events*:

(i)   Paul organises and completes the collection in Galatia - C.
(ii)   The Corinthians start a collection for Jerusalem - S.
(iii) The Corinthians question Paul regarding the collection - C.
(iv) Paul addresses the questions of the Corinthians - P.

---

[4] Petersen, *Rediscovering Paul*, 48.
[5] The concept of an epistolary 'praesens' is borrowed from Altman, *Epistolarity*, 127, who uses this concept in terms of the ideological and temporal reference point within the intra-textual discourse.

(v)   Paul's answer reaches the Corinthians - (P)F.
(vi) The collection is to be modelled on that of the Galatians - F.
(vii) The collection should not be delayed until Paul's arrival - F.
(viii) The Corinthians must put money aside for the collection on Sundays - F.
(ix) The Corinthians must appoint a delegation to take the collection to Jerusalem - F.
(x)   Paul is underway to, and arrives in Corinth - F.
xi)   Paul personally discharges the Corinthian delegation to Jerusalem with a letter of recommendation - F.
(xii) Paul probably also accompanies them on the journey to Jerusalem - F.

In terms of the poetic sequence of 1 Corinthians 16,1-4, number (iv), Paul's intra-textual response to the questions of the Corinthians, is placed first. It is followed by the discourse on the collection, which also anticipates the organisation and completion of the Galatian collection endeavour (i); the start of the Corinthian collection (ii); the question(s) on the part of the Corinthians (iii), and the arrival of the letter with Paul's answer in Corinth (v). This is followed by Paul's directives concerning the organisation of the Corinthian collection along the lines of the Galatian effort (vi), as well as by number (viii), the manner in which money should be set aside for the collection, and number (viii), the instruction that the Corinthians should not delay this project until Paul's arrival (vii and x). From numbers xi-xii the chronological sequence and poetic sequence are identical.

5.3. The apostolic directives for a successful collection effort in 1 Corinthians 16,1-4

Paul's response to the question of the Corinthians at the beginning of 1 Corinthians 16,1-4, serves to stress his own apostolic authority as broker of the heavenly patrons, but also emphasises the hierarchical distance between him and his readers. Paul believed himself to be under the control of divine forces far greater than himself. Therefore he presents himself to the Corinthians as being endowed with the necessary divinely assigned authority to head the organisation of the collection. As the inferior party in this relationship, the Corinthians were therefore dependent on Paul, who was in possession of the necessary information about the collection that would enable them to successfully complete this project. The only legitimate option for them was to obediently follow his instructions. But Paul's apostolic authority was not merely limited to his supervision over the Corinthians. The Galatians also fell under his jurisdiction. And their obedience to his instructions led to the successful completion of their collection effort. Therefore, the Corinthians had to imitate the Galatians' exemplary behaviour.

Paul indicates that his directions in verses 2-4 are a duplication of his instructions to the Galatians. These instructions thus serve as the blueprint for any successful collection effort. But the reference to the Galatians in verse 1 fulfils yet another function. It points to the *ecumenical nature* of the collection. This project not only serves as a visual symbol of the unity between the Pauline communities and the Jerusalem church, but also between the various Pauline communities. The fact that Paul could expect of the Corinthians to follow the same instructions as the Galatians, reflects a bond between them based upon their common faith. As a matter of fact, only on the basis of the κοινωνία between his communities could the apostle have organised a cognate collection effort, a λογεία,[6] for Jerusalem.

In verse 2, Paul provides information regarding the practical organisation of the collection in terms of:

(a) *the persons involved in the collection in Corinth*: Paul states that the entire Christian community should be involved (ἕκαστος ὑμῶν), not only the prosperous members. Assistance to the poor was not the responsibility of a privileged few, who had a surplus of possessions. It was the responsibility of all Christians, irrespective of their social status or economical position, to assist those more needy than themselves. Within the context of 1 Corinthians, Paul apparently does not suppose that every single person in the Christian community should contribute to the collection. Ἕκαστος rather refers to the responsibilities of the heads of the various Christian households in terms of the λογεία. Since the Christian *patresfamiliarum* were responsible for the religious life of their families,[7] it was the logical move for Paul to place them under obligation in order to contribute to the collection on behalf of all members in their households.

---

[6] The term λογεία refers to the actual activities of gathering the contributions of the various churches - Fee, *The First Epistle to the Corinthians*, 812.

[7] The available information in the New Testament points to the important role of *patresfamiliarum* in the conversion of their families and the formation of believing communities. 'Conversion of households fixed the character of the Christian fellowship; the embryo of the community was a family and the household turned into a congregation." - Sandnes, "Equality within Patriarchal Structures", 153. However, some individuals who belonged to the Christian community in Corinth, and who probably did not have the support of households, such as slaves and women who individually joined the community (e.g., 1 Cor 7,12ff.), had to personally take responsibility to save up an amount on their own.

(b) *The temporal parameters within which the collection was to be undertaken*: Paul states that believers should put money aside for the collection κατὰ μίαν σαββάτου, on the first day of the week. Following the Jewish calendar,[8] Paul expects of the Corinthians to save up some money for the collection on a weekly basis; more specifically, on the Sunday, which probably already at this early stage already took on a special significance as the day on which Christ's resurrection was celebrated in early Christian circles.[9] Although it is difficult to determine what specific meanings were actually attached to the Sunday within the various early Christian communities, we could assume that from very early on, it served as an identity marker in Pauline Christianity, over against the Sabbath as a distinctive Jewish identity marker.[10] On Sunday the communal meal was celebrated, and believers also, probably before sunrise and/or after sundown, gathered for worship in their house-churches.[11] Thus Sunday co-determined the character of Pauline Christianity. Over against Jewish groups who gathered on the Sabbath, the Pauline communities formed part of the new eschatological people of God who came together on their own special day; the day of their Messiah's victory over the powers of death and destruction.

Apart from Paul's instruction that the Corinthians had to set aside money for Jerusalem on Sundays, they also had to complete this project before his own arrival in the city. It was expected of them to gradually build up a significant fund through their weekly savings, in order that Paul could make the final arrangements for the delivery of the collection to Jerusalem, at the time of his arrival.

(c) *The nature of their contributions*: Paul does not specify that believers had to bring their contributions to the assembly on the Sunday, but the fact that they had to privately put away money for this purpose on Sundays, determined the nature of the collection as a *religious undertaking*. It was not merely a λογεία; it was also a χάρις, a gift of love on the part of the Corinthians (16,3), and, as such, also formed part of their religious responsibilities. On the very same day on which they celebrated their faith in an organised, manner, they also had to give visible expression to their bond with believers in the Jerusalem church. These material 'sacrif-

---

[8] E.g., Conzelmann, *Der erste Brief an die Korinther*, 365; Fee, *First Epistle to the Corinthians*, 813f.

[9] Cf. Wolff, *Der erste Brief des Paulus an die Korinther*, 429f. The laying aside of money on the Sunday instead of on the Sabbath so as to accommodate Jewish believers, who were not allowed to handle money on the Sabbath, apparently did not play a role here, as Orr & Walther, *1 Corinthians*, 355, suppose.

[10] Cf. in this regard, Neyrey, *Paul, in Other Words*, who deals with the various Jewish and Pauline boundary markers in terms of holy space, time, people, etc.

[11] See e.g., Becker, *Paulus*, 269.

ices' from the income they had earned during the week as small farmers, artisans, builders, businessmen, etc., had to be undertaken within the private sphere of their houses. This was probably done to avoid competition and envy among rich and poor believers if the collection was taken up during their meetings, or to avoid any maladministration of a communal fund.[12]

Paul does not prescribe a specific amount, such as a tithe, to be put aside for the collection by individuals in Corinth. He only states that each member should contribute in proportion to 'whatever profit he makes' (ὅ τι ἐὰν εὐοδῶται[13]). In this (intentionally?) ambiguous expression, Paul leaves it to the discretion of believers to decide on the amount that they will put aside for the collection, but then it should at least be in accordance with "whatever success or prosperity may have come their way that week."[14] The implication is clear: these individual contributions should be substantial, but also proportional.[15]

In spite of Paul's silence regarding a prescribed contribution from the Corinthians, his remarks in verses 3-4 indicates that he anticipated a significant collection from them. For instance, he advises them to appoint delegates who would transport the collection to Jerusalem after his own arrival in Corinth. Paul would definitely not have proposed such a symbolic gesture if he had thought that this sum was insignificant. These delegates would also serve as the personal link between Corinth and the church in Jerusalem. At the same time, their presence would also serve as a safeguard against any rumours of maladministration of the collection funds.[16]

To emphasise the necessity of a large contribution on the part of the Corinthians, Paul also states in verse 4 that he will only accompany the Corinthian delegation to Jerusalem if the gift is worthy of it.[17] As the

---

[12] Large numbers of Corinthians worked in the various manufactories in the city. Corinth was well known for its lamp and pottery manufacture, as well as for its work in bronze and marble sculpture. These manufactures created many local jobs, as did the large building projects in the city; the organisation and hosting of numerous local games and various forms of entertainment, and the providing of various services to the large stream of merchants, travellers and tourists to the city - Engels, *Roman Corinth*, Ch.2-3.

[13] Barrett, *A Commentary on the First Epistle to the Corinthians*, translates τι ἐὰν εὐοδῶται as a present subjunctive.

[14] Fee, *First Epistle to the Corinthians*, 814.

[15] The same view is expressed by Orr & Walther, *1 Corinthians*, 356, who also state that the putting away of funds for Jerusalem was done on a family basis and kept at home because of the lack of appropriate organisation and banking facilities.

[16] Klauck, *1. Korintherbrief*, 124.

[17] It is difficult to explain the ambiguous expression: ἐὰν δὲ ἄξιον ᾖ. Orr & Walther, *1 Corinthians*, 356f., understand this impersonal adjective as a reference to Paul's itinerary ("... if his schedule is suitable, the delegation from Corinth would join

divinely appointed apostle who is responsible for the proclamation of the good news throughout the Graeco-Roman world, Paul implies that his itinerary is already set (cf. v. 5ff.). He cannot occupy himself with trivialities, such as an inferior collection, that will not serve its basic purpose, namely to address the needs of the poor in the Jerusalem church. Therefore, he alludes to a personal inspection and an evaluation of the Corinthian collection effort upon his arrival before committing himself to travel to Jerusalem. If he eventually decides to go to Jerusalem, the Corinthian delegates may then accompany him (σὺν ἐμοὶ πορεύσονται), not *viceversa*.

Paul's authority is further underscored by his remark that he will issue letters of recommendation to each member of the Corinthian delegation to ensure that they would be shown the necessary hospitality by fellow believers *en route* to Jerusalem, and that they would also be received in a friendly manner by the Jerusalem community.[18] Letters of recommendation within the Graeco-Roman world usually granted messengers the same authority as that of their senders.[19] Since they 're-presented' their senders, they could only act within the mandate endorsed by the former. In this regard, the Corinthian delegates were to be sent out under Paul's name to deliver the collection. They would be entrusted with his apostolic authority, as his signature on the letters of recommendation would have indicated to all the churches along the way, as well as to the Jerusalem church.

5.4. Paul's autocratic leadership style and the organisation of the collection

Paul's claims to honour and authority were closely bound up with the fact that he was the 'official' representative and broker of God and Christ. But, at the same time, he was also a typical group-orientated person whose loyalties lay with the communities under his supervision (as 'in-groups'), and

---

his delegation"). On his part, Conzelmann, *Der erste Brief an die Korinther*, 363, translates this expression as follows: 'Wenn es eurer Meinung entspricht." However, the most logical explanation would be to view the collection (χάρις - v. 3) as the subject of this clause, implying that if a substantial amount had been put together by the Corinthians, Paul might accompany the delegation to Jerusalem - so Wolff, *Der erste Brief des Paulus an die Korinther*, 430.

[18] Hospitality was a highly regarded virtue in the ancient world. In ancient Israel (cf. e.g. Gen 18,1-8; 19,1-8), early Christianity (e.g., Heb 13,1f.; 3 Jn 5-8), and also in the Graeco-Roman world, we have numerous examples of hospitality - cf. Klauck, *Der zweite und dritte Johannesbrief*, 95-97.

[19] See the discussion on letters of recommendation in Klauck, *Antike Briefliteratur*, 75-79.

the Jerusalem church (as a 'secondary group'). Because the acknowledgement by the Jerusalem church of his position as apostle of the Gentiles and benefactor was a matter of the highest significance to Paul, he did not hesitate to use his authority within the orbit of his own communities to get the collection successfully off the ground. At the same time, although Paul's personal goals did not normally precede his group's goals, his personal honour was closely tied up with the completion of the collection. The positive response of Jerusalem to this contribution would not only redress the personal humiliation he experienced in Antioch, but would also serve as the visible repayment of the debt he incurred at the Jerusalem meeting with the 'pillar-apostles'. However, these personal concerns functioned mostly beneath the surface structure in his references to the collection. As a collectivist, who indulged in activities that were intended for the common good of his own communities, Paul, on the surface structure of his texts, interpreted the collection as an undertaking that would benefit all in his churches. He carefully avoided any self-concerned focus on this project (apart from, perhaps, Rom 15,25ff. - cf. Chapter 6). Of course this does not imply that there was an antithesis between Paul's own views on the collection and that of his communities. His collection was their collection. More correctly, he turned his views of the collection into theirs! If the collection failed, Paul would be brought to shame in public because of his failure to live up to his part of the reciprocal relationship with the 'pillar-apostles'; but so would his communities. And if the collection effort succeeded, Paul would be duly honoured as benefactor of Jerusalem; as would his communities. However, Paul ultimately stood at the head of the collection. He could therefore legitimately lay claim to the most honour if the project succeeded (just as he would experience the most humiliation if it failed). A successful collection effort would imply that Paul measured up to the social and cultural expectations that constituted his apostolic identity in the eyes of his own communities, as well as in the eyes of Jerusalem.

On the basis of the asymmetric distribution of power, which Paul perceived to exist between himself and his communities, he claimed the right to exercise influence over the formulation and reproduction of the symbolic orders that defined and shaped the nature and identity of the collection. In Corinth it implied following an autocratic strategy. The reason was simple: This strategy worked in the Galatian churches. Their successful collection effort was a testimony to the effectiveness of Paul's control over the collection process in terms of:

(a) *The setting of (long-term and short-term) goals*: Paul's goal was to address Jerusalem's poverty. In order to attain this goal, he set some short-term goals for the Galatians and the Corinthians. This included the completion of their collection efforts within a specific time frame through the setting aside of money on Sundays. The appointment of local delegates to escort the collection to Jerusalem (16,2-3) also formed part of these short-term goals.

(b) *The monitoring and evaluation of the various stages of the collection*: the second phase of the Corinthian collection effort involved Paul's personal presence. He had to determine whether the believers had followed his instructions, and whether they had put together enough money in order to justify his accompanying the collection to its final destination.

Paul's instructions regarding the local collection efforts; his appointment of helpers, and his personal control over the project's progress, all point to the fact that the collection was not a spontaneous effort. On the contrary, it was a carefully planned and well-managed project.

5.5. The crisis in Corinth and the new intra-textual relationship between Paul and the Corinthian believers

5.5.1. The situation between 1 Corinthians 16 and 2 Corinthians 1-9

Paul's general style and tone, as well as his own intra-textual role and the role conferred upon the readers in 2 Corinthians 8-9, differ noticeably from that of 1 Corinthians 16,1-4, and from that of 1 Corinthians in general. Instead of the autocratic style of 1 Corinthians 16, very few explicit commands or instructions concerning the collection are to be found in 2 Corinthians 8-9. Paul rather limits himself to some advisory remarks, while, at the same time, emphasising the spiritual maturity and positive attributes of his readers. Over against the hierarchical distance between himself and the Corinthians in 1 Corinthians 16, Paul bridges the distance between them in 2 Corinthians 8-9, by, in anti-structural fashion, adopting a *very mild* patriarchal role. Since the collection project in Corinth came to a halt because of the disturbed relations between the apostle and the believers after the delivery of 1 Corinthians, and due to the intrusion of some people from the outside who stirred up the church, Paul had to drastically change his strategies. This he had to do in order to ensure the completion of the collection.

In view of the available information in 2 Corinthians 1-9, we may construct the following scenario for the situation between the writing of 1 Corinthians and 2 Corinthians 1-9:[20] Shortly after the dispatching of 1 Corinthians, people who preached a different gospel infiltrated the Corinthian community. When hearing of this, probably from Titus after he returned from Corinth for his first visit to organise the collection (2 Cor 8,6),[21] Paul

---

[20] I am here indebted to the views of Klauck, *2. Korintherbrief*, 5-7.
[21] So Barnett, *Second Epistle to the Corinthians*, 387.

changed his itinerary. He undertook an unannounced 'Zwischen-besuch' to Corinth (cf. 2 Cor 12,14; 13,1). Unfortunately, this led to a public confrontation with a prominent member of the community who apparently sided with the intruders in their strong criticism of Paul's apostolic ministry. After this conflict (cf. 2 Cor 2,5; 7,12) the apostle hastily departed, deeply humiliated. He then wrote a letter from Ephesus (cf. 2 Cor 2,4; 7,8)

> ... den wir aufgrund von 2,4 den Tränenbrief nennen (vgl. 7,8) und der eine scharfe Abrechnung mit allen Kräften in der Gemeinde enthalten hat, die sich gegen Paulus stellten und an seiner Autorität zweifelten.[22]

This letter, delivered by Titus, is partly preserved in 2 Corinthians 10-13.[23]

In the *Letter of Tears*, Paul not only defends the true nature of his apostleship, but also refers to the problem of financial support from Corinth (2 Cor 11,7ff.; 12,13ff.). Apparently his own policy of refusing material support from the Christian communities that he established, in order to prevent any possible claims on the side of patrons to his 'clientele-loyalties', provided his opponents with an ideal opportunity to cast a shadow of doubt over the collection, and also over his own integrity. They probably spread rumours that Paul misappropriated the collection funds, as well as that he insulted the Corinthians by refusing to accept their money to provide for his own livelihood.[24] Within the network of patronage relationships operative in Roman Corinth, and apparently also under believers in the city, the latter accusation could have caused some of the socially influential members (= patrons) to rally behind the intruders. By that time, they were already up in arms over Paul's denouncement of some believers from their ranks in 1 Corinthians, especially those who tried to exercise their right to pursue their own agendas at the expense of other, less influential, members of the Christian community.[25] The apostle's rejection of patronage when it led to the turning of a blind eye to immoral behaviour, or when it operated as a system of social control, was not taken that well in Corinth.[26]

---

[22] Klauck, *2. Korintherbrief*, 6.
[23] See also Pesch, *Paulus kämpft um sein Apostolat*, 62-70; Becker, *Paulus*, 234.
[24] See also Murphy-O'Connor, *Paul. A Critical Life*, 319.
[25] See this regard, Chow, *Patronage and Power*, Ch.2.
[26] Correctly, Marshall, *Enmity in Corinth*, 257f. In this regard, Winter, *Seek the Welfare of the City*, 60, goes too far when he states that Paul was determined to see the abolition of patronage within his communities, since he wanted to create a new class of benefactors who did good without any expectations of reciprocity or repayment. Paul's efforts in this regard should rather be understood in terms of providing a particular religious dimension to reciprocal relationships. He viewed God as the indirect object of Christian beneficence. At the same time, bestowal of benefits by believers functioned as 're-payments' for God's eschatological gifts. In situations where Paul was assured that his communities understood these principles, he did in fact accept monetary gifts. E.g., while

Fortunately for Paul, the response from the Corinthians to his 'tearful' letter was positive. He heard this good news when he eventually met with Titus in Macedonia (2 Cor 2,12f.). The latter returned from Corinth with information that the person who earlier challenged Paul's honour in public was reprimanded in a meeting of the entire community (2 Cor 2,6). In response, Paul soon afterwards wrote his *Letter of Reconciliation* (the present 2 Cor 1-9), around 56 CE, which was also delivered by Titus.

5.6. Paul's textual strategies in 2 Corinthians 8-9

Paul finds himself in an *argumentative situation* anew in 2 Corinthians 8-9.[27] Although the *Letter of Tears* succeeded in eliciting the desired response from the Corinthians, their collection project was still on hold. Paul is therefore faced with the challenge of 'moving' the Corinthians once again from one ideological position to another in 2 Corinthians 8 and 9, that is from their refusal to complete the collection to renewed participation therein.

Argumentation aims at influencing and changing the evaluative attitudes, as well as the behavioural response of the receptors through the use of specific strategies.[28] Various interactional strategies are operative on the different levels of 2 Corinthians 8-9, such as *discourse strategies* (which deals with the interaction between the interlocutors and the langu-age used in the production of the different verbal utterances), and *semantic*

---

working in Thessalonica, Paul received money from the Philippians to provide for his own livelihood (Phil 4,4ff.), and also from some Macedonian believers (probably also the Philippians) while working in Corinth (2 Cor 11,9). In response, Paul, on his part, was prepared to enter into a particular reciprocal relationship with the Philippians. Not only did he gratefully accept their gifts (Phil 4,11-13), but he also placed this relationship within the sphere of religious reciprocity by praying that God would return their gift (Phil 4,19f.).

[27] Without becoming engaged in the debate regarding concepts such as argumentation and persuasion (cf., e.g. Siegert, *Argumentation bei Paulus*, 16-22; Cohen, "Classical Rhetoric and Modern Theories of Discourse", 69-84), I understand the 'argumentative situation' as an ideal intra-textual creation where the implicit author endeavours, through the use of various strategies and arguments, to move his intended readers to share his ideological viewpoints. The overall impact of all textual indicators on the latter, both on the surface structure and the deep structure of the text (so as to elicit the desired response in terms of their full, critical participation in the situation under discussion) must be taken into consideration in this regard.

[28] A strategy could be defined as "... a property of a cognitive interaction plan that controls the optimal realisation of a set of goals" - Van Dijk, "Cognitive and Conversational Strategies in the Expression of Ethnic Prejudice", 380. Cf. also Joubert, "Persuasion in the Letter of Jude", 75-87, esp. 75-77.

strategies (which are related to the establishment of the meaning of the discourse).

The socially determinative functions of Paul's persuasive strategies in 2 Corinthians 8-9 will acquire our attention in the rest of this chapter. However, before engaging in an analysis of 2 Corinthians 8-9, Paul's basic textual strategy in these chapters, in terms of the *assignment of new roles* to the interlocutors, will be addressed. This change of the roles of the intra-textual personages over against 1 Corinthians 16, together with the creation of a new intra-textual discourse situation, points to the dramatic impact of the postponement of the collection in Corinth on Paul's textual strategies.[29]

5.7. Paul's patriarchal role in 2 Corinthians 8-9

In the *praescriptio* of 1 and 2 Corinthians, Paul presents himself as ἀπόστολος χριστοῦ Ἰησοῦ, whereas the Corinthians are addressed as ἐκκλησία τοῦ θεοῦ (1 Cor 1,1-2; 2 Cor 1,1). These explicit roles assigned to the interlocutors, reflect, and at the same time also determine, their status and respective positions within the epistolary discourse.[30] In his role as apostle Paul clearly commands the centre stage. As the normative broker of the μυστήριου τοῦ θεοῦ (1 Cor 2,1), he possesses the necessary authority to demand total obedience to his instructions from the Corinthians (1 Cor 7,8; 16,1-4). Although Paul does make use of his apostolic authority, he frequently alternates this role in the course of the Corinthian correspondence by, at times explicitly, but more often implicitly, presenting himself in an intimate way as a typical 'father-figure' towards the Corinthians as his 'children' (e.g., 1 Cor 4,14-15; 2 Cor 6,13; 12,14-16).[31]

In 1 Corinthians 4,15, Paul explicitly refers to his 'patriarchal' relationship with the Corinthians: ἐὰν γὰρ μυρίους παιδαγωγοὺς ἔξητε ἐν χριστῷ, ἀλλ οὐ πολλοὺς πατέρας, ἐν γάρ Χριστῷ Ἰησοῦ διὰ τοῦ

---

[29] In this regard the extra-textual context was the crucial determinant of Paul's rhetorical choices, and his and his audience's new intra-textual roles. According to Du Toit, "Persuasion in Romans 1,1-17", 197: "... if within the textual construction the real readers do not recognize themselves, as well as the real author (as far as they know him), they will experience the argument as unconvincing. The exercise will lose its credibility and fail."

[30] Cf. also Joubert, "Behind the Mask of Rhetoric": 101-112, esp. 102f. See Craffert, "Pauline Household Communities", 309-341, for a discussion of the socio-historical nature of Pauline communities.

[31] See in this regard the views on Paul's patriarchal role in Meeks, *The First Urban Christians*, Best, *Paul and his Converts*, 29-58, and Peterman, *Paul's Gift from Philippi*, 172-174.

εὐαγγελίου ἐγὼ ὑμᾶς ἐγέννησα. As a matter of fact, this *parent-child relationship* is frequently applied to the interaction between Paul and the Corinthians. For instance, Paul instructs the Corinthians as his 'children' (1 Cor 4,17; 7,1-40); admonishes them (2 Cor 2,8); regulates their conduct (2 Cor 13,11); expects of them to imitate his behaviour, and be obedient to him (1 Cor 3,1-2; 2 Cor 2,9). At the same time, Paul, as the 'loyal father', states that he is not only saving up an 'inheritance' for them (2 Cor 12,14), but that he is even prepared to sacrifice his own life for them (2 Cor 12, 15). He is also cheered by their good deeds (2 Cor 7,16), and constantly prays for them (2 Cor 13,9).[32]

In his role as patriarchal figure, Paul still holds the leading position in the discourse. The role conferred upon the readers in this regard is one of *obedience*, but also of child-like *trust in him*. By adopting this role, Paul does, however, in anti-structural fashion, break through the strict hierarchical relationship that should actually exist between him and the Corinthians. At the same time this father-child relationship places much implicit pressure on the intended readers to conform to their father's wishes.[33]

As part of Paul's textual strategy in 2 Corinthians 8-9, he does not emphasise the hierarchical distance between himself and the Corinthians, as is the case in 1 Corinthians 16,1-4. Both the 'autocratic apostle figure' of 1 Corinthians 16, who could assert himself as being in a position to give direct orders and exercise complete control over all aspects of the collection, and the 'immature believers', who were ignorant as to the correct behaviour regarding to the collection, are now replaced by 'new' intra-textual personages.

In 2 Corinthians 8-9 Paul acts as a mild father figure who, on the surface structure of the text, only offers his advise to his 'mature children' who experience spiritual abundance (ἐν παντὶ περισσεύετε, πίστει καὶ λογω καὶ γνώσει καὶ πάσῃ σπουδῇ - 8,7).[34] Instead of issuing commands, or unilaterally taking charge of the organisation of the collection, Paul now

---

[32] This patriarchal role serves as an important intra-textual proof of Paul's goodwill towards the Corinthians, while, at the same time, it also reflects on his own integrity and credibility. Paul's emphasis on his fatherly integrity in 2 Corinthians 1-9 is further supported by the repeated recollection of his own virtues, persecution, suffering, hard work, and selfless care for his communities (2 Cor 6,4ff.; 11,8ff.).

[33] According to Holmberg, *Paul and Power*, 79: "...we find in all letters, except Romans, the conception of apostolic fatherhood and imitation, which, as a description of the relation between the apostle and the local church is milder and at the same time more demanding than a list of rights and obligations. It is milder because it signifies an affectionate relation, but it is also more demanding - when are you free from the obligation of respecting and obeying 'father', and when have you repaid the debt of gratitude to the person who has given you life (eternal)?"

[34] Although he explicitly addresses the Corinthians as ἀδελφοί (8,1), Paul acts out his patriarchal role throughout Chapter 8-9. He does not treat them as his equals, that is, as

rather opts to teach by way of example (cf. the references to the behaviour of the Macedonians [8,1-5] and that of Christ [8,9]). At the same time, he also emphasises his abundant love for them (8,8); offers his advice to them in their own interest (8,10); is concerned about their socio-economic position (8,13), and boasts to others about them (8,24; 9,2-3).[35]

5.7.1. The 'potestas' of the paterfamilias

In order to understand more fully the meanings inherent in this 'father-child' relationship between Paul and the Corinthians, we need to briefly focus on the typical role-expectations, responsibilities and functions of Roman fathers and children during the first century as the socio-historic framework..

The *paterfamilias*, the oldest surviving male ascendant, formally headed the Roman *familia*. All members of the *familia* were subjected to his lifelong authority or *potestas,* unless, of course, he terminated it himself - for instance by the adoption of a *filius* into another family, or by *emancipatio.*[36] This *potestas*, which was legally recognised and protected, provided the *paterfamilias* with the right of life and death over his descendants (*vitae necisque potestas*). He had the power to decide whether a newborn child was to be allowed into the family, or exposed to die. At the same time the *paterfamilias* possessed formal ownership over all property in possession of his *familia*. He could legitimately disown or expel his sons from their *domus*, and even sell them off as slaves or have them imprisoned. Furthermore, the head of the household had considerable influence over the marriage of his offspring. Not only did his sons and daughters need his consent to get married, but the law also gave him enough leverage to force them into marriages against their will. At the same time he could also unilaterally dissolve his children's marriages by imposing a divorce.[37]

---

brothers, even though the hierarchical distance between them is not as acute as in 1 Cor 16,1-4. Cf. also the infomative discussion on family in 1John by Van der Watt, "Ethics in First John", 491-511.

[35] In 2 Corinthians 9 Paul follows an even more informal style than in Chapter 8. He switches from the first person plural to singular in references to himself. This implies that he, within the progression in the intra-textual discourse, supposes a positive change of attitude on the part of his readers regarding himself and the collection.

[36] So, Dixon, *The Roman Family*, 40.

[37] The *paterfamilias* was only legally forbidden to break off the marriage of his children from the second half of the second century CE - Treggiari, *Roman Marriage*, 459ff.

Patria potestas formed the backbone of Roman society; it was a palladium of Romanism.[38] However, the available literary evidence does not support the notion of peculiarly oppressive or violent father-son relationships in the Roman world. Invocation of the father's *vitae necisque potestas* against his sons, or *exheredatio* (disinheritance) was not a daily occurrence. Neither was corporeal punishment accepted everywhere, as Plutarch, Seneca and Horace make clear. Whipping of children was actually eschewed by them, because it could inculcate a servile mentality by treating children in a contemptible way.

Patria potestas should be understood in terms of the power invested in the father as head of the *familia*. Roman law protected his power, although *patresfamiliarum* very seldom used their powers to the fullest extent. It was expected of children to wholeheartedly submit themselves to the *potestas* of their fathers, since filial obedience brought honour and public esteem to the position of the *paterfamilias* in the eyes of others. It pointed to the fact that he was able to discipline and control his family.

5.7.2. 'Pietas' and the family

Pietas, when related to relations within the family, reflects the reciprocal obligations and the (affectionate) devotion on the part of fathers and children to each other. "Parents were obliged to look after the best interests of their children, just as children were obliged to respect and protect their parents."[39] The ideal of *pietas* was frequently stressed as the basis of *patria potestas*. It was impressed on Roman fathers not to abuse their powers by maltreatment of their families. For instance, the Roman *censor*, during the time of the Republic, also fulfilled the function of ensuring that the paterfamilias acted in accordance with the tradition of the forefathers (*mos majorum*), and *pietas*.[40] Dixon[41] also identifies a so-called 'sentimental idea of the family' that flourished from the time of the late Republic onwards, where the ideal of *concordia* between husband and wife was frequently emphasised, as well as the extension of affection to children. Philosophers, such as Cicero, Seneca and Plutarch, encouraged fathers to love their children even more than their own wealth and honour, to be proud of them, to take special interest in their studies, to cherish high ambitions for them, to care about their physical and moral well-being, and to be concerned about their future marriages, etc.[42]

---

[38] Schulz, *Classical Roman Law*, 142.
[39] Saller, *Patriarchy*, 111-112.
[40] Lassen, "The Roman Family", 103-120, esp. 107.
[41] Dixon, "The Sentimental Idea of the Roman Family, 99-113.
[42] Cf. Joubert, "Managing the Household", 215.

5.7.3. Reciprocity between parents and children

According to Dio Chrysostom (*Oratio* 75.6), the relationship between children and parents was one of the most important reciprocal relationships. Greek and Roman writers alike confirm this view.[43] Xenophon (*Mem.* II.2,1-13), for instance, refers to the discussion between Socrates and his son Lamprocles, where the latter is reminded at length of his debts toward his parents for his birth, rearing and education. Cicero (*De Off.* 1,58), in turn, states that a man's responsibility works both ways, to parents and children, but the greater obligation would be to his parents: "... country would come first, and parents, for their services have laid us under the heaviest obligation; next come children and the whole family, who look to us for support and can have no other protection." Later in *De officiis,* Cicero also adds the responsibility to the gods (1,60), that should take centre stage followed by one's country, parents, children, and kinsmen.

Ancient writers are convinced that parental benefactions are based upon their love for their children, but also on the expectation of future recompense. In return for the gift of life, education, and security, children must show respect to their parents, be obedient to them, and also care for them in their old age. These responsibilities actually had to continue until after the death of the parents, since it was also the responsibility of children to ensure a decent burial for them.

5.7.4. Metaphorical use of familial terms

The father metaphor played a significant role in Roman life. For instance, the title *parens patriae* was offered to Cicero by the *Princeps Senatus* after saving the Republic from Cataline's conspiracy. Caesar was also conferred the title *pater patriae* in 45 or 44 BCE, while Augustus officially received the same title in 2 BCE. With the reign of Augustus a so-called 'patriarchal religion' took shape in the Empire.[44] After becoming *pontifex maximus* in 12 CE, and after identifying family gods with that of the state, the imperial ruler became an image of divine rule. Jupiter (Zeus) was now regarded as the paternal guardian of the state. His rule as father of the gods and mankind provided the analogy for the 'patriarchal' reign of the emperors. Stevenson[45] points out that both the Greeks and the Romans also devel-

---

[43] See in this regard Stevenson, "Ideal Benefactor", 421-436.

[44] Augustus was soon pictured as saviour and the new founder of Rome. Since Romulus was the first to be called the father of Rome, it made political sense to link the figures of Romulus and Augustus. The latter probably functioned as the physical embodiment of the lost ideals of Romulus in his role as *pater patriae*, (that is, the universal patron) of the *populus Romanus*.

[45] Stevenson, "Ideal Benefactor", 421ff.

oped a concept of the ideal benefactor, and frequently used the father analogy to designate such figures. During the first two centuries of the Christian era, this ideal benefactor-beneficiary relationship seems to have been applied particularly to relationships involving the Roman emperor.[46] The state was also referred to as 'fatherland' (*patria*, πάτρα, πατρίς), its produce sustained life, it united people as in a family, it provided shelter and the fatherland, its laws regulated the lives of all its 'children,' etc.

5.7.5. Summary

Paul's use of patriarchal language should be understood within the framework of the altered relationship between him and the Corinthians after their collection effort came to a halt. In order to prepare them once more for a favourable disposition to the collection, and to elicit their adherence, Paul creates a new intra-textual rhetorical situation in 2 Corinthians 8-9. This strategy involves the adaptation of new roles by the interlocutors, as well as a new textual strategy. In order to bridge the hierarchical and ideological distance between himself and the Corinthians, Paul opts for a mild patriarchal role, while portraying his readers as mature children who now only need his fatherly advice.

Paul's use of patriarchal language should be understood against the framework of the family, the primary social institution in the ancient Mediterranean world. According to Roman people's common-sense knowledge, the *paterfamilias* possessed lifelong *potestas* over all his children. Obedience to his authority was therefore expected of all members of his *famila*. In spite of the theoretically extreme powers vested in the *paterfamilias*, this was tempered by the principle of *pietas*, the dutiful affection of fathers and children towards each other. According to the generally accepted view, parental benefits placed children in permanent debt to them. As part of the repayment of their debt of gratitude, it was expected of children to show respect to their parents and to take care of them in their old age. Patriarchal imagery was also used metaphorically to give expression to and legitimise existing political realities, such as the reign of the gods and the emperor. Patriarchal language also provided a handy 'vehicle' to depict the image of the ideal benefactor in the Graeco-Roman world.

The metaphorical application of family language by Paul in 2 Corinthians 8-9 anti-structurally bridges the hierarchical gap between him and the Corinthians within the intra-textual discourse. Over against Paul's apostle role, which reflects his position as mediator/broker of the heavenly patrons

---

[46] Stevenson, "Ideal Benefactor", 424. From the time of Homer the (potential or actual) benefactor was actually framed in procreative/tuletary terms; that is, the power to give, sustain and protect life.

(cf. Chapter 3), his patriarchal role is related to his position in terms of the believers under his supervision. In other words, Paul's apostolic role symbolises his claim to authority as the officially assigned representative of God, while his patriarchal role points to his position as the head of his churches as a new, fictive, family.

Paul's patriarchal role does not diminish his authority in any way. In this role he only acts less strictly than what his apostolic-role demands of him. But within this familial relationship the implicit pressure on the Corinthians is probably much greater to adhere to Paul's fatherly 'advice' than within an explicit authoritarian situation such as depicted in 1 Corinthians 16,1-4. Within the framework of the ancient Mediterranean family, the responsibilities of children were clearly demarcated: They had to show lifelong obedience to their *paterfamilias*. Disobedience signalled disrespect, and posed a serious threat to their position within the *familia*. At the same time, due to the asymmetric nature of the reciprocal relationship between children and their parents, the former remained permanently indebted to them. Since all these stereotyped meanings are invoked by Paul's careful use of patriarchal language, the implications for the Corinthians in terms of the collection are obvious: nothing less than their full cooperation and compliance with Paul's wishes would be a satisfactory response to his fatherly advise and instructions.

5.8. 2 Corinthians 8-9: Salvaging the collection

5.8.1. 2 Corinthians 8,1-6: An agonistic exemplum

In Chapter 4 we have already dealt with the exemplary Macedonian collection attempt within the framework of religious reciprocity. In a nutshell, verses 1-5 point to the astounding effect which God's grace had on the Macedonians. In spite of severe testing and intense poverty, they were full of joy. At the same time, of their own accord, they contributed generously and beyond their means, to the collection.

Paul instructs by way of example in verses 1-5.[47] In this regard, the example of the successful Macedonian collection serves to accentuate the differences between their collection and that of the Corinthians, while at

---

[47] The *exemplum* or 'paradeigma' forms an important form of appeal to the reason ('logos') within the Aristotelian 'proofs', or means of persuasion (cf. *Rhet* 1356a). The term 'pistis' used by Aristotle in this regard, is usually translated as 'proof', but in fact it has a broader semantic range, also encompassing the related qualities of trustworthiness and credibility. It also "... extends to objects and means used to secure trust or belief" - Carey, "Rhetorical Means of Persuasion, 26.

the same time presenting a summary of particular features of the exemplars' actions which are relevant to Paul's argument.[48] The reference to the outstanding moral character traits of the Macedonians (cf. 8,2-3), and their felicitous religious response to God and to Paul (8,5), serve to elicit a particular disposition on the part of the intended readers towards the collection and towards Paul. But what response did Paul in fact anticipate on their part? Did he have the Macedonians' exemplary conduct in mind, where it should serve as a model to be imitated by the readers? Were the latter, analogous to the Macedonians, also to give them to God and to Paul? A straightforward affirmation or denial of these questions will not suffice. It would seem that, implicit to the account of the Macedonians' behaviour in verses 1-5, there is an appeal to the Corinthians to imitate their brethren,[49] but, on the other hand, Paul does not explicitly commend the actions of the Macedonians as a model for his readers.[50] At the same time he does not merely hold up the example of the Macedonians to shame the Corinthians.[51] Perhaps we should seek for an answer from another angle of incidence, namely from the framework of social reciprocity, which serves, as the interpretative framework for Paul's various conceptualisations of the collection.

The *agonistic* ancient Mediterranean culture turned most forms of social interaction between benefactors and beneficiaries into agonistic contests for personal honour, as well as for the securing of sought after goods and services (cf. Chapter 2). Well aware of the impact of this agonistic mentality on reciprocal relations, Paul, rather surprisingly, applies these principles at the beginning of his collection discourse by narrating the successful collection attempt of Macedonia to the Corinthians. Paul thus deliberately creates an *implicit rivalry* between these two beneficiaries in the reciprocal relationship with Jerusalem by emphasising that the Macedonians did *everything* according to the book.[52] They received God's grace, and in response, gave themselves to him and to Paul. The Macedonians then contributed to the collection beyond their material means. This placed them in the favourable position as would-be benefactors of Jerusalem.

The *exemplum* in verse 1-5 is intentionally constructed to put the Corinthians under pressure from the start of the discourse, on account of

---

[48] Cf. in this regard the discussion of the functions of *exempla* by Stowers, *The Diatribe and Paul's Letter to Romans*, 171-173.

[49] So Betz, *2 Corinthians 8 & 9*, 54.

[50] So Furnish, *2 Corinthians*, 415.

[51] See in this regard the views of Harvey, *Renewal through Suffering*, 83.

[52] Religious rivalry for honour was often found between members of religious associations, or within various associations worshiping the same deities in the ancient world - cf. Ascough, "The Completion of a Religious Duty", 598.

their own despondent performance with regards to the collection. According to Murphy-O'Connor:[53] "The example of the Macedonians is introduced in such a way as to permit the Corinthians' self-respect to function as an internal incentive." Perhaps it should be stated in even stronger terms: Within this agonistic intra-textual context it is expected of the Corinthian believers not merely to match the behaviour of Macedonia, but to actually surpass it. A superficial echo of Macedonia's conduct would not suffice. Only a large financial contribution to the collection from the Corinthians, that would match their own exemplary spiritual gifts (cf. 8.7), would suffice.[54] The message to them is thus unequivocal: If they do not become involved in the collection, they would seriously endanger their own integrity within the church. Their present negative behaviour casts a shadow of doubt over their allegiance and commitment to group norms.

Assuming the success of this agonistic introduction to the collection (in terms of the readers' acceptance of the challenge to complete the collection so as to dissolve the dissonance they experienced in verses 1-5), Paul refers to the return of Titus to Corinth in verse 6.[55] In fact, Paul says that he 'urgently requested' (παρακαλεῖν) Titus to return to the city once more to complete the collection. In line with his 'mild' patriarchal role, Paul still refrains from the use of authoritative language, as well as from avowing his own virtues. He rather opts for an 'indirect' form of persuasion by referring to the imminent visit of Titus. Since the outstanding moral character traits of this apostolic envoy, such as his piety and trustworthiness, as well as his goodwill towards the believing community in Corinth, have already been established in 2 Corinthians 7,6(ff.), the mere mention of his return conveys in itself an unmistakable appeal to the Corinthians.[56]

In summary: Paul's introduction to the *topos* of the collection in 2 Corinthians 8,1-6 is not intended to create a sympathetic disposition on the

---

[53] Murphy-O'Connor. *Paul. A Critical Life*, 314.

[54] Within the familial context of 2 Cor 8-9, the behaviour of Macedonia places further implicit pressure on the Corinthians. The Macedonians acted out their role as 'loyal children' of Paul, since they closely followed his instructions on the collection. The spiritually mature Corinthians, who belong to the same family of believers, could therefore not afford to be outdone by their brethren in this regard.

[55] This loyal helper of Paul was also present at the Jerusalem meeting (Gal 2, 1-10), and apparently, shortly after the dispatchment of 1 Corinthians, paid a personal visit to Corinth to put Paul's remarks on the collection in 1 Cor 16,1-4 into practice. However, due to the presence of the intruders in the church, he returned to Paul without accomplishing this goal. But shortly afterwards he was dispatched to Corinth again as the bearer of the *Letter of Tears*.

[56] So also Furnish, *2 Corinthians*, 415.

side of his readers to himself, or, for that matter, to the Macedonians. He deliberately devises an agonistic situation through his carefully chosen references to the outstanding conduct of the Macedonians. This serves to highlight the differences between the Corinthians and the Macedonians regarding their respective collection attempts. Paul, in his reference to the visit of Titus to Corinth, anticipates the success of his textual strategy in terms of the creation of a competitive spirit in the Corinthians that will secure their renewed participation in the collection.

5.9. 2 Corinthians 8,7-9: The Christ-event as basis for the Corinthian collection

5.9.1. Testing the spiritual integrity of the Corinthians

In a new section (vv. 7-9), marked by the conjunction ἀλλά, Paul explicitly focuses on the role of the Corinthians in the collection. This is done by way of an appeal to them to complete the collection (v. 7), as well as putting their ἀγάπη to the test by referring to the σπουδῇ of the Macedonians (v. 8). But the chiastic christological statement in verse 9 provides the basic motivation. Paul makes it evident that the participation of the Corinthians in the collection is not based upon their own spiritual wealth, or on their agonistic competition of love with the believers in Macedonia (v. 8), but on the poverty of Christ who, through his suffering and death, enriched them spiritually.

After the 'agonistic introduction' (vv. 1-6), Paul turns his attention to the outstanding spiritual virtues of the Corinthians in verse 7. Their περίσσευμα, in terms of *charismata* such as faith, speech, and knowledge (cf. also 1 Cor 1,5; 12,8-9), presupposes the active presence of the very same divine χάρις in their lives that actually moved the Macedonians to overflow in joy and generosity (cf. 8,2). But the Corinthians also excel in Paul's own love for them (καὶ τῇ ἐξ ἡμῶν ἐν ὑμῖν ἀγάπη - cf. also 2 Cor 2,4).

In Paul's first reference to himself in Chapter 8, he openly reaffirms his fatherly love for his 'spiritually mature children'. This reference to the virtues of the Corinthians and Paul's love, at the same time prepares the ground for the paraenetic call (v. 7b) to them to also overflow in this 'benevolence' ('the collection').[57] According to Paul spiritual wealth must lead to the sharing of material wealth with others. "... 'Das Überströmen', die

---

[57] The subjunctive clause: ἵνα ...περισσεύητε here functions as an imperative.

Verwandlung der eigenen Geistesgaben in einen Reichtum anderen zugute, ist ihm Kennzeichen für die Wahrheit der Charismen."[58]

In terms of Paul's textual strategy, the repetition of περισσεύειν in verse 7a and b; the reference to the collection as χάρις; the reference to the Corinthians' spiritual gifts (v. 7a), as well as the patriarchal role of Paul, all serve to create an intimate relationship between the interlocutors. But, at the same time, these aspects place the readers under pressure to broaden the scope of their faith by also excelling in the collection. They must, in other words, now furnish concrete proof of their sharing in God's gifts.

In the event that the camouflaged command in verse 7 could have created the impression that Paul has again begun to dictate to the Corinthians, he immediately 'corrects' himself by qualifying the preceding statement (v. 8a; cf. also the change from the first person plural to the singular): οὐ κατ' ἐπιταγὴν λέγω.[59] However, although verse 7b seems more prescriptive than the apparent mild remarks in verse 8, the opposite is actually the case on the rhetorical level of the text. On the surface structure, Paul's hesitance to give orders might be due to the fact that in deliberative rhetoric (as is the case here in 8,1-15), commands are out of order.[60] But the mere fact that Paul also links the collection to his readers' basic value system (through his testing of their love), places much more pressure on the Corinthians than any explicit command in fact would. We could actually speak of a *Steigerung* between verses 7 and 8. Whereas the link between the readers' spiritual gifts and the collection is emphasised in verse 7, their love is brought into play in verse 8. And, as they knew from 1 Corinthians 12-14 (where the *Steigerung* from spiritual gifts to love is basic to Paul's argument), ἀγάπη forms the heart of the Christian life, far surpassing even the most impressive *charismata* in value. The most logical object of their love within this context would surely be Paul, their spiritual father, who has just confessed his own love for them (v. 7b). The Corinthians are therefore obliged to respond in a fitting manner by obeying his wish, namely to become involved in the collection, again.[61]

In verse 8b Paul also makes use of *comparison*, a basic ancient rhetorical technique,[62] when he states that, in the view of the zeal of others ('the Macedonians'), he is putting the love of the Corinthians to the test. In other words, the eagerness of the Macedonian believers towards the collection (vv. 1-5) provides the standard against which the behaviour of the

---

[58] Theobald, *Die überströmende Gnade*, 280.
[59] See also Söding, *Das Liebesgebot bei Paulus*, 151.
[60] So Betz, *2 Corinthians 8 & 9*, 39.
[61] Other objects of their love would also include Christ and the Jerusalem believers - Wolff, *Der zweite Brief des Paulus an die Korinther*, 171.
[62] Cf. Talbert, "Money Management in Early Christianity", 359-370.

Corinthians is now tested. Since the Macedonians have already passed this test, because of the genuineness of their love and their zeal for the collection, Paul refers to them once again within the framework of the intra-textual 'rivalry' between the Macedonians and the Corinthians. Paul's remarks indicate that he is not unjust in putting the Corinthians to this test, because:

(a) both the Macedonians and the Corinthians share in God's χάρις;

(b) both have Paul as their spiritual father, who loves them and who has mediated God's salvation for them; and

(c) both possess the necessary zeal (σπουδή).[63]

Since the Corinthians have more than once indicated their zeal to Paul (cf. 2 Cor 7,7; 8,7), they have no legitimate excuse for not becoming involved in the collection.

The readers still find themselves in an *agonistic* situation in verse 8. What has been implicit in the *exemplum* of the Macedonian collection effort, is now (carefully) spelled out to them in verse 8b: they have to pass the standard set by Macedonia. But this test is qualified in terms of the principle of Christian love. It is thus not a typical *agonistic* competition where the participants should cause insult or humiliation to each other. What Paul has in view is more or less what Seneca referred to as: "... the most honourable contest (*contentio*) of conquering benefits with benefits" (*Ben*.I.4.3-4). Within such a situation it should be the aim of the debtors not only to equal the gift bestowed upon them, but also to actually surpass it in deed and spirit. In Paul's view the Corinthians possess the right spiritual 'equipment' to give concrete expression to this ideal.

The christological statement in verse 9 presents the second *exemplum* within the argumentative context of 2 Corinthians 8-9.[64] According to Paul, the grace/kindness (χάρις!)[65] of Christ caused him to voluntarily exchange his pretemporal heavenly glory for a humble earthly existence (cf. also 2 Cor 5,21; Phil 2,5-11).[66] This condensed reference to the Christ-

---

[63] The term σπουδή is often used in administrative letters and in decrees. E.g., in the decree for Iunia Theodora, a resident of Corinth (c. 43 CE - cf. Pleket, *Epigraphica*. Vol II), she is honoured for her σπουδή towards the Lycinans.

[64] Gnilka, "Die Kollekte der paulinischen Gemeinden für Jerusalem", 314, comes even closer to the truth when he states: "... mit diesen Worten wird weniger Christus als Beispiel vorgestellt, sondern das Erlösungswerk beschworen, in das sie einbezogen wurden und dessen innerer Struktur der Entäußerung und liebenden Hingabe sie entsprechen sollen."

[65] "Da die 'Gnade' auch das Synonym für die 'Kollekte' ist, kann er (Paul) die in Christus begründete Heilstat in einen direkten Bezug zur Kollekte setzen und mit demselben Wort bezeichnen" - Beckheuer, *Paulus und Jerusalem*, 135.

[66] Contrary to Dunn, *Christology in the Making*, 121ff., and Murphy-O'Connor, *The Theology of the Second Letter to the Corinthians*, 83, who both view 2 Cor 8,9 as a reference to the type of death that Christ accepted, I share the views of scholars who interpret 2 Cor 8,9 as a reference to Christ's incarnation (e.g., Talbert, "Money

event, from his pre-existent glory (cf. the metaphoric expression: πλούσιος ὤν), to his incarnation and sacrificial death, enabled a new existence for the Corinthians (cf. the emphatic placement of δι᾽ ὑμᾶς in. 9): "Seine Armut vollzieht sich in der Menschwerdung; sie zielt auf seinen schmählichen Kreuzestod."[67] The poverty of Christ became their spiritual affluence. Due to his sacrifice they are now ὑπὸ χάριν (cf. also Rom 6,14). Whereas the χάρις τοῦ θεοῦ (8,1) provides the foundation for the περισσεία of the Macedonians and the Corinthians (8,1-5.7), the χάρις τοῦ χριστοῦ provides the very reason for their sharing in God's gracious gifts. Thus, the Corinthians now live in a symbolic universe encompassed by the χάρις of Christ, as the foundation of their existence, and the χάρις of God that fills their life-world with overflowing joy and spiritual gifts.

Does the *exemplum* of Christ serve as a model to be emulated by the Corinthians? Apparently not, since Paul in his chiastic construction focuses on the poverty of Christ that has spiritually enriched the Corinthians, and not on the fact that the latter should also imitate his poverty. The admonition implicit to this christological statement is rather that, since the lives of the Corinthians have been changed by the gifts from the heavenly benefactors, they, in terms of the principles of religious reciprocity, must now respond with an appropriate sign of gratitude. As to an adequate response: "das 'Gnadenwerk' der Kollekte ist eine adäquate Frucht der Gnade Christi."[68]

In summary: After offering his praise for the outstanding spiritual gifts of the Corinthians, and assuring them of his own fatherly love (v. 7a), Paul requests of them to be generous in terms of the collection (v. 7b). To Paul the possession of spiritual gifts and generosity go hand in hand. An *agonistic* testing of the love of the Corinthians follows in verse 8, with the σπουδή of Macedonia as the standard for their behaviour. Whereas the spiritual gifts of the Corinthians have been brought into play in verse 7, Paul, by way of a *Steigerung* in verse 8, also involves their ἀγάπη in the collection. In verse 9 the collection is given its ultimate theological grounding in Paul's christological reference to the sacrifice of Christ for the sake

---

Management in Early Christianity", 363, and Dietzfelbinger, "Sohn und Gesetz", 121.) The close relationship between 2 Cor 8,9 and the 'hymn' in Phil 2,5-11 has also been discussed from various perspectives, although in recent research this relationship is often rejected (e.g. Karrer, *Jesus Christus im Neuen Testament*, 316). For our purposes it is sufficient to note that Paul follows the same basic structure in condensed form in 2 Cor 8,9 as in Phil 2,5-11: both texts deal with the humiliation of Christ. However, the victorious return of Christ to his heavenly dwelling is absent in 2 Cor 8,9.

[67] Klauck, *2. Korintherbrief*, 68.
[68] Zeilinger, *Krieg und Friede*, 275.

of the Corinthians. This sacrifice forms the basis for their spiritual wealth and their sharing in the divine gifts. The only proper response to the χάρις τοῦ θεοῦ καὶ τοῦ χριστοῦ in this context would be to become involved in the χάρις for Jerusalem again.

5.10. 2 Corinthians 8,10-12: The nature of the contributions of the Corinthians

5.10.1. Overview of the structure

In 2 Corinthians 8,10-15 Paul directly addresses the collection project in Corinth. In the first sub-section, verses 10-12, he offers his fatherly γνώμη in this regard. This 'advice' involves a command to complete the collection (v. 11a), and an explanation concerning the concrete nature of the contributions expected from the Corinthians (vv. 11b-12). In the second sub-section, verses 13-15, Paul reflects theologically on the principle of ἰσότης, which implies that both Jerusalem and Corinth should benefit equally from their social interaction. To substantiate his views, he, in a carefully constructed chiasm, deals with the principle of balanced reciprocity (vv. 13b-14), before also quoting a prooftext from Scripture (v. 15).[69]

Returning to verses 10-12, the repetition of no less than five 'structure markers' within the short space of three verses, validates view-ing it as a unit: τὸ ποιῆσαι (vv. 10c; 11a); τὸ θελεῖν (vv. 10c; 11b); ἡ προθυμία (vv. 11b; 12a); τὸ ἐπιτελεσεῖν (vv. 11a. c), and ἐχεῖν (vv. 11c; 12b.c).

5.10.2. Instructions for the conduct of the beneficiaries

As the caring father, who acts for the common good of his family (συμφέρει), Paul offers his advice to the spiritually mature Corinthians in relation to their collection effort (v. 10). This collection had started with the visit of Titus to their city (8,6) roughly a year previously.[70] Paul's γνώμη is linked to the earlier accomplishments of the Corinthians, and to their positive attitude regarding the collection (as the required disposition

---

[69] Since the structure and contents of verses 13-15 have already been dealt with in Chapter 4, a few cursory remarks in this regard would suffice.

[70] Contra Windisch, *Der zweite Korintherbrief*, 253, τοῦτο in v. 10 does not refer to the collection that is undertaken to the advantage of the Corinthians, but rather to Paul's fatherly advice. This advice is offered for their own benefit so as to enable them to participate in the collection according to the principles Paul lay down for his communities. Therefore γὰρ links what has preceded with the following remarks in verses 10b-11.

from any grateful beneficiary).[71] Advancing from this positive linkage of the collection to the Corinthians' past activities, Paul moves to the present situation in verse 11a, with the only explicit imperative in 2 Corinthians 8-9: ἐπιτελέσατε,[72] ordering them to complete the collection. Paul does this because he is of the opinion that the intra-textual discourse has progressed to such an extent (mainly because of the bridging of the hierarchical distance between the interlocutors), that he can now afford to act more prescriptively. Yet, Paul immediately qualifies his command by referring back to the earlier goodwill and willingness of the Corinthians (cf. the repetition of τὸ θελεῖν in verses 10c and 11b, as well as προθυμία in verses 11b and 12a), thereby shifting the responsibility back to them. The Corinthians had publicly proven their good intentions towards the collection; therefore it would be in contradiction to their previous commitments to the obligations of their group, not to become involved in the collection once again.

In a rather unusual phrase, Paul (v. 11c) turns his attention to the size of the material contribution of the Macedonians, a matter of great importance in benefit exchanges. By reiterating his previous statement in 1 Corinthians 16,2, albeit in a somewhat different manner, Paul states that one should give according to what one possesses (cf. the repetition of ἐχεῖν in verses 11c and 12c), and not according to what one does not have (v. 12b). Following the principle of proportionate giving, popular in Jewish wisdom tradition,[73] Paul emphasises that he does not expect more of the Corinthians than what is humanly possible. In this way he deliberately moderates his call to give, and therewith, the explicit pressure on the readers, by stating that one should give in accordance to what one may have (καθὸ ἔχῃ). This principle is repeated in verse 13a where Paul says that one should not alleviate the plight of others at the expense of one's own affliction.

If the Corinthians were to follow Paul's fatherly advice, their contribution would be εὐπρόσδεκτος, that is, acceptable. The majority of scholars

---

[71] Lang, *Die Briefe an die Korinther*, 320, notes that in verse 10 "... das Tun vor dem Wollen genannt wird." This is probably done to fit in with the carefully structured wording of verse 10a-b, where the same order between doing and willingness is maintained.

[72] On the basis of his investigation of the use of ἐπιτελέω in the Graeco-Roman world, Ascough, "The Completion of a Religious Duty", concludes that this verb was mainly used with reference to religious duties. He states that Paul, who was always receptive to the shared cultural experiences of his audiences, uses this verb in 2 Cor 8 to appeal to the Corinthians' sense of religious duty.

[73] Cf. Bultmann, *Der zweite Brief an die Korinther*, 256f.

take God to be the object in this regard.⁷⁴ I would propose, however, that Paul here has both God and Jerusalem in view. Although he does not provide an explicit object, thus leaving a 'gap' in the text for the intended readers to fill in, the latter know that Paul, up till this point in the discourse, has placed the collection within the framework of the χάρις of God and Christ. He also made use of such 'provocative' terms as ἐπιτελέω, ἀγάπη, and περισσεύω to emphasise the religious responsibilities of the Corinthians towards the collection. From verses 13(ff.) Paul explicitly focuses on the reciprocal interaction between the Corinthians and Jerusalem. Therefore, in verse 12, he now also hints at the acceptability of the collection for Jerusalem, as an introduction to this theme. Verse 12 thus communicates to the readers that their *active willingness* (πρόκειμαι) to donate to the collection out of their own means, would be accepted gratefully by both God and Jerusalem. In terms of his profile of the ideal beneficiaries, Paul here once again comes close to the views of Seneca for whom the intention of the giver is also more important than what is given (*Ben*. I.6.1). The joy and gratefulness on the part of the Corinthians for the benefits they had received from their benefactors should, according to Paul, prompt them to readily give something back in return. Similar to Seneca (*Ben*. IV.3,1f.), Paul assures the Corinthians that the right attitude on their part would stir a joyful response under the recipients, which, in turn, would be ample reward for their efforts.

In verses 11-14, Paul also develops the principle of *proportionality* in terms of the nature of the contributions of the Corinthians. In verse 11 he states that there should be proportionality between willingness (ἡ προθυμία τοῦ θέλειν) and the accomplishment itself (τὸ ἐπιτελέσαι). In verse 12 proportionality between the size of the Corinthians' possessions and their quantitative contributions is emphasised. In verse 13-14 proportionality within the reciprocal exchange between Corinth and Jerusalem, in terms of the nature of the gifts exchanged between them in the present and in the future, receives emphasis.⁷⁵

In summary: In verses 10-12 Paul strategically shifts his emphasis to the past accomplishments of the Corinthians with regards to the collection as a leverage to coerce them into active involvement in this project once more. He assures them that their previous positive attitude, when activated again, would be sufficient to turn their donation into an acceptable gift, both to God and to the Jerusalem church. At the same time, they are assured that

---

⁷⁴ E.g., Furnish, *2 Corinthians*, 407, and Wolff, *Der zweite Brief des Paulus an die Korinther*, 172. In Rom 15,31 εὐπρόσδεκτος is used with reference to the acceptability of the collection in the eyes of Jerusalem.

⁷⁵ Cf. Joubert, "Behind the Mask of Rhetoric", 109.

they only have to contribute to the collection in relation to their financial means. Paul sketches his own ideal in terms of the Corinthian collection effort (v. 12): If they would activate their previous willingness, it would lead to the successful completion of the collection, as well as to a positive response on the side of the recipients, namely God (as indirect object of their benefactions), and Jerusalem (as the other party in the reciprocal relationship).

5.11. 2 Corinthians 8,10-15: The deliberate tension between rivalry and realism

In 2 Corinthians 8,10-15 Paul stresses that the Corinthians are not under any moral obligation to contribute to the collection more than what they can afford. The probable reasons for this emphasis are threefold:

(a) Paul apparently heard from Titus that the Corinthians were afraid that the collection would place a heavy financial burden on their shoulders. He now responds by pointing out that neither God nor he expects of them any excessive financial sacrifices in this regard.

(b) Paul, in terms of his over-zealous emphasis on the exemplary behaviour of Macedonia in verses 1-5 and 8, realised in the course of the textual discourse that he overstated his case. In order to place matters in perspective, he now changes his approach (from v. 10ff. onwards) by explaining to the readers that they do not have to suffer material shortage in order to help the impoverished Jerusalem community. At the same time, the readers are also reminded of the nature of their reciprocal relationship with Jerusalem: The latter will soon reciprocate their gifts, thus placing them in the role of benefactors (v. 14). In this way there will be ἰσότης. Nobody within this relationship will be in need of anything, materially or spiritually. As a matter of fact, God personally guarantees this 'equality'. as the quotation from Exodus 16,18 illustrates (v. 15).[76]

(c) A third, and within the context the most probable, possibility is that Paul follows a particular textual strategy here, whereby he creates a deliberate tension between verses 1-9, and verses 10-15. Whereas he (in the first five verses) points to the practical effects of God's grace on the Macedonians, as well as on the sacrifice of Christ (v. 9), Paul spells out the underlying (mild!) principles that the Corinthians actually have to follow in terms of their contributions (vv. 10-15).

---

[76] Murphy-O'Connor, *The Theology of the Second Letter to the Corinthians*, 85, notes that this quotation from Ex. 16 is not intended to be emulated by the readers, but rather to illustrate the nature of God's involvement in the collection.

From verse 10-15 the *agonistic* context, created in verse 1-5, is replaced by Paul's emphasis of the principle of proportionality, thus making it clear that the Corinthians do not have to make any unnecessary sacrifices regarding the collection. However, in spite of Paul's emphasis of these mild principles, the readers also know that the Macedonians did in fact do more than what even God expected of them. Under extremely difficult circumstances they gave far beyond their means! This unresolved tension between principle and practice, between what God demands and what certain believers are prepared to do in his service, is intentionally created by Paul. Through this strategy he conveys the message to his readers that the above mentioned principles are not unattainable ideals. In fact they could even be surpassed in practice. But it depends on the readers themselves to determine when they have complied with God's expectations and principles regarding the collection. The spiritually mature Corinthians have to actualise these principles according to their own material means, but also with Macedonia ever present, in the back of their minds.

5.12. 2 Corinthians 8,16-24: Paul's commendation of Titus and his helpers

5.12.1. The Letter of Recommendation

Paul appropriately commends Titus in verses 16-24 as the bearer of the *Letter of Reconciliation* (2 Cor 1-9), and as the person responsible for the practical completion of the collection in Corinth, as well as the two representatives accompanying him. Letters of recommendation, as well as sections of letters that were written within this genre, suppose a triangular relationship between author, recipients and the carrier of the letter. In particular, these letters emphasise the integrity of the letter carrier, as well as the friendly relationship between the latter and the author; the existing bond of friendship between the author and the recipients, and the request to the latter to receive the carrier of the letter in the same manner as the author would have been received by them.[77]

Paul's letter of recommendation (vv. 16-24) is not only intended to commend Titus and the other helpers accompanying him to Corinth. The suspicions raised concerning the apostle after the writing of 1 Corinthians that he misappropriated the collection funds, have not yet been adequately addressed up till this point. This problem had to be dealt with in order to insure the smooth transferral of the collection funds to Jerusalem; hence

---

[77] See Klauck, *Antike Briefliteratur*, 76.

the references to Paul's own integrity, as well as to that of Titus, and to the delegates from other Christian communities. As a matter of fact, the moral character and reliability of these people involved in the official organisation of the collection are of more importance at this stage, than their identities.

5.12.2. *2 Corinthians 8:16-17: Affirmation of the integrity of Titus*

The moral integrity of Titus had already been established in 2 Corinthians 7,6(ff.). Because of the central role of Titus in the Corinthian collection, Paul does not hesitate to reconfirm his goodwill toward the Corinthians in 8,16-17. Paul starts his commendation in verse 16a with a conventional thanksgiving formula (χάρις δὲ τῷ θεῷ) to honour God for the σπουδή of Titus for the Corinthians.[78] He makes it clear that, due to divine inspiration, the same zeal that the Macedonians have previously displayed toward the collection (v. 8), and which the Corinthians have shown toward Paul (v. 7), is now also present in the heart of Titus. As part of the new family of believers they all portray the same moral character traits towards others within their group, as well as towards the collection. The integrity of Titus is further underlined in Paul's statement that the former did not understand his appeal (παράκλησις) to return to Corinth as a heavy burden (v. 17). Due to his 'utter sincerity' (σπουδαιότερος), he actually heeded Paul's urging by deciding to go there on his own initiative (αὐθαίρετος).

The similarities between the extraordinary behaviour of Titus and the Macedonians are clear. Both reflect the same self-sacrificing behaviour for the common good of their fellow believers. In the case of the Macedonians, their zeal prompted them to contribute beyond their means to the collection, whereas in the case of Titus, he, of his own accord, decided to go to Corinth to complete the collection. The presence of divinely infused zeal is thus the driving force which 'moves' believers to walk the second mile in terms of the collection. Within this context Paul's commendation of Titus is not only intended to create the necessary goodwill on the part of the readers towards him, but to also keep them under pressure to 'channel' the σπουδή in their own lives in the right direction (that is, towards the collection).

---

[78] It is not immediately clear what the expression: τὴν αὐτὴν σπουδὴν means. Does it refer to the same zeal as Paul? (so e.g., Barrett, *A Commentary on the Second Epistle to the Corinthians*, 227; Wendland, *Die Briefe an die Korinther,* 221), or the same zeal as the Macedonians? (e.g. Windisch, *Der zweite Korintherbrief*, 261; Kremer, *2. Korintherbrief*, 76), or the zeal of the Corinthians for Paul (cf. 7,11.12; 8,7)? From the context of 2 Cor 8 it would seem as if Paul had the zeal of both the Macedonians and the Corinthians in mind.

5.12.3. 2 Corinthians 8,18-22: Commendation of the envoys, and reconfirmation of Paul's loyalty to group norms

In verses 18-22, Paul commends the brothers appointed by the other Pauline communities to assist with the completion of the collection in Corinth (cf. the epistolary aorists in verses 18 and 22). At the same time he switches from the first person singular in his reference to Titus (cf. verses 16-17; 23a) to the first person plural in his references to the envoys from the churches (vv. 18-22; 23b).[79] In line with typical Jewish practices, Paul includes two envoys in this delegation,[80] with Titus as the obvious leader. The identity of these envoys, who are only identified as 'brothers', has sparked much debate and speculation. In spite of the various solutions offered in this regard,[81] we are only left with a short description of their Christian virtues, which qualified them for this task.

The first brother is a person of high reputation (ἔπαινος). He is well known and respected in all the Pauline communities (διὰ πασῶν τῶν ἐκκλησιῶν) for his commitment to the principles of the gospel (ἐν τῷ εὐαγγελίῳ - v. 18).[82] Moreover, he is an officially elected representative of these churches as one of Paul's travelling companions (συνέκδημος - v. 19). As to how these procedures took place, we are left in the dark. Was this brother appointed by more than one Christian community? Did it take place through a 'democratic' show of hands, as χειροτονεῖν (when taken literally) seems to imply? Did the Pauline communities expect of their apostle to take this brother along in order to ensure the integrity of their own participation in the collection? Or did Paul request of them to send one of their officially appointed envoys to Corinth to help him solve the problems there? Although we do not have any clear-cut answers to these

---

[79] It is not so easy to determine whether the first person plural in verses 19-22 is inclusive of Paul, his helpers, and all his communities, or whether it refers to Paul and his helpers, or only to Paul. In verses 18 and 22, where the verb συνεπέμψαμεν is repeated, Paul undoubtedly has himself in mind, since only he possessed the necessary authority within the realm of his churches to send out delegates on important missions of this nature. Apparently Paul is also the subject in verses 20-21 (the plural thus functions as a literary plural). However, on the rhetorical level of the text, Paul deliberately uses the first person plural in an ambiguous manner so as to also include his helpers and all the Pauline communities (also the intended readers) within his collection effort.

[80] See Klauck, *2. Korintherbrief*, 70-71.

[81] Hughes, *Paul and the Second Epistle to the Corinthians*, 312-316, offers an informative discussion of the various solutions presented in this regard.

[82] Contra Jager, *De Tweede Brief aan die Korinthiers*, 158, Paul does not explicitly say that this brother was involved in the proclamation of the gospel (although the possibility that he could have been involved in such activities should not be discarded). At most Paul wants to emphasise the integrity of this brother when it came to the heart of the Christian life: his loyalties to the gospel was well-known within the orbit of Paul's communities.

questions, we may deduce from the remarks in verse 18(ff.) that Paul did not only change his authoritarian rhetorical style after the negative reception of 1 Corinthians 16,1-4, but also his organisational strategies. Over against his earlier optimism that he himself could unilaterally conduct matters in terms of the completion of the collection in Corinth (cf. 1 Cor 16,4), he now had to turn for assistance to his communities that had already successfully completed their efforts. Obviously, due to ideological- and 'security' reasons, Paul did not plan to take the collection to Jerusalem all by himself (cf. 1 Cor 16,4).[83] But these envoys were probably not included in all the local collection efforts up till the Corinthian crisis. The untimely problems in Corinth caused Paul to adjust his own strategies by requesting the presence of two of the well-known envoys from other communities to help see matters through.

In his commendation of the first brother, Paul emphasises that this person's presence will ensure that the collection (χάρις), which is administered by Paul (and his communities), will accomplish the following functions:

(a) It will show the glory of the Lord (πρὸς τὴν τοῦ κυρίου δόξαν).[84] The religious nature of this undertaking as a means to giving expression to the believers' gratitude for all the benefits from the Lord (that is, Christ), is once more explicitly underlined (cf. Chapter 4).

(b) The collection will reflect the goodwill (προθυμία) of Paul, but also the goodwill of all his communities, including the Corinthians. The concrete steps taken by the apostle to ensure that no further suspicions would be levelled against him, would thus not only secure his own honour, but also that of his communities. In the end, it was also their collection, their repayment of their debt of gratitude to the Lord and to Jerusalem. Therefore, their honour would also be compromised if their apostle's integrity was brought into disrepute. Hence Paul's statement that he, and all those involved in the collection, took particular care not to give any cause to anybody to point a finger in terms of the supervision of this large sum (cf.

---

[83] Murphy-O'Connor, *Paul - A Critical Life*, 345, points to the dangers involved in transporting large amounts of money in antiquity. Although we do not know how much money Paul collected, it was probably a significant amount, as he indicates in verse 20. Therefore, in order to ensure the safety of this money, Paul commanded the assistance of companions to escort him to Jerusalem. At the same time the very presence of these envoys in the Holy City would function as visible proof of the effectiveness of Paul's Law-free mission (cf. Chapter 6).

[84] Αὐτοῦ is omitted in the most important manuscripts: B C D*F G L, etc. In spite of the suggestion of Barrett, *A Commentary on the Second Epistle to the Corinthians*, 217, n.2, that the inclusion of αὐτοῦ would present us with a more difficult reading, and therefore more likely with the correct text, the external evidence outweighs his arguments.

the *hapax legomena*: ἀδροτής) that is being administered by them (v. 20).[85]

The commendation of the second brother follows in verse 22. Although nothing is said about his appointment by any Christian community, Paul (v. 23) does include him between the ἀπόστολοι ἐκκλησιῶν, which indicates a link of sorts with one of the communities within Paul's sphere of influence. The fact that he is referred to as τὸν ἀδελφὸν ἡμῶν also indicates his close ties with Paul. It could be that the apostle personally requested this person's services in the Corinthian collection attempt, while the churches officially appointed the other brother.[86] Although this person's identity is also shrouded in mystery, his moral virtues, which qualify him to be included in the 'apostolic trio' together with Titus and the other renowned brother, is mentioned: His zeal has often been tested by Paul in various situations (in terms of the administration of funds?), and he had passed these tests with flying colours.

In summary: In 2 Corinthians 8,8-22 Paul commends the two brothers who are to form the delegation tasked with completing the collection in Corinth because of their involvement in the gospel (v. 18), and their trustworthiness and zeal (v. 22). The presence of the first brother, in particular, would assure that the religious aims of the collection are met, namely to honour Christ, as well as to confirm the goodwill and integrity of Paul and all other persons involved in this project. Paul takes particular care to emphasise his own moral integrity in this regard, in order to elicit the sympathy of his readers within the intra-textual discourse, but also to make it clear that he did not act in opposition to the norms and expectations of other believers and God.

---

[85] In this way Paul draws a sharp distinction between himself and the religious charlatans who were active in the Roman world, but also to counter the defamatory stories in Corinth that he embezzled the collection funds.

[86] See in this regard Betz, *2 Corinthians 8 & 9*, 78. The fact that Paul is less cautious and more personal in his commendation of the second brother could also indicate a good relationship between them. It could well be that he was one of the Macedonians who assisted Paul financially (cf. e.g. 2 Cor 12,9). This seems all the more probable in the view of Paul's remarks in 9,2 where he refers to his earlier boasting about the readiness of the Corinthians to the Macedonians, and then, directly afterwards in 9,3, refers to the arrival of these brothers in Corinth. It would not make much sense to emphasise his boasting to the Macedonians about Corinth's willingness if a Macedonian delegate was not included between these brothers. On the other hand, we could also speculate whether the first renowned brother did not belong to the Galatian churches, which by this time have successfully completed their collection effort and had already appointed their envoys to take the collection to Jerusalem. Due to the strained relations between them and Paul after the completion of their collection effort, the apostle reacted in a more formal manner in his commendation of their representative.

5.12.4. 2 Corinthians 8,23-24: The authorisation of the 'apostolic trio,' and Paul's appeal to the Corinthians

In verse 23a Paul, once again, switches to the first person singular when he commends Titus apart from the other brothers as his partner and co-worker.[87] As an esteemed partner, Titus was to play a key role in the successful completion of the collection. The two 'apostles' of the Pauline churches were to accompany him. Here we have an

> ... etwas anderen Apostolatsbegriff als den bei Paulus gewohnten. Apostel ist in dieser Konzeption jeder Gesandte, der auf Weisung einer Gemeinde mit bestimmten Aufträgen unterwegs ist.[88]

They are further designated by the title: δόξα χριστοῦ. Because of their faithfulness to their appointment by their communities, and their dispatch to Corinth by Paul, they thus also reflected the glory of the resurrected Christ.

On the basis of the Paul's reconfirmation of the integrity of the apostolic trio, he requests of the Corinthians to respond appropriately by receiving them in love (v. 24). In this way, they would take the first concrete steps in giving expression to Paul's earlier appeal to them to make their love visible by becoming involved in the collection once more (8,8). In preparation for the next theme (cf. 9,1ff.), Paul adds another thrust to his appeal by stating that the reception of these envoys in Corinth should correspond to his own fatherly boasting about them in the other Pauline communities. The reputation of the Corinthians within the new family of God is thus on the line. If they do not respond in an appropriate manner to Paul's request, they would bring shame upon themselves and on their spiritual father.

5.13. 2 Corinthians 9,1-5: Motivation for the sending of the delegation to Corinth

5.13.1. Overview of the structure

In spite of the views of a number of scholars that the diction of 9,1 points to the beginning of a new letter,[89] we actually have a *"Wiederaufnahme des Hauptthemas nach dem exkursartigen Stück über die Boten,"*[90] in verse

---

[87] See Ollrog, *Paulus und seine Mitarbeiter*, 77.

[88] Klauck, *2. Korintherbrief*, 71.

[89] So e.g., Georgi, *Der Armen zu gedenken*, 50-51, and Héring, *The Second Epistle of St. Paul to the Corinthians*, 65.

[90] Klauck, *2. Korintherbrief*, 1986, 72. See also Dahl, *Studies in Paul*, 39.

9,1ff, while Paul also builds upon the remark in 8,24 concerning his own pride in the Corinthians. In this new section (9,1-5), dominated by Paul's fatherly boasting about the Corinthians' goodwill, the implied readers are drawn into an *agonistic situation* once more. In verse 2, where Paul motivates his introductory statement in 9,1, the readiness of the Corinthians to contribute to the collection is presented as the basis for his boasting.[91] In verse 3, he refers to his dispatching of the 'apostolic trio' to Corinth to ensure that this boasting was not in vain. Paul's fears concerning the failure of the Corinthian collection effort, are *repeated* from a different perspective in verse 4 in his reference to his upcoming visit to Corinth in the company of some Macedonians (v. 4), before explains more fully the function of the delegation to Corinth (v. 5).

5.13.2. Paul's boasting

Through his use of the figure of *praeteritio* in 9,1,[92] Paul once again emphasises the spiritual maturity of his readers, on the surface structure of the text. His knowledge of their readiness to complete the collection (οἶδα γὰρ τὴν προθυμίαν ὑμῶν -v. 2a), provides the basis for his statement regarding his redundancy to write to them. But in spite of this remark, Paul persists with the topic of the collection in 9,2(ff.), because this willingness by the Corinthians has still not delivered the desired result. On the deep structure, the *praeteritio* in 9,1b thus functions as a forceful persuasive technique to impel the Corinthians to complete their service for the followers of Christ in Jerusalem (cf. the *terminus technicus* for the collection: διακονία εἰς τοὺς ἁγίους which is also used in 8,2 9,12; 1 Cor 16,15; Rom 15,25.31).[93]

Paul reiterates the willingness (προθυμία) of his readers towards the collection (9,2), which formed a vital part of his argument of proportionality in 8,10ff. But this time their willingness is placed within an *agonistic context* when Paul states that he boasted to the Macedonian believers (= their 'rivals' within this *agonistic* situation) about their eagerness to complete the collection during his earlier visit to Macedonia (cf. 2 Cor 1,15-16;

---

[91] Contra Bultmann, *Der zweite Brief an die Korinther*, 258, Paul's remark: περισσόν μοί ἐστιν τὸ γράφειν ὑμῖν, is not a surprise after everything he said concerning the collection in Chapter 8, since in 9,2a he explains the meaning of this expression.

[92] According to Klauck, *2. Korintherbrief*, 72, Paul, with his use of this figure: "... gibt vor, das Thema bestenfalls zu streifen, schafft sich dadurch aber tatsächlich die Ausgangsbasis für eine ausführlichere Behandlung."

[93] More correctly, as Paul has also indicated in the introduction to the *Letter of Reconciliation* (2 Cor 1,1), he has all the believers in the various house churches in the province of Achaia in mind (9,2c). Not merely those in the capital city, Corinth, but also those in places such as Cenchreae (cf. Rom 16,1), should be moved to become engaged in the collection once more.

2,13; 7,5ff.). Paul's fatherly pride about the initial readiness of the Corinthians thus served as a stimulus to the Macedonians, or at least to the majority of them (as τοὺς πλείονας indicates), to follow suit. He thus used the same *'agonistic* strategies' in Macedonia as employed here and in 8,1-5, although in reversed order, to persuade them to commit themselves to the collection. The zeal (τὸ ζῆλος) of the Corinthians was presented to the Macedonians, in order to challenge their loyalties to the common interests of their group. The result of Paul's persuasive strategies in Macedonia is, of course, well known.

The completion of the Macedonian collection has left Paul with a potentially embarrassing situation: If the Corinthians refused to commit themselves to the collection, it would imply that he had exaggerated, if not actually twisted the truth in his boasting about their readiness.[94] If it were to become clear that his boasting was in vain in this matter (v. 3), his patriarchal integrity ('telling the truth'), as well as that of his readers ('living up to their promises'), would be seriously compromised within the orbit of the Pauline communities. Therefore, Paul underlines the task of the delegation to Corinth in order to avert the triggering of the chain of negative events envisioned in verses 3b-4.

Paul anticipates a third visit by himself to Corinth in the presence of Macedonian delegates *en route* to Jerusalem to finally deliver the collection funds (cf. v.4). He restates his fears about the Corinthian collection, but in a somewhat different manner than in verse 3. Anticipating the scenario in the event of the failure of the 'apostolic trio's' mission, Paul now refers to the humiliation of himself (cf. the use of the first person plural in verses 3-4) and the readers if the Macedonian delegation were to show up in Corinth, only to find the Corinthians unprepared.[95] It would be a sad reflection of their highly acclaimed spiritual attributes, as well as of Paul's public reputation (and his ability to build churches).

After the strong challenge to the Corinthians' honour in view of the impending visit of the brothers, and soon afterwards, that of himself and Macedonians, Paul once more elaborates on the task of the first delegation (v. 5). It would be their duty to help prepare the Corinthian 'gift/blessing' (εὐλογία) for Jerusalem which they had pledged in advance (προαγγέλλ-

---

[94] Harvey, *Renewal through Suffering*, 88, carefully states: "... there may be a little rhetorical exaggeration here. But Paul almost seems to concede this when he expresses his anxiety that they may turn out in the event to have been 'unprepared'...."

[95] Because of its wide spectrum of possible meanings, the term ὑπόστασις (cf. the expression: ἐν τῇ ὑποστάσει ταύτῃ), is difficult to translate. E.g., Héring, *Second Epistle of St. Paul to the Corinthians*, 66, translates it as "in this eventuality". But it makes better sense to understand it in its 'classical sense' as a plan or a project, referring specifically to the collection - so, e.g., Wolff, *Der zweite Brief des Paulus an die Korinther*, 182.

ομαι).⁹⁶ To ensure that the true nature of the collection was served, the 'apostolic trio' had to see to it that the Corinthians took up their role as grateful beneficiaries in their relationship with Jerusalem once more.⁹⁷ Obviously the most important sign of gratitude within any social exchange relationship of this nature was to pay one's debts to one's benefactors.⁹⁸

In order to alleviate the external pressure on his readers, Paul makes it clear that the delegation would not place any unrealistic demands on them. They would only ensure that the gift of love from Corinth would be completed for the right reasons, namely to show their gratitude for the spiritual benefits they had received from Jerusalem, and not because it was unilaterally demanded from them by Paul. As a matter of fact, the Corinthians only had to live up to their earlier promises.

In summary: Well-aware of the serious threat that the Corinthians' 'ingratitude' held for their own, as well as for his own moral integrity within the early Christian movement, Paul (2 Cor 9,1-5) creates an agonistic situation again to persuade them to become involved in the collection. His boasting to the Macedonians about the Corinthians' (vv. 2-4) serves as a particularly effective rhetorical tool to intensify the intra-textual 'rivalry' between the readers and the Macedonians. Paul attains a 'heightened *agonistic* effect' by referring to the positive response of the Macedonians to the Corinthian προθυμία. If their own willingness and zeal could prompt the Macedonians to contribute beyond their own means to the collection, the former would have no other option than to complete their good intentions of more than a year previous.

---

⁹⁶ According to Harvey, *Renewal through Suffering*, 89, εὐλογία should be understood as a thanksoffering made in response to benefits received. Following Dunn, *The Theology of Paul the Apostle*, 711, Paul wants the Corinthians to see the collection as an act of generosity, not as an act of extortion.

⁹⁷ Paul deliberately emphasises the contrast between εὐλογία and πλεονεξία: Whereas the latter points to the "... spirit of a selfish, greedy person who gives only because he is forced to do so" - Bratcher, *A Translator's Guide to Paul's Second Letter to the Corinthians*, London, 97f., εὐλογία in turn points to a gift which carries with itself a certain blessing.

⁹⁸ In Seneca's view the reluctance of debtors to return benefits is the greatest sin, and the most common of all the vices (*Ben.* I.1.2, 13).

5.14. 2 Corinthians 9,6-10: God's gracious gifts lead to generosity

5.14.1. Overview of the structure

As a subsection of 2 Corinthians 9,6-15, which deals with God's conferral of gifts and the effects thereof on the lives of the recipients (cf. Chapter 4), Paul metaphorically applies *agrarian imagery* to give expression to God's abundant χάρις in the lives of the Corinthians in verses. 6-10. In an admonition to the readers (v. 7), which is introduced through two parallel structured lines (v. 6), Paul in vv. 6-7 deals with the principle of sowing and reaping. He relates this *'Bauernregel'* to the inner attitude of the givers (v. 7), and to God's reaction to those who display the right attitude to possessions (vv. 7-8). Hereafter, Paul's understanding of the relationship between God's encompassing gifts and their results in the lives of the recipients, in terms of the principle of αὐταρκεία (v. 8), is sanctioned by means of a quotation from Scripture (v. 9). Agrarian imagery is applied in verse 10, in order to explain the nature of God's involvement in the Corinthians' sharing of material and spiritual gifts with others.

5.14.2. The metaphorical use of agrarian imagery

Agrarian imagery, which is applied in verses 6-10 in relation to the collection, was frequently used in ancient Israelite society.[99] In the Graeco-Roman world agrarian imagery was also well known.[100] As a matter of fact, the wide range of texts from the various ancient Mediterranean cultures that deal with agricultural imagery in the form of proverbs, adages, religious rites, folk wisdom, the household economy and religion, point to the existence of a supra-cultural 'agrarian ideology' that formed part of the majority of Mediterranean people's 'common sense' knowedge.

It is not surprising that agrarian imagery permeated all facets of ancient social reality, since

> ... die Landwirtschaft hatte im Römischen Reich wirtschaftlich eine Vorrangstellung.
> ... Die große Mehrheit der Bevölkerung arbeitete in der Landwirtschaft.[101]

A complex of secondary reflection on agrarian imagery in ancient philosophical and religious circles was therefore to be expected.[102] Paul also

---

[99] "Die Erfahrung göttlichen Segens ist in der Bibel oft an das Geschehen von Aussaat und Ernte gebunden" - Klauck, *2. Korintherbrief*, 73. More specifically: the idea that one must reap whatever one has sown, formed one of the axioms of Jewish wisdom tradition (cf. e.g., Ps 126,5; Prov 11,21.24.26.30; 22,8; Job 4,8; Sir 7,3).

[100] Cf. Betz, *2 Corinthians 8 & 9*, 98.

[101] Stegemann & Stegemann, *Urchristliche Sozialgeschichte*, 30.

drew from this pre-Christian (and pre-Jewish) ideological complex with its principal component, the emphasis on the religious aspect of sowing and reaping (cf. Gal 6,7b-8). For his Corinthian readers this agrarian image was also well known, since roughly 207 square kilometres of the *territorium* of the city-state of Corinth supported different forms of agriculture in Paul's time. Although Corinth was not a typical 'agro-city' whose economy was based on urban farmers commuting to their fields and back, around 8,000 inhabitants of the city at this time were directly supported by agricultural production.[103]

In the first of the two chiastically constructed, parallel lines in verse 6, introduced by an elliptic citation formula (τοῦτο δέ), Paul applies a well-known 'Bauernregel'[104] with regard to the collection, by emphasising that sparse sowing yields a small harvest. The opposite idea is expressed in the second chiasm, which is added to this rule in order to create a maxim: Generous sowing leads to a generous harvest. Here the adverbial phrase, ἐπ' εὐλογίας, emphasises the bounty that goes hand in hand with a good harvest. In terms of the collection (as εὐλογία) it implies that a gift, which is freely and spontaneously bestowed, constitutes a blessing to the recipients.

In his role as the mild father figure, Paul refrains from prescribing any specific amount to be donated to the collection by the Corinthians. It is for each person to sow as he sees fit (v. 7ab). Giving is a matter of personal conviction. One's heart, as the centre of all thought and emotions, and the working place of the Spirit (cf. Gal 4,6; 2 Cor 3,2-3; Rom 5,5) should determine the size of one's material response. This emphasis on the correct moral resolution by the givers (v. 7), could be taken either as a 'rectification' of the maxim in verse 6, which might have left the readers with the impression that there is a direct causal relationship between giving and receiving, or as a further clarification of the nature of the blessings involved in the 'correct way of giving'. Perhaps the latter view would come the closest to Paul's aims (v. 7a-b) where he deliberately shifts the emphasis away from the size of the Corinthians' contributions to their inner orientation. Two principles are laid down here to ensure the correct disposition on their part: They must not give grudgingly (μὴ ἐκ λύπης), or

---

[102] Betz, *2 Corinthians 8 & 9*, 98-99, traces this 'agrarian theology' back to ancient Greek sources (such as Hesiod), and also points to the impact thereof on Hellenistic-Jewish literature.

[103] Engels, *Roman Corinth*, 27ff. states that, although the *territorium* of the city-state of Corinth was around 825 square kilometres, only about 207 square kilometre was capable of supporting any kind of agriculture. Due to the problem of distance from the city (and the time factor involved), agriculture was not the main source of income of the city, but rather its manufactures and its service economy.

[104] So Windisch, *Der zweite Korinthebrief*, 276.

give under constraint for fear of censure (ἐξ ἀνάγκης). Just as Seneca (cf. *Ben.* II.1.1ff.), Paul once again stresses the right attitude that should be exhibited by the givers. In other words, the contributions of the Corinthians should be spontaneous. They should not be miserly in their yield to Paul's coaxing by being manipulated into an undertaking, without the corresponding inner commitment on their part.[105]

To provide the necessary sanction for these principles, Paul (v. 7c) alludes to Proverbs 22,8 (LXX), which states that God loves a cheerful giver. This typical Jewish idea of God's approval of the person who gives from the correct inner orientation, provides support for Paul's view of the direct involvement of God in the reciprocal relationship between the Corinthians and Jerusalem. To give grudgingly would not only throw a shadow of doubt over their relationship with Jerusalem, but it would also reflect badly on their own gratefulness for God's eschatological benefits to them.

Paul changes the perspective in verse 8 by applying the principle of sowing and reaping to God's χάρις and its effects on the moral life (and contributions) of the Corinthians. "Hatte er bisher aus der Sicht der Spender gesprochen, so richtet er nun den Blick auf Gott, den Geber aller Gaben. Damit expliziert er, was im Begriff der εὐλογία angelegt ist."[106] The same God who loves cheerful givers, is also the powerful God (δυνατεῖ δὲ ὁ θεὸς) who is in the position to richly endow the Corinthians with the fullness of his grace.

The result of the active χάρις of God in the lives of the Corinthians is αὐτάρκεια, self-sufficiency (cf. also Phil 4,11-13). This concept, which played such an important role in Stoic thought (in terms of the ideal of inward contentment which in turn leads to material and spiritual independence from others), is now applied to the Corinthian collection attempt. But αὐτάρκεια does not bear its full technical meaning here, as elsewhere in Hellenistic philosophy. Although Paul latches on to the popular understanding of αὐτάρκεια within his society, he, at the same time, fills this provocative term with new meaning: According to him the divine χάρις *always* (πάντοτε) provides *in all* the Corinthians' needs (ἐν παντί), both materially and spiritually. As a matter of fact, his grace is not merely sufficient, it is abundant and inexhaustible, thus enabling the Corinthians to actually to excel (περισσεύειν) in all good works. The αὐτάρκεια that

---

[105] Here Paul's principles actually turn against themselves, on the rhetorical level of the text. Although he explicitly emphasises the inner moral freedom of the Corinthians, this very principle places further pressure on the them to complete the collection. Should they refuse to participate in the collection, they would be brought to shame within the orbit of the Christian communities. But, on the other hand, should they participate, they would be left with no other moral option than to do it 'out of their own free choice' and with cheerful hearts.

[106] Theobald, *Die überströmende Gnade*, 293.

is experienced by them as a result of this divine grace, does not lead to their total independence from others in terms of their financial and spiritual needs. Paul rather implies that God's *χάρις* provides them with enough resources in all areas of their life in order to use it to the advantage of fellow believers.

The Corinthians cannot selfishly keep God's riches to themselves; they must let it 'flow' to others through their good works, by which Paul obviously has the collection in mind. The message to the readers is clear: They once more need to become fully aware of the nature of God's blessings in their lives in order to turn into grateful beneficiaries who would joyfully adhere to the principles laid down in verse 7.

By way of a typical citation formula (καθὼς γέγραπται), Paul quotes from Psalm 111,9 (LXX) in vv. 6-10, in order to lend Scriptural support to his view that the person who has experienced God's goodness freely shares his material possessions with the needy.[107] By 'sowing' his possessions lavishly (σκορπίζειν) in the fertile ground of people's lives who are in need of his 'material αὐτάρκεια', the righteous person is the embodiment of the agrarian maxim according to this citation in verse 6.[108] But at the same time, he also lives up to God's ideal of the 'model giver' (v. 7c), since his δικαιοσύνη leads to ceaseless deeds of lovingkindness towards others.

As an integral part of Paul's strategy to persuade his readers by means of the use of agrarian imagery and quotations from, and allusions to Scripture in this section, the utilisation of Psalm 111,9 conveys the message to the readers that they should constantly open their hearts and pockets to those less fortunate than themselves. As a matter of fact, πάντοτε in verse 8 (related to αὐτάρκεια of the objects of God's grace) is affirmed by the Scriptural citation in verse 9, that true righteousness in the life of the faithful remains forever. Therefore, the Corinthians have no legitimate excuse not to complete their collection project. As people who, according to Paul's own public testimony, partake of God's abundant grace, they

---

[107] Scholars are divided as to the subject of the 'scattering' in verse 9: God or the righteous man? Without getting involved in all the arguments in this regard (cf. the useful overview of the various options by Furnish, *2 Corinthians*, 448f.), the fact that: (a) Ps 111,9 refers not to God but to the righteous man who engages in deeds of righteousness or almsgiving; (b) the logical link between 2 Corinthians 9,6; 7b; 8 (and 9) in terms of the cheerful giver who is prepared to generously 'sow' in order to reap a generous harvest of blessing; (c) the repetition of the idea of permanence in terms of the effects of God's grace in verses 8 and 9, and (d) the reference to δικαιοσύνη in verses 9 and 10 (with the believers clearly as the objects in the latter verse), we may conclude that Paul has the recipients of God's grace in mind in v. 9. .

[108] See also Wilk, *Die Bedeutung des Jesajabuches für Paulus*, 335.

must give expression to his consistent work in their lives through contributing generously to the collection for the poor.

In order to assure the readers that they do not have to fear any hardship for themselves after the indirect, but very real, pressure on them to contribute, as read in verses 6-9, Paul (v. 10) makes explicit use of agrarian imagery. By drawing some words and phrases from the prophetic texts of Isaiah 55,10 ("seed for the sower and bread for food") and Hosea 17,18 ("the fruits of your righteousness"), he applies the examples of God's provision for the needs of those in the horticultural sphere of activity to the situation of the Corinthians. They are assured that the very same God, who ensures that the farmers have seed to sow and that there is daily bread on their tables, will also provide them with 'seed' (that is, with the necessary material means). As a result, they will have enough to share with their poor fellow believers in Jerusalem. When they begin to use their possessions in this way, they will actually experience a big harvest in return (πληθυνεῖ τὸν σπόρον ὑμῶν), which will enable them to have even more 'seed' to sow in the lives of others in need. Multiplicity is thus the key. By giving generously and cheerfully, believers will, according to Paul, experience the miracle, due to God's grace in their lives, that they actually would have even more to give in future.

In line with his understanding of the collection as a three-way reciprocal relationship between the Corinthians (as a *pars pro toto* for the Pauline communities), Jerusalem, and God, Paul also states that the fruit of the Corinthians' righteousness will grow. In other words, by doing what God expects of them, they will not only experience αὐτάρκεια on a material level, but also in terms with their relationship with God. Giving money to those in need is not an inferior spiritual undertaking. It forms part of an encompassing involvement in the lives of others. But more importantly, through the sharing of their possessions, they are actually giving to God as the indirect object of their benefactions, who in turn will reciprocate in an encompassing way.

In summary: God takes care of all the needs of cheerful and generous givers, both materially and spiritually. This is the message to the Corinthians in 2 Corinthians 9,6-10. In order to address their concerns that a large contribution may entail economic hardship for them, Paul, by means of the use of agrarian imagery, makes it evident that God's abundant χάρις in their lives will provide them with the necessary means, that they would always experience αὐτάρκεια. Therefore, they will have sufficient means to sow liberally (which also means cheerfully and freely) in the lives of the needy believers in Jerusalem in full confidence that God will bestow a liberal harvest.

5.15. Conclusion

5.15.1. Paul's persuasive strategies and the collection in the Corinthian correspondence

1 Corinthians 16,1-4 presents us with the picture of an authoritative apostle who unilaterally takes charge of the organisation of all aspects of the collection, from its conceptualisation to its eventual delivery in Jerusalem. Until writing 1 Corinthians, this strategy of Paul apparently delivered the desired results, as his reference to the Galatian collection effort (1 Cor 16,1) illustrates. But, due to the negative reception of 1 Corinthians and the intrusion of outsiders in Corinth with a different gospel, their collection effort drew to an abrupt halt. This serious threat to the success of the collection from the Corinthians, as one of the potentially major contributors to this project, is masterfully handled by Paul in 2 Corinthians 8-9. As a matter of fact, these chapters reveal Paul at his best "... in terms of religious leadership. His consummate skill in the art of persuasion underlines how much he has matured in a single year."[109]

Paul's basic textual strategy in 2 Corinthians 8-9, which involves the assignment of new roles to the interlocutors, serves to anti-structurally bridge the hierarchical gap between him (as the mild patriarchal figure) and the Corinthians (as his spiritually mature children) within the intra-textual discourse. Within this more intimate discourse situation, in which he still maintains the superior position, Paul creates a deliberate *agonistic situation* at the beginning of the *topos* of the collection by an elaborate description of the Macedonian collection attempt (8,1-6). Pressure is placed on the Corinthians to outdo them right from the start. This rivalry is continued into the second section (2 Cor 8,7-9), where the ἀγάπη of the Corinthians is tested against the σπουδή of the Macedonians. In the rest of 2 Corinthians 8, Paul replaces the *agonistic* rivalry between the readers and Macedonia with a discussion of the principle of *proportionality*. This principle is related to the contributions of the Corinthians and the expected return-gifts within the framework of the reciprocal relationship between them and Jerusalem (8,10-15). Titus is also commended, as well as the two brothers who are underway to Corinth to complete the collection (2 Cor 8,16-24). However, in 2 Corinthians 9,1-5 the intra-textual *agonistic* rivalry between the readers and the Macedonians surfaces again when the initial goodwill of the Corinthians is presented as the reason for the successful Macedonian collection. This is followed by a discussion of the results of the grace of God in the lives of its recipients (2 Cor 9,10-15).

---

[109] Murphy-O'Connor, *Paul - A Critical Life*, 314.

In both 2 Corinthians 8 and 2 Corinthians 9 the same basic themes are present, although there is evident development in Paul's argument from Chapter 8 to Chapter 9:

(a) In the first sections of each chapter the readers are drawn into an *agonistic* rivalry of love between themselves and the Macedonians (cf. 2 Cor 8,1-6; 7-9, and 2 Cor 9,1-5).

(b) In the following sections the *fears* of the readers, that their contribution might place them in a financially precarious position, are addressed (cf. 2 Cor 8,11-15; 2 Cor 9,6-15).

Regarding the progression in terms of Paul's argument from 2 Corinthians 8-9, it is clear that, whereas the readers are not addressed in the first *agonistic* section (2 Cor 8,1-6), they are explicitly drawn into the argument in 2 Corinthians 9,1-5. At the same time the 'direction' of the rivalry is reversed in Chapter 9. In 2 Corinthians 8,1-6, the *exemplum* of the Macedonian collection serves to create the necessary intra-textual competition, whereas in 2 Corinthians 9,1-5 the initial προθυμία of Corinth serves as a trigger for the successful Macedonian collection (which rhetorically functions as a forceful leverage to coax the Corinthians into the collection so as to save their own honour).

Paul is not only interested in involving the Corinthians in the collection again, but also to elicit a *large contribution* from them. This is clear from:

(a) Paul's discussion of the generous attempt by the Macedonians, in spite of their abysmal poverty (8,3-4);

(b) the reference to the big gift (ἁδρότης) from the various communities that is presently ministered by Paul and his helpers (8,20);

(c) the emphasis on the generous contributions from the righteous (9,6-10), and the prayer of thanksgiving from Jerusalem for the liberal donation from Corinth (9,13).

All these examples point to the fact that an insignificant contribution would not suffice (cf. also 1 Cor 16,1-4). Constant *pressure* is therefore applied on the readers to live up to Paul's aim of a substantial collection by, amongst others: the use of the *exempla* of Macedonia (8,1-5) and Christ (8,9); the emphasis of the same presence of God's χάρις in their own lives that inspired the Macedonians to complete the collection (cf. 8,1; 9,8); Paul's stressing of his fatherly love for, and boasting about them (8,7; 9,2-4); the positive attitude of Titus and the brothers towards them (8,16-24); the upcoming visit of Paul and the Macedonians to Corinth (9,4), and the expected positive response of Jerusalem to the collection (9,11-14).

Well-aware of the constant pressure that is applied to the implied readers within the course of the intimate intra-textual collection discourse, Paul also *explicitly* addresses their fears that their contribution would place them in a financial predicament (8,11-15; 9,6-15). In terms of the readers' fears, there is also a development in Paul's argument. In 8,10-15 he reassures the Corinthians by stating that they should only contribute to the collection in accordance to their possessions, while he also uses the principle of ἰσότης to explain that, within the parameters of the reciprocal relationship with Jerusalem, they do not have anything to fear. Just as they are now addressing Jerusalem's needs, the latter will in future address any spiritual needs that they might have. In 9,6-15, however, the readers are drawn into the sphere of God's encompassing gifts, which will lead to material (and spiritual) αὐτάρκεια. In other words, God's active grace in their lives will provide them with the necessary means to contribute generously to the collection. Paul's emphasis thus shifts from the two-way reciprocal interchange between Corinth and Jerusalem in Chapter 8, to the three-way relationship between these groups and God in Chapter 9.

The intra-textual progression in terms of Paul's arguments is not only limited to the agonistic rivalry between the Corinthians and the Macedonians, or to the readers' fears, but also to the ideological position of the intended readers. While Paul explicitly admonishes them to become involved in the collection again at the beginning of the collection discourse (cf. e.g., 8,7; 11), the emphasis at the end of the discourse shifts to the successful completion of the Corinthian collection attempt, and to the positive response from Jerusalem (9,11-14). Paul thus supposes that the ideological distance between himself and the intended readers has been successfully bridged in the course of 2 Corinthians 8 and 9.

During the intra-textual discourse in chapter 8-9, the Corinthian readers changed from people with abundant spiritual gifts (8,7) and προθυμία (9,2), but who, alas, still did not complete the collection, to people who (will) give clear proof of their faithful submission to the gospel of Christ (9,13) by fulfilling their beneficial duties towards Jerusalem. Therefore Paul closes this successful intra-textual discourse in 9,15 with a fitting doxology that forms an *inclusio* together with 8,1.

5.15.2. Theological conceptualisation of the collection in 2 Corinthians 8-9

In 2 Corinthians 8-9 we obtain a glimpse into Paul's conceptualisation of the collection within the sphere of his own communities. Although we do not possess any information on his strategies and theological conceptualisations of the collection in the Christian communities in Galatia and Macedonia (and Asia?), we may assume that Paul went about it in more or less the same manner as he did here in 2 Corinthians 8-9. His indication that he used the same organisational strategies in Galatia (1 Cor 16,1), as well as the same persuasive strategies in Macedonia (2 Cor 9,2), substantiates this understanding.

The framework of benefit exchange formed the basis of Paul's theological reflections. According to Paul the collection formed part of a three-way reciprocal relationship between God, the various believing communities under his supervision, and Jerusalem. Within this relationship the collection functioned as the Pauline communities' repayment of their debt of gratitude to God. At the same time, the collection also served as a sign of their gratitude for the spiritual benefits which they received from the church in Jerusalem, who in turn, would soon reciprocate with the necessary bestowals of honour.

Paul superimposes the basic interpretative framework of the collection with various theological meanings as part of his ideological reflection on this project. In this regard, the *active χάρις of God* forms the key concept to explain the nature of God's presence within the Pauline communities, as well as the impact of his presence on the successful completion of the collection. According to Paul, God's grace is present in an overwhelming way in the lives of believers (cf. the use of περισσεύειν in 8,2.8,7ab; 9,8.12). The same grace that moved the Macedonians to such great heights (8,1) is also active under the Corinthians (8,7.9). God's grace provides abundantly in all the needs of its recipients, both on material and spiritual levels (9,8). The active presence of this divine grace leads to spiritual wealth (πλουτεῖν - 8,9; 9,11) and to αὐτάρκεια, the latter two enable the recipients to become involved in activities which address the wellbeing of fellow believers (9,8).

When believers become aware of, and open their lives to God's power, they selflessly sacrifice their own material means for the sake of others, as the exemplary behaviour of the Macedonians (8,1-5) makes clear. As a matter of fact, their wealth consists in generously assisting those who are in need (9,11). In the words of Theobald: "Dieses 'Überströmen' (of God's grace - SJ) bezeichnet das Aufbrechen eines inneren Reichtums, der nach außen drängt und mit Macht seinen sichtbaren Ausdruck sucht."[110] This implies the beginning of a situation of assistance, sharing and harmony between believers that is nothing less than the eschatological fulfilment of the words of Scripture (8,15). The positive response of the Judean recipients of these benefactions (prayers of thanksgiving) in turn leads to an increase in God's honour (9,12). At the same time, due to the recipients' intercession for their helpers, the latter's lives are even further enriched by God's grace (9,14). According to Paul, the bestowal of God's grace thus sets a chain of positive events in motion in the lives of the recipients, and in all those who are assisted by them, which eventually also increases God's own glory and honour.

---

[110] Theobald, *Die überströmende Gnade*, 302.

God's grace is further explained by the χάρις τοῦ χριστοῦ, who sacrificed his own heavenly glory so that those believers may overflow in spiritual wealth (8,9). Within this new sphere, encompassed by the grace of God and Christ, believers cannot but become involved in activities that would increase God's glory and address other believers' needs. As a matter of fact, the effect of God's grace creates the necessary προθυμία (8,11.12.19; 9,2), σπουδή (cf. 8,7.8.16), and ἀγάπη (8,8.24) in the recipients that leads to deeds of righteousness towards others (9,9). Stated differently: God's 'sowing' in the lives of believers produces a generous harvest, since it changes the recipients from self-centred individuals, who are only inter-ested in securing their own welfare, to people who do not hesitate to part joyfully from their material means for the common good of others (8,2-3; 9,7).

In view of Paul's emphasis on the grace of God, it is not surprising that he also refers to the collection as χάρις (cf. 8,6.7.19): a gracious service. The recipients of God's abundant χάρις cannot but participate in a project that will 'overflow' through the extension and mediation of his grace to fellow believers. This is accentuated through another technical term for the collection: διακονία (8,4; 9,1.12.13), which gives expression to the nature of this undertaking as a selfless service from the Pauline communities that is intended to bring financial relief to Jerusalem. As a concrete expression of the instructions of the earthly Jesus concerning true greatness within the circle of his followers (cf. Mk 10,42-45), the collection as διακονία in turn shifts the emphasis from the self-interests of the Corinthians to the needs of their fellow believers.

Even stronger emphasis is placed on the sacrificial nature of the collection in Paul's use of the term λειτουργία in 9,12. Here the collection is given a cultic understanding as a spiritual sacrifice from Paul and his communities to Jerusalem. The collection is not just a mere caritative project. As a spiritual gift, it also functions as a blessing to Jerusalem, as well as an act of worship. Yet another term for the collection: εὐλογία ('gift/blessing' - 9,5), also emphasises this point. In Paul's view, the collection will remove the material obstacles that hinder the church in Jerusalem from being fully effective in God's service. It would enable them to fulfil their spiritual role as intercessors for Paul's various believing communities.

For Paul, the collection was a benefit that functioned to repay his own and his communities' debt of gratitude. But, at the same time, it was an unique form of repayment within the parameters of a particular reciprocal relationship, since it was simultaneously the *result and the sign of God's active grace*. Since it was intended to be a blessing to Jerusalem, it had to be given freely and joyously. But did Jerusalem receive it in this spirit? This is the question we must now address in Chapter 6.

Chapter 6

Success and Failure? The Delivery of the Collection in Jerusalem

6.1. Success at last!

After years of organisation, planning, theological reflection and crisis management, Paul was finally ready to transport the collection to its final destination at the beginning of 57 CE: Jerusalem. This much is clear from Romans 15,25-26. The envisaged ceremonial delivery of the funds, and the anticipated positive response from the Jerusalem community (cf. 2 Cor 9,11-14) would be the culmination of many years of hard work for Paul. Old wounds would finally be healed in Jerusalem. Paul's Law-free mission would be reconfirmed, and his own position as apostle of the Gentiles and benefactor of Jerusalem would be publicly recognised. At the same time his communities (who were to be represented by their envoys) would also share in their apostle's moment of glory. Not only would the legitimacy of their position within the new eschatological people of God be acknowledged, but they would also be raised to the level of benefactors within the reciprocal relationship with Jerusalem.[1] At least, this is probably how Paul initially envisioned the delivery of the collection.

Ever since Paul took up the collection project during or about 52 CE in order to repay his 'debt of gratitude' towards Jerusalem, he conceptualised this project from various theological angles of incidence. In this process he elicited the co-operation of (all?) his communities in the collection. Although Paul (in Rom 15,26) only refers to the financial support from the Macedonians and Achaians, we may assume that the Galatians also completed their collection project successfully and probably also the Christian communities in Asia (and Roman Galatia?).

---

[1] Achtermeier, *Romans*, 230f., has a different view on the nature of the (reciprocal) relationship between Jerusalem and Paul's communities. He is of the opinion that the acceptance of the collection would imply that these two groups, who were mutually indebted to one another, would then be on equal footing.

In Acts 20,4 Luke refers to a number of (but definitely not all[2]) env-oys from Paul's communities who accompanied him during his 'collection journey' to Jerusalem, namely Sopater from Beroea, Aristarchus and Secundus from Thessalonica, Gaius from Derbe in Roman Galatia; Timothy (as Paul's junior colleague, not as a delegate of a local church[3]), and Tychicus and Trophimus from Asia. Although Luke's list is incomplete, it at least bears witness to the fact that the collection was successfully completed in most, if not in all the major centres of Paul's missionary activities.

Paul effectively addressed the numerous logistic and theological problems that he encountered in the course of the collection project. Even the stubborn Corinthians were eventually persuaded to take up their responsibilities regarding the collection once more, as Romans 15,26 indicates. Given the major obstacles that the apostle had to face in this process, such as a limited infrastructure and weak communication systems; large distances between his communities; animosity towards his message from the inhabitants of the Graeco-Roman cities, and various crises in his communities, the eventual completion of the collection was nothing less than remarkable. It served as a concrete proof of Paul's ability to effectively manage the communities under his supervision. Their obedience to his instructions regarding the collection reconfirmed his status as their apostle and spiritual father! At the same time the collection also gave visible expression to the κοινωνία, the bond of fellowship among the various Pauline communities. Neither the big distances between them, nor any cultural differences eventually stood in the way of an united effort to repay their common debt of gratitude to Jerusalem, and in this way address the financial plight of Jerusalem's poor.

Apart from the positive functions the completion of the collection fulfilled within the sphere of Paul's communities, it at the same time also served as the apostle's personal claim to honour. Paul's basis of power in the Christian communities in the Graeco-Roman world, which was now stronger than ever, would be publicly reconfirmed with Jerusalem's acceptance of the collection. At the same time, the initial expectations of the leadership of the Jerusalem church during the meeting with Paul during 48 CE (namely that he had access to the necessary sources to realise their request to take care for their poor) would also be validated.

The completion of the collection was nothing less than a personal victory for Paul. His own public position within his communities was once again as secure as it could be. The quarrelsome Corinthians adhered to his instructions, as did the Galatians with their differing ideological views. By

---

[2] Correctly so, Roloff, *Die Apostelgeschichte*, 1988, 296.
[3] So Bruce, *The Acts of the Apostles*. 424. Cf. also Ollrog, *Paulus und seine Mitarbeiter*, 52ff.

subjecting their personal interests to that of their group, these and other Pauline communities committed themselves to a common goal, namely to repay their debt to Jerusalem by means of a tangible gift. All that now remained was for Jerusalem to embrace this gracious gift from Paul and his communities.

6.2. Romans 15: Preparing for the delivery of the collection

The successful completion of the collection among the Pauline communities implied the transportation of the funds to Jerusalem. Not only did logistic matters, such as the gathering of the contributions from the various communities, have to be carefully co-ordinated, but the security of this large sum of collected money also had to be ensured during the long ship and land journey to Jerusalem. At the same time, there were also high costs involved in terms of the fare of the various envoys.[4] Apart from these practical matters, the relationship between Jerusalem and Paul's communities occupied much of the apostle's thoughts. His theological reflection on the collection until now largely focused on his communities' responsibilities towards Jerusalem. But now Paul had to shift his attention to the expected impact and symbolic value of the collection on present and future relations between himself, Jerusalem and his communities. Another crisis lurked on the horizon, as Paul's earnest request to the Romans to pray that his collection may be acceptable to the church in Jerusalem in Romans 15,30-31 indicates (... ἡ διακονία μου ἡ εἰς ’Ιερουσαλὴμ εὐπρόσδεκτος τοῖς ἁγίοις γένηται).[5] In order to comprehend Paul's doubts regarding the positive response from Jerusalem to the collection, we need to look at Romans 15 briefly once more, before turning our attention to the final delivery of the collection in Jerusalem.

6.2.1. A New ideological angle of incidence on the collection

Romans 15 is not only important because it presents us with Paul's final written 'testament' on the collection, but also because it is a reflection of his views *after* the successful completion of this undertaking within the orbit of his own communities. We are thus presented with a different ideological angle of incidence on the collection in Romans 15, over against

---

[4] Georgi, *Der Armen zu gedenken*, 88.

[5] Schmithals, *Römerbrief*, 539, concludes from the absence of a second ἵνα in the reference to the unfaithful Judeans and the Jerusalem church in v. 31 that we should understand the reaction from the latter as being dependent upon the initial response from the Judeans. "Das führt zu dem Verständnis, daß Paulus nicht 'eine doppelte Befürchtung' ausspricht..., sondern nur von einer Furcht bewegt wird, die sich nach zwei Seiten entfaltet."

Paul's earlier texts where he was mainly concerned with securing the co-operation of his communities in this project.⁶ Paul speaks from a position of strength within the reciprocal relationship with Jerusalem. He and his communities had officially fulfilled their responsibilities as beneficiaries. It was now up to Jerusalem to either accept their gift, and thus ensure the continuance of the reciprocal relationship, or to reject it, and thereby threaten the unity of the early Christian movement. Rejection of the collection would be a flagrant insult to Paul and his communities (and to the views they represented). While the symbolical importance of the Jerusalem church had already begun to decline in the eyes of the Graeco-Roman Christian communities, Jerusalem would run the risk of derailing themselves into an inferior position as a sectarian, or even worse: a heretic, faction within the parameters of the early Christian movement, if they rejected this gift.

6.2.2. Securing the bond of unity

In Romans 15 Paul's emphasis notably shifts to the *koinonia* between his churches and Jerusalem. Of course there is still continuity with the apostle's earlier views on the collection. The framework of benefit exchange is still presented as the basis of the relationship between Jerusalem and his communities (15,27), while the provocative nature of the collection, as a spiritual sacrifice from his communities, is also emphasised (v. 27; cf. also 2 Cor 9,12). However, the bond of unity between them and Jerusalem receives particular emphasis in Romans 15, as Paul's marked use of κοινωνία/κοινωνεῖν in verses 25-26 makes clear.⁷ This reciprocal bond of fellowship between the two major groups within the early Christian movement was of great importance to Paul. As mentioned earlier (cf. Chapter 4), he took particular care not to turn his communities into an independent movement that existed in isolation from, or in opposition to the Jerusalem church. Since Paul was convinced that the existing boundaries between Jews and Gentiles were dissolved by the Christ-event, it was his responsibility to give visible expression to this unity. And what better way was there, than through this διακονία that he, as the head of the collection, was now personally taking it to Jerusalem (15,25.31)? The collection was nothing less than a *'Zeichen eines lebendigen Gemeinschafts-*

---

⁶ Scholars often fail to distinguish carefully between Paul's earlier theological conceptualisations of the collection within the parameters of his own communities (as reflected in Gal 2; 1 Cor 16, and 2 Cor 8-9), and his reflection on this project after its successful completion in Rom 15, where we have a different ideological perspective on the collection.

⁷ On linguistic level, Paul's repetition of the concepts κοινωνία/κοινωνεῖν in vv. 25-26, as well as διακονία/διακονεῖν (vv. 25; 31), and εὐδοκεῖν (vv. 26-27), indicates where his emphasis in terms of the collection rests in the present situation.

bewußtseins' between Paul's churches and Jerusalem.[8] But the acceptance of these funds by Jerusalem was crucial. It would serve as the visible confirmation of the existing bond of unity between them.[9]

6.2.3. Paul as 'diakonos' of the sacred ministry to Jerusalem

Over against Paul's earlier uses of διακονία (cf. 2 Cor 8,4; 9,1.12.13), he now explicitly relates this concept to his own responsibility and function regarding the collection (Rom 15,25, 31). As the would-be benefactor of the Jerusalem church, he was now on the verge of fulfilling his own duties to Jerusalem. But even now, and in line with his 'Christian reinterpretation' of the system of benefit exchange, Paul understands his role in the collection as that of a *servant*. He is not going to Jerusalem to further his personal agenda at the expense of the Jerusalem church, but to serve them.[10] At the same time, Paul is not on some errand for Macedonia and Achaia either.[11] He is also on his way to Jerusalem as apostle of the Gentiles and benefactor of God's people in Jerusalem.

Although it is basic to the system of public/private benefaction in the Graeco-Roman world that benefactors had to be duly honoured, Paul does not give any indication that he is seeking public recognition. Could there have been another reason, apart from the apostle's own service-oriented attitude towards benefit exchange, that caused him to refrain from referring to any 'tangible' honours from Jerusalem? Perhaps his fears that his διακονία would not be acceptable (εὐπρόσδεκτος) to the ἅγιοι, provides an indication. Paul's strong appeal to the Romans in verses 30-31 to earnestly strive in their prayers (cf. the *hapax legomenon*: συναγωνίζομαι, which emphasises the principle of *agonistic* exertion) that he might be delivered from the disobedient Judeans, and that his collection might be accepted by the mother church, points to his awareness of the existence of a different ideology in Jerusalem, and even among the Jerusalem believers. This ideology could pose a serious threat to the acceptance of the collection and to the unity of the early Christian movement (cf. below).[12]

---

[8] Cf. Hainz, *Koinonia bei Paulus*, 380.

[9] Stuhlmacher, *Der Brief an die Römer*, 214.

[10] This is in line with Paul's views that Christian benefactors should act like servants who constantly seek the welfare of others, and not personal rewards (cf. e.g. Phil 2,3-4; Rom 12,9ff). In other words, Christians are to assist others and bestow benefits upon them, irrespective of their response - Winter, *Seek the Welfare of the City*, ch. 3.

[11] *Contra* Collins, *Diakonia*, 220 who is of the opinion that Paul uses the term 'diakonia' in this passage to indicate that he is acting "in an official capacity as the appointed courier of the churches."

[12] Cf. in this regard Dunn, *Romans 9-16*, 878ff., and Stuhlmacher, *Der Brief an die Römer*, 215.

In anticipation of the possible rejection of the collection by the Jerusalem church, Paul in Rom 15,25ff. deliberately steers away from the mention of any possible role-reversals between Jerusalem and himself or his communities, as he had done earlier in 2 Corinthians 8,13-15. He rather emphasises the fulfilment of his own responsibilities in terms of the delivery of the collection.

As head of the collection project, it is Paul's responsibility to deliver it to its final destination. But this is no mere administrative task, as his use of the concepts λειτουργέω (v. 27) and ἐπιτελέω (v. 28) indicates.[13] Investing the collection with a 'sacral-liturgical aura',[14] Paul implies that his visit to Jerusalem is not only hazardous because of the differing ideologies of his Judean opponents and the Jerusalem church. The very nature of the collection also poses a serious threat to his safety. As a provocative cultic venture, the collection threatens the 'secure' ideological borders that Judean believers drew around themselves in terms of 'outsiders' (the Gentiles) and 'insiders' (the Jews), and between the cultic and profane spheres. The acceptance of the collection would place Jerusalem under obligation to broaden their own horizons by accepting Paul's gospel, as well as by recognising his churches as full partners within the new eschatological Israel of God.[15]

6.2.4. Redefining 'success'

Aware of the fact that the collection would probably not be accepted with open arms in Jerusalem, Paul 'rationalises' this possibility in terms of the redefinition of his own ideological position, as well as that of his communities, towards Jerusalem in Romans 15. His earlier optimism in 2 Corinthians 9,11-14, that Jerusalem would respond to the collection with prayers of thanksgiving and bestowals of honour, now makes way for the realism of an expected hostile reception. Anticipating the position of his own churches in such an event, Paul deliberately shifts the focus from any future 'rewards,' to the *honourable fulfilment* of his churches' duties. In this regard, Paul, through his reference to the moral debt of the Macedonians and the Achaians (cf. the use of ὀφειλέτης and ὀφειλεῖν in v. 27), which they gratefully repaid, presents his communities as ideal beneficiar-

---

[13] Ascough, "Completion of a Religious Duty", 592, refers to cultic inscriptions where ἐπιτελεῖν is used in conjunction with λειτουργεῖν (cf. Rom 15,27).

[14] Martin, *2 Corinthians*, 251.

[15] However, all efforts of creating 'koinonia' would be of no avail if the material needs of Jerusalem were not effectively addressed. In its function as a 'sacred ministry' the collection was therefore primarily directed towards removing Jerusalem's financial problems. Only through the physical delivery of the contributions from Paul's communities could the various symbolic meanings that were attached to the collection be fully realised.

ies. They fulfilled their responsibilities within the reciprocal relationship with Jerusalem, irrespective of the response from the latter.

In Paul's reflection in Romans 15 on the role of his churches within the reciprocal relationship with Jerusalem, he once again comes close to Seneca's ideal of the true benefit as a virtue (*virtus*), which is to be desired because of itself, not for any external advantages it may hold for the givers (*Ben.* IV.20.1). According to both Paul and Seneca, *the intentions* of the givers determined the moral character of their actions within reciprocal interchanges. As people who joyfully repaid their debts to Jerusalem, the Pauline communities, from this perspective, reflect the 'correct' inner orientation. They viewed the collection as a gift, not as an investment or a loan to Jerusalem. Therefore, their collection effort ended in success, since they fulfilled the role of *model beneficiaries*, which, at the same time, also released them from their reciprocal obligations towards Jerusalem.

As the 'ideal' would-be benefactor himself, Paul persists in his plans of personally delivering the collection to Jerusalem, in spite of the expected negative response from the side of the mother church. His personal honour does not permit him to be derailed from his responsibilities by the expected ingratitude of Jerusalem. Since he has freed himself from all self-centred motives, the 'success' of the collection is not bound up with a favourable reaction from Jerusalem, but with the successful completion and delivery thereof.

In 15,28 Paul refers to his own function in terms of the collection as the "sealing of a fruit to Jerusalem" (σφραγισάμενος αὐτοῖς τὸν καρπὸν τοῦτον). The delivery of the collection is thus the culmination of the agreement reached at the Jerusalem meeting a few years earlier (Gal 2,10). It provides concrete proof that Paul remained faithful to his commitments. The collection is also proof that the seed of God's χάρις in the lives of his communities bore fruit (cf. 2 Cor 9,6ff.).

After the completion of his duty in delivering the collection, Paul has a new mission field in view in the western parts of the Roman Empire, as he explains in verse 28. He has no intention of turning the delivery of the collection into an eschatological pilgrimage of the nations to Jerusalem as a sign of the imminent end of the world. He also does not want to elicit a 'mass conversion' from the Judeans when they see Gentiles pouring into the Holy City with gifts.

6.3. Paul in Jerusalem

Paul and his companions began the collection-journey to Jerusalem at the beginning of 57 CE. In Acts, Luke presents us with an itinerary of the apostle from Corinth through Macedonia, via Philippi by boat to Troas (Acts 20,5). From there the party travelled to Assos (20,13), Mytilene (20,14), Samos and Milete (20,15), and then further via Kos and Rhodos to Patara (21,1). Hereafter Paul and the delegates travelled in a southerly direction to Tyre (21,3), and then via Ptolemais (21,7) to Caesarea (21,8), which eventually brought them to Jerusalem.[16] Although Luke narrates Paul's meeting with the leadership of the Jerusalem church in Acts 21,17(ff.), he is silent about the actual delivery of the collection. As a matter of fact, his only reference to Paul's delivery of the collection to Jerusalem is to be found in the apostle's speech before Felix in Acts 24,17 where he is quoted, saying that the reason for his visit to Jerusalem was to bring alms to his people and to sacrifice (ἐλεημοσύνας ποιήσων εἰς τὸ ἔθνος μου ... καὶ προσφοράς).[17] Luke's silence about Jerusalem's response to the collection could be explained in various ways:

(a) *Luke's sources on the collection were limited*: He had no knowledge as to the outcome of Paul's delivery of the collection, or to the importance Paul attached to the positive response from the side of Jerusalem. According to Lohse:

> Dem Berichterstatter, der einige Jahrzehnte nach den Ereignissen schrieb, war offensichtlich nicht bekannt, welche Bedeutung Paulus diesem Zeichen der Solidarität der Heidenchristen mit der Mutterkirche in Jerusalem beigemessen hatte.[18]

(b) *The collection was delivered in secret*: The Jerusalem leadership's sensitivity to the social circumstances of the socially destitute in their

---

[16] Cf. informative discussions of Paul's itinerary by Riesner, *Die Frühzeit des Apostels Paulus*, 269, and Lohse, *Paulus*, 257ff..

[17] On the basis of Paul's references to the collection in his letters, the majority of scholars take this expression to refer to the collection - cf. e.g., Witherington, *The Acts of the Apostles*, 712, and Jervell, *Die Apostelgeschichte*, 571. Hyldahl, *Die Paulinische Chronologie*, 127, suggests that Acts 24,17 captures the true nature of the collection as a gift that was not merely intended for the Jerusalem church, but for all Israel. However, Paul's earlier theological conceptualisations of the collection point to an undertaking that from start to finish took place within the boundaries of the early Christian movement. His remarks in 2 Cor 8,10-15, and 9,11-14 would not have made any sense if he did not have the Jerusalem Christians in mind. As to Luke's reference to the collection as a form of almsgiving in Acts 24,17, Bruce, *The Acts of the Apostles*, 480, notes that Luke, according to his presentation of Paul as the loyal Hellenistic Jew, rightly refers to the collection as a form of almsgiving since it was intended for the poor.

[18] Lohse, *Paulus*, 259. In contrast Jervell, *Die Apostelgeschichte*, 498, n.562, suggests that Luke did not elaborate on the collection because it was well-known to Luke's readers.

midst, and their fears for the negative reaction from fellow Jews, caused them to settle for nothing less than a private delivery ceremony.[19]

(c) *The contemporary irrelevance of the collection*: At the time when Acts was written, a good thirty to forty years after the events recorded in Acts 21,17(ff.) took place, Luke, although he knew about the collection, is silent about it, because it does not have any direct relevance to his own ideological agenda.

(d) *The collection was refused by Jerusalem*: According to Roloff:

> Rekonstruiert man die Vorgänge in dieser Weise, so findet auch das Schweigen des Lukas seine Erklärung. Er übergeht die Kollekte nicht etwa, weil sie in seinen Augen unwichtig gewesen wäre, sondern - paradoxerweise - weil er von ihrer überragenden Bedeutung wußte! Ihm war aus seinen Quellen bekannt, daß die Jerusalemer das Opfer der Heiden nicht angenommen haben.[20]

We may assume that, contrary to (a) above, Luke did in fact possess some basic knowledge about the collection project. Although his sources were limited, and although he mixed up his information on the collection (cf. Chapter 3), he was aware of the fact that Paul eventually took the collection to Jerusalem (cf. Acts 24,17). Regarding (b), it is unlikely that the collection would have been delivered in secret. The symbolical presence of the delegates that accompanied Paul to Jerusalem, as well as the 'public' nature of the collection within Paul's communities, renders this possibility highly improbable. Number (c) does present a viable explanation for Luke's silence about the collection. Since it was not his aim to write an 'objective history' of the early church, we should be cognisant of his own reinterpretation and selective use of the material at his disposal. However, this still does not provide a final solution, because of Luke's indications that he at least knew some important details concerning the collection, such as the basic reason for the collection; the main parties involved; (some of) the theological meanings attached to this project; the delivery journey to Jerusalem; and Paul's meeting with the Jerusalem leadership. Therefore, we should also seriously consider (d), the *refusal of the collection* by Jerusalem. According to a number of scholars, Paul's fear in Romans 15,30-31 that Jerusalem would not accept the collection, provides sufficient textual support in favour of this possibility.[21] But in order to come to a more nuanced position, we should also take cognisance of Luke's understanding of the meeting between Paul and the Jerusalem leadership in Acts 21,17(ff.). Although he only had a rudim-

---

[19] This would be in line with the views of Seneca who states that the person who experiences humiliating circumstances should be helped in private. Glorious benefits should, however, be given publicly (*Ben*.II.9.1).

[20] Roloff, *Die Apostelgeschichte*, 312.

[21] Cf., e.g., Pesch, *Die Apostelgeschichte II*, 222; Gnilka, *Paulus von Tarsus*, 155.

entary idea of what took place during this meeting, he does in fact provide us with a basic outline from which we may construct the following scenario:

6.3.1. New nationalistic sentiments in the Jerusalem Church

James and the elders were opposed to Paul's circumcision-free gospel (Acts 21,21). Due to heightened nationalistic sentiments in Jerusalem during this time,[22] they were under extreme pressure from fellow Judeans and church members to demonstrate their loyalties to the Jewish way of life. Any unconditional acceptance of the collection under these circumstances would compromise their own position, since it would also signal their acceptance of Paul's gospel.[23] The earlier agreement between the δοκοῦντες and Paul (cf. Gal 2, 1-10) was therefore under threat, since the (new) Jewish converts did not feel themselves bound to the reciprocal responsibilities implied in this relationship with a 'heretic' such as Paul, who was labelled in Jerusalem as a dangerous antinominist (Acts 21,21). However, at the same time, James was also under pressure from Paul and the large delegation to accept the collection, which he, James, as the only remaining of the 'dokountes' in Jerusalem, requested a few years earlier.

6.3.2. The compromise

During the meeting with the Jerusalem church leadership, Paul, in all probability, put forward a strong case for the acceptance of the collection. In particular: His basic theological motivation that the collection functioned as a sign of the *koinonia* between his churches and Jerusalem, as well as a spiritual sacrifice from the former (Rom 15,25ff.), placed James in a moral dilemma. He knew that outright rejection of this sacrifice would sever the link between Jerusalem and the Christian movement under Paul's supervision. On the other hand, unconditional acceptance thereof would threaten his own legitimacy as leader of the Jerusalem church, not to speak of the negative reaction from the nationalistic Judeans. Therefore, according to Luke, James proposed a public gesture that would satisfy both himself and his "... right-wing constituency that Paul still remained a

---

[22] Cf. the overview of the socio-political turmoil in Judea and the impact thereof on the Jerusalem church by Schenke, *Die Urgemeinde*, 248-250.

[23] After the departure of Peter, the Jerusalem church began to adhere more strictly to Jewish religious practices and rituals, such as circumcision and dietary laws (cf. Acts 21,20). Over against the earlier 'liberal' sentiments of the church towards circumcision, as embodied in the resolutions of the Jerusalem meeting (Acts 15; Gal 2), and in Peter's proclamation of the gospel of the Messiah to non-Jews (Acts 10), the Jerusalem church now strictly aligned itself with Jewish ideologies and practices.

practising Jew, and that his antinomian reputation was unjustified."[24] Specifically: James expected of Paul to undergo the purification rite expected of all Jewish people returning from pagan territory who wanted to enter the temple, as well as to pay for the Nazarite vows of four Torah-observant members of the Jerusalem community (cf. Acts 21,23-24). Only after Paul had completed this honourable deed in the Temple, would the Jerusalem church 'officially' accept the collection. This strategy would not only relieve the Jerusalem church from a heavy financial burden, but it would also safeguard them against any negative reactions from fellow Judeans. If Paul 'passed this test,' that is, if Jewish worshippers accepted his presence in the temple, the Jerusalem church could safely follow suit. But if Paul's presence in the temple led to some form of unrest, he would have to bear the consequences himself, since he did not officially represent the Jerusalem church.

Paul agreed to this proposal. In spite of the lack of literary information to this effect, we may, however, assume that Paul demanded that the costly Nazarite vows (cf. Num 6,1-21) were to be paid from the collection money. Not only did his own financial position necessitate such a demand, but also his view that the collection was, in the first instance, intended to address the financial needs of the Jerusalem church. In this way Paul would ensure that Jerusalem profited from the collection funds from the very start. This 'solution' would give concrete expression to his own role as 'benefactor-servant' of this material gift of love to Jerusalem, and to the bond of fellowship between them. Along these lines, Paul's ideological conceptualisation of the collection, in terms of the relationship between himself, his churches and Jerusalem as reflected in Romans 15,25(ff.), would at least be partly realised.

This compromise, which apparently suited both James and Paul, is credited by Luke only to the leadership of the Jerusalem community and not to Paul. But, as Murphy-O'Connor correctly notes,[25] Paul in all probability played an active part in the finding of a solution at this meeting that would not compromise his own interests and that of his communities. It is unthinkable that Paul, who until now addressed the various threats to the collection within the sphere of his own communities, did not once again reflect on some new strategies after he had expressed his fears as to the positive reception of the collection in Romans 15,31-32. Although Romans 15 presents us with the last words from Paul on this matter, we should not assume that these represent his final views on the collection. Since Paul was well aware of the sentiments of the Jerusalem church

---

[24] Murphy-O'Connor, *Paul - A Critical Life*, 349f. See also Jervell, *Die Apostelgeschichte*, 527.

[25] Cf. Murphy-O'Connor, *Paul - A Critical Life*, 350f.

towards himself, he envisioned some public gesture on his part to demonstrate his own loyalties to the faith of his forefathers.

The solution reached at the initial meeting between James and Paul was never concluded because of Paul's arrest in the temple. After ending up in Roman custody, the collection was out of his hands. Whether his companions returned the funds to their churches, or gave it to Jerusalem, we shall never know. But at least Paul tasted some success for a short time (even though it happened under dangerous circumstances at that!), by acting as public benefactor of the Jerusalem church through his paying of the Nazarite vows.

Chapter 7

Conclusion

7.1. The interpretative framework for the collection

The collection was the result and the concrete expression of the reciprocal relationship between the Jerusalem leadership and Paul, and also between the Jerusalem church and the rapidly growing early Christian movement under Paul's supervision. *Benefit exchange* provided the basic interpretative framework that informed the collection, from Paul's initial theological conceptualisation to the eventual delivery thereof. The apostle did not develop his different theological conceptualisations of this project in isolation from the formative impact of the ideological and cultural scripts from his *Umwelt*.

The various theological interpretations of the collection reverberated within the parameters of the exchange relationship between Paul and Jerusalem, and their respective obligations as beneficiaries and benefactors in this regard. More specifically, as a religious undertaking, the collection was understood by Paul as forming part of a three-way reciprocal relationship between God, the Pauline communities and Jerusalem. Within this overarching framework, the collection was related to the nature of God's involvement in the lives of the givers, in terms of his overflowing χάρις (cf. 2 Cor 8,1-6); the impact of the Christ-event on the latter (2 Cor 8,9), and the relationship between God's gifts and believers' generous sharing of their material possessions with others (2 Corinthians 9,6-15).

7.2. The 'performative' functions of Paul's theological reflection on the collection

Paul's theological reflections on the collection were primarily related to his efforts within the orbit of his own communities to secure their full participation in the collection. Paul addressed specific questions and/or crises pertaining to the completion of this project (cf. 1 Cor 16,1-4; 2 Cor

8-9; Gal 2,1-10). But his reflections were also intended to secure his own role as apostle and benefactor in the eyes of Jerusalem. However, he carefully avoided any self-centred remarks that might have indicated that he was seeking personal satisfaction to the detriment of his churches. As the typical group-oriented person, who constantly laboured for the honour of God and the well-being of the communities under his supervision, Paul presented himself as a honourable figure, who paid his debts to God and to fellow believers (cf. Gal 2,10). His integrity in terms of the collection was therefore inseparably interwoven with his living up to the expectations of Jerusalem to address the needs of their poor.

7.3. Paul's reinterpretation of the basic principles of benefit exchange

Although Paul placed the collection within the interpretative framework of Graeco-Roman benefit exchange, he also reinterpreted some of its basic tenets in terms of his own understanding of the Christ-event. Nowhere is this more evident than in Romans 15,25(ff.), where Paul depicts his role in the delivery of the collection as that of a *diakonos*. Instead of seeking personal honour, he presents himself as going to Jerusalem to seek the welfare of fellow believers in Romans 15. At the same time, Paul redefines the predisposition of his Christian givers regarding reciprocal relationships. Instead of following the typical Graeco-Roman principle of giving as a return, Paul shifts their emphasis from the expected return gifts to their own positive inner orientation, irrespective of the reaction on the side of the recipients. In this regard Paul's view of the ideal givers is very similar to that of Seneca as expressed in his *De Beneficiis*.[1] Paul, in his communication of these principles to his communities, thus deliberately modifies the typical Graeco-Roman attitudes towards the needy. In spite of munificent forms of assistance, Graeco-Roman benefactors generally used their benefactions to increase their own honour, and not so much to alleviate the want of others. Although Paul was not using the financial situation of Jerusalem as a basic motivation to involve his communities in the collection, he nevertheless uses the references to their poverty (cf. 2 Cor 9,12; Gal 2,10; Rom 15,26) to impress upon his communities that they are morally obliged to assist their poor brethren in Jerusalem. Paul's letters, therefore, simultaneously present us with his own conceptualisation of the collection in order to address the contingent needs of his commun-

---

[1] At the same time, the apostle's views also come close to that of Jesus with regards to giving to the poor, as expressed in the various Jesus-traditions (cf. e.g., Mark 10,17-31; Matt 40-48; Lk 6,33).

ities, and his coherent Christian reinterpretation of the basic principles of benefit exchange.

7.4. The completion of the collection

The collection was primarily intended to address Jerusalem's poverty. Paul, therefore, expected nothing less than a significant contribution from his communities. Through the bestowal of this benefit on Jerusalem, their financial plight would be relieved and the reciprocal relationship strengthened through the latter's grateful response in the form of the bestowal of tangible honours. At least this is how Paul conceptualised the delivery of the collection while it was still in progress within his communities (2 Cor 9,11-14). Unfortunately, not all of these ideals were realised, as the Lukan account (Acts 21,17ff.) of Paul's final meeting with the Jerusalem leadership indicates. Shortly afterwards, Paul's capture in the temple brought an abrupt end to the collection project, at least from the perspective of the apostle's early Christian biographers.

In spite of the unfortunate ending to the collection, this imaginative project could be described as a success, particularly within the sphere of the Pauline communities. Not only did Paul effectively address the numerous obstacles that threatened the completion of the collection, but his own communities, through their combined efforts to submit the collection as a gracious service to Jerusalem, eventually also gave visible expression to their common bond of unity. The Jerusalem community apparently did not reject the collection outright. The Lukan version of Paul's 'collection-visit' points to the devising of a solution by Paul and James that was intended to address the negative attitude from Jerusalem, as well as to ensure the eventual acceptance of the collection (cf. Chapter 6).

The role and impact of the collection within the early Christian movement could scarcely be overestimated! The sheer physical effort that went into the organisation and the administration of this imaginative project under the Christian communities spread out through Galatia, Macedonia, Achaia, and Asia, as well as Paul's own time and energy that went into the project, in the end paid the necessary dividends. It led to the existential involvement of most members of Paul's communities in a service for fellow believers in Judea, whom the majority of them had never even met. Obviously, these believers' basic knowledge of the system of social exchange provided an ideal foundation for Paul's various theological conceptualisations on the collection. But, the fact that they were willing to give visible expression to their compassion for fellow-believers' plight on such a large scale points to Paul's successful communication of the theological principles inherent to the collection.

Perhaps present-day churches should once again pay serious attention to the principles inherent to the Pauline collection. Analogous caritative projects could serve as powerful witnesses to the overflowing grace of God in our troubled world. What better way is there to make God's presence felt than through the generous and joyful bestowal of benefits on fellow believers in need? Such efforts to address the situation of the socially destitute could at the same time give concrete expression to the bond of fellowship between God's people. Obviously, caritative projects of this nature entail personal sacrifice. But, in the words of Oscar Cullmann: "... ohne Opfer ist die Einheit der Kirche unmöglich."[2]

---

[2] Cullmann, *Katholiken und Protestanten*, 17.

Bibliography

ABEL, K., "Seneca. Leben und Leistung", in: W. Haase (ed.), *ANRW* II.32.2. Berlin Walter De Gruyter.
ACHTERMEIER, J., *Romans*, Atlanta: John Knox Press, 1985.
ALFÖLDY, G., *The Social History of Rome* Tr. by D. Braund & F. Pollock. Totowa: Barnes & Noble Books, 1985.
ALTMAN, J.G., *Epistolarity. Approaches to a Form*, Columbus: Ohio State University Press, 1982.
ASCOUGH, R.S., "The Completion of a Religious Duty: The Background of 2 Cor 8.1-5", in: *NTS* 42 (1996) 584-599.
BACHMANN, M., *Sünder oder Übertreter: Studien zur Argumentation in Gal 2,15ff.*, WUNT 59, Tübingen: Mohr-Siebeck, 1992.
BADIAN, E., *Foreign Clientelae (264-70 B.C.)*, Oxford: Clarendon, 1958.
BAR-ILAN, M., "Illiteracy in the Land of Israel in the First Centuries C.E.", in: S. Fishbane & S. Schoenfeld (eds.), *Essays in the Social-Scientific Study of Judaism and Jewish Society*, Hoboken, New York: Ktav, 1992, 46-61.
BARNETT, P., *The Second Epistle to the Corinthians*, NICNT, Grand Rapids: Eerdmans, 1997.
BARRETT, C.K., *A Commentary on the First Epistle to the Corinthians* BNTC, London: Black, 1968
-, *A Commentary on the Second Epistle to the Corinthians*, BNTC, London: A & C Black, ²1979 (1973).
-, *Paul. An Introduction to his Thought*, London: SPCK, 1994.
BARTSCH, H.W., "... 'Wenn ich ihnen diese Frucht versiegelt habe'. Röm 15,28. Ein Beitrag zum Verständnis der paulinischen Mission", in: *ZNW* 63 (1972) 95-107.
BASORE, J.W., *Seneca, Moral Essays*. Vol III: *De Beneficiis*, London: Heinemann, 1975.
BAUR, F.C., *Geschichte der christlichen Kirche. I. Teil*, Leipzig: Nationales Druckhaus, 1969 (1863).
BECKER, J., *Paulus: Der Apostel der Völker*, Tübingen: Mohr Siebeck, ²1992.
-, "Der Brief an die Galater", in: J. Becker & U. Luz, *Die Briefe an die Galater, Epheser und Kolosser, Thessalonicher und Philemon*, NTD 8/1, Göttingen: Vandenhoeck, 1998, 9-106.
BECKER, L.C., *Reciprocity*, London: Routledge & Kegan Paul, 1986.
BECKHEUER, B., *Paulus und Jerusalem. Kollekte und Mission im theologischen Denken des Heidenapostels*, EHS.T 23, Frankfurt am Main: Peter Lang, 1997.
BEKER, J.C., "Recasting Pauline Theology: The Coherence-Contingency Scheme as Interpretative Model", in: J. M. Bassler (ed.), *Pauline Theology. Volume 1: Thessalonians, Philippians, Galatians, Philemon*, Minneapolis: Fortress, 1991.
BEN-DAVID, A., *Talmudische Ökonomie*, Hildesheim: Georg Olms, 1974.
BENEDUM, J., "Arztinschriften aus Kos", in: *ZPE* 25 (1991) 265-276.

BENNER, A.R. & FORBES, F.H., *The Letters of Alchiphron, Aelian and Philostratus*, LCL, London: Heinemann, 1979.
BENNER, P., *Die Politik des P. Claudius Pulcher: Untersuchungen zur Denautierung des Clientelwesens*, Historia Einzelschriften 50, Stuttgart, 1987.
BERGER, K., "Almosen für Israel. Zum historischen Kontext der paulinischen Kollekte", in: *NTS* 23 (1977) 180-203.
BERGER, P. & LUCKMANN, T., *The Social Construction of Reality*, London: Penguin, 1966.
BEST, E., *Paul and his Converts*, Edinburgh: T & T. Clark, 1988.
BETZ, H.D, *Galatians*, Hermeneia, Philadelphia: Fortress, 1979.
-, *2 Corinthians 8 and 9, A Commentary on Two Administrative Letters of the Apostle Paul*, Hermeneia Philadelphia: Fortress Press, 1985.
BLAU, P.M., *Exchange in Power and Social Life*, London: Wiley, 1964.
BLEICKEN, J., *Verfassungs-und Sozialgeschichte des Römischen Kaiserreiches*, Band 1, UTB 838, Paderborn: Ferdinand Schöningh, [2]1981.
BLOCH, M., *The Historian's Craft*, New York: Ktav, 1953.
BOERS, H., *The Justification of the Gentiles. Paul's Letters to the Galatians and Romans*, Peabody: Hendrickson, 1994.
BOISSEVAIN, J., *Friends of Friends: Networks, Manipulators, and Coalitions*. New York: St. Martin's Press, 1974.
BOLKESTEIN, H., *Wohltätigkeit und Armenpflege im vorchristlichen Altertum*, Utrecht: A. Oosthoek, 1939.
BOLYKI, J., *Jesu Tischgemeinschaften*, WUNT 2/ 96, Tübingen: Mohr Siebeck, 1998.
BORMANN, L., *Philippi. Stadt und Christengemeinde zur Zeit des Paulus*, NT.S 78, Leiden: Brill, 1995.
BORNKAMM, G., *Paulus*, Stuttgart: Kohlhammer, 1969.
BORSE, U., *Der Standort des Galaterbriefes*, BBB 41, Köln: Peter Hanstein, 1972.
-, *Der Brief an die Galater*, RNT, Regensburg: Friedrich Pustet, 1984.
BOTHA, P.J.J., "Community and Conviction in Luke-Acts", in: *Neotest.* 29/2 (1995) 145-165.
BÖTTGER, P.C., "Paulus und Petrus in Antiochien. Zum Verständnis von Galater 2,11-21", in: *NTS* 37 (1991) 77-100.
BRÄNDLE, R., "Geld und Gnade (zu II Kor 8,9)", in: *ThZ 41* (1985) 264-271.
BRATCHER, R.G., *A Translator's Guide to Paul's Second Letter to the Corinthians*, London: UBS, 1983.
BREYTENBACH, C., *Paulus und Barnabas. Studien zu Apostelgeschichte 13f.; 16,6; 18,23 und den Adressaten des Galaterbriefes*, AGJU 38, Leiden: Brill, 1996.
BRUCE, F.F., *The Epistle to the Galatians*, NIGTC, Exeter: Paternoster, 1982.
-, *The Acts of the Apostles. The Greek Text with Introduction and Commentary*, Grand Rapids: Eerdmans, [3]1990 (1951).
BULTMANN, C., *Der Fremde im antiken Juda. Eine Untersuchung zum sozialen Typenbegriff 'ger' und seinem Bedeutungswandel in der alttestamentlichen Gesetzgebung*, FRLANT 153, Göttingen: Vandenhoeck, 1992.
BULTMANN, R., *Der zweite Brief an die Korinther*, KEK, Hrsg. von E. Dinkler, Göttingen: Vandenhoeck, 1976.
CAPPER, B.J., "Reciprocity and the ethic of Acts", in: I.H. Marshall & D. Peterson (eds.), *Witness to the Gospel. The Theology of Acts*, Grand Rapids: Eerdmans, 1998, 499-518.
CAREY, C., "Rhetorical Means of Persuasion", in: I. Worthington (ed.), *Persuasion*, London: Routledge, 1994, 26-46.

CARNEY, T.F., *The Shape of the Past. Models and Antiquity*. Lawrence, Coronado Press, 1975.
CARY, E., *The Roman Antiquities of Dionysius of Halicarnassus* LCL 319, Cambridge, London 1937, Repr. 1968.
CHOW, J.K., *Patronage and Power. A Study of Social Networks in Corinth*, JSNTS, Sheffield: JSOT Press, 1992.
CLARKE, M.L., "Poets and Patrons at Rome", in: *GaR* 25 (1978) 46-54.
COHEN, D., "Classical Rhetoric and Modern Theories of Discourse", in: I. Worthington (ed), *Persuasion: Greek Rhetoric in Action*, London: Routledge, 1994, 69-84.
COLLINS, J.N., *Diakonia. Re-interpreting Ancient Sources*, Oxford: Oxford University Press, 1990.
COLLINS, M.S., "Money, Sex and Power: An Examination of the Role of Women as Patrons of the Ancient Synagogues", in: P. J. Haas (ed.), *Rediscovering the Role of Women. Power and Authority in Rabbinic Jewish Society*, Atlanta: Scholars Press, 1992, 7-22.
CONZELMANN, H., *Der erste Brief an die Korinther*, KEK 5, Göttingen: Vandenhoeck, ²1981 (1969).
COOK, K.S. (ed.), *Social Network Theory*, London: Sage Publications, 1987.
CRAFFERT, P.F., "The Pauline Household Communities: Their Nature as Social Entities", in: *Neotest.* 32/2 (1998) 309-341.
CRANFIELD, C.E.B., *A Critical and Exegetical Commentary on the Epistle to the Romans*, Vol. II Edinburgh: Clark, 1979.
CULLMANN, O., *Katholiken und Protestanten. Ein Vorschlag zur Verwirklichung christlicher Solidarität*, Basel, Reinhardt, 1958.
CURCHIN, L.A., "Social Relations in Central Spain: Patrons, Freedmen and Slaves in the Life of a Roman Hinterland", in: *AncSoc* 18 (1987) 75-90.
DAHL, N.A., *Studies in Paul. Theology for the Early Christian Mission*, Minneapolis: Augsburg, 1977.
DANKER, F.W., "2 Peter 1: A Solemn Decree", in: *CBQ* 40 (1978) 64-82.
-, *Benefactor: Epigraphic Study of a Graeco-Roman and New Testament Semantic Field*, St. Louis: Clayton, 1982.
DIBELIUS, M., *Aufsätze zur Apostelgeschichte*. Hrsg. von H. Greeven, Göttingen: Vandenhoeck, ³1957.
DIETZFELBINGER, C., "Sohn und Gesetz: Überlegungen zur paulinischen Christologie", in: C. Breytenbach & H. Paulsen (Hrsg.), *Anfänge der Christologie*. (FS. für Ferdinand Hahn), Göttingen: Vandenhoeck, 1991, 111-130.
DINKLER, E., "Der Brief an die Galater", in: *VF* (1953/55) 175-183.
DIXON, S., "A Family Business: Women's Role in Patronage and Politics at Rome 80-44 BC", in: *CM* 43 (1983) 91-112.
-, "The Sentimental Idea of the Roman Family", in: B. Rawson (ed.), *Marriage, Divorce and Children in Ancient Rome*, Baltimore: John Hopkins University Press, 1987.
-, *The Roman Family*, Baltimore: John Hopkins University Press, 1992, 99-113.
DODD, B.J., "Christ's Slave, People Pleasers and Galatians 1.10", in: *NTS* 42 (1996) 90-104.
DOMMERSHAUSEN, W., *Die Umwelt Jesu. Politik und Kultur in neutestamentlicher Zeit*, Freiburg: Herder, 1977.
DONAHUE, J.R., "Windows and Mirrors: The Setting of Mark's Gospel", in: *CBQ* 57 (1995) 1-26.
DOUGLAS, M., "No Free Gift", in: M. Mauss, *The Gift. The Form and Reason for Exchange in Archaic Societies*, London: Routledge, 1990, vii-xviii.

DRUMMOND, A., "Early Roman Clientes", in: A. Wallace-Hadrill (ed.), *Patronage in Ancient Society*, London: Routledge, 1989, 89-116.
DUNCAN-JONES, R., *The Economy of the Roman Empire: Quantitative Studies*, Cambridge: Cambridge University Press, 1982.
-, "The Procurator as Civic Benefactor", in: *JRS* 64 (1974), 79-85.
DUNN, J.D.G., *Christology in the Making: a New Testament Inquiry into the Origins of the Doctrine of the Incarnation*, London: SCM Press, 1980.
-, *Romans 9-16*, Dallas: Word, WBC 38b, 1998.
-, The Theology of Galatians: The Issue of Covenantal Nomism, in: J.M. Bassler (ed.), *Pauline Theology*, Augsburg: Fortress, 1991, 125-146.
-, *The Epistle to the Galatians*, Peabody: Hendrickson, BNTC IX, 1993.
-, *The Theology of Paul's Letter to the Galatians*, Cambridge: Cambridge University Press, 1993.
-, *The Theology of Paul the Apostle*, Grand Rapids: Eerdmans, 1998.
DU TOIT, A.B., "Persuasion in Romans 1,1-17", in: *BZ* 41 (1989) 192-209.
-, "Vilification as a Pragmatic Device in Early Christian Epistolography", in: *Bib* 75 (1994) 402-414.
EAGLETON, T., *Ideology: An Introduction*, London: Verso, 1991.
ECKERT, J., "Die Kollekte des Paulus für Jerusalem", in: P.G. Müller & W. Stenger (Hrsg.), *Kontinuität und Einheit* (FS F. Mußner), Freiburg: Herder, 1981.
ECKSTEIN, H.J., *Verheißung und Gesetz. Eine exegetische Untersuchung zu Galater 2,15-4,7*, WUNT 86, Tübingen: Mohr Siebeck, 1996.
EDLUND, I.E.M., "Invisible Bonds: Clients and Patrons through the Eyes of Polybios", in: *Klio* 59 (1977) 129-136.
EISENSTADT, S.N. & RONIGER, L., *Patrons, Clients and Friends. Interpersonal Relations and the Structure of Trust in Society*, London: Cambridge University Press, 1984.
ELLIOTT, J.H., *What is Social-Scientific Criticism?*, Minneapolis: Fortress, 1993.
-, "Patronage and Clientage", in: R. Rohrbaugh (ed.), *The Social Sciences and New Testament Interpretation*, Peabody: Hendrickson, 1996, 144-158.
ENGBERG-PEDERSEN, T., "Plutarch to Prince Philopapus on How to Tell a Flatterer from a Friend", in J. T. Fitzgerald (ed.), *Friendship, Flattery and Frankness of Speech*, Leiden: Brill, 1996, 61-79.
ENGELS, D., *Roman Corinth. An Alternative Model for the Classical City*, Chicago: University of Chicago Press, 1990.
ERSKINE, A., "The Romans as Common Benefactors", in: *Historia* 43 (1994) 70-87.
ESLER, P.F., "Making and Breaking an Agreement Mediterranean Style: A New Reading of Galatians 2,1-4", in: *Interp.* 3 (1995) 285-314.
FEE, G.D., *The First Epistle to the Corinthians*, NICNT, Grand Rapids: Eerdmans, 1987.
FINLEY, M., *Politics in the Ancient World*, Cambridge: Cambridge University Press, 1983.
FITZGERALD, J.T., "Friendship in the Greek World Prior to Aristotle", in: J.T. Fitzgerald (ed.), *Friendship, Flattery and Frankness of Speech: Studies on Friendship in the New Testament World*, NT.S 82, Leiden: Brill, 1996, 13-34.
FREYNE, S., *Galilee from Alexander the Great to Hadrian: 323 BCE to 135 C.E.: A Study of Second Temple Judaism*, Wilmington: Glazier, 1980.
FUNG, R.Y.K., *The Epistle to the Galatians*, NICNT, Grand Rapids: Eerdmans, 1988.
FURNISH, V.P., *2 Corinthians*, AncB 32a, London: Doubleday, 1984.
GARDNER J.F. & WIEDEMANN, T., *The Roman Household: A Source Book*, New York: Routledge, 1991.

GARNSEY, P., "Famine in Rome", in: P. Garnsey & C.R. Whittaker (eds), *Trade and Famine in Classical Antiquity*, Cambridge: Cambridge Philological Society, 1983, 56-64.
-, *Famine and Food Supply in the Graeco-Roman World: Responses to Risk and Crisis*, Cambridge: Cambridge University Press, 1988.
GARNSEY, P. & SALLER, R.P., *The Roman Empire. Economy, Society and Culture*, London: Duckworth, 1987.
GARNSEY, P. & WOOLF, G., "Patronage of the Rural Poor in the Roman World", in: A. Wallace-Hadrill (ed.), *Patronage in Ancient Society*, London: Routledge, 1989, 153-170.
GASTON, L., "Paul and the Law in Galatians 2-3", in: P. Richardson (ed.), *Anti-Judaism in Early Christianity*, Waterloo: Wilfrid Laurier University Press, 1986, 127-154.
-, "Israel's Misstep in the Eyes of Paul", in: K.P. Donfried (ed.), *The Romans Debate. Revised and Expanded Edition*, Edinburgh: T. & T. Clark, 1991, 309-326.
GAUTHIER, P., *Les cités grecques et leurs bienfaiteurs. Contribution a l'histoire des institutions*, BCH Supp XII, Paris 1985.
GEORGI, D., *Der Armen zu gedenken. Die Geschichte der Kollekte des Paulus für Jerusalem*, Neukirchen: Neukirchener Verlag, Zweite durchgesehene und erweiterte Auflage 1994.
GEWALT, D., "Neutestamentliche Exegese und Soziologie", in: *EvTh 31* (1971) 87-99.
GIDDENS, A., *Central Problems in Social Theory*, London: MacMillan, 1979.
-, *New Rules of Sociological Method. A Positive Critique of Interpretative Sociologies*, London: Hutchinson, 1976.
GILL, D.W.J., "Achaia", in: D. W. J. Gill & C. Gempf (eds.), *The Book of Acts in its First Century Setting*, Vol 2: *The Book of Acts in its Graeco-Roman Setting*, Grand Rapids: Eerdmans, 1994, 433-454.
GNILKA, J., "Die Kollekte der paulinischen Gemeinden für Jerusalem als Ausdruck ekklesialer Gemeinschaft", in: R. Kampling & T. Söding (Hrsg.), *Ekklesiologie des Neuen Testaments* (FS Karl Kertelge), Herder: Freiburg, 1996.
-, *Paulus von Tarsus: Apostel und Zeuge*, HThK, Suppl VI; Herder: Freiburg, 1996.
GOULDNER, A.W., "The Norm of Reciprocity: A Preliminary Statement", in: *ASR 25/2* (1960) 161-178.
GREGORY, C.A., *Gifts and Commodities*, London: Academic Press, 1982.
GRUEN, E.S., *The Hellenistic World and the Coming of Rome I*, Los Angeles: University of California Press, 1984.
HAACKER, K., *Paulus. Der Werdegang eines Apostels*, SBS 171, Stuttgart: Katholisches Bibelwerk, 1997.
HAENCHEN, E., *Die Apostelgeschichte*, KEK 3, Göttingen: Vandenhoeck, ³1977.
HAINZ, J., "Gemeinschaft (κοινωνία) zwischen Paulus und Jerusalem (Gal 2,9f.)", in: W. Stenger & P.G. Müller, *Kontinuität und Einheit*, (FS F. Mußner), Freiburg: Herder, 1981, 30-42.
-, *Koinonia*, BU 16, Regensburg: Friedrich Pustet, 1982.
-, "Koinonia bei Paulus", in: L. Bornmann, K.D. Tredici, A. Standhartinger (Hrsg.), *Religious Propaganda and Missionary Competition in the New Testament World* (FS D. Georgi), NT.S 74, Leiden: Brill, 1994, 375-392.
HALL, D.R., "St. Paul and Famine Relief: A Study in Galatians 2,10", in: *ExpT 82* (1970-71) 309-311.
HANDS, A.R., *Charities and Social Aid in Greece and Rome*, Ithaca: Cornell, 1968.
HANSON, K.C., & OAKMAN, D.E., *Palestine in the Time of Jesus*, Philadelphia: Fortress, 1998.

HARRILL, J.A., *The Manumission of Slaves in Early Christianity*, HUT 32, Tübingen: Mohr Siebeck, 1995.
HARVEY, E.A. *Renewal through Suffering. A Study of 2 Corinthians*, Edinburgh: T. & T. Clark, 1996.
HAYS, R.B., *The Moral Vision of the New Testament. A Contemporary Introduction to New Testament Ethics*, Edinburgh: T. & T. Clark, 1996.
HENDRIX, H., "Benefactor/Patron Networks in the Urban Environment: Evidence from Thessalonica", in: L. M. White (ed.), *Social Networks in the Early Christian Environment: Issues and Methods for Social History*, Atlanta: Scholars Press, 1992, 39-58.
HENGEL, M., *Eigentum und Reichtum in der frühen Kirche. Aspekte einer frühchristlichen Sozialgeschichte*, Stuttgart: Calwer, 1972.
-, *Zur urchristlichen Geschichtsschreibung*, Stuttgart: Kohlhammer, ^{2}1984.
-, *The Pre-Christian Paul*, Valley Forge: Trinity, 1991.
-, & SCHWEMER, A.M., *Paul between Damascus and Antioch. The Unknown Years*, Westminster John Knox: Louisville, 1997.
HÉRING, J., *The Second Epistle of St. Paul to the Corinthians*, London: Epworth, 1967.
HERMAN, G., *Ritualised Friendship and the Greek City*, Cambridge: Cambridge University Press, 1987.
HESTER, J.C., "The Rhetorical Structure of Galatians", in: *JBL 103* (1984) 223-33.
HILLER VON GÄRTRINGEN, F., *Inschriften von Priene*, 1908. Repr. Berlin: De Gruyter 1968.
HÖFFE, O., *Aristoteles*, München: C. H. Beck, 1996.
HOLL, K., "Der Kirchenbegriff des Paulus in seinem Verhältnis zu dem Urgemeinde", in: *Gesammelte Aufsätze zur Kirchengeschichte. Band 2: Der Osten*, Darmstadt: Wissenschaftliche Buchgesellschaft, 1964 [1928].
HOLMBERG, B., *Paul and Power. The Structure of Authority in the Primitive Church as Reflected in the Pauline Writings*, Philadelphia: Fortress, 1978.
HOLZBERG, N., *Martial*, Heidelberg: Carl Winter, 1988.
HORN, F.W., *Glaube und Handeln in der Theologie des Lukas*, GTA, Göttingen: Vandenhoeck und Ruprecht, 1983.
HORRELL, D.G., "Paul's Collection: Resources for a Materialist Theology", in: *EpRe* 22 (1995) 74-83.
-, *The Social Ethos of the Corinthian Correspondence. Interests and Ideology from 1 Corinthians to 1 Clement*, Edinburgh: T. & T. Clark, 1996.
HORSLEY, R.A., *Archaeology, History, and Society in Galilee. The Social Context of Jesus and the Rabbis*, Valley Forge: Trinity Press, 1996.
HÜBNER, H., *Biblische Theologie des Neuen Testaments. Band 2: Die Theologie des Paulus*, Göttingen: Vandenhoeck 1993.
HUGHES, F.W., "Rhetorical Criticism and the Corinthian Correspondence", in: S. E. Porter & T. H. Olbricht (eds.), *The Rhetorical Analysis of Scripture: Essays from the 1995 London Conference*, JSNTS 146, Sheffield: Sheffield Academic Press, 1997, 336-350.
HUGHES, P.E., *Paul and the Second Epistle to the Corinthians*, NICNT, Grand Rapids: Eerdmans, 1962.
HYLDAHL, N., *Die Paulinische Chronologie*, AThD XIX, Leiden: Brill, 1986.
INWOOD, B., "Politics and Paradox in Seneca's *De Beneficiis*", in: A. Laks & M. Schofield (eds.), *Justice and Generosity. Studies in Hellenistic Social and Political Philosophy*, Cambridge: Cambridge University Press, 1995, 241-266.
JAGER, J.H., *De Tweede Brief aan die Korinthiers*, Kampen: Van den Berg, 1978.

JAMESON, M., "Famine in the Greek World", in: P. Garnsey & C. R. Whittaker (eds.), *Trade and Famine in Classical Antiquity*, Cambridge: Cambridge Philological Society, 1983, 6-16.
JEREMIAS, J., "Sabbatjahr und neutestamentliche Chronologie", in: *ZNW* 27 (1928) 98-103.
-, *Jerusalem zur Zeit Jesu. Eine kulturgeschichtliche Untersuchung zur neutestamentlichen Zeitgeschichte*, Göttingen: Vandenhoeck, ³1962.
JERVELL, J., *Die Apostelgeschichte*, KEK 3, Göttingen: Vandenhoeck, 1998.
JEWETT, R., *The Thessalonian Correspondence: Pauline Rhetoric and Millenarian Piety*, FFNT, Philadelphia: Fortress Press, 1986.
JONES, C.P., *The Roman World of Dio Chrysostom*, Cambridge: Cambridge University Press, 1978.
JOUBERT, S.J., "Behind the Mask of Rhetoric: 2 Corinthians 8 and the Intra-Textual Relation between Paul and the Corinthians", in: *Neotest.* 26 (1992), 101-112.
-, "Managing the Household. Paul as *Paterfamilias* of the Christian Household Group in Corinth", in: P.F. Esler (ed.), *Modelling Early Christianity*, London: Routledge, 1995, 213-223.
-, "Persuasion in the Letter of Jude", in: *JSNT* 58 (1995) 75-87.
KARRER, M., *Jesus Christus im Neuen Testament*, Göttingen: Vandenhoeck, NTD 11, 1998.
KÄSEMANN, E., *An die Römer*, HNT, Tübingen: Mohr Siebeck, ³1974.
KECK, L., "The Poor among the Saints in the New Testament", in: *ZNW* 56 (1965) 100-129.
-, "The Poor among the Saints in Jewish Christianity and Qumran", in: *ZNW* 57 (1965) 54-78.
KENNEDY, G.A., *New Testament Interpretation through Rhetorical Criticism*, Chappel Hill: University of North Carolina Press, 1984.
KENT, J.H., *The Inscriptions 1926-1950*, No. 153 (Corinth: Results of Excavations, VIII/3), Princeton: Princeton University Press, 1966.
KERN, P.H., *Rhetoric and Galatians. Assessing an Approach to Paul's Epistle*, ShTSMS 101, Cambridge: Cambridge University Press, 1998.
KIDD, R.M., *Wealth and Beneficence in the Pastoral Epistles*, SBL.DS 122, Atlanta: Scholars Press, 1990.
KIM, S., "The 'Mystery' of Rom 11.25-6 Once More", in: *NTS* 43 (1997) 412-429.
KLAUCK, H.J., *1. Korintherbrief*, NEB 7, Würzburg: Echter Verlag, 1984.
-, *2. Korintherbrief*, NEB 8, Würzburg: Echter 1986.
-, "Die Hausgemeinde als Lebensform im Urchristentum", in: *Gemeinde, Amt, Sakrament*, Würzburg: Echter, 1989, 11-28.
-, "Die Armut der Jünger in der Sicht des Lukas", in: *Gemeinde, Amt, Sakrament*, Würzburg: Echter, 1989, 160-195.
-, "Gütergemeinschaft in der klassischen Antike in Qumran und im Neuen Testament", in: *Gemeinde, Amt, Sakrament*, Würzurg: Echter, 1989, 69-100.
-, *Der zweite und dritte Johannesbrief*, EKK 23/2, Neukirchen-Vluyn: Neukirchener Verlag, 1992.
-, "Der Gott in dir (Ep 41,1). Autonomie des Gewissens bei Seneca und Paulus", in: *Alte Welt und neuer Glaube. Beiträge zur Religionsgeschichte, Forschungsgeschichte und Theologie des Neuen Testaments*, NTOA 29, Göttingen: Vandenhoeck, 1994.
-, *Die religiöse Umwelt des Urchristentums I: Stadt und Hausreligion, Mysterienkulte, Volksglaube*, KThS 9,1, Stuttgart: Kohlhammer, 1995.

-, *Die religiöse Umwelt des Urchristentums* II: *Herrscher und Kaiserkult, Philosophie, Gnosis*, KThS 9,2, Stuttgart: Kohlhammer, 1996.
-, *Neutestamentliches Oberseminar. Ein Reader*, Würzburg, 1997.
-, *Die antike Briefliteratur und das Neue Testament*, UTB 2022, Paderborn: Schöningh, 1998.
-, *Vom Zauber des Anfangs: Biblische Besinnungen*, Franziskanische Impulse 3, Werl: Dietrich-Coelde, 1999.
KRAUSE, J., *Spätantike Patronatsformen im Westen des Römischen Reiches*, Vestigia 38, München: C. H. Beck, 1987.
KREMER, J., *2. Korintherbrief*, SKK 8, Stuttgart: Kohlhammer, 1990.
KRIEGER, M., *A Window to Criticism*, Princeton: Princeton University Press, 1964.
LANG, F., *Die Briefe an die Korinther*, NTD 7, Göttingen, Vandenhoeck, 1986.
-, "Paulus und seine Gegner in Korinth und in Galatien", in: P. Schäfer et al (Hrsg), *Geschichte - Tradition - Reflexion*. Band III: *Frühes Christentum* (FS M. Hengel), Tübingen: Mohr Siebeck, 1996, 417-434.
LARFELD, W., *Griechische Epigraphik*, München: C. H. Beck, 1914.
LASSEN, E.M., "The Roman Family: Ideal and Metaphor", in: H. Moxnes (ed.), *Constructing Early Christian Families: Family as Social Reality and Metaphor*, 1997.
LATEGAN, B.C., "Levels of Reader Instruction in the Text of Galatians", in: *Semeia 48* (1989) 171-184.
LEGRAND, L., " 'That We Remember the Poor' (Gal 2:10): The Conclusion of the Jerusalem Synod according to Gal 2:10", *ITS* 32 (1995) 161-173.
LENSKI, F., *Power and Privilege. A Theory of Social Stratification*. New York: McGraw-Hill, 1966.
LÉVI-STRAUSS, C., *Les Structures Elémentaires de la Parenté*, Paris: Maiton, 1971.
-, "The Principle of Reciprocity", in: L.A. Coser & B. Rosenberg, *Sociological Theory*, New York: MacMillan, 1957.
LÉVY-BRUHL, C., *How Natives Think*, New York: Arno Press, 1979 [1926].
LIEBENAM, W., *Zur Geschichte und Organisation des römischen Vereinswesens*. 3 *Untersuchungen*, Aalen: Scientia (Neudruck der Ausgabe Leipzig 1890), 1964.
LOHSE, E., *Paulus. Eine Biographie*. München: C. H. Beck, 1996.
LONGENECKER, R.N., *Galatians*, WBC 41, Dallas: Word, 1990.
LUCKMANN, T., *Life-World and Social Realities*, London: Heinemann, 1983.
LÜDEMANN, G., *Paulus, der Heidenapostel I: Studien zur Chronologie*, FRLANT 123, Göttingen: Vandenhoeck, 1980.
-, *Das frühe Christentum nach den Traditionen der Apostelgeschichte. Ein Kommentar*. Göttingen: Vandenhoeck, 1987.
LYONS, G., *Pauline Autobiography. Toward a New Understanding*, SBL.DS 73, Atlanta: Scholars Press, 1985.
MACDONALD, M.Y., *The Pauline Churches: A Socio-historical Study of Institutionalization in the Pauline and Deutero-Pauline Writings*, Cambridge, 1988.
MACMULLEN, R., *Roman Social Relations: 50 B.C. to A.D. 284*. New Haven: Yale University Press, 1974.
-, "The Epigraphic Habit in the Roman Empire", in: *AJP* 103 (1982) 233-246.
MALHERBE, A.J., *Ancient Epistolary Theorists*, SBLSBS 19, Atlanta: Scholars Press, 1988.
-, "Seneca on Paul as Letter Writer", in: B. A. Pearson (ed.), *The Future of Early Christianity* (FS H. Koester), Minneapolis: Fortress, 1991, 414-421.

MALINA, B.J., "The Social Sciences and Biblical Interpretation", in: *Interp.* 37 (1983) 229-42.
-, "Patron and Client: The Analogy behind Synoptic Theology", in: *Forum* 4/1 (1988) 2-32.
-, & NEYREY, J.H., "Conflict in Luke-Acts: Labelling and Deviance Theory", in: J. H. Neyrey (ed.), *The Social World of Luke-Acts: Models for Interpretation*, Peabody: Hendrickson, 1991, 97-124.
- & -, *Portraits of Paul. An Archaeology of Ancient Personality*. Louisville: Westminster John Knox, 1996.
MALINOWSKI, B., *Argonauts of the Western Pacific*, New York: Dutton, 1961.
MARBÖCK, J., *Gottes Weisheit unter uns. Zur Theologie des Buches Sirach*, Herder's Biblische Studien 6, Freiburg: Herder, 1995.
MARSHALL, P., *Enmity in Corinth: Social Conventions in Paul's Relations with the Corinthians*, WUNT 23, Tübingen: Mohr Siebeck, 1987.
MARTIN, R.P. *2 Corinthians*, WBC 40, Waco: Word, 1986.
MATERA, F.J., *Galatians*, Collegeville: Liturgical Press, 1992.
MAURACH, G., *Seneca. Leben und Werk*, Darmstadt: Wissenschaftliche Buchgesellschaft, 1991.
MAUSS, M., *The Gift. The Form and Reason for Exchange in Archaic Societies*, London: Routledge, 1990
MCKNIGHT, S., "The Collection", in: G. F. Hawthorne; R. P. Martin, & D. G. Reid, (eds), *Dictionary of Paul and his Letters*, Leicester: SPCK, 1993, 143-147.
MCLEAN, B.H., "Galatians 2.7-9 and the Recognition of Paul's Apostolic Status at the Jerusalem Meeting: A Critique of G. Luedemann's Solution", in: *NTS* 37 (1991) 67-76.
MEEKS, W.A., *The First Urban Christians. The Social World of the Apostle Paul*, New Haven, 1983.
MERKLEIN, H., " 'Nicht aus Werken des Gesetzes...' Eine Auslegung von Gal 2,15-21", in: *Studien zu Jesus und Paulus II*, WUNT 105, Tübingen: Mohr Siebeck, 1998, 303-315.
MEYER, E.A., "Explaining the Epigraphic Habit in the Roman Empire: The Evidence of Epitaphs", in: *JRS* 80 (1990) 74-96.
MEYERS, E.M., "Galilean Regionalism: A Reappraisal", in: W. S. Green [ed.], *Approaches to Ancient Judaism*, Vol 5, Chico, CA: Scholars Press, 1985, 125-131.
MILLAR, F., *The Roman Empire and its Neighbours*, London, Morrison & Gibb, ²1981.
MILLER, W., Cicero, *De Officiis*, (LCL) London: Heinemann, 1975.
MILLETT, P., "Patronage and its Avoidance in Classical Athens", in A. Wallace-Hadrill (ed.), *Patronage in Ancient Society*, London: Routledge, 1989, 15-48.
MITCHELL, A.C., "Greet the Friends", in: J. T. Fitzgerald (ed.), *Friendship, Flattery and Frankness of Speech*, Leiden: Brill, 1996, 203-226.
MITCHELL, M.M., *Paul and the Rhetoric of Reconciliation*, HUT 28, Tübingen: Mohr-Siebeck, 1991.
MOO, D., *The Epistle to the Romans*, NICNT, Grand Rapids, Eerdmans, 1996.
MOORE, G.F., *Judaism in the First Centuries of the Christian Era. The Age of the Tannaim. Vol 1*, Cambridge: Harvard University Press, ⁹1962.
MOTT, S.C., "The Power of Giving and Receiving: Reciprocity in Hellenistic Benevolence", in: G. Hawthorne (ed.), *Current Issues in Biblical and Patristic Interpretation* (FS M. Tenney), Grand Rapids: Eerdmans, 1975, 60-72.

MOXNES, H., "Patron-Client Relations and the New Community in Luke-Acts", in: J. H. Neyrey (ed.), *The Social World of Luke-Acts*, Peabody: Hendrickson, 1991, 241-270.
MUNCK, J., *Paulus und die Heilsgeschichte*, Kopenhagen: Aarhuus, 1954.
MURPHY-O'CONNOR, J., *The Theology of the Second Letter to the Corinthians*, Cambridge: University Press, 1991.
-, *St. Paul's Corinth. Texts and Archaeology*, Expanded Edition, GNS 6, Collegeville: Liturgical Press, 1992.
-, *Paul - A Critical Life*, Oxford: Claredon Press, 1996.
MURRAY, O., "Introduction", in: P. Veyne, *Bread and Circuses. Historical Sociology and Political Pluralism*, London: Penguin, 1990.
MUßNER, F., *Der Galaterbrief*, HThK IX, Freiburg: Herder, 1974.
NANOS, M.D., *The Mystery of Romans. The Jewish Context of Paul's Letter*, Minneapolis: Fortress, 1996.
NEYREY, J.H., *Paul, in Other Words: A Cultural Reading of his Letters*, Louisville: Westminster John Knox, 1990.
-, *Honor and Shame in the Gospel of Matthew*, Louisville: Westminster John Knox, 1998.
NICKLE, K.F., *The Collection: A Study in Pauline Strategy*, Napierville: Allenson, 1966.
NICOLS, J., "Pliny and the Patronage of Communities", in: *Hermes* 108 (1980) 365-385.
- "Patronage in Ancient Society: A Review of Wallace-Hadrill (ed.)", in: *Gnomon* 64 (1992) 129-135.
NIEBUHR, W., *Heidenapostel aus Israel. Die jüdische Identität des Paulus nach ihrer Darstellung in seinen Briefen*, WUNT 62, Tübingen: Mohr Siebeck, 1992.
OAKMAN, D.E., *Jesus and the Economic Questions of his Day. Studies in the Bible and Early Christianity 8*, Lewiston, Queenston: Edwin Mellen Press, 1986.
OEGEMA, G.S., *Für Israel und die Völker. Studien zum alttestamentlich-jüdischen Hintergrund der paulinischen Theologie*, NT.S 95, Leiden: Brill, 1999.
OEPKE, A., *Der Brief des Paulus an die Galater*, THNT 9, Berlin: Evangelische Verlagsanstalt, ³1973.
OGG, G., *The Odessey of Paul*, New Jersey: Jervell, 1968.
OLLROG, W.H., *Paulus und seine Mitarbeiter*, WMANT 50, Neukirchen-Vluyn: Neukirchener Verlag, 1979.
OPPENHEIMER, A., *The Am Ha-Aretz*, Leiden: Brill, 1977.
ORR, W.F. & WALTHER, J.A., *1 Corinthians*, AncB 32, New York: Doubleday, 1976.
OSIEK, C. & BALCH, D.L., *Families in the New Testament World. Households and House Churches*. Louisville: Westminster John Knox, 1997.
OVERMAN, J.A., "The Diaspora in the Modern Study of Ancient Judaism", in: J. A. Overman & R. S. MacLennan (eds.), *Diaspora Jews and Judaism. Essays in Honor of, and in Dialogue with A. T. Kraabel*, Atlanta: Scholars, 1992, 63-78.
PALLAS, D.I., CHARITONDIS, S. & VENENCIE, J., "Inscriptions Lyciennes trouvées a Solômos pres de Corinthe", in: *BCH* 83 (1959) 496-508.
PAPATHOMAS, A., "Das agonistische Motiv 1 Kor 9.24ff. im Spiegel zeitgenössischer dokumentarischer Quelle", in: *NTS* 43 (1997) 223-241.
PESCH, R., *Die Apostelgeschichte (Apg 1-12)*, EKK V/I, Zürich: Benziger/Neukirchener Verlag, 1986.
-, *Paulus kämpft um sein Apostolat. Drei weitere Briefe an die Gemeinde Gottes in Korinth*, Freiburg: Herder, 1987.
PETERMAN, G.W., *Paul's Gift from Philippi. Conventions of Gift Exchange and Christian Giving*, MSSNTS 92, Cambridge: Cambridge University Press, 1997.

PETERSEN, R.N., *Rediscovering Paul. Philemon and the Sociology of Paul's Narrative World*, Philadelphia: Fortress, 1985.
PLEKET, H.W., *Epigraphica Vol II: Texts on the Social History of the Greek World*, TMUA 41, Leiden: Brill 1969.
PLUMMER, A. *A Critical and Exegetical Commentary on the Second Epistle of Paul to the Corinthians*, ICC 47, Edinburgh: T & T Clark, 1915 (repr. 1978).
PORTER, S.E., "Paul of Tarsus and his Letters", in: S.E. Porter (ed.), *Handbook of Classical Rhetoric in the Hellenistic Period 330 B.C - A. D. 400*, Leiden: Brill, 1997, 533-585.
PRELL, M., *Armut im antiken Rom. Von den Gracchen bis Kaiser Diokletian*. Stuttgart: Steiner, 1997.
PRICE, S.R.F., *Rituals and Power. The Roman Imperial Cult in Asia Minor*. Cambridge: Cambridge University Press, 1986 (repr 1987).
QUAß, F., *Die Honoratiorenschicht in den Städten des Griechischen Ostens. Untersuchungen zur politischen und sozialen Entwicklung in hellenistischer und römischer Zeit*. Stuttgart: Steiner Verlag, 1993.
RAJAK, T., "Benefactors in the Graeco-Jewish Diaspora", in: P. Schäfer et al (Hrsg.), *Geschichte – Tradition – Reflexion*, Band 1: Judentum (FS. M. Hengel), Tübingen: Mohr Siebeck, 1996, 305-319.
RAWSON, E., "The Eastern Clientelae of Clodius and the Claudii", in: *Historia* 22 (1973) 219-239.
REED, J.T., "The Epistle", in: S.E. Porter (ed.), *Handbook of Classical Rhetoric in the Hellenistic Period 330 B.C - A. D. 400*, Leiden: Brill, 1997, 171-193.
REUMANN, J., "Contributions of the Philippian Community to Paul and to Earliest Christianity", in: *NTS* 39 (1993) 438-457.
RICKMAN, G., *The Corn Supply of Ancient Rome*, Oxford: Claredon Press, 1980.
RIESNER, R., *Die Frühzeit des Apostels Paulus. Studien zur Chronologie, Missionsstrategie und Theologie*, WUNT 71, Tübingen: Mohr Siebeck, 1994.
ROHDE, J., *Der Galaterbrief*, ThHK 9; Berlin: Evangelische Verlagsanstalt, 1988.
ROLOFF, J., *Die Apostelgeschichte*, NTD 5, Göttingen: Vandenhoeck, 1981.
RUSSELL, R., "The Idle in 2 Thess 3:6-12: An Eschatological or a Social Problem?", in: *NTS* 34 (1988) 105-119.
RUTGERS, L.V., *The Hidden Heritage of Diaspora Judaism*, Leuven: Uitgeverij Peeters, 1998.
SALLER, R.P., *Personal Patronage under the Early Empire*, Cambridge: Cambridge University Press, 1982.
-, *Patriarchy, Property and Death in the Roman Family*, Cambridge: Cambridge University Press, 1994.
SAMPLEY, J.P., *Pauline Partnership in Christ*, Philadelphia: Fortress, 1980.
SANDERS, E.P., *Judaism: Practice and Belief, 63 BCE - 66 CE*, London: SCM, 1992.
SANDNES, K.O., "Equality within Patriarchal Structures: Some New Testament Perspectives on the Christian Fellowship as a Brother- or Sisterhood and a Family", in: H. Moxnes (ed.), *Constructing Early Christian Families. Family as Social Reality and Metaphor*. London: Routledge, 1997, 150-166.
SCHENKE, L., *Die Urgemeinde. Geschichtliche und theologische Entwicklung*. Stuttgart: Kohlhammer Verlag, 1990.
SCHLIER, H., *Der Brief an die Galater*, KEK 7, Göttingen: Vandenhoeck, [5]1971 (1949).
SCHMITHALS, W., *Der Römerbrief. Ein Kommentar*, Gütersloh: Gerd Mohn, 1988.

SCHNACKENBURG, R., "Die Einheit der Kirche und die koinonia-Gedanken", in: F. Hahn, K. Kertelge & R. Schnackenburg (Hrsg.), *Einheit der Kirche. Grundlegungen im Neuen Testament*, Freiburg: Herder, 1979, 52-93.
SCHNEIDERS, S.M., *The Revelatory Text: Interpreting the New Testament as Sacred Scripture*, San Francisco: Harper, 1992.
SCHNELLE, U., *Gerechtigkeit und Christusgegenwart*, GTA 24, Göttingen: Vandenhoeck, ²1986.
SCHRAGE, W., *Der Erste Brief an die Korinther* (1 Kor 1,1-6,11), EKK 7/1, Neukirchen: Neukirchener Verlag, 1991.
SCHROEDER, F.M., "Friendship in Aristotle", in: J. T. Fitzgerald (ed.), *Graeco-Roman Perspectives on Friendship*. Atlanta: Scholars Press, 1996, 6-16.
SCHULZ, F., *Classical Roman Law*, Aalen: Scientia Verlag, 1992.
SCHWANKL, O., "Lauft so, daß ihr gewinnt. Zur Wettkampfmetaphorik in 1 Kor 9", in: *BZ* (1997) 174-191.
SCHWARTZ, D.R., "Ishmael ben Phiabi and the Chronology of Provincia Judaea", in: *Studies in the Jewish Background of Christianity*, WUNT 60, Tübingen: Mohr Siebeck, 1992.
SCOTT, J.M. *Paul and the Nations. The Old Testament and Jewish Background of Paul's Mission to the Nations with Special Reference to the Destination of Galatians*, WUNT 84, Tübingen: Mohr Siebeck, 1993.
SEARLE, J.R., *The Construction of Social Reality*, London: Penguin, 1995.
SECCOMBE, D., "Was there Organized Charity in Jerusalem before the Christians?", in: *JThS* 29 (1978), 140-143.
SEGAL, A.F., *Paul the Convert. The Apostolate and Apostasy of Saul the Pharisee*, New Haven: Yale University Press, 1990.
SHARPLES, R.W., *Stoics, Epicureans and Sceptics. An Introduction to Hellenistic Philosophy*. London: Routledge, 1996.
SHELTON, J., *As the Romans Did*. New York: Oxford University Press, 1988.
SHERWIN-WHITE, A.N., *The Letters of Pliny the Younger: A Historical and Social Commentary*. Oxford: Oxford University Press, 1966.
SHURDEN, S.H., *The Christian Response to Poverty in the New Testament Era*. Michigan: Michigan Microfilms International, 1970.
SIEGERT, F., *Argumentation bei Paulus, gezeigt an Röm 9-11*. WUNT 34, Tübingen: Mohr Siebeck, 1985.
SÖDING, T., *Das Liebesgebot bei Paulus: Die Mahnung zur Agape im Rahmen der paulinischen Ethik*, NTA 26, Münster: Aschendorff, 1995.
-, "Zur Chronologie der paulinischen Briefe", in: *BN 56* (1991), 57-58, repr. in: T. Söding, *Das Wort vom Kreuz*, WUNT 93, Tübingen: Mohr Siebeck, 1997, 3-30.
-, " 'Apostel der Heiden' (Röm 11,3). Zur paulinischen Missionspraxis, in: T. Söding, *Das Wort vom Kreuz*, WUNT 93, Tübingen: Mohr Siebeck, 1997, 185-195
-, "Der Erste Thessalonicherbrief und die frühe paulinische Evangeliumsverkündigung. Zur Frage einer Entwicklung der paulinischen Theologie", in: T. Söding, *Das Wort vom Kreuz*, WUNT 93, Tübingen: Mohr Siebeck 1997, 31-56.
-, "Die Gegner des Apostels Paulus in Galatien. Beobachtungen zu ihrer Evangeliumsverkündigung und ihrem Konflikt mit Paulus", in: T. Söding, *Das Wort vom Kreuz*, WUNT 93, Tübingen: Mohr Siebeck, 1997, 132-152.
SØRENSEN, V., *Seneca. Ein Humanist an Nero's Hof.* München: C. H. Beck, ²1985.
SPERBER, D., "Patronage in Amoraic Palestine (c. 220-400): Causes and Effects", in: *Journal of the Economic and Social History of the Orient 14* (1971) 120-132.

SPICQ, C., "εὐεργεσία, " *Theological Lexicon of the New Testament*, Volume 2, Peabody: Hendrickson, 1994, 107-113.
STEGEMANN, E.W. & STEGEMANN, W., *Urchristliche Sozialgeschichte. Die Anfänge im Judentum und die Christusgemeinden in der mediterranen Welt*, Stuttgart: Kohlhammer, 1995.
STEVENSON, T.R., "The Ideal Benefactor and the Father Analogy in Greek and Roman Thought", in: *CQ* 42 (1992) 421-436.
STOWERS, S.K., *The Diatribe and Paul's Letter to Romans*, SBL.DS 57, Chico, CA: Scholars Press, 1981.
STRACK, H.L. & BILLERBECK, P., *Das Evangelium nach Matthäus erläutert aus Talmud und Midrasch. Band 1*, München: C.H. Beck ('sche Verlagsbuchhandlung), 1922.
STUHLMACHER, P., *Das Paulinische Evangelium 1. Vorgeschichte*, FRLANT 95, Göttingen: Vandenhoeck, 1968.
-, *Der Brief an die Römer*, NTD 6, Göttingen: Vandenhoeck, 1989.
SUHL, A., *Paulus und seine Briefe. Ein Beitrag zur paulinischen Chronologie*, StNT 11, Gütersloh: Kaiser, 1975.
SVENBRO, J., *Phrasikleia: An Anthropology of Reading in Ancient Greece*, Ithaca: Cornell University Press, 1993.
TALBERT, C.H., "Money Management in Early Christianity: 2 Corinthians 8 and 9", in: *Review and Expositor* (1989) 359-370.
TANNEHILL, R.C., *The Narrative Unity of Luke-Acts. A Literary Interpretation. Volume 2: The Acts of the Apostles*. Minneapolis: Fortress, 1990.
TAYLOR, N., *Paul, Antioch and Jerusalem. A Study in Relationships and Authority in Earliest Christianity*, JSNTS 66, Sheffield: JSOT Press, 1992.
THEOBALD, M., *Die überströmende Gnade. Studien zu einem paulinischen Motivfeld*, FzB 22, Würzburg: Echter, 1982.
THOMPSON, J.B., *Studies in the Theory of Ideology*. Cambridge: Polity Press, 1984.
THURÉN, L., "Hey Jude! Asking for the Original Situation and Message of a Catholic Epistle", in: *NTS* 43 (1997) 451-65.
TOULOUMAKOS, J., "Zum römischen Gemeindepatronat im griechischen Osten", in: *Hermes 11* (1988) 304-324.
TOWNER, M.H., "Mission Practice and Theology under Construction (Acts 18-20)", in: I.H. Marshall & D. Peterson (eds.), *Theology of Acts*, 1998, 417-436.
TREGGIARI, S., *Roman Marriage: 'Iusti Coniuges' from the Time of Cicero to the Time of Ulpian*, Oxford: Oxford University Press, 1991.
TROBISCH, D., *Die Paulusbriefe und die Anfänge der christlichen Publizistik*, Gütersloh: Kaiser, 1994.
UMBACH, H., *In Christus getauft – von der Sünde befreit: Die Gemeinde als Sündenfreier Raum bei Paulus*, Vandenhoeck & Ruprecht: Göttingen, 1999.
VAN DER WATT, J.G., "Ethics in First John: A Literary and Socioscientific Perspective", in: *CBQ* 61 (1999) 491-511.
VAN DIJK, T.A., "Cognitive and Conversational Strategies in the Expression of Ethnic Prejudice", in: *Text 3* (1983) 377-385.
VEYNE, P., *Bread and Circuses. Historical Sociology and Political Pluralism*, London: Penguin, 1990.
VYHMEISTER, N.J., "The Rich Man in James 2: Does Ancient Patronage Illumine the Text?", in: *AUSS* 33 (1995) 265-283.
WACHOLDER, B.Z., "The Calendar of Sabbatical Cycles during the Second Temple and the Early Rabbinic period", in: *HUCA* 44 (1973) 153-196.

WALLACE-HADRILL, A., "Patronage in Roman Society: From Republic to Empire", in: A. Wallace-Hadrill (ed.), *Patronage in Ancient Society*, London: Routledge, 1989, 63-88.
WALTER, N., "Apostelgeschichte 6,1 und die Anfänge der Urgemeinde in Jerusalem", in: *NTS* 29 (1983) 370-393.
WATSON, F., *Paul, Judaism and the Gentiles. A Sociological Approach*, MSSNTS 56, Cambridge: Cambridge University Press, 1986.
WEHNERT, J., *Die Reinheit des christlichen Gottesvolkes aus Juden und Heiden. Studien zum historischen und theologischen Hintergrund des sogennanten Aposteldekres*. FRLANT 172, Göttingen: Vandenhoeck, 1997.
WEHR, L., *Petrus und Paulus - Kontrahenten und Partner. Die beiden Apostel im Spiegel des Neuen Testaments, der Apostolischen Väter und früher Zeugnisse ihrer Verehrung*, NTA 30, Münster: Aschendorff, 1996.
WEISER, A., *Die Apostelgeschichte I*, ÖTK 5/I-II, Gütersloh: Gerd Mohn, 1981.
WENDLAND, H.D., *Die Briefe an die Korinther*, NTD 7, Göttingen: Vandenhoeck, ^{15}1980.
WESTERMANN, C., *Genesis 12-36: A Commentary*, Minneapolis: Augsburg Publishers, 1985.
WHITE, L.M., *Building God's House in the Roman World. Architectural Adaptation among Pagans, Jews and Christians, Baltimore*: John Hopkins 1990.
-, "Morality Between Two worlds: A Paradigm of Friendship in Philippians", in: D.L. Balch, E. Fergusson & W.A. Meeks (eds.), *Greeks, Romans and Christians*, 1990, 201-215.
WHITE, P., "The Friends of Martial, Status and Pliny and the Dispersal of Patronage", in: *HSCP* 79 (1975) 265-300.
WILCKENS, U., *Der Brief an die Römer, 3. Teil: Rom 12-16*, EKK 6/3, Neukirchen: Neukirchener Verlag, 1982.
WILK, F., *Die Bedeutung des Jesajabuches für Paulus*, FRLANT 179, Göttingen: Vandenhoeck, 1998.
WINDISCH, H., *Der zweite Korintherbrief*, KEK, Göttingen: Vandenhoeck, 1970.
WINTER, B.W., "Secular and Christian Responses to Corinthian Famines", in: *TynB* 40 (1989) 86-106.
-, *Seek the Welfare of the City. Christians as Benefactors and Citizens*. Grand Rapids: Eerdmans, 1994.
-, "Acts and Food Shortages", in: D.W.J. Gill & C. Gempf (eds.), *The Book of Acts in its First Century Setting*, Vol 2: *The Book of Acts in its Graeco-Roman Setting*, Grand Rapids: Eerdmans, 1994, 59-78.
WISEMAN, T.P., " 'Pete nobiles amicos.' Poets and Patrons in Late Republican Rome", in: B. K. Gold (ed.), *Literary and Artistic Patronage in Ancient Rome*, Austin: University of Texas Press, 1982.
WITHERINGTON (III), B., *Conflict and Community. A Socio-Rhetorical Commentary of 1 and 2 Corinthians*. Grand Rapids, Eerdmans, 1995.
-, *The Acts of the Apostles. A Socio-Rhetorical Commentary*, Grand Rapids: Eerdmans, 1997.
-, *The Paul Quest. The Renewed Search for the Jew of Tarsus*, Leicester: InterVarsity, 1998.
-, *Grace in Galatia*, Edinburgh: T&T Clark, 1998.
WOLFF, C., *Der zweite Brief des Paulus an die Korinther*, ThHK 8, Berlin: Evangelische Verlagsanstalt, 1989.

-, *Der erste Brief des Paulus an die Korinther,* ThHK 7, Leipzig: Evangelische Verlagsanstalt, 1996.
ZEILINGER, F., *Krieg und Friede in Korinth. Kommentar zum 2. Korintherbrief des Apostels Paulus. Teil 1: Der Kampfbrief. Der Versöhnungsbrief. Der Bettelbrief.* Wien: Böhlau Verlag, 1992.

Index of Modern Authors

Abel, K., 40
Achtermeier, J., 204
Alföldy, G., 26
Altman, J.G., 157
Ascough, 4, 133, 174, 181, 209
Ascough, R.S., 4, 133, 174, 181, 209
Bachmann, M., 78
Badian, E., 23, 24, 25, 62
Balch, D.L., 30, 35, 234
Bar-Ilan, M., 12
Barnett, P., 3, 113, 135, 137, 148, 165
Barrett, C.K., 3, 86, 134, 141, 142, 161, 185, 187
Bartsch, H.W., 2, 73
Basore, J.W., 18
Baur, F.C., 91
Becker, J., 78, 87, 90, 121, 124, 160, 165,
Becker, L.C., 19
Beckheuer, B., 4, 88, 89, 122, 133, 178
Beker, J.C., 6
Ben-David, A., 107
Benedum, J., 53
Benner, A.R., 45
Benner, P., 61
Berger, K., 3, 73, 89, 131
Berger, P., 10
Best, E., 167
Betz, H.D., 73, 76-100, 104, 117, 128, 134, 140, 142, 144, 147, 148, 174, 177, 188, 193, 194
Billerbeck, P., 96
Blau, P.M., 19, 22, 46, 150
Bleicken, J., 27, 62
Bloch, M., 14
Boers, H., 79, 84
Boissevain, J., 28
Bolkestein, H., 39, 94, 98
Bolyki, J., 118
Bormann, L., 23, 27, 61, 70, 127, 129

Bornkamm, G., 78
Borse, U., 75, 77
Botha, P.J.J., 92
Böttger, P.C., 117
Brändle, R., 2
Bratcher, R.G., 192
Breytenbach, C., 76, 223
Bruce, F.F., V, 76, 205, 211
Bultmann, C., 96
Bultmann, R., 135, 181, 190
Capper, B.J., 111
Carey, C., 173
Carney, T.F., 15
Cary, E., 60
Charitondis, S., 55
Chow, J.K., 22, 35, 70, 127, 165
Clarke, M.L., 31
Cohen, D., 166
Collins, J.N., 128, 208
Collins, M., 34, 94
Conzelmann, H., 160, 162
Cook K.S., 19
Craffert, P.F., 167
Cranfield, C.E.B., 128, 132
Cullmann, O., 219
Curchin, .A., 24
Dahl, N.A., 189
Danker, F.W., 51, 53
Dibelius, M., 92
Dietzfelbinger, C., 179
Dinkler, E., 86
Dixon, S., 28, 169, 170
Dodd, B.J., 81, 82
Dommershausen, W., 107
Donahue, J.R., 12
Douglas, M., 19, 20
Drummond, A., 24
Duncan-Jones, R., 32, 55

Index of Modern Authors

Dunn, J.D.G., 76, 81, 86, 104, 105, 118, 119, 123, 130, 133, 136, 178, 192, 208
Du Toit, A.B., 81, 167
Eagleton, T., 9
Eckert, J., 1, 89
Eckstein, H.J., 77
Edlund, I.E.M., 29, 60, 65
Eisenstadt, S.N., 24, 63
Elliott, J.H., 8, 9, 14, 15
Engberg-Pedersen, T., 36
Engels, D., 155, 161, 194
Erskine, A., 63, 64
Esler, P.F., 120, 227
Fee, G.D., 159-161
Finley, M., 59
Fitzgerald, J.J.T., 69, 224, 229, 232
Forbes, F.H., 45
Freyne, S., 99
Fung, R.Y.K., 1
Furnish, V.P., 3, 134, 136, 174, 175, 182, 196
Gardner J.F., 34
Garnsey, P., 11, 27, 29, 33, 56, 61, 69, 98, 109, 110, 225, 227
Gaston, L., 120, 131
Gauthier, P., 51
Georgi, D., VII, 2, 3, 78, 87-89, 121, 137, 141, 190, 206, 225
Gewalt, D., 89
Giddens, A., 9, 11
Gill, D.W.J., 125, 225, 234
Gnilka, J., 1, 87, 90, 103, 116, 142, 144, 146, 178, 212
Gouldner, A.W., 19
Gregory, C.A., 20, 21, 147
Gruen, E.S., 59
Haacker, K., 82
Haenchen, E., 111
Hainz, J., 2, 84, 129, 137, 208
Hall, D.R., 89
Hands, A.R., 39, 41, 54
Hanson, K.C., 12
Harrill, J.A., 25
Harvey, E.A., 174, 191, 192
Hays, R.B., 141
Hendrix, H., 68
Hengel, M., VIII, 80, 84, 90, 92, 109, 112, 228, 231
Héring, J., 189, 191
Herman, G., 69
Hester, J.C., 78

Hiller von Gärtringen, F., 52
Höffe, O., 38, 39
Holl, K., 89
Holmberg, B., 1, 73, 168
Holzberg, N., 31
Horn, F.W., 111
Horrell, D.G., 4, 9
Horsley, R.A., 99
Hübner, H., 79
Hughes, F.W., 78
Hughes, P.E., 186
Hyldahl, N., 1, 78, 211
Inwood, B., 43, 48, 51
Jager, J.H., 186
Jameson, M., 56
Jeremias, J., 109, 111
Jervell, J., 211, 214, 230
Jewett, R., 78
Jones, C.P., 55, 57
Joubert, S.J., I, VIII, 61, 81, 117, 127, 166, 167, 170, 182
Karrer, M., 179
Käsemann, E., 89
Keck, L., 89
Kennedy, G.A., 78
Kent, J.H., 52, 65
Kern, P.H., 79
Kidd, R.M., 5, 39, 54, 55
Kim, S., 86
Klauck, H.J., V, VII, 33, 34, 40, 42, 55, 79, 90, 98, 111-113, 126, 134, 136, 137, 139, 143, 144, 156, 161, 162, 164, 165, 179, 184, 186, 189, 190, 193
Krause, J., 23, 69
Kremer, J., 185
Krieger, M., 12
Lang, F., 10, 135, 142, 145, 181, 221
Larfeld, W., 54
Lassen, E.M., 170
Lategan, B.C., 78
Legrand, L., 3, 88, 90
Lenski, F., 107
Lévi-Strauss, C., 19, 22
Lévy-Bruhl, C., 120
Liebenam, W., 33
Lohse, E., 3, 122, 124, 211
Longenecker, R.N., 78
Luckmann, T., 10
Lüdemann, G., 1, 86, 89, 91, 111, 129
Lyons, G., 82
MacDonald, M.Y., 3

MacMullen, R., 33
Malherbe, A.J., 79, 102
Malina, B.J., VII, 5, 15, 82, 83, 120, 127
Malinowski, B., 21
Marböck, J., 96, 97
Marshall, P., 19, 48, 70, 165, 222, 233
Martin, R.P., VIII, 92, 136, 142, 145, 209, 222, 229
Matera, F.J., 90
Maurach, G., 42, 50
Mauss, M., 19, 20, 223
McKnight, S., 3
McLean, B.H., 87, 102
Meeks, W.A., 73, 167, 234
Merklein, H., 117
Meyer, E.A., 52
Meyers, E.M., 99
Millar, F., 108
Miller, W., 18
Millett, P., 23, 59
Mitchell, A.C., 63, 78
Mitchell, M.M., 63, 78
Moo, D., 128, 130
Moore, G.F., 96
Mott, S.C., 49, 138
Moxnes, H., 63, 228, 231
Munck, J., 2, 3
Murphy-O'Conner, J., 116, 120, 155, 165, 175, 178, 183, 187, 198, 214
Murray, O., 12, 19
Mußner, F., 76, 85, 105, 224, 225
Nanos, M.D., 133
Neyrey, J.H., VII, 82, 83, 120, 121, 160, 229, 230
Nickle, K.F., VII, 3, 131, 146
Nicols, J.J., 28, 32, 62, 63, 66
Niebuhr, W., 80, 82
Oakman, D.E., 12, 107
Oegema, G.S, 76
Oepke, A., 80, 87
Ogg, G., 109
Ollrog, W.H., 189, 205
Oppenheimer, A., 108
Orr, W.F., 160, 161
Osiek, C., 30, 35
Overman, J.A., 96, 230
Pallas D.I., 55
Papathomas, A., 84
Pesch, R., 91, 93, 165, 212
Peterman, G.W., 17, 49, 50, 55, 94, 97, 99, 167

Petersen, R.N., 83, 157
Pleket, H.W., 55, 178
Plummer, A., 142
Porter, S.E., 79, 226, 231
Prell, M., 30, 33, 57, 62, 68, 130, 149
Price, S.R.F., 53
Quaß, F., 25, 51, 52, 56, 57, 64
Rajak, T., 34, 52, 55, 94
Rawson, E., 65, 223
Reed, J.T., 79
Reumann, J. 4
Rickman, G., 56
Riesner, R., 1, 76, 108, 125, 211
Rohde, J., 77
Roloff, J., 92, 205, 212
Roniger, L., 24, 63
Russell, R., 63
Rutgers, L.V., 96
Saller, R.P., 19, 23, 27-29, 33, 56, 59, 69, 98, 110, 170
Sampley, J.P., 101
Sanders, E.P., 107, 119
Sandnes, K.O., 159
Schenke, L., 74, 75, 92, 108, 112, 213
Schlier, H., 75, 89, 100, 102, 130
Schmithals, W., 130, 132, 206
Schnackenburg, R., 130, 232
Schneiders, S.M., 12
Schnelle, U., 77
Schrage, W., 155
Schroeder, F.M., 54
Schulz, F., 170
Schwankl, O., 43, 84
Schwartz, D., 109
Schwemer, A.M., 92
Scott, J.M., 76
Searle, J.R., 9
Seccombe, D., 110
Segal, A.F., 96, 125
Sharples, R.W., 41
Shelton, J., 23
Sherwin-White, A.N., 28
Shurden, S.H., 110
Siegert, F., 166
Söding, T., V, 77, 78, 123, 131, 134, 177, 225, 232
Sørensen, V., 41
Sperber, D., 94
Spicq, C., 40
Stegemann, E.W., 18, 107, 193
Stegemann, W., 18, 107, 194
Stevenson, T.R., 40, 171, 172

Stowers, S.K., 174
Strack, H.L., 96
Stuhlmacher, P., 80, 208
Suhl, A., 1
Svenbro, J., 12
Talbert, C.H., 178, 179, 233
Tannehill, R.C., 92
Taylor, N., 78
Theobald, M., 136, 142, 144, 146, 148, 177, 195, 201
Thompson, J.B., 9
Thurén, L., 81
Touloumakos, J., 62, 64, 65
Towner, M.H., 147
Treggiari, S., 169
Trobisch, D., 2
Umbach, H., 117
Van der Watt, J., 169
Van Dijk, T.A., 166
Venencie, J., 55
Veyne, P., 19, 27, 38, 39, 52, 53, 57, 59, 68, 149, 230
Vyhmeister, N.J., 63
Wacholder, B.Z., 109

Wallace-Hadrill, A., 24, 27, 28, 59, 224, 225, 229, 230, 234
Walter, N., 111, 221
Walther, J.A., 160, 161
Watson, F., 117
Wehnert, J., 84, 87, 109, 117, 119
Wehr, L., 78, 117, 121
Weiser, A., 92
Wendland, H.D., 185
Westermann, C., 95
White, L.M., 31, 34, 70, 226
White, P., 31
Wiedemann, T., 34
Wilckens, U., 128, 130
Wilk, F., 196
Windisch, H., 136, 141, 180, 185, 194
Winter, B.W., 22, 51, 63, 110, 125, 165, 208, 226
Wiseman, T.P., 24
Witherington (III), B., 3, 78, 79, 92, 113, 119, 136, 211
Wolff, C., 3, 135, 137, 142-144, 160, 162, 177, 182, 191
Woolf, G., 11, 61, 69
Zeilinger, F., 128, 136, 140, 145, 179

Index of Passages

Ancient Texts

Alciphron			*Antiquitates Romanae*	60-63
Letters of Fishermen			Eusebius	
10.5	45		*Hist. Eccl.*	110
Aristotle				
Nicomachean Ethics	37		Josephus	
III-IV	37		*Antiquitates*	
IV.1	39		3,320	109
IV.3	48		18,90	108
IV.2.1-15	38		18,328-9	100
VIII.1	54		20,2	109
VIII.8.9	47, 54		20,51-53	109, 110, 113
VIII.14	54		*Bello Judaicum*	
Art of Rhetoric			5,410	108
1356a	173		*Contra Apionem*	
1361a 28-43	38, 39		II.74-78	94
1361a43-1361b3	39		II.185-6	94
Polis 21	140		II.205	94
			II.217	93
Arrian				
Epictetio Dissertationes			Juvenal	
II.9.12	49		*Satires*	
			3.189	35
Cicero			VII.1-97	35
De Officiis				
1.47	18		Isocrates	
1.48	48, 103		*Aeropagiticus*	
1.58	171		31-35	38-39
Verres				
II.2.154	66		Lucian	
			Nigrinius	
Dio Chrysostom			22	66
Oratio				
46,2-13	57		Martial	
66.2	53, 55, 56		*Epigrams*	
75.6	37		1.59	35
75.7	53		3.7	35
Dionysius of Halicarnassus			3.8	34

5.22	35	*Moralia*	
6.88	35	582	40
7.72	31	820B	54
		822B	56
Philo		*Romulus*	
Cherubim		XIII.5	60
122-123	98		
De Decal.		Seneca	
1.4-7	98	*De Beneficiis*	
De Virtue		– See discussion of contents	40-51
82-84	98	I.4.2	18
Plant.		I.4.3-4	178
126-131	138	I.6.1	182
Quis Rer. Div. Her.		II.1.1	195
141-206	140	II.23-25	91, 103
Spec. leg.		II.35.1.1	103
1.95	138	IV.3.1	182
1.283	138	IV.20.1	210
		V.4.2	27
Philodemus		VI.33.3-34-5	105
On Household Management		VI.34.2-3	29, 34
23.22-36	31	VI.41.1-2	41, 102
		VII.15.3	103
Pliny the Younger		*De Brev. Vit.*	
Epistulae	28	1.4	36
I.19	29		
II.9.2	28	Tacitus	
II.13.19	36	*Annals*	
III.12.2	34	6,13	112
III.6.14	54		
IV.1.4-5	31	Theophrast	
IV.17	30	*Characters*	36
VII.3	30		
X.12	29	Xenophon	
X.51	29	*Mem.*	
		II.2.1	171
Plutarch		*Oeconomicus*	
Quomondo adulator ab amico Internoscatur	36	2.1-18	54

Early Jewish Texts

1 Maccabees		Mishnah	
6,58	100	*Peah*	110
11,50. 62	100		
13,45	100	Sirach	
		3,14	97
2 Maccabees		3,30	97
11,26	100	29,8-13	97

Tobit
2,11-14	96	12,9	97
4,10	97		

Early Christian texts

Tertullian
Apologetica
39,7   57

Biblical texts

Old Testament

Genesis
18,1-8   162
19,1-8   162
33   95

Exodus
2,15ff   95
16,18   141, 143, 183

Numbers
6,1-21   214

Deuteronomy
15,1-18   95
15,8   96
24,17-22   95

Judges
8,5-9.35   95

1 Samuel
25   95

2 Samuel
14,22   95

2 Kings
4,8-17   95
8   110
10,15   100

2 Chronicles
20,10-1   95

Ezra
10,19   100

Job
4,8   193

Psalms
103,6   96
111,9   196
126,5   193
146,7-9   96

Proverbs
11,21   193
11,24   193
11,26   193
11,30   193
22,8   193

Isaiah
55,10   197
61,6   133
66,20   133

Index of Passages

Ezekiel
17,18   101

Hosea
17,18   197

New Testament

Matthew
14-34   121
40-48   217

Mark
10,17-31   217

Luke
6,33   217
7,1-10   99

Acts
4,3-37   92
4,32-35   111
4,36   92
6,1-7   111,112
8,1   91
8,12   85
9,7   92
9,11   90
9,30   90
10   213
11,28   108
11,27ff   91
11,29   92
11,19-30   91
11,27-30   89, 91, 92, 108
12,25   92
13   92
14   92
15   92, 213
16,6   77, 126
16,6-11   125
16,12ff   125
17,1   125
17,10ff   125
17,15ff   125
18,1ff   125
18,23   77, 126
19,23ff   147
20,4   205
20,5   211
20,5-12   125
20,13-14   125, 211
20,15   211
20,15-38   125
21,1   211
21,3   211
21,7   211
21,8   211
21,10   213
21,17ff   7, 211, 212, 218
21,21   213
21,23-24   214
22,3   90
24,17   92, 211, 212
35,14   85

Romans
1,5   136
1,8ff   80
5,5   194
6,14   179
11,25   86, 123
11,26   86, 123
12,1-2   137
12,9-21   129, 208
15   131, 133, 134, 136, 153, 206, 207, 209, 210, 214, 218
15,15   136, 191
15,16   133, 145
15,22-33   128
15,25   2, 124, 133, 169, 214, 217
15,25-31   2
15,25-27   77, 128, 151, 204
15,25   92, 124, 205
15,26   90, 205, 113, 218
15,27   89, 132, 141, 144, 150, 209
15,28   133
15,30-31   206, 208, 212
15,31   92, 123, 133, 191
15,31-32   214
16,1   190

1 Corinthians
1,1-2   126, 167
1,4ff   80

1,5	176	4,15	146
1,12	123	5	153
2,1	127, 167	5,20	127
2,7	127	5,21	178
3,1-2	168	6,13	167
3,10	136	7,5	191
3,22	123	7,6	175, 185
4,1	127	7,7	178
4,14-15	168	7,8	165
4,17	168	7,12	165
5,9	156	7,16	168
7,1-40	168	8-9	2, 7, 124, 134, 135, 144, 146, 153, 155, 156, 164, 166, 167, 168, 172, 173, 178. 181, 184, 198-201, 216
7,1	156		
7,8	167		
7,25	156		
7,30	136		
8,1	156	8	130, 142, 198, 189
9,5	123	8,1-5	152, 199
9,16	125	8,1-6	134, 135, 138, 139, 199, 173, 175, 198, 209, 216
12-14	177		
12,1	156		
12,8-9	176	8,1	145
14,1	131	8,4	90, 92, 128, 208
16	156, 157, 164, 167, 168	8,6	164
		8,7-9	176, 198, 199
16:1-4	2, 4, 7, 124, 156-158, 164, 167, 168, 173, 187, 198, 199, 216	8,7	142, 178
		8,8-22	188
		8,10-15	180, 183, 198
16,1	90, 128, 156, 198, 200	8,10-12	180
16,2	90, 181	8,11-15	199
16,4	187	8,13-15	130, 140, 144, 151
16,5	157	8,16-24	184, 198
16,12	156	8,16-17	185
16,15	128, 190	8,18-22	186
16,17	156	8,19-20	92
		8,23-24	189
2 Corinthians		9,1-5	189, 192, 198, 199
1,1	126, 167	9,1	90, 92, 128, 189, 208
1,11	146	9,2	200
1-9	77, 78, 134, 164, 166, 184	9,6-15	193, 199, 209, 216
		9,6	210
1,15-16	190	9,6-10	193, 197
2,4	165, 176	9,10-15	198
2,5	165	9,11-14	151, 152, 204, 209, 219
2,6	166		
2,8	168	9,11-15	144, 150, 209
2,9	168	9,12-14	142, 143
2,12	166	9,12	90, 128, 207, 208, 217
2,13	191	10-13	77, 78, 127, 134, 164, 165
3,2-3	194		
4,6	127	11,7	165
4,7-18	136	12,1-5	127

12,2	127	4,13-15	77, 126
12,13	165	4,21	122
12,14-16	167	5.14	117
12,14	165, 168	6,7b-8	194
12,15	168		
13-15	130, 168, 209	*Philippians*	
13,1	165	1,11	133
13,9	168	1,22	133
13,11	168	1,30	44
		2,1-11	129
Galatians		2,3-4	208
1-2	82, 83, 92, 93, 118, 127	2,5-11	178, 179
		2,16	44, 84, 125
1	127	2,17	137
1,10	81, 214	3,12-14	44
1,11-2,21	80	4,4	166
1,18-19	105	4,11-13	166, 195
1,18	76	4,19	166
1,21	76		
2	81, 90, 91, 92, 105, 106, 132	1 *Thessalonians*	
		1,1-2	80
2,1-10	73, 75, 80, 83, 85, 90, 103, 104, 114, 213, 217	1,1	126
		3,9	147
		2,14	122, 123
2,2	84, 93		
2,4	76, 84	*Philemon*	
2,6-10	100	2,1-11	129
2,7-10	86, 87	2,5-11	179
2,7-8	87	2,16	125
2,10	2, 6, 7 17, 77, 78, 80, 88, 89, 100, 102, 103, 113, 116, 130, 151, 153, 210, 217	4,11-13	195
		Hebrews	
2:11-14	77, 116, 117	13,1f.	162
3,28	122		
4,6	194	3 *John*	
		5-8	162

Index of Subjects

Acts (Book of), 7, 13, 77, 85, 89, 90, 91, 92, 105, 108, 110-113, 125, 147, 205, 210-214, 218
Agrarian imagery, 193
Antioch, 6, 75, 76-78, 83, 85, 87, 91, 92, 93, 99-106, 113, 114, 116-124, 163
   Conflict in Antioch, 77, 121, 122, 123, 125
   The Antiochene collection, 89, 91, 92
Apostle, 73, 123, 136, 192
   Paul as apostle (*see also* Paul), 73
Barnabas, 6, 76, 77, 80, 89, 91- 93, 100-102, 104, 105, 107, 117
Benefaction, 37, 40, 68
   benefits, 43, 44, 47
   collective benefaction, 57
   euergetism, V, 11, 38, 39, 51, 53, 55, 57, 59, 60, 63, 64, 67, 68, 69, 70, 94, 97, 98, 149
   honorary decrees, 51, 63, 65, 66, 93
   honorary inscriptions, 65
   ingratitude, 41, 42, 48, 95, 192, 210
Benefactor
   agonistic attitude, 49, 54
   civic benefactors, 55
   private benefactors, 37, 56
   reciprocal interchange, 18, 22, 40, 59, 200, 210
   social approval, 45, 46, 150
Benefactor *see also* Benefaction, 17, 40, 51, 53, 55, 69, 102, 171, 172
Benefit exchange, 6, 7, 11, 38, 69-74, 90, 91, 93, 97, 99, 102, 104, 106, 114, 126, 129, 131, 134, 139, 143, 148, 149, 150, 152, 181, 201, 207, 208, 218
   social exchange, 8, 11, 14-24, 40, 41, 44, 46, 47, 49, 51, 58, 59, 67, 69, 70, 74, 90, 96, 97, 99, 132, 149, 152, 153, 192, 219
   gift exchange, 15, 20, 74, 94, 107
   Jewish benefit exchange, 95

Christ, 74, 81, 82, 101, 112, 119, 121, 122, 127, 129, 133, 137-139, 148, 150, 160, 162, 169, 176, 178, 179, 180, 182, 184, 187, 189, 190, 200, 202
   poverty, 5, 39, 89, 90, 111, 112, 129, 130, 136, 146, 148, 163, 173, 176, 179, 199, 218, 219
   sacrifice, 94, 129, 133, 138, 139, 168, 179, 180, 184, 201, 202, 207, 211, 213
Clients (*see* Patronage), 24, 29, 224
Collection, 1, 3, 4, 131, 135, 146,
   agreement at the Jerusalem meeting (*see also* Jerusalem church), 86
   bond of unity, 207, 219
   caritative functions, 1, 146
   chronology, 13, 76, 125
   delivery, 5, 73, 92, 104, 138, 145, 148, 150, 151, 153, 160, 164, 198, 204, 206, 209, 210-212, 217, 218, 219
   eschatological provocation, 4
   financial support, 165, 204
   gratitude, V, 18, 27, 29, 32, 36, 42, 44, 46, 48, 49, 50, 52, 55, 58, 91, 94, 99, 102, 103, 114, 128, 131, 138, 139, 141, 144-146, 148, 149, 150-152, 168, 172, 179, 187, 188, 192, 201, 203-205
   interpretative framework, 4, 5, 8, 11, 13, 17, 51, 58, 69, 73, 74, 82, 116, 126, 131, 150, 152, 156, 174, 201, 217, 218
   needs of the poor in Jerusalem (*see* the poor, Jerusalem church), 134, 151
   organisation, 4, 5, 10, 14, 15, 20, 74, 101, 112, 114, 124, 129, 156, 158, 159, 161, 162, 169, 185, 198, 204, 219
   reciprocal relationships, 6, 8, 11, 18, 94, 97, 140, 147, 166, 171, 218

Index of Subjects and Names

Rejection, 114, 207
religious reciprocity, 134, 138, 166, 173, 179
sacred ministry, 133, 208, 209
size of the contributions, 146
success, 7, 45, 84, 149, 161, 175, 176, 198, 209, 210, 215, 219
tangible honours, 219
theological reflection on the collection, 133, 144, 150, 206, 217
Corinthians, 3, 22, 73, 76-78, 113, 123, 124, 128, 131, 134-205, 209, 217, 221, 222, 224, 226, 227, 229-234
  conflict, 15, 25, 26, 40, 61, 72, 77, 93, 106, 117, 118, 121-125, 129, 165
  ideal beneficiaries, 182, 210
  recipients, 44, 68
  spiritual gifts, 129, 131, 132, 134, 143, 144, 151, 175, 177, 179, 180, 193, 200
Diakonia, 128, 208, 223
Equality ('isotes' – *see also* Collection), 159
Family, 28, 169, 170, 223, 228, 231
Famine, 56, 89, 98, 109, 110, 225, 227
Galatians (Letter to), 1, 73, 75-106, 113, 114, 116-120, 122, 126, 129, 132, 151, 158, 159, 163, 204, 206
  recipients, 7, 41, 44, 45, 46, 50, 57, 58, 74, 76, 92, 98, 99, 130, 141, 145, 149, 150, 152, 153, 182, 183, 184, 193, 194, 196, 199, 201, 202, 218
  structure, 10, 17, 40, 51, 67, 69, 77, 78, 80, 88, 122, 136, 137, 140, 144, 155, 157, 163, 166, 169, 177, 179, 180, 190, 193
Gifts
  see God, Benefaction, 20, 21, 46, 147
God, 6, 10, 34, 63, 73, 74, 81, 82, 83, 86, 87, 94, 96, 97, 100, 101, 104, 118, 119, 122-128, 131, 133, 135, 136, 138, 139, 142-153, 160, 162, 166, 173-175, 177-179, 182-185, 189, 193, 195-204, 208-210, 217, 218
  active grace, 136, 143, 145, 150, 152, 200, 203
  benefactor, 5, 7, 8, 22, 31, 32, 38, 39, 40, 43-52, 55, 57, 58, 63-65, 68, 69, 71, 72, 95, 97, 102-104, 106, 113, 115, 118, 133, 143, 147, 153, 163, 172, 173, 204, 208, 210, 215, 218
  gifts, 3, 6, 7, 8, 17-22, 35, 38, 39, 43, 44, 47-50, 58, 68, 69, 73, 90, 95, 96, 99, 107, 130-139, 142-147, 149, 152, 166, 177, 179, 180, 183, 193, 200, 210, 217, 218
  honour, 11, 20, 22, 26, 28, 32-35, 38, 39, 43, 50, 52, 54, 55-58, 64, 66, 68, 71, 86, 90, 93, 95, 98, 101, 115, 119, 121, 124, 125, 127, 130, 138, 147, 148, 150-153, 162, 166, 170, 171, 174, 175, 185, 188, 189, 192, 199, 201, 202, 205, 209, 210, 218
Grace (*charis*), 119, 234
Gratitude, 48, 138
Gregory, C.A., 20, 21, 147
Group, 227
  collective/ dyadic personality, 120
  norms, 9, 10, 40, 175, 186, 189
Ideology, 8, 9
Ingratitude, 47
Israel *see also* Judaism, 1, 2, 3, 12, 76, 80, 82, 88, 89, 95, 97, 122, 123, 128, 131, 142, 162, 209, 211
James, 7, 63, 82, 85, 86, 101, 105, 117, 118, 119, 123, 132, 213-215, 219,
  theological views, 5, 75, 114, 123
Jerusalem, 2, 4-8, 10, 15, 17, 73, 74, 75, 76-80, 82-93, 99-126, 128-137, 139, 140-163, 174-185, 187, 188, 190-192, 195, 197-215, 217-219
Jerusalem church
  elders, 213
  rejection of the collection (*see also* Collection), 7, 153, 209
  status in the early church, 106
Jerusalem church *see also* Jerusalem, James, Paul, 6, 7, 8, 10, 74, 75, 84, 86, 87, 89-91, 112, 113, 116-123, 129, 132-134, 137, 149, 151, 153, 159, 160, 162, 163, 183, 205-209, 211, 213-215, 217
Jerusalem meeting, 6, 75, 77, 80, 83, 86, 87-93, 99, 104, 106, 116-118, 132, 146, 151, 163, 175, 210, 213
  the 'dokountes', 107, 115, 118, 119, 213
Judaism, 34, 90, 96, 107, 117, 118, 155, 221, 224, 229, 230, 231, 234

Judea, 5, 88, 92, 107-111, 123, 124, 131, 213, 219
Macedonians, 129, 136, 137, 139, 146, 169, 173-179, 181, 184, 185, 188, 190-192, 199-201, 204, 210
Models, 15,
Naherwartung, 114
Patronage, 12, 14, 19, 22-29, 31-37, 59, 62, 63, 66, 67, 69, 70, 94, 127, 165
  clients, 24, 29
  patronage of communities, 32, 63, 67
Paul, 2-8, 10-11, 13, 15, 17, 19, 22, 44, 49, 50, 55, 59, 71, 73-94, 96-97, 99-219,
  benefactor, 17, 40, 51, 53, 55, 69, 102, 171, 172
  boasting, 188-192, 200
  honourable figure, 218
  leadership style, 162
  patriarchal role, 22, 164, 167, 168, 169, 172, 173, 175, 177
  slave - *see also* Apostle, 81, 82
Pauline communities, 8, 22, 73, 74, 93, 128, 129, 132, 139-143, 146-148, 151, 152, 159, 160, 167, 186, 187, 189, 191, 197, 201, 202, 205, 206, 210, 217, 219

Persuasion, 81, 117, 166, 167, 174
  discourse situation, 167, 198
  intra-textual roles, 75, 167
  rhetoric, 38, 78, 79, 166, 167, 183, 223, 227, 229, 231
  textual strategy/ies, 166, 167, 168, 172, 176, 177, 184, 198
Peter
  Cephas, 76, 82, 85, 105, 117, 118
  request to Paul (*see also* Jerusalem meeting), 81, 119
Peter *see also* Apostle, Jerusalem church, 17, 51, 77, 86, 87, 93, 101, 105, 117-121, 123, 124, 213,
Reciprocity, 1, 6, 19, 22, 49, 90, 111, 171
  agonistic contests (*see also* agonistic attitude to life), 22, 43, 174
  balanced reciprocity, 22, 45, 90, 103, 134, 140, 149, 152, 180
Romans (Letter to), 76, 77, 89, 108, 123, 124, 128, 129, 130, 132, 133, 141, 146, 151, 153, 167, 168, 172, 174, 204, 205, 206, 207, 208, 209, 210, 212, 214, 218
  recipients, 44, 68
  structure, 78, 226
Titus, 76, 80, 135, 165, 166, 175, 176, 181, 183-186, 188-200

Wissenschaftliche Untersuchungen zum Neuen Testament
Alphabetical Index of the First and Second Series

Ådna, Jostein: Jesu Stellung zum Tempel. 2000. *Volume II/119.*
Anderson, Paul N.: The Christology of the Fourth Gospel. 1996. *Volume II/78.*
Appold, Mark L.: The Oneness Motif in the Fourth Gospel. 1976. *Volume II/1.*
Arnold, Clinton E.: The Colossian Syncretism. 1995. *Volume II/77.*
Avemarie, Friedrich und *Hermann Lichtenberger* (Ed.): Bund und Tora. 1996. *Volume 92.*
Bachmann, Michael: Sünder oder Übertreter. 1992. *Volume 59.*
Baker, William R.: Personal Speech-Ethics in the Epistle of James. 1995. *Volume II/68.*
Balla, Peter: Challenges to New Testament Theology. 1997. *Volume II/95.*
Bammel, Ernst: Judaica. Volume I 1986. *Volume 37* – Volume II 1997. *Volume 91.*
Bash, Anthony: Ambassadors for Christ. 1997. *Volume II/92.*
Bauernfeind, Otto: Kommentar und Studien zur Apostelgeschichte. 1980. *Volume 22.*
Bayer, Hans Friedrich: Jesus' Predictions of Vindication and Resurrection. 1986. *Volume II/20.*
Bell, Richard H.: Provoked to Jealousy. 1994. *Volume II/63.*
– No One Seeks for God. 1998. *Volume 106.*
Bergman, Jan: see *Kieffer, René*
Bergmeier, Roland: Das Gesetz im Römerbrief und andere Studien zum Neuen Testament. 2000. *Volume 121.*
Betz, Otto: Jesus, der Messias Israels. 1987. *Volume 42.*
– Jesus, der Herr der Kirche. 1990. *Volume 52.*
Beyschlag, Karlmann: Simon Magus und die christliche Gnosis. 1974. *Volume 16.*
Bittner, Wolfgang J.: Jesu Zeichen im Johannesevangelium. 1987. *Volume II/26.*
Bjerkelund, Carl J.: Tauta Egeneto. 1987. *Volume 40.*
Blackburn, Barry Lee: Theios Anēr and the Markan Miracle Traditions. 1991. *Volume II/40.*
Bock, Darrell L.: Blasphemy and Exaltation in Judaism and the Final Examination of Jesus. 1998. *Volume II/106.*
Bockmuehl, Markus N.A.: Revelation and Mystery in Ancient Judaism and Pauline Christianity. 1990. *Volume II/36.*
Böhlig, Alexander: Gnosis und Synkretismus. Teil 1 1989. *Volume 47* –Teil 2 1989. *Volume 48.*
Böhm, Martina: Samarien und die Samaritai bei Lukas. 1999. *Volume II/111.*
Böttrich, Christfried: Weltweisheit – Menschheitsethik – Urkult. 1992. *Volume II/50.*
Bolyki, János: Jesu Tischgemeinschaften. 1997. *Volume II/96.*
Büchli, Jörg: Der Poimandres – ein paganisiertes Evangelium. 1987. *Volume II/27.*
Bühner, Jan A.: Der Gesandte und sein Weg im 4. Evangelium. 1977. *Volume II/2.*
Burchard, Christoph: Untersuchungen zu Joseph und Aseneth. 1965. *Volume 8.*
– Studien zur Theologie, Sprache und Umwelt des Neuen Testaments. Ed. by D. Sänger. 1998. *Volume 107.*
Byrskog, Samuel: Story as History - History as Story. 2000. *Volume 123.*
Cancik, Hubert (Ed.): Markus-Philologie. 1984. *Volume 33.*
Capes, David B.: Old Testament Yaweh Texts in Paul's Christology. 1992. *Volume II/47.*
Caragounis, Chrys C.: The Son of Man. 1986. *Volume 38.*
– see *Fridrichsen, Anton.*
Carleton Paget, James: The Epistle of Barnabas. 1994. *Volume II/64.*
Ciampa, Roy E.: The Presence and Function of Scripture in Galatians 1 and 2. 1998. *Volume II/102.*
Crump, David: Jesus the Intercessor. 1992. *Volume II/49.*
Deines, Roland: Jüdische Steingefäße und pharisäische Frömmigkeit. 1993. *Volume II/52.*
– Die Pharisäer. 1997. *Volume 101.*
Dietzfelbinger, Christian: Der Abschied des Kommenden. 1997. *Volume 95.*
Dobbeler, Axel von: Glaube als Teilhabe. 1987. *Volume II/22.*
Du Toit, David S.: Theios Anthropos. 1997. *Volume II/91.*
Dunn, James D.G. (Ed.): Jews and Christians. 1992. *Volume 66.*
– Paul and the Mosaic Law. 1996. *Volume 89.*
Ebertz, Michael N.: Das Charisma des Gekreuzigten. 1987. *Volume 45.*
Eckstein, Hans-Joachim: Der Begriff Syneidesis bei Paulus. 1983. *Volume II/10.*
– Verheißung und Gesetz. 1996. *Volume 86.*

Ego, Beate: Im Himmel wie auf Erden. 1989. *Volume II/34*
Ego, Beate und *Lange, Armin* sowie *Pilhofer, Peter(Ed.):* Gemeinde ohne Tempel - Community without Temple. 1999. *Volume 118.*
Eisen, Ute E.: see *Paulsen, Henning.*
Ellis, E. Earle: Prophecy and Hermeneutic in Early Christianity. 1978. *Volume 18.*
- The Old Testament in Early Christianity. 1991. *Volume 54.*
Ennulat, Andreas: Die 'Minor Agreements'. 1994. *Volume II/62.*
Ensor, Peter W.: Jesus and His 'Works'. 1996. *Volume II/85.*
Eskola, Timo: Theodicy and Predestination in Pauline Soteriology. 1998. *Volume II/100.*
Feldmeier, Reinhard: Die Krisis des Gottessohnes. 1987. *Volume II/21.*
- Die Christen als Fremde. 1992. *Volume 64.*
Feldmeier, Reinhard und *Ulrich Heckel* (Ed.): Die Heiden. 1994. *Volume 70.*
Fletcher-Louis, Crispin H.T.: Luke-Acts: Angels, Christology and Soteriology. 1997. *Volume II/94.*
Förster, Niclas: Marcus Magus. 1999. *Volume 114.*
Forbes, Christopher Brian: Prophecy and Inspired Speech in Early Christianity and its Hellenistic Environment. 1995. *Volume II/75.*
Fornberg, Tord: see *Fridrichsen, Anton.*
Fossum, Jarl E.: The Name of God and the Angel of the Lord. 1985. *Volume 36.*
Frenschkowski, Marco: Offenbarung und Epiphanie. Volume 1 1995. *Volume II/79* - Volume 2 1997. *Volume II/80.*
Frey, Jörg: Eugen Drewermann und die biblische Exegese. 1995. *Volume II/71.*
- Die johanneische Eschatologie. Band I. 1997. *Volume 96.* - Band II. 1998. *Volume 110.* - Band III. 2000. *Volume 117.*
Freyne, Sean: Galilee and Gospel. 2000. *Volume 125.*
Fridrichsen, Anton: Exegetical Writings. Ed. von C.C. Caragounis und T. Fornberg. 1994. *Volume 76.*
Garlington, Don B.: 'The Obedience of Faith'. 1991. *Volume II/38.*
- Faith, Obedience, and Perseverance. 1994. *Volume 79.*
Garnet, Paul: Salvation and Atonement in the Qumran Scrolls. 1977. *Volume II/3.*
Gese, Michael: Das Vermächtnis des Apostels. 1997. *Volume II/99.*
Gräßer, Erich: Der Alte Bund im Neuen. 1985. *Volume 35.*

Green, Joel B.: The Death of Jesus. 1988. *Volume II/33.*
Gundry Volf, Judith M.: Paul and Perseverance. 1990. *Volume II/37.*
Hafemann, Scott J.: Suffering and the Spirit. 1986. *Volume II/19.*
- Paul, Moses, and the History of Israel. 1995. *Volume 81.*
Hamid-Khani, Saeed: Relevation and Concealment of Christ. 2000. *Volume II/120.*
Hannah, Darrel D.: Michael and Christ. 1999. *Volume II/109.*
Hartman, Lars: Text-Centered New Testament Studies. Ed. by D. Hellholm. 1997. *Volume 102.*
Heckel, Theo K.: Der Innere Mensch. 1993. *Volume II/53.*
- Vom Evangelium des Markus zum viergestaltigen Evangelium. 1999. *Volume 120.*
Heckel, Ulrich: Kraft in Schwachheit. 1993. *Volume II/56.*
- see *Feldmeier, Reinhard.*
- see *Hengel, Martin.*
Heiligenthal, Roman: Werke als Zeichen. 1983. *Volume II/9.*
Hellholm, D.: see *Hartman, Lars.*
Hemer, Colin J.: The Book of Acts in the Setting of Hellenistic History. 1989. *Volume 49.*
Hengel, Martin: Judentum und Hellenismus. 1969, ³1988. *Volume 10.*
- Die johanneische Frage. 1993. *Volume 67.*
- Judaica et Hellenistica. Band 1. 1996. *Volume 90.* - Band 2. 1999. *Volume 109.*
Hengel, Martin and *Ulrich Heckel* (Ed.): Paulus und das antike Judentum. 1991. *Volume 58.*
Hengel, Martin und *Hermut Löhr* (Ed.): Schriftauslegung im antiken Judentum und im Urchristentum. 1994. *Volume 73.*
Hengel, Martin and *Anna Maria Schwemer:* Paulus zwischen Damaskus und Antiochien. 1998. *Volume 108.*
Hengel, Martin and *Anna Maria Schwemer* (Ed.): Königsherrschaft Gottes und himmlischer Kult. 1991. *Volume 55.*
- Die Septuaginta. 1994. *Volume 72.*
Herrenbrück, Fritz: Jesus und die Zöllner. 1990. *Volume II/41.*
Herzer, Jens: Paulus oder Petrus? 1998. *Volume 103.*
Hoegen-Rohls, Christina: Der nachösterliche Johannes. 1996. *Volume II/84.*
Hofius, Otfried: Katapausis. 1970. *Volume 11.*
- Der Vorhang vor dem Thron Gottes. 1972. *Volume 14.*
- Der Christushymnus Philipper 2,6-11. 1976, ²1991. *Volume 17.*

- Paulusstudien. 1989, ²1994. *Volume 51.*
Hofius, Otfried und Hans-Christian Kammler: Johannesstudien. 1996. *Volume 88.*
Holtz, Traugott: Geschichte und Theologie des Urchristentums. 1991. *Volume 57.*
Hommel, Hildebrecht: Sebasmata. Band 1 1983. *Volume 31* – Band 2 1984. *Volume 32.*
Hvalvik, Reidar: The Struggle for Scripture and Covenant. 1996. *Volume II/82.*
Joubert, Stephan: Paul as Benefactor. 2000. *Volume II/124.*
Kähler, Christoph: Jesu Gleichnisse als Poesie und Therapie. 1995. *Volume 78.*
Kammler, Hans-Christian: Christologie und Eschatologie. 2000. *Volume 126.*
- see Hofius, Otfried.
Kamlah, Ehrhard: Die Form der katalogischen Paränese im Neuen Testament. 1964. *Volume 7.*
Kelhoffer, James A.: Miracle and Mission. 1999. *Volume II/112.*
Kieffer, René and Jan Bergman (Ed.): La Main de Dieu / Die Hand Gottes. 1997. *Volume 94.*
Kim, Seyoon: The Origin of Paul's Gospel. 1981, ²1984. *Volume II/4.*
- „The 'Son of Man'" as the Son of God. 1983. *Volume 30.*
Kleinknecht, Karl Th.: Der leidende Gerechtfertigte. 1984, ²1988. *Volume II/13.*
Klinghardt, Matthias: Gesetz und Volk Gottes. 1988. *Volume II/32.*
Köhler, Wolf-Dietrich: Rezeption des Matthäusevangeliums in der Zeit vor Irenäus. 1987. *Volume II/24.*
Korn, Manfred: Die Geschichte Jesu in veränderter Zeit. 1993. *Volume II/51.*
Koskenniemi, Erkki: Apollonios von Tyana in der neutestamentlichen Exegese. 1994. *Volume II/61.*
Kraus, Wolfgang: Das Volk Gottes. 1996. *Volume 85.*
- see Walter, Nikolaus.
Kuhn, Karl G.: Achtzehngebet und Vaterunser und der Reim. 1950. *Volume 1.*
Laansma, Jon: I Will Give You Rest. 1997. *Volume II/98.*
Labahn, Michael: Offenbarung in Zeichen und Wort. 2000. *Volume II/117.*
Lange, Armin: see Ego, Beate.
Lampe, Peter: Die stadtrömischen Christen in den ersten beiden Jahrhunderten. 1987, ²1989. *Volume II/18.*
Landmesser, Christof: Wahrheit als Grundbegriff neutestamentlicher Wissenschaft. 1999. *Volume 113.*
Lau, Andrew: Manifest in Flesh. 1996. *Volume II/86.*

Lichtenberger, Hermann: see Avemarie, Friedrich.
Lieu, Samuel N.C.: Manichaeism in the Later Roman Empire and Medieval China. ²1992. *Volume 63.*
Loader, William R.G.: Jesus' Attitude Towards the Law. 1997. *Volume II/97.*
Löhr, Gebhard: Verherrlichung Gottes durch Philosophie. 1997. *Volume 97.*
Löhr, Hermut: see Hengel, Martin.
Löhr, Winrich Alfried: Basilides und seine Schule. 1995. *Volume 83.*
Luomanen, Petri: Entering the Kingdom of Heaven. 1998. *Volume II/101.*
Maier, Gerhard: Mensch und freier Wille. 1971. *Volume 12.*
- Die Johannesoffenbarung und die Kirche. 1981. *Volume 25.*
Markschies, Christoph: Valentinus Gnosticus? 1992. *Volume 65.*
Marshall, Peter: Enmity in Corinth: Social Conventions in Paul's Relations with the Corinthians. 1987. *Volume II/23.*
McDonough, Sean M.: YHWH at Patmos: Rev. 1:4 in its Hellenistic and Early Jewish Setting. 1999. *Volume II/107.*
Meade, David G.: Pseudonymity and Canon. 1986. *Volume 39.*
Meadors, Edward P.: Jesus the Messianic Herald of Salvation. 1995. *Volume II/72.*
Meißner, Stefan: Die Heimholung des Ketzers. 1996. *Volume II/87.*
Mell, Ulrich: Die „anderen" Winzer. 1994. *Volume 77.*
Mengel, Berthold: Studien zum Philipperbrief. 1982. *Volume II/8.*
Merkel, Helmut: Die Widersprüche zwischen den Evangelien. 1971. *Volume 13.*
Merklein, Helmut: Studien zu Jesus und Paulus. Volume 1 1987. *Volume 43.* – Volume 2 1998. *Volume 105.*
Metzler, Karin: Der griechische Begriff des Verzeihens. 1991. *Volume II/44.*
Metzner, Rainer: Die Rezeption des Matthäusevangeliums im 1. Petrusbrief. 1995. *Volume II/74.*
- Das Verständnis der Sünde im Johannesevangelium. 2000. *Volume 122.*
Mittmann-Richert, Ulrike: Magnifikat und Benediktus. 1996. *Volume II/90.*
Mußner, Franz: Jesus von Nazareth im Umfeld Israels und der Urkirche. Ed. by M. Theobald. 1998. *Volume 111.*
Niebuhr, Karl-Wilhelm: Gesetz und Paränese. 1987. *Volume II/28.*
- Heidenapostel aus Israel. 1992. *Volume 62.*
Nissen, Andreas: Gott und der Nächste im antiken Judentum. 1974. *Volume 15.*
Noack, Christian: Gottesbewußtsein. 2000. *Volume II/116.*

Noormann, Rolf: Irenäus als Paulusinterpret. 1994. *Volume II/66.*
Obermann, Andreas: Die christologische Erfüllung der Schrift im Johannesevangelium. 1996. *Volume II/83.*
Okure, Teresa: The Johannine Approach to Mission. 1988. *Volume II/31.*
Oropeza, Brisio J.: Paul and Apostasy. 2000. *Volume II/115.*
Ostmeyer, Karl-Heinrich: Taufe und Typos. 2000. *Volume II/118.*
Paulsen, Henning: Studien zur Literatur und Geschichte des frühen Christentums. Ed. von Ute E. Eisen. 1997. *Volume 99.*
Park, Eung Chun: The Mission Discourse in Matthew's Interpretation. 1995. *Volume II/81.*
Philonenko, Marc (Ed.): Le Trône de Dieu. 1993. *Volume 69.*
Pilhofer, Peter: Presbyteron Kreitton. 1990. *Volume II/39.*
- Philippi. Volume I 1995. *Volume 87.*
- see *Ego, Beate.*
Pöhlmann, Wolfgang: Der Verlorene Sohn und das Haus. 1993. *Volume 68.*
Pokorný, Petr und *Josef B. Souček:* Bibelauslegung als Theologie. 1997. *Volume 100.*
Porter, Stanley E.: The Paul of Acts. 1999. *Volume 115.*
Prieur, Alexander: Die Verkündigung der Gottesherrschaft. 1996. *Volume II/89.*
Probst, Hermann: Paulus und der Brief. 1991. *Volume II/45.*
Räisänen, Heikki: Paul and the Law. 1983, ²1987. *Volume 29.*
Rehkopf, Friedrich: Die lukanische Sonderquelle. 1959. *Volume 5.*
Rein, Matthias: Die Heilung des Blindgeborenen (Joh 9). 1995. *Volume II/73.*
Reinmuth, Eckart: Pseudo-Philo und Lukas. 1994. *Volume 74.*
Reiser, Marius: Syntax und Stil des Markusevangeliums. 1984. *Volume II/11.*
Richards, E. Randolph: The Secretary in the Letters of Paul. 1991. *Volume II/42.*
Riesner, Rainer: Jesus als Lehrer. 1981, ³1988. *Volume II/7.*
- Die Frühzeit des Apostels Paulus. 1994. *Volume 71.*
Rissi, Mathias: Die Theologie des Hebräerbriefs. 1987. *Volume 41.*
Röhser, Günter: Metaphorik und Personifikation der Sünde. 1987. *Volume II/25.*
Rose, Christian: Die Wolke der Zeugen. 1994. *Volume II/60.*
Rüger, Hans Peter: Die Weisheitsschrift aus der Kairoer Geniza. 1991. *Volume 53.*
Sänger, Dieter: Antikes Judentum und die Mysterien. 1980. *Volume II/5.*
- Die Verkündigung des Gekreuzigten und Israel. 1994. *Volume 75.*
- see *Burchard, Chr.*
Salzmann, Jorg Christian: Lehren und Ermahnen. 1994. *Volume II/59.*
Sandnes, Karl Olav: Paul – One of the Prophets? 1991. *Volume II/43.*
Sato, Migaku: Q und Prophetie. 1988. *Volume II/29.*
Schaper, Joachim: Eschatology in the Greek Psalter. 1995. *Volume II/76.*
Schimanowski, Gottfried: Weisheit und Messias. 1985. *Volume II/17.*
Schlichting, Günter: Ein jüdisches Leben Jesu. 1982. *Volume 24.*
Schnabel, Eckhard J.: Law and Wisdom from Ben Sira to Paul. 1985. *Volume II/16.*
Schutter, William L.: Hermeneutic and Composition in I Peter. 1989. *Volume II/30.*
Schwartz, Daniel R.: Studies in the Jewish Background of Christianity. 1992. *Volume 60.*
Schwemer, Anna Maria: see *Hengel, Martin*
Scott, James M.: Adoption as Sons of God. 1992. *Volume II/48.*
- Paul and the Nations. 1995. *Volume 84.*
Siegert, Folker: Drei hellenistisch-jüdische Predigten. Teil I 1980. *Volume 20* – Teil II 1992. *Volume 61.*
- Nag-Hammadi-Register. 1982. *Volume 26.*
- Argumentation bei Paulus. 1985. *Volume 34.*
- Philon von Alexandrien. 1988. *Volume 46.*
Simon, Marcel: Le christianisme antique et son contexte religieux I/II. 1981. *Volume 23.*
Snodgrass, Klyne: The Parable of the Wicked Tenants. 1983. *Volume 27.*
Söding, Thomas: Das Wort vom Kreuz. 1997. *Volume 93.*
- see *Thüsing, Wilhelm.*
Sommer, Urs: Die Passionsgeschichte des Markusevangeliums. 1993. *Volume II/58.*
Souček, Josef B.: see *Pokorný, Petr.*
Spangenberg, Volker: Herrlichkeit des Neuen Bundes. 1993. *Volume II/55.*
Spanje, T.E. van: Inconsistency in Paul?. 1999. *Volume II/110.*
Speyer, Wolfgang: Frühes Christentum im antiken Strahlungsfeld. Band I: 1989. *Volume 50.* – Band II: 1999. *Volume 116.*
Stadelmann, Helge: Ben Sira als Schriftgelehrter. 1980. *Volume II/6.*
Stenschke, Christoph W.: Luke's Portrait of Gentiles Prior to Their Coming to Faith. *Volume II/108.*
Stettler, Hanna: Die Christologie der Pastoralbriefe. 1998. *Volume II/105.*

Wissenschaftliche Untersuchungen zum Neuen Testament

Strobel, August: Die Stunde der Wahrheit. 1980. *Volume 21.*
Stroumsa, Guy G.: Barbarian Philosophy. 1999. *Volume 112.*
Stuckenbruck, Loren T.: Angel Veneration and Christology. 1995. *Volume II/70.*
Stuhlmacher, Peter (Ed.): Das Evangelium und die Evangelien. 1983. *Volume 28.*
Sung, Chong-Hyon: Vergebung der Sünden. 1993. *Volume II/57.*
Tajra, Harry W.: The Trial of St. Paul. 1989. *Volume II/35.*
– The Martyrdom of St.Paul. 1994. *Volume II/67.*
Theißen, Gerd: Studien zur Soziologie des Urchristentums. 1979, ³1989. *Volume 19.*
Theobald, Michael: see *Mußner, Franz.*
Thornton, Claus-Jürgen: Der Zeuge des Zeugen. 1991. *Volume 56.*
Thüsing, Wilhelm: Studien zur neutestamentlichen Theologie. Ed. von Thomas Söding. 1995. *Volume 82.*
Thurén, Lauri: Derhetorizing Paul. 2000. *Volume 124.*
Treloar, Geoffrey R.: Lightfoot the Historian. 1998. *Volume II/103.*
Tsuji, Manabu: Glaube zwischen Vollkommenheit und Verweltlichung. 1997. *Volume II/93.*
Twelftree, Graham H.: Jesus the Exorcist. 1993. *Volume II/54.*
Visotzky, Burton L.: Fathers of the World. 1995. *Volume 80.*
Wagener, Ulrike: Die Ordnung des „Hauses Gottes". 1994. *Volume II/65.*
Walter, Nikolaus: Praeparatio Evangelica. Ed. by Wolfgang Kraus und Florian Wilk. 1997. *Volume 98.*
Wander, Bernd: Gottesfürchtige und Sympathisanten. 1998. *Volume 104.*
Watts, Rikki: Isaiah's New Exodus and Mark. 1997. *Volume II/88.*
Wedderburn, A.J.M.: Baptism and Resurrection. 1987. *Volume 44.*
Wegner, Uwe: Der Hauptmann von Kafarnaum. 1985. *Volume II/14.*
Welck, Christian: Erzählte 'Zeichen'. 1994. *Volume II/69.*
Wilk, Florian: see *Walter, Nikolaus.*
Williams, Catrin H.: I am He. 2000. *Volume II/113.*
Wilson, Walter T.: Love without Pretense. 1991. *Volume II/46.*
Zimmermann, Alfred E.: Die urchristlichen Lehrer. 1984, ²1988. *Volume II/12.*
Zimmermann, Johannes: Messianische Texte aus Qumran. 1998. *Volume II/104.*

For a complete catalogue please write to the publisher
Mohr Siebeck · Postfach 2030 · D–72010 Tübingen.
Up-to-date information on the internet at http://www.mohr.de

www.ingramcontent.com/pod-product-compliance
Lightning Source LLC
Chambersburg PA
CBHW050436240426
43661CB00055B/2404